# THE BOOK CALLED ISAIAH

# The Book Called Isaiah

## *Deutero-Isaiah's Role in Composition and Redaction*

H. G. M. WILLIAMSON

CLARENDON PRESS · OXFORD
1994

*Oxford University Press, Walton Street, Oxford* OX2 6DP
*Oxford New York Toronto*
*Delhi Bombay Calcutta Madras Karachi*
*Kuala Lumpur Singapore Hong Kong Tokyo*
*Nairobi Dar es Salaam Cape Town*
*Melbourne Auckland Madrid*
*and associated companies in*
*Berlin Ibadan*

*Oxford is a trade mark of Oxford University Press*

*Published in the United States*
*by Oxford University Press Inc., New York*



*British Library Cataloguing in Publication Data*
*Data available*

*Library of Congress Cataloging in Publication Data*
*Williamson, H. G. M. (Hugh Godfrey Maturin), 1947–*
*The book called Isaiah : Deutero-Isaiah's role in composition and redaction*
*Includes bibliographical references and indexes.*
*1. Bible. O.T. Isaiah—Authorship. 2. Bible. O.T. Isaiah–*
*–Criticism, interpretation, etc. I. Title.*
*BS1515.5.W56 1994 224'.1066—dc20 93–47670*
*ISBN 0–19–826360–0*

*1 3 5 7 9 10 8 6 4 2*

*Typeset by Regent Typesetting, London*
*Printed in Great Britain*
*on acid-free paper by*
*Biddles Ltd., Guildford and King's Lynn*

Dedicated to
the President and Fellows
of Clare Hall, Cambridge
1985–1992

# PREFACE

RECENT research on the book of Isaiah has been dominated by discussions of its unity, and the present work seeks to make a contribution to this continuing enterprise. As the opening chapter indicates, however, an unsettling division is developing between those who continue to operate within the established tradition of historical-critical study of the Old Testament and those who believe that we should move beyond this to various forms of post-critical literary readings. This disagreement about a correct method and approach in biblical interpretation is by no means confined to Isaiah, of course, but because multiple authorship of this book is so widely agreed it raises some of the underlying issues in a particularly acute form.

Many scholars, who I suspect form a 'silent majority', still cling to the hope that ultimately it should be possible to reconcile these divergent approaches at the rational level if the redactional processes that lead from diversity to unity could be more intensively explored. Undoubtedly, much of the evidence necessary to undertake this fully is lost to us, but at the same time awareness of the problem can sometimes enable us to trace elements of it in areas that were inevitably overlooked by earlier generations of scholars. An underlying theme of this book, therefore, is the argument that approaches to the unity of Isaiah should be pursued by way of a more intense application of traditional methods rather than an ignoring or bypassing of them.

If I am right, my conclusions will have important implications for interpretation, and some readers may be disappointed that I have not developed these further. To have done so, however, would have been to write a completely different book. In my opinion, which is an inevitable consequence of what has just been said, interpretation should follow critical analysis. If the latter is mistaken, interpretation will be askew. I have, therefore, confined myself here to arguing for one—perhaps the most—significant phase in the composition of Isaiah; only if it is found acceptable will it be possible to move on to interpretation in a different and more appropriate genre.

A rudimentary form of parts of this book formed the substance of the Gheens Lectures delivered at the Southern Baptist Theological Seminary in Louisville, Kentucky, in April 1990; I am most grateful to the President, staff, and students for their generous hospitality on that occasion. In addition, a rewritten form of part of Chapter 5 was delivered as the 1993 Henton Davies Lecture at Regent's Park College, Oxford, where again I was most graciously received, while the discussion of Isa. 11: 11-16 and related passages discussed in Chapter 6 formed the basis of a paper read to the IOSOT meeting in Paris in July 1992.

On all these and other occasions I have benefited from discussions with a number of friends and colleagues. In particular, I am grateful for the detailed comments on a draft of nearly the whole book by Dr John Day and Dr Jeremy Hughes. Especially helpful have been conversations over a number of years with Dr Knud Jeppesen of Aarhus University.[1] From his publications it will be seen that our approaches differ in a number of ways even while we share in common certain fundamental convictions regarding the composition of Isaiah. I am very appreciative of the stimulus which these conversations have provided in working out my own position.

In order not to interrupt the flow of the argument unnecessarily, I have included discussion of most of the relevant text-critical issues involved in a separate Appendix. In the main text, an asterisk (*) indicates that I have adopted an emendation, while a dagger (†) indicates that I follow the MT even though it has been challenged by others. All passages so marked are discussed in the Appendix. Commentaries on Isaiah are generally cited by author's name alone, and a list of these follows the list of abbreviations. Other works are cited by an abbreviated title after a full reference on their first appearance. Both they and the commentaries are all, of course, listed in full in the Bibliography.

I am grateful to the Delegates of the Oxford University Press for

[1] His major treatment of Deutero-Isaiah is included in his dissertation *Groeder ikke saar saare! Studieri Mikabogens sigte*. (Being in Danish, this is not accessible to me, but Dr Jeppesen has kindly provided me with an English summary.) Briefer treatments on particular passages include 'The Cornerstone (Isa. 28: 16) in Deutero-Isaianic Rereading of the Message of Isaiah', *ST* 38 (1984), 93–9, and 'The *maśśā' Bābel* in Isaiah 13–14', *PIBA* 9 (1985), 63–80.

accepting this book for publication, and to Hilary O'Shea for her careful and courteous editorial supervision. Most of the book was written while I was still a Fellow of Clare Hall, Cambridge; it is therefore appreciatively dedicated to my colleagues there during those happy years.

H. G. M. WILLIAMSON
*Christ Church, Oxford*
*September 1993*

# CONTENTS

# LIST OF ABBREVIATIONS

| | |
|---|---|
| AB | The Anchor Bible |
| *ActOr* | *Acta Orientalia* |
| *AHw* | W. von Soden, *Akkadisches Handwörterbuch* (Wiesbaden, 1965–81) |
| *AJSL* | *American Journal of Semitic Languages and Literatures* |
| AnB | Analecta Biblica |
| AOAT | Alter Orient und Altes Testament |
| *ASTI* | *Annual of the Swedish Theological Institute* |
| ATD | Das Alte Testament Deutsch |
| *AV* | *Authorized Version* |
| *BA* | *Biblical Archaeologist* |
| BAT | Die Botschaft des Alten Testaments |
| BDB | F. Brown, S. R. Driver, and C. A. Briggs, *A Hebrew and English Lexicon of the Old Testament* (Oxford, 1907) |
| BET | Beiträge zur biblischen Exegese und Theologie |
| BETL | Bibliotheca Ephemeridum Theologicarum Lovaniensium |
| BEvT | Beiträge zur evangelischen Theologie |
| *BHS* | *Biblia Hebraica Stuttgartensia* |
| *BibSac* | *Bibliotheca Sacra* |
| *BJRL* | *Bulletin of the John Rylands Library* |
| BKAT | Biblischer Kommentar, Altes Testament |
| *BN* | *Biblische Notizen* |
| BSt | Biblische Studien |
| BWANT | Beiträge zur Wissenschaft vom Alten und Neuen Testament |
| *BZ* | *Biblische Zeitschrift* |
| BZAW | Beihefte zur *Zeitschrift für die alttestamentliche Wissenschaft* |
| *CBQ* | *Catholic Biblical Quarterly* |
| CBQMS | *Catholic Biblical Quarterly*, Monograph Series |
| CBSC | Cambridge Bible for Schools and Colleges |
| ConB | Coniectanea Biblica |
| *DISO* | Ch.-F. Jean and J. Hoftijzer, *Dictionnaire des inscriptions sémitiques de l'ouest* (Leiden, 1965) |
| EB | Études bibliques |
| ET | English translation |
| *ETL* | *Ephemerides Theologicae Lovanienses* |

| | |
|---|---|
| *EvTh* | *Evangelische Theologie* |
| *ExpT* | *Expository Times* |
| GK | *Gesenius' Hebrew Grammar as edited and enlarged by the late E. Kautzsch*, ET A. E. Cowley (2nd edn., Oxford, 1910 = 28th German edn., 1909) |
| HK | Handkommentar zum Alten Testament |
| HSAT | Die Heilige Schrift des Alten Testaments |
| HSM | Harvard Semitic Monographs |
| *HTR* | *Harvard Theological Review* |
| ICC | International Critical Commentary |
| *IEJ* | *Israel Exploration Journal* |
| *ITQ* | *Irish Theological Quarterly* |
| *JBL* | *Journal of Biblical Literature* |
| *JJS* | *Journal of Jewish Studies* |
| *JNES* | *Journal of Near Eastern Studies* |
| Joüon | P. Joüon, *Grammaire de l'Hébreu biblique* (Rome, 1923) |
| *JQR* | *Jewish Quarterly Review* |
| *JSOT* | *Journal for the Study of the Old Testament* |
| JSOTS | *Journal for the Study of the Old Testament*, Supplement Series |
| *JSS* | *Journal of Semitic Studies* |
| *JTS* | *Journal of Theological Studies* |
| KAT | Kommentar zum Alten Testament |
| KHAT | Kurzer Hand-Commentar zum Alten Testament |
| LecD | Lectio Divina |
| LXX | The Septuagint |
| MT | Masoretic Text |
| NCB | New Century Bible |
| *NEB* | *New English Bible* |
| N.F. | neue Folge |
| NICOT | The New International Commentary on the Old Testament |
| *NRT* | *Nouvelle Revue Théologique* |
| NS | New Series |
| OBO | Orbis Biblicus et Orientalis |
| ÖBS | Österreichische Biblische Studien |
| OBT | Overtures in Biblical Theology |
| OTL | Old Testament Library |
| *OTS* | *Oudtestamentische Studiën* |
| Pesh. | The Peshiṭta |
| *PIBA* | *Proceedings of the Irish Biblical Association* |
| *RB* | *Revue biblique* |
| *REB* | *Revised English Bible* |
| *RQ* | *Revue de Qumrân* |
| *RSV* | *Revised Standard Version* |

| | |
|---|---|
| *RV* | *Revised Version* |
| SBLDS | Society of Biblical Literature Dissertation Series |
| SBS | Stuttgarter Bibelstudien |
| SBT | Studies in Biblical Theology |
| *ScrH* | *Scripta Hierosolymitana* |
| *SEÅ* | *Svensk Exegetisk Årsbok* |
| *SJOT* | *Scandinavian Journal of the Old Testament* |
| *SJT* | *Scottish Journal of Theology* |
| SOTSMS | The Society for Old Testament Study Monograph Series |
| SP | Samaritan Pentateuch |
| SP-B | Studia Post-Biblica |
| SSN | Studia Semitica Neerlandica |
| *ST* | *Studia Theologica* |
| SVT | Supplements to *Vetus Testamentum* |
| Targ. | The Targum |
| *TGl* | *Theologie und Glaube* |
| ThB | Theologische Bücherei |
| ThSt | Theologische Studien |
| *ThZ* | *Theologische Zeitschrift* |
| *TWAT* | G. Botterweck and H. Ringgren (eds.), *Theologisches Wörterbuch zum Alten Testament* (Stuttgart, 1970–) |
| *TynB* | *Tyndale Bulletin* |
| UBL | Ugaritisch-biblische Literatur |
| *VD* | *Verbum Domini* |
| Vg. | The Vulgate |
| *VT* | *Vetus Testamentum* |
| WBC | Word Biblical Commentary |
| WMANT | Wissenschaftliche Monographien zum Alten und Neuen Testament |
| *ZAW* | *Zeitschrift für die alttestamentliche Wissenschaft* |
| *ZDPV* | *Zeitschrift des deutschen Palästina-Vereins* |
| *ZTK* | *Zeitschrift für Theologie und Kirche* |

# COMMENTARIES ON ISAIAH


| | |
|---|---|
| Auvray | P. Auvray, *Isaïe 1–39* (Sources bibliques; Paris, 1972). |
| Beuken | W. A. M. Beuken, *Jesaja II–III* (De Prediking van het Oude Testament, 4 vols; Nijkerk, 1979–89). |
| de Boer | P. A. H. de Boer, *Second-Isaiah's Message* (*OTS* 11; Leiden, 1956). |
| Bonnard | P.-E. Bonnard, *Le Second Isaïe: Son disciple et leurs éditeurs: Isaïe 40–66* (EB; Paris, 1972). |
| Clements | R. E. Clements, *Isaiah 1–39* (NCB; Grand Rapids, Mich., and London, 1980). |
| Delitzsch | F. Delitzsch, *Commentar über das Buch Jesaia* (Leipzig, 1889$^{4}$) = ET *Biblical Commentary on the Prophecies of Isaiah* (Edinburgh, 1890) . |
| Dillmann | A. Dillmann, *Der Prophet Jesaia* (Kurzgefasstes exegetisches Handbuch zum Alten Testament; Leipzig, 1890; 6th edn. by R. Kittel, Leipzig, 1898). |
| Duhm | B. Duhm, *Das Buch Jesaja übersetzt und erklärt* (HK 3/1; Göttingen, 1892; 4th edn., 1922). |
| Eichrodt | W. Eichrodt, *Der Herr der Geschichte: Jesaja 13–23 und 28–39* (BAT 17/II; Stuttgart, 1967). |
| Elliger | K. Elliger, *Deuterojesaja*, i. *Jesaja 40,1–45,7* (BKAT xi/1; Neukirchen-Vluyn, 1978). |
| Fischer | J. Fischer, *Das Buch Isaias* (HSAT 7; Bonn, 1937). |
| Fohrer | G. Fohrer, *Das Buch Jesaja* (3 vols., Zürcher Bibelkommentare; Zurich and Stuttgart, 1964–67$^{2}$). |
| Gray | G. B. Gray, *A Critical and Exegetical Commentary on the Book of Isaiah I–XXVII* (ICC; Edinburgh, 1912). |
| Hayes and Irvine | J. H. Hayes and S. A. Irvine, *Isaiah, the Eighth-Century Prophet: his Times and his Preaching* (Nashville, 1987). |
| Hermisson | H.-J. Hermisson, *Deuterojesaja 45,8–25* (BKAT 11/7; Neukirchen-Vluyn, 1987). |

Kaiser — O. Kaiser, *Das Buch des Propheten Jesaja Kapitel 1–12* (ATD 17; Göttingen, 1981$^5$) = ET *Isaiah 1–12: A Commentary* (OTL; London, 1983$^2$); *Der Prophet Jesaja Kapitel 13–39* (ATD 18; Göttingen, 1973) = ET *Isaiah 13–39: A Commentary* (London, 1974).

Kessler — W. Kessler, *Gott geht es um das Ganze: Jesaja 56–66 und Jesaja 24–27* (BAT 19; Stuttgart, 1967$^2$).

Kissane — E. J. Kissane, *The Book of Isaiah* (Dublin, 1941).

König — E. König, *Das Buch Jesaja, eingeleitet, übersetzt und erklärt* (Gütersloh, 1926).

Lowth — R. Lowth, *Isaiah: A New Translation; with a Preliminary Dissertation, and Notes, Critical, Philological, and Explanatory* (London, 1824).

McKenzie — J. L. McKenzie, *Second Isaiah: Introduction, Translation, and Notes* (AB; Garden City, NY, 1968).

Marti — K. Marti, *Das Buch Jesaja* (KHAT 10; Tübingen, 1900).

Miscall — P. D. Miscall, *Isaiah* (Sheffield, 1993).

Muilenburg — J. Muilenburg, 'The Book of Isaiah, Chapters 40–66', in G. A. Buttrick (ed.), *The Interpreter's Bible*, v (New York and Nashville, Tenn., 1956), 381–773.

North — C. R. North, *The Second Isaiah: Introduction, Translation and Commentary to Chapters xl–lv* (Oxford, 1964).

Oswalt — J. N. Oswalt, *The Book of Isaiah, Chapters 1–39* (NICOT; Grand Rapids, Mich., 1986).

Procksch — O. Procksch, *Jesaia I* (KAT 9/1; Leipzig, 1930).

Schoors — A. Schoors, *Jesaja* (Boeken van het Oude Testament, 9; Roermond, 1972–3).

Scott — R. B. Y. Scott, 'The Book of Isaiah, Chapters 1–39', in G. A. Buttrick (ed.), *The Interpreter's Bible*, v (New York and Nashville, Tenn., 1956), 151–381.

Skinner — J. Skinner, *The Book of the Prophet Isaiah, Chapters I.–XXXIX. with Introduction and Notes* (CBSC; Cambridge, 1897).

Snaith — N. H. Snaith, 'Isaiah 40–66: A Study of the Teaching of the Second Isaiah and its Consequences', in H. M. Orlinsky and N. H. Snaith, *Studies on the Second Part of the Book of Isaiah* (SVT 14; Leiden, 1977$^2$), 135–264.

Torrey — C. C. Torrey, *The Second Isaiah: A New Interpretation* (Edinburgh, 1928).

Vermeylen — J. Vermeylen, *Du prophète Isaïe à l'apocalyptique: Isaïe, I–XXXV, miroir d'un demi-millénaire d'expérience religieuse en Israël* (EB; 2 vols; Paris, 1977–8).

Volz — P. Volz, *Jesaia II* (KAT 9; Leipzig, 1932).

Wade — G. W. Wade, *The Book of the Prophet Isaiah* (London, 1929²).

Watts — J. D. W. Watts, *Isaiah 1–33* and *Isaiah 34–66* (WBC 24–5; Waco, 1985 and 1987).

Westermann — C. Westermann, *Das Buch Jesaja Kapitel 40–66* (ATD 19; Göttingen, 1981⁴) = ET *Isaiah 40–66. A Commentary* (OTL; London, 1969).

Whybray — R.N. Whybray, *Isaiah 40–66* (NCB; London, 1975).

Wildberger — H. Wildberger, *Jesaja,* i. *Jesaja 1–12* (BKAT 10/1; Neukirchen-Vluyn, 1980²); ii. *Jesaja 13–27* (BKAT 10/2; Neukirchen-Vluyn, 1978); iii. *Jesaja 28–39: Das Buch, der Prophet und seine Botschaft* (BKAT 10/3; Neukirchen-Vluyn, 1982).

# I

## Recent Study of the Book Called Isaiah

ONE of the best-known and most widely accepted critical hypotheses concerning the composition of the Old Testament is that the book of Isaiah was not entirely, or even largely, written by the eighth-century Judaean prophet. This theory, first developed in the modern period[1] by J. C. Döderlein,[2] steadily gained ground during the nineteenth century[3] until it was developed into its classical form by Duhm in his commentary of 1892.[4] According to Duhm, not only are the three major divisions of Isaiah to be ascribed to authors of three different historical periods, so that it has become customary to speak of Proto-, Deutero-, and Trito-Isaiah (chapters 1–39, 40–55, and 56–66 respectively), but even within these major

[1] For a discussion of Ibn Ezra's anticipation of this view in the twelfth century, see U. Simon, 'Ibn Ezra between Medievalism and Modernism: The Case of Isaiah xl–lxvi', in J. A. Emerton (ed.), *Congress Volume: Salamanca 1983* (SVT 36; Leiden, 1985), 257–71.

[2] The development of Döderlein's position between 1781 and 1788 is documented by J. M. Vincent, *Studien zur literarischen Eigenart und zur geistigen Heimat von Jesaja, Kap. 40–55* (BET 5; Frankfurt am Main, 1977), 17–21. Vincent helpfully locates Döderlein's work in its intellectual context (mentioning especially the importance of Spinoza), notes the anticipation of Döderlein by J. B. Koppe in 1779–80, and discusses the differences between his approach and that of his contemporary Eichhorn, in whose Introduction the composition of Isaiah was given extended treatment: see J. G. Eichhorn, *Einleitung ins Alte Testament* (Leipzig, 1787²), iii. 52–102. (I regret that the first edition of 1783 is not available to me.)

[3] The clearest indication of this comes from the change of mind by the moderately conservative Delitzsch in the fourth edition of his commentary on Isaiah; note S. R. Driver's introduction to the English translation of this edition on pp. vii–xv, reprinted from *ExpT* 1 (1889–90), 197–201, and H.-J. Kraus, *Geschichte der historisch-kritischen Erforschung des Alten Testaments* (Neukirchen-Vluyn, 1969²), 230–41. The extent to which Delitzsch 'surrendered to the critical theory of multiple authorship' is minimized by R. K. Harrison (*Introduction to the Old Testament* (London, 1970), 770–1). For a fuller discussion of nineteenth-century trends in the study of Isaiah prior to the publication of Duhm's commentary, see E. J. Young, *Studies in Isaiah* (London, 1954), 9–38.

[4] This commentary was revised more than once, so that it is now normal to refer to the fourth edition of 1922.

divisions later material is also to be separated out. This is best known with regard to his isolation of four so-called servant songs in Deutero-Isaiah (42: 1–4; 49: 1–6; 50: 4–9; 52: 13–53: 12), which Duhm regarded as later additions to the text written originally in the margins or in spaces between sections, but also within Proto-Isaiah he found many examples of material which had been added subsequently to the work of the eighth-century prophet.

In adopting this principle of multiple authorship as the starting-point for the present investigation, one or two points deserve emphasis, even though this is not the place, nor is there today any real need, for a full exposition of the reasons that have led to the acceptance of this conclusion.[5] First, in view of repeated accusations,[6] it should be emphasized that this opinion is not necessarily motivated by a wish to circumvent the possibility of predictive prophecy. Indeed, there remains plenty of 'prediction', both general and specific, within Deutero-Isaiah itself, for example, if the bulk of Isaiah 40–55 is to be dated before the end of the period of Babylonian exile, and indeed it has frequently been maintained that part of the purpose of the concluding chapters of Isaiah was precisely to answer the problems raised by the apparent failure of these predictions to be borne out by the experience of the return and post-exilic restoration.[7]

Secondly, the strongest argument has always seemed to me to be that, in chapter 41 in particular, Deutero-Isaiah uses the argument from prophecy in order to encourage faith in the new message which is now being proclaimed. If a prophet maintains that certain things which have been prophesied in the past have been accurately fulfilled, so that now one may have confidence in the reliability of the new predictions being made, the argument both presupposes an acceptance of the validity of predictive prophecy, and also demands that the speaker should himself be located after the fulfilment of those predictions. The text itself thus requires us to accept that part of it comes either from a period substantially later than the work of whoever wrote the earlier part, or, if the 'former things'

[5] See e.g. S. R. Driver, *An Introduction to the Literature of the Old Testament* (Edinburgh, 1913[9]), 236–44.

[6] e.g. O. T. Allis, *The Unity of Isaiah* (London, 1951), echoing many earlier apologists.

[7] e.g. R. P. Carroll, *When Prophecy Failed: Reactions and Responses to Failure in the Old Testament Prophetic Traditions* (London, 1979), 152–5.

refer to the initial rise of Cyrus, chronicled in 41: 2–4,[8] then from a point in time later than that initial rise; either way, we are brought down to a time far too late to be within the lifetime of Isaiah of Jerusalem.

Thirdly, again despite objections, weight must still be given to the view that we should take seriously the historical standpoint which the writer presupposes for himself. S. R. Driver's classic formulation of this argument bears repetition:

> In the present prophecy there is no *prediction* of exile: the exile is not announced as something still future; it is *presupposed*, and only the *release* from it is *predicted*. By analogy, therefore, [that is, with Jeremiah and Ezekiel] the author will have lived in the situation which he thus presupposes, and to which he continually alludes.[9]

To deny the force of this point by suggesting that, without indicating what he was doing, an earlier prophet projected himself fully into the standpoint of far later readers seems to introduce an element of deception into his work that I should be reluctant to concede; it would appear to be quite as reprehensible as that of which conservative scholars accuse those who hold to multiple authorship with regard, for instance, to the heading in Isa. 1: 1.

Naturally, a great deal more could be said about the subject than this, and we shall see that the situation is in any case far more complicated than the simple threefold division of Isaiah implies, but this must suffice for the moment to enable us to enquire what scholars have made of this fact of multiple authorship by way of explanation.[10]

Confining ourselves to the period from Duhm to the present day, we may categorize the suggestions which have been made into six main groups. (1) Duhm himself hardly addressed the question directly, for it emerges from the composition history which he sketches in the introduction to his commentary that in his view the two major halves of the book developed independently of one

[8] This was maintained with regard to some of the relevant passages by, e.g., C. R. North, 'The "Former Things" and the "New Things" in Deutero-Isaiah', in H. H. Rowley (ed.), *Studies in Old Testament Prophecy* (Edinburgh, 1957), 111–26.

[9] S. R. Driver, *Introduction*, 237.

[10] For other surveys of research, see J. Vermeylen, 'L'Unité du livre d'Isaïe', and G. I. Davies, 'The Destiny of the Nations in the Book of Isaiah', both in J. Vermeylen (ed.), *The Book of Isaiah* (BETL 81; Leuven, 1989), 11–53 and 93–120 respectively, and D. Carr, 'Reaching for Unity in Isaiah', *JSOT* 57 (1993), 61–80.

another and were only combined at a very late stage. Chapters 40–66 were already in their present form by this time ('etwa am Ende des 3. Jahrh.' (p. xx) ), though some additions to 1–39 are to be dated even later. In particular, he deduces from the apparent ascription of a citation of Isa. 44: 28 to Jeremiah in 2 Chron. 36: 22–3 = Ezra 1: 1–3 that Isaiah 40–66 may have been attached to the book of Jeremiah in the Chronicler's day, or at least that it was not yet reckoned to be part of the book of Isaiah.[11]

It would appear that many who followed Duhm similarly saw little or no need to explain how or why this diverse material came together as a single book. As Vermeylen has correctly pointed out,[12] the emphasis of these scholars was always to establish the separate composition of the later parts of the book, something which was understandable when the view still needed to be established, but which became increasingly myopic once it had become widely accepted. The few desperate attempts made at an explanation have never been found satisfying, sometimes even to those who proposed them.[13] Most widely cited is the conjecture[14] that the combination was due to purely material considerations—the need to fill a complete and precious scroll by combining two shorter works into something approximately the same length as Jeremiah, Ezekiel, and the 'book' of the twelve minor prophets.[15] However, quite apart from all that will be said below, the fact that this consideration does not seem to have been a material cause in determining the length of other biblical books renders the theory questionable. As Haran has pointed out, there is no ancient evi-

[11] See, however, H. G. M. Williamson, *Ezra, Nehemiah* (WBC 16; Waco, 1985), 10, for an alternative explanation.

[12] Vermeylen, 'L'Unité', 13.

[13] See e.g. Fohrer as cited in n. 17 below.

[14] This conjecture is usually cited in the form given it by R. H. Pfeiffer, *Introduction to the Old Testament* (London, 1952), 415. In fact, the suggestion is far older; it is not dissimilar to the suggestion already advanced by Eichhorn (*Einleitung*, iii. 81–2), who associates it, however, with his 'anthological' approach to the composition of the book; more precisely, see e.g. W. R. Smith, *The Prophets of Israel and their Place in History* (London, 1895²), 211–13, and A. F. Kirkpatrick, *The Doctrine of the Prophets* (London, 1917³), 363. Kirkpatrick further anticipates some more modern proposals by suggesting as additional reasons that Deutero-Isaiah was in some sense a disciple of Isaiah and that there has been influence from the very name of 'Isaiah' itself: 'Where could the great prophecy of Israel's deliverance from Babylon be more fitly placed than in the volume of the prophet whose name proclaimed the message of *Jehovah's salvation*?' (p. 364).

[15] Taking the number of pages in *BHS* as a very rough and ready guide, the figures are 104, 115, 94, and 95 respectively.

dence whatsoever for the copying of shorter books, such as the five *megillot*, on a single scroll.[16] Similarly, evidence is entirely lacking for the proposal that the author of the second half of the book also happened to be called Isaiah, thus causing the two parts to be juxtaposed.[17] Such theories are clearly nothing less than guesses born of desperation.

It may seem surprising to some that I should also wish to include the monograph of O. H. Steck on Isaiah 35[18] in this first category. Steck's main concern in this work is to demonstrate by way of a detailed comparison of Isaiah 35 with 32–4, on the one hand, and 40: 1–11, on the other, that it was written as a bridge passage, a redactional join, between the two main parts of the book as a whole. He is insistent that it did not originate independently, but that it was specifically composed for its present setting. He then goes on to identify some other passages which are also part of this redaction, notably 11: 11–16; 27: 12–13; and 62: 10–12, and further argues that some other material was added to the now united book at an even later stage. He proposes that the initial redaction took place at the very end of, or just after, the period of Persian rule, and that the later phases continued until well into the third century BC.

This summary does not attempt to do justice to all aspects of Steck's careful analysis, which includes many observations of importance for our overall theme, and to which inevitably we must return (see Chapter 8 below). Nor do I wish to play down the significance of the fact that he is grappling seriously with the kind of questions which Duhm and his successors left unanswered. But his

16 See M. Haran, 'Book-Size and the Device of Catch-Lines in the Biblical Canon', *JJS* 36 (1985), 1–11. Admittedly, the case of the twelve minor prophets might be adduced as evidence to the contrary, but this exception is more apparent than real. As far back as our external evidence reaches, the Twelve have been regarded as a single book, and it appears that this appreciation stretches back to the final stages of their redaction and canonical ordering; see P. R. House, *The Unity of the Twelve* (JSOTS 97; Sheffield, 1990), 10. House's starting-point is thus secure, even if not all the results of his subsequent analysis carry conviction. Without question, the empirical evidence on the size of scrolls in ancient times points clearly to the conclusion that this was not a determinative factor in deciding the length of 'books' beyond the obvious point that some large books had to be accommodated on more than a single scroll.

17 See E. Sellin and G. Fohrer, *Einleitung in das Alte Testament* (Heidelberg, 1965[10]), 410 = ET G. Fohrer, *Introduction to the Old Testament* (London, 1970), 375.

18 O. H. Steck, *Bereitete Heimkehr: Jesaja 35 als redaktionelle Brücke zwischen dem Ersten und dem Zweiten Jesaja* (SBS 121; Stuttgart, 1985).

work belongs in this category for the simple reason that in his opinion the two major parts of Isaiah developed initially in apparently complete isolation from one another.[19] In other words, the redaction associated with chapter 35 is wholly secondary from the point of view of a total composition history of the book. As with Duhm, no place is found for any inherent connection between the various parts of the book at the level of initial composition itself.

(2) The second group of scholars that we must consider argues for a much closer connection between the various parts of Isaiah by way of postulating an Isaianic school of disciples, to which the authors of each of the later parts belonged. In terms of the history of scholarship, this seems to have been the earliest proposal by those who denied authorial unity to attempt to account for the development of the book as we now have it on internal grounds rather than as the result of a mere juxtaposition of originally unrelated works.

The idea that Isaiah of Jerusalem established a school of disciples was postulated primarily by Mowinckel.[20] It was developed notably with relevance to our present concerns by Jones in an influential article of 1955.[21] Jones concentrated on three significant moments in the composition and transmission of Isaianic material. First comes Isaiah's own commitment to writing of (some of) his oracles 'amongst my disciples' (8: 16), 'a community who hold in their midst the written prophetic *torah* or תְּעוּדָה' (p. 237). As illuminated

[19] 'Diese Redaktion richtet sich auf zwei, offensichtlich bisher voneinander unabhängige, bereits schriftlich festformulierte Bücher' (p. 101). He regards it as probable that the joining together of the two books and the redactional composition of chapter 35 were part of the same process.

[20] See S. Mowinckel, *Prophecy and Tradition: The Prophetic Books in the Light of the Study of the Growth and History of the Tradition* (Oslo, 1946), 67–70, where he states that it is a development of his earlier views published in *Jesajadisiplene: Profitien fra Jesaja til Jeremia* (Oslo, 1926). The earliest systematic representative of this approach was apparently G. Margoliouth, 'Isaiah and Isaianic', *The Expositor*, 7th ser., 9 (1910), 525–9, though even he had predecessors; see e.g. Delitzsch, 28–9 = ET 38–9. Vermeylen ('L'Unité', 16 n. 20), also lists a number of other scholars who have favoured this approach, to which might be added J. Schreiner, 'Das Buch jesajanischer Schule', in J. Schreiner (ed.), *Wort und Botschaft: Eine theologische und kritische Einführung in die Probleme des Alten Testaments* (Würzburg, 1967), 142–62. The suggestion of K. Elliger (*Deuterojesaja in seinem Verhältnis zu Tritojesaja* (BWANT 63; Stuttgart, 1933) ) and others that Trito-Isaiah was a disciple of Deutero-Isaiah is, of course, a separate issue.

[21] D. R. Jones, 'The Traditio of the Oracles of Isaiah of Jerusalem', *ZAW* 67 (1955), 226–46.

by Jeremiah 32 and 36, Isaiah 8 attests 'both the single prediction made to contemporaries but also written down that the fulfilment might be recognised as Yahweh's work and the writing down of a number of oracles in condensed form that they also might stand as a witness, when the day comes, that Yahweh had declared it beforehand' (p. 237).

Secondly, Jones surveys the material in Isaiah 1–5 in order to show how this material of Isaiah was shaped and expanded by Isaiah's disciples so as to apply it to the situation following the fall of Jerusalem in 587 BC. Finally, and most briefly, he directs attention to a third stage, 'represented by that greatest of all Isaiah's disciples whose work is now shown over and over again to reveal close knowledge of the teaching of Isaiah of Jerusalem' (p. 245). Without going into detail, Jones suggests that 'the former things' which 'have come to pass' (42: 9, with parallels elsewhere) refer specifically to the previously collected oracles of Isaiah as they now reached him in edited form by way of the school of disciples.

Jones's article was avowedly programmatic, and did not set out to provide all the evidence necessary to establish his case. It deals most fully with what he calls 'the first significant moment in the process of transmission', uses chapters 1–5 only by way of illustration of the second, and is sketchy in the extreme with regard to the third. This is appropriately, therefore, the very point which the other major representative of this line of interpretation, J. H. Eaton,[22] seeks to develop more fully. Eaton starts out with a major attempt to establish the probability that Isaiah founded a school of disciples. This is based both on general considerations and particularly again on Isa. 8: 16–18. In contrast with Jones, however, he places more emphasis on oral tradition than on a written deposit. Then, after a brief survey of the work of this school down to the period of the exile, he turns his attention to chapters 40–66 in order to argue that they 'can reasonably be regarded as a continuation of the work of the Isaianic society' (p. 152). This he does both by thematic considerations, such as the promise of deliverance based on ideas drawn from the pre-exilic New Year Festival and by attention to certain aspects of the content and style of these

[22] J. H. Eaton, 'The Origin of the Book of Isaiah', *VT* 9 (1959), 138–57. See also his *Festal Drama in Deutero-Isaiah* (London, 1979), and 'The Isaiah Tradition', in R. Coggins, A. Phillips, and M. Knibb (eds.), *Israel's Prophetic Tradition: Essays in Honour of Peter R. Ackroyd* (Cambridge, 1982), 58–76.

chapters, though, with the exception of the phrase 'The Holy One of Israel', these turn out on examination to be less specific than might at first have been supposed. Nevertheless, they enable Eaton to conclude that study of the book of Isaiah as a whole should prove worthwhile.

Whereas, as I hope to show later, there are aspects of Jones's and Eaton's observations which prove to be of value, it may nevertheless be questioned whether their explanation by way of a school of disciples is satisfactory. In addition to those scholars, such as G. Fohrer, who have difficulty with their interpretation of 8: 16, it has been pointed out that there is really no evidence for the existence of such a school after the time of Isaiah nor any explanation of where or how it could have maintained itself in comparative isolation during a period of more than two centuries. Furthermore, Clements[23] observes that the argument is circular, the existence of the group being allegedly attested from the book itself, and he asks in what meaningful sense one may speak of a 'disciple' so long after the prophet's death, and how such a 'disciple' could have the liberty to introduce so much new material. It remains to be seen, therefore, whether the observations on which this theory is based cannot be more reasonably explained without recourse to the dubious hypothesis of a school of disciples of the prophet.

(3) We come now to what may be regarded as the modern period of study of the 'unity' of Isaiah. During the past fifteen years or so this has become the subject of increasing interest to scholars, and a steady flow of publications bears witness to the fact that the subject has moved to the centre stage of Isaianic studies. Nevertheless, there remain several related but still distinct approaches which require classification.

We may begin with the largest group, which can be generally categorized as theories concentrating on redaction history. We have already seen that Steck's work might have been included here were it not for the fact that he sees the process of redactional linkage starting so late, well after the time when the major blocks of the book were already approaching their present form. By contrast, we are looking now at studies which see the process of composition and redaction as more closely associated, though the disentangling

[23] R. E. Clements, 'The Unity of the Book of Isaiah', *Interpretation*, 36 (1982), 117–29 (119).

of quite what this involves will prove to pose one of the major difficulties for this view.

Before coming to the recent advocates of this approach, we should pause to take note of an earlier precursor which, perhaps because it now appears to have been ahead of its time, has not always received the attention it deserves, at least in English-speaking circles. In 1968 J. Becker published an unpretentious little volume[24] in which he argued that the work of Isaiah was subjected to a major redaction in or just after the exile. He both identified passages in 1–39 which belonged to this and argued in addition for its close association, if not identity with, the composition of 40–66.[25] Isaiah 40 seemed to him to be designed deliberately to follow 39, while the theme of 'the former things and the new things' in 40–8 also appeared to be designed as an 'ad hoc construction' to forge a redactional link between the two parts of the book. He summarized the major themes and motives which linked these redactional sections of Isaiah as follows: 'The people are forgiven and return to their land in a new Exodus; Yahweh's kingly rule begins on Zion and his glory is revealed; those returning home from exile increase miraculously both in number and power; the nations come on pilgrimage to Zion while the enemies of Israel are judged' (p. 42; my translation). Finally, he noted in particular a theocratic tendency in the redaction which reapplied the material about the Davidic dynasty in Isaiah's own work to the later community.

Other works which require consideration here are less ambitious than Becker's. Mention should be made of a series of articles by P. R. Ackroyd[26] in which, without attempting an answer to the question of how this came about, he points to the suitability of certain sections to an analysis of the book as a whole. Thus, following in the wake of some earlier observations by Melugin,[27] he argues that

[24] J. Becker, *Isaias—der Prophet und sein Buch* (SBS 30; Stuttgart, 1968).

[25] It should be noted that on p. 37 he expresses doubts about a separate book of 'Deutero-Isaiah'.

[26] Note especially 'Isaiah i–xii: Presentation of a Prophet', in *Congress Volume: Göttingen, 1977* (SVT 29; Leiden, 1978), 16–48, and 'Isaiah 36–39: Structure and Function', in W. C. Delsman *et al.* (eds.), *Von Kanaan bis Kerala: Festschrift für Prof. Mag. Dr. J. P. M. van der Ploeg O.P. zur Vollendung des siebzigsten Lebensjahres am 4. Juli 1979* (AOAT 211; Neukirchen-Vluyn, 1982), 3–21, both conveniently reprinted, together with several other articles which are relevant to this topic, in *Studies in the Religious Tradition of the Old Testament* (London, 1987). It is surprising that Vermeylen does not include these articles in his survey of research (see above, n. 10).

[27] R. F. Melugin, *The Formation of Isaiah 40–55* (BZAW 141; Berlin, 1976).

chapters 36–9 function effectively as a join between the first part of the book and chapters 40–55, and further that this is strengthened by the particularly close links between 36–9 and 6: 1–9: 6. Similarly, in a study of chapters 1–12 he suggests that as they are assembled now they help to answer the question why the prophet Isaiah came to be so highly regarded and why such a large corpus of material came to be assembled under his name. He does not generally study specific connections with chapters 40–55 in this article, but we may note his analysis of chapter 12 as a suitable colophon to what precedes and as providing some particularly close links with the later part of the book.

Somewhat different in its approach is the work of Rendtorff,[28] who argues on the basis of a number of phrases and themes in Deutero-Isaiah which recur in Proto- and Trito-Isaiah for a tight redactional association of the three parts of the book. Within this analysis, certain chapters, such as 1, 12, 35, and 40, stand out as being particularly significant for this process. Furthermore, it emerges that chapters 40–55 are central to the development of the book as a whole, Proto-Isaiah being edited with an eye towards what follows, and 56–66 serving to bind both earlier parts together. A brief but neat example of Rendtorff's procedure is furnished by his handling of the use of *ṣedeq/ṣ^e^dāqâ*. In 1–39 he finds that it is frequently associated with *mišpāṭ*, whereas in 40–55 it stands in association with words from the root *yšʿ*. In the first part, therefore, it stands for human righteousness, in contrast to the second, where it refers to divine salvation. In 56: 1, however, which introduces Trito-Isaiah, we find these two usages drawn together in juxtaposition:

Keep ye judgment [*mišpāṭ*] and do righteousness [*ṣ^e^dāqâ*];
For my salvation [*y^e^šûʿ*â] is near to come, and my righteousness [*ṣ^e^dāqâ*] to
be revealed.

In terms of strictly composition history, Rendtorff's conclusions are not quite clear in one respect, namely, whether Deutero-Isaiah wrote with knowledge of, or under the influence of, any part of chapters 1–39. However, his description of 40–55 as 'eine durchkomponierte und in sich geschlossene Einheit' (p. 318) seems to

[28] R. Rendtorff, 'Zur Komposition des Buches Jesaja', *VT* 34 (1984), 295–320.

imply that he did not. Similarly, in his *Introduction*[29] he concludes that Deutero-Isaiah 'could have existed independently before being inserted into the present composition'.

Finally in this section, reference should be made to Vermeylen's recent article on the subject (see above, n. 10), which naturally builds to some extent on his earlier major analysis of Isaiah 1–35.[30] In some respects, Vermeylen's approach could be compared with that of Steck, for he too regards the combination of Proto- and Deutero-Isaiah as a late phase in the development of the book. This is especially so as regards Proto-Isaiah, which he argues was still an independent work when it was brought to something very close to its present form by an eschatological redaction around 480 BC. Deutero-Isaiah, too, was an independent composition in its original state, but this is where Vermeylen's view takes a new turn. Following some who have begun to question the substantial unity of 40–55, he suggests that this 'original state' was far briefer than the work we now have, but that around the time of Nehemiah it was expanded redactionally as part of the process of associating it with 1–39. Isa. 40: 1–3, 5, for instance, was shaped in parallel with chapter 1, so that the new part of the book now opens with a word of consolation which closely echoes and yet reverses that which opens the first part of the book. Finally, Trito-Isaiah's many links with all that precedes are explained by the theory that they were written by this self-same redactor. Thus, in Vermeylen's view, the processes of composition and redaction are more closely intertwined than Steck implies.

A review of the works outlined in this section reveals some notable gains, particularly in most cases along the lines of the challenge to read parts of Isaiah 1–39 in the light of 40–55 (or 66).[31] And this work is now being taken further by other scholars, most notably Sweeney,[32] who virtually take this as a given starting-point in works devoted to 1–39 alone. (This is also the appropriate point at which to refer again to the work of K. Jeppesen, mentioned in the Preface.) What is lacking, however, is any sustained consideration

[29] R. Rendtorff, *The Old Testament: An Introduction* (London, 1985), 200 = *Das Alte Testament: Eine Einführung* (Neukirchen-Vluyn, 1983), 211.

[30] J. Vermeylen, *Du prophète Isaïe à l'apocalyptique: Isaïe, I–XXXV, miroir d'un demi-millénaire d'expérience religieuse en Israël* (EB; 2 vols.; Paris, 1977–8).

[31] Vermeylen is an obvious exception here, however.

[32] M. A. Sweeney, *Isaiah 1–4 and the Post-Exilic Understanding of the Isaianic Tradition* (BZAW 171; Berlin, 1988).

of the question whether the original nucleus of 1–39 had any influence, not only on the redaction, but also on the composition, of 40–55, which emerges so clearly from the work of Rendtorff as the central body of material for consideration in the growth of the book as a whole.

(4) In the context of recent studies, the question just raised has been approached step by step in the work of Clements. Following the publication of his commentary and various related studies,[33] he first wrote explicitly on 'The Unity of the Book of Isaiah' in 1982. In this article he argued that the overall structure of the book showed signs of editorial planning and further that his own and others' redactional studies suggested that this was not a late and superficial stage in the book's development. In particular, 'this renders it perfectly possible and feasible that the great unnamed prophet of Isaiah 40–55 . . . could have known and made allusion to the earlier prophetic collection now embedded in Isaiah 1–35' (p. 124). After some discussion, which in my opinion does not show awareness of the full amount of material that ought to be considered, Clements equivocates; Isaiah 40–55 certainly 'complements' the earlier chapters of the book, but he leaves open the question 'whether the original prophet of the exile saw this, or whether it was a circle of later editors who felt the appropriateness of adding his message to that of Isaiah' (p. 128).

Three years later Clements had made up his mind, regarding it now as most probable that 'from the outset, the material in chs. 40–55 was intended to develop and enlarge upon prophetic sayings from Isaiah of Jerusalem'.[34] This he attempted to establish on the basis of two fundamental themes and several other possible ones. The two fundamental themes are, first, Israel's blindness and deafness, which occurs several times in 40–55 and is thought to find its origin in the account of Isaiah's commissioning in 6: 9–10 (it also occurs in the later 29: 18 and 35: 5), and, second, the divine election of Israel, by which Deutero-Isaiah reverses First Isaiah's repeated emphasis that God has rejected his people. The group of

[33] R. E. Clements, *Isaiah 1–39* (NCB; Grand Rapids, Mich., and London, 1980); *Isaiah and the Deliverance of Jerusalem: A Study of the Interpretation of Prophecy in the Old Testament* (JSOTS 13; Sheffield, 1980); 'The Prophecies of Isaiah and the Fall of Jerusalem in 587 BC', *VT* 30 (1980), 421–36.

[34] R. E. Clements, 'Beyond Tradition-History: Deutero-Isaianic Development of First Isaiah's Themes', *JSOT* 31 (1985), 95–113 (101).

'possibles' comprises the theme of witnesses, the way in which 44: 26 counterbalances 6: 11, and the divine summons by means of God's 'raising a signal'.

Most recently, Albertz has followed very much in Clements's footsteps with an article whose title is revealing: 'Das Deuterojesaja-Buch als Fortschreibung der Jesaja-Prophetie'.[35] He first points to the fact that the prologue to Deutero-Isaiah builds programmatically on some central passages in First Isaiah, notably Isaiah 6 (see further Chapter 3 below), and then examines some other connections between the two parts of the work, particularly that of God's 'plan', and the likelihood that 'the former things' refer to this plan as outlined in the Assyrian redaction of First Isaiah.

This is a convenient place at which to mention a number of studies which seek to identify other themes which characterize the book of Isaiah as a whole, even though not all by any means believe that these can be used to settle the question of how far the various parts of the book can be related at the level of composition. Of course, those who defend unity of authorship have always appealed to this argument, and a recent example is the commentary of Oswalt,[36] who suggests that 'The book . . . seeks to answer the question: How can a sinful, corrupt people become the servants of God?' (p. 21). On the other hand, Dumbrell,[37] who does not specifically argue for unity of authorship, though he comes close to it and one suspects that it may be part of his hidden agenda,[38] proposes with equal confidence the theme of 'Yahweh's interest in and devotion to the city of Jerusalem', and he writes that 'If the book is read as a unit there is an *overmastering* theme which may be said effectively to unite the whole' (p. 112).

Undoubtedly, it is possible to trace such themes in the various parts of the book, and it would be surprising if human ingenuity could not devise ways of making them 'tell a story' that might suggest the work of a single mind. The problem remains, however,

[35] R. Albertz, 'Das Deuterojesaja-Buch als Fortschreibung der Jesaja-Prophetie', in E. Blum, C. Macholz, and E. W. Stegemann (eds.), *Die Hebräische Bibel und ihre zweifache Nachgeschichte: Festschrift für Rolf Rendtorff zum 65. Geburtstag* (Neukirchen-Vluyn, 1990), 241–56.

[36] J. N. Oswalt, *The Book of Isaiah, Chapters 1–39* (NICOT; Grand Rapids, Mich., 1986).

[37] W. J. Dumbrell, 'The Purpose of the Book of Isaiah', *TynB* 36 (1985), 111–28.

[38] Note his equally guarded language in *The Faith of Israel: Its Expression in the Books of the Old Testament* (Leicester, 1989), 98–100.

that such arguments are not persuasive to those who are not already convinced, both because such divergent suggestions can be advanced and because they lack firm control; how is one to know if the relevant passages come from a single author or from several writing on the same theme?

Others who write on this subject are more cautious, describing what they see without drawing broader, critical conclusions from their analysis. Mention here should be made of Roberts,[39] who writes, 'If there is any one concept central to the whole Book of Isaiah, it is the vision of Yahweh as the Holy One of Israel' (p. 131). Roberts then traces the implications of this central affirmation, such as that Yahweh alone is Lord, in ways that effectively suggest a synchronic theological reading of the book. Similarly, J. Jensen undertakes a study of 'Yahweh's Plan in Isaiah and in the Rest of the Old Testament',[40] from which he concludes that 'In general there is little that resembles Isaiah's use of this terminology to designate Yahweh's control of history, except in Deutero-Isaiah and some other later sections of the Isaiah collection' (p. 455). Studies such as these are suggestive of the possibility that the various authors of the book may have had an eye on one another, so to speak, but, as has been mentioned, they do not set out with that issue in view and thus the material they present cannot be used for that purpose without further analysis.

One writer who is very much aware of these problems of method in his presentation of an Isaianic theme is G. I. Davies; indeed, his study of 'The Destiny of the Nations in the Book of Isaiah' is explicitly undertaken to examine the extent to which such a thematic analysis may be able to contribute to the current debate. Having collected the relevant material and sketched some of the views that I have also outlined, he turns to consider the relationship between the two. Although Davies is impressed with some of the links, both phraseological and thematic, which his study has revealed between chapters 1–39 and 40–55, he is not convinced that they establish Deutero-Isaiah's dependence on Proto-Isaiah, because influence from other sources, such as Jeremiah 50–1, is equally plausible. He is more open to the probability of overarching

[39] J. J. M. Roberts, 'Isaiah in Old Testament Theology', *Interpretation*, 36 (1982), 130–43; see also J. G. Gammie, *Holiness in Israel* (OBT; Minneapolis, 1989), ch. 3.

[40] *CBQ* 48 (1986), 443–55. Jensen's study should now be modified in the light of W. Werner, *Studien zur alttestamentlichen Vorstellung vom Plan Jahwes* (BZAW 173; Berlin, 1988), though contrast the article of Albertz mentioned above, n. 35.

redactional activity, but ultimately he suggests that the unity of the book derives not so much from its compilers as from the tradition which underlies it, 'and that means above all the Jerusalem cult tradition with its cosmic and universal perspective' (p. 119). This is a valuable study which raises important methodological issues to which we must return later; suffice it to say for the moment that we shall need to ask whether Davies's proposal, which furnishes a possible explanation for the unifying effect of one single theme, will be sufficient to account for all the material when other, quite separate themes are brought into the picture.

(5) Another group of studies focuses on the topic of the structural unity of the book. An early but influential attempt in this direction was made by Liebreich,[41] who drew attention to numerous verbal parallels as a means of dividing the book into its main sections. Most of these were limited to sections within the major divisions of Isaiah, but two were of further reaching consequence, namely the heavy density of parallels between chapters 1 and 65–6, and the connections between chapters 39 and 40. The effects of these are to tie the two main parts of Isaiah together, and to suggest that it has been consciously given final shape by the 'envelope' pattern in which the end matches the beginning.

While Liebreich concentrated on verbal parallels, Lack developed similar observations by drawing in themes, imagery, and theology,[42] and included in this was a brief sketch of a history of redaction (pp. 142–5), even though his primary interest lay elsewhere. Some aspects of the work of both these scholars, particularly as regards the relationship between the beginning and the end of the book of Isaiah, have been influential on several of the later studies which have already been mentioned.[43]

[41] L. J. Liebreich, 'The Compilation of the Book of Isaiah', *JQR* NS 46 (1955–6), 259–77; 47 (1956–7), 114–38.

[42] See R. Lack, *La Symbolique du Livre d'Isaïe: Essai sur l'image littéraire comme élément de structuration* (AnB 59; Rome, 1973).

[43] See, in particular, Sweeney (*Isaiah 1–4*, 21–4), who strengthens Lack's case with a further impressive series of verbal echoes; on the closing chapters of Isaiah, note also the studies of W. A. M. Beuken, 'Isaiah Chapters lxv–lxvi: Trito-Isaiah and the Closure of the Book of Isaiah', in J. A. Emerton (ed.), *Congress Volume: Leuven 1989* (SVT 43; Leiden, 1991), 204–21, and A. J. Tomasino, 'Isaiah 1.1–2.4 and 63–66, and the Composition of the Isaianic Corpus', *JSOT* 57 (1993), 81–98. Carr ('Reaching for Unity in Isaiah') voices some timely warnings against pressing such markers of structural unity too far and concludes that 'no editor intervened deeply enough into the book to make it all conform to an overall conception' (p. 78).

Far more extensive and ambitious is a proposal by Brownlee,[44] which has now been worked out in detail by his pupil Evans.[45] Noting that there is a space between chapters 33 and 34 in 1QIsa[a], he tentatively proposed that the book as we have it has been edited as a two-volume work. With chapter 1 bracketed as an introduction to the whole, each 'volume' is divided into seven sections, and it is suggested that the first section of volume one parallels the first of volume two, and so on. In support of this, Evans draws attention to a number of verbal and thematic links between each section.

Proposals such as this are difficult to evaluate. It is of interest to note, however, that at least one of the parallels (chapters 6–8 and 36–40) includes two sets of correspondences to which attention has been independently drawn by others, such as Ackroyd and Rendtorff, whereas it takes no account of others, notably that between chapters 1 and 65–6 just referred to, which have received a widespread measure of agreement. Furthermore, some scholars seem simply to be more receptive to such analyses than others. We should note here as of interest, however, that Brownlee and Evans offer as a partial explanation of their scheme that it was consciously shaped by editors of Isaiah who 'intercalated' sections from one part of Isaiah into another.

(6) A final group of studies, though again differing widely amongst themselves, may be bracketed together by virtue of the fact that they do not believe that an approach to the book of Isaiah by way of tracing the history of its composition will ever lead to a satisfactory understanding of the present form of the work. The context within which the text is read—whether in ancient or modern times—becomes a controlling factor for interpretation. In particular, reference must be made to Childs's 'canonical' approach,[46] which by no means wishes to deny the validity of the conclusions of historical-critical research, but which nevertheless affirms that they are of tangential significance to the enterprise of biblical interpretation within the community of faith. As regards Isaiah, Childs's understanding of 'the former things', which, like some others we have noted, he refers to the prophecies of First Isaiah, leads him to

44 W. H. Brownlee, *The Meaning of the Qumrân Scrolls for the Bible, with Special Attention to the Book of Isaiah* (New York, 1964), 247–59.

45 C. A. Evans, 'On the Unity and Parallel Structure of Isaiah', *VT* 38 (1988), 129–47.

46 B. S. Childs, *Introduction to the Old Testament as Scripture* (London, 1979).

affirm that 'In the light of the present shape of the book of Isaiah the question must be seriously raised if the material of Second Isaiah in fact ever circulated in Israel apart from its being connected to an earlier form of First Isaiah' (p. 329). It lies outside his interests, however, to pursue this question further. While this task has been undertaken in a useful study by Meade,[47] it is noticeable (and commendable) that he places much greater weight on more conventional redaction-historical concerns.

More radical still are approaches by way of the 'new' literary and reader-response criticism.[48] On the one hand, there is the attempt by Watts[49] to lay out the whole book in the format of an extensive, two-volumed commentary according to a 'reader-oriented' approach, his 'reader', however, being located at the time of the book's completion, *c.*435 BC (p. xxiv). It is something of a disappointment, however, that Watts rarely pauses to justify his reading, which, as reviewers have remarked, contains many idiosyncratic features. On the other hand, Conrad[50] and Webb[51] have undertaken studies more from the standpoint of the modern reader.

I have no intention of becoming embroiled in the debate about appropriate methods for the study of the Old Testament. Whereas I find many acute observations in the works of both Webb and Conrad on which I may therefore occasionally draw later, and while I have no wish to deny the validity of what they are doing, viewed from a certain standpoint, their work goes beyond my present interest. They may be justified in claiming that their approach is in one sense more objective, and hence 'valid', than speculations about the growth of the book of Isaiah, but that need not imply that such speculations are illegitimate or without interest. Having started from a historical-critical approach (namely, the fact

47 D. G. Meade, *Pseudonymity and Canon: An Investigation into the Relationship of Authorship and Authority in Jewish and Earliest Christian Tradition* (Grand Rapids, Mich., 1987), 26–43.

48 The unconscious links between Childs's approach and that of some forms of 'New Criticism' are explored in J. Barton, *Reading the Old Testament: Method in Biblical Study* (London, 1986), chs. 6–12.

49 J. D. W. Watts, *Isaiah 1–33* and *Isaiah 34–66* (WBC 24–5; Waco, 1985 and 1987). Note too Miscall's brief commentary on the book as a whole, which pays particular attention to 'intertextuality'.

50 E. W. Conrad, *Reading Isaiah* (OBT; Minneapolis, 1991).

51 B. G. Webb, 'Zion in Transformation: A Literary Approach to Isaiah', in D. J. A. Clines, S. E. Fowl, and S. E. Porter (eds.), *The Bible in Three Dimensions: Essays in Celebration of Forty Years of Biblical Studies in the University of Sheffield* (JSOTS 87; Sheffield, 1990), 65–84.

of multiple authorship), it seems reasonable also to seek a historical explanation for the ramifications of that starting-point which further work has revealed.

With this last remark in mind, what conclusions can be drawn from this selective, but I trust reasonably representative, survey of recent work on the 'unity' of Isaiah which may guide our future research? Three points seem to emerge clearly as being in pressing need of resolution.

First, it has become clear that one crucial question is the extent to which, if at all, Deutero-Isaiah may have been written in conscious dependence on and in elaboration of the work of Proto-Isaiah. We have seen that many who favour the redactional unity of the book nevertheless wish to deny this possibility, while others, as yet only a small minority, have made a tentative start towards an affirmative answer. In seeking to advance the discussion of this issue, there are, as Davies has reminded us, important issues of method which must be tackled if conclusions are to be soundly based.

Secondly, we have had repeated cause to notice that the question of how links between the various parts of Isaiah arose has frequently not been asked. Many scholars have observed connections of various sorts between Proto- and Deutero-Isaiah, but they have remained content with this descriptive task. The time has surely come, from the point of view of a historical-literary critic, to ask not only 'what?', but also 'how?' and 'why?'

Finally, the possibility of converse influence, that is to say from the later on to the earlier parts of the book, needs further clarification along the same lines. Redaction critics, such as Becker and Sweeney, have again drawn attention to some striking features in this regard, but without always pressing on to consider the historical and literary rationale for the evidence which they have uncovered.

These three topics will be taken up in turn in what follows, and the suggestion made, perhaps somewhat naïvely, that the answers to all three are very closely related. 'Simple' solutions to such complicated issues invite a scornful response from some, but to others, such as myself, they retain a (possibly dangerous) fascinating attraction. Before turning to that in detail, however, I must outline in the next chapter some limitations, presuppositions, and considerations of method which will govern the remainder of the work.

# 2

# Limitations, Presuppositions, and Method

IT will not have escaped notice that the survey of recent work on the book of Isaiah in the previous chapter has had little to say about the concluding section of the book, usually known as Trito-Isaiah (chapters 56–66). This is not by any means because of lack of scholarly attention to this section in recent years, but rather because it is not my intention to deal with it except in so far as it impinges directly on a consideration of chapters 1–55. Important as the study of Trito-Isaiah may be in its own right, it is the issue of the relationship between the first two major parts of the book of Isaiah which has emerged as being in more pressing need of elucidation, and this can for the most part be undertaken without sustained consideration of the problems raised by the composition of Trito-Isaiah.

This conscious limitation to the following discussion can be easily justified. There is widespread agreement that from the point of view of both composition and redaction Trito-Isaiah is dependent on what precedes and thus to some extent can be treated separately. This can be most simply observed from the fact that there are numerous citations of and allusions to both earlier parts of Isaiah. This has long been observed so far as chapters 40–55 are concerned,[1] and recent work has gone on to emphasize that this is no less true with regard to chapters 1–39. The comments of Rendtorff to this effect were noted in the previous chapter, and to them should be added in particular the more detailed and extensive studies of Beuken and Steck.[2] While recent studies continue to

[1] See e.g. W. Zimmerli, 'Zur Sprache Tritojesajas', in *Festschrift für Ludwig Köhler* (Bern, 1950), 62–74 = *Gottes Offenbarung: Gesammelte Aufsätze zum Alten Testament* (ThB 19; Munich, 1963), 217–33.

[2] W. A. M. Beuken (in addition to his commentary), 'Isa. 56: 9–57: 13—An Example of the Isaianic Legacy of Trito-Isaiah', in J. W. van Henten *et al.* (eds.), *Tradition and Re-interpretation in Jewish and Early Christian Literature: Essays in Honour of Jürgen C. H. Lebram* (SP-B 36; Leiden, 1986), 48–64; 'Isaiah Chapters

reflect a great diversity of opinion regarding many aspects of the composition of these chapters,[3] this discussion is therefore generally conducted without significant attention to the problems of the growth of the earlier part of the book. It is assumed that Trito-Isaiah is a separate composition, later in date than at any rate the bulk of Isaiah 1–55. To avoid complicating further what is already a detailed argument in the following chapters, it therefore seems reasonable to proceed without the distraction of attention to a series of issues which, it is widely agreed, should be treated separately for the most part.

There are two related aspects of recent study, however, which require a note of caution at this point. On the one hand, there is a strong likelihood that parts of chapters 1–55 may have been edited at a late stage in the light of 56–66. (The suggestion that Isaiah 1 and 65–6 are redactionally related was mentioned in the previous chapter, for instance.) Naturally, where such suggestions impinge on the discussion of these earlier chapters below, due account will be taken of them.

On the other hand, Steck has maintained that it is possible to correlate some of the phases of the redaction of chapters 1–55 with the stages which he proposes in the development of chapters 56–66. This arises from his radically new understanding of the nature of the material in Trito-Isaiah. In contrast with previous studies, which have usually assumed either that Trito-Isaiah is the work of a single prophet or that it comprises the fragments of a number of elements of originally independent prophecy moulded together in various redactional stages to form the present work, Steck argues that this section of the book is to be understood as the product of redactional reflection on the gradually developing book of Isaiah as a whole. Far from being the work of a separate prophet or prophets, it is the result of purely literary activity which cannot be understood apart from its function within the form of the book for which it was explicitly written. As already noted, he finds that most of this already presupposes the combined work of Proto- and Deutero-

lxv–lxvi'; Steck's articles, together with much new material, have now been conveniently collected in *Studien zu Tritojesaja* (BZAW 203; Berlin and New York, 1991).

[3] In addition to the work of Beuken and Steck, reference may be made to the recent major studies of Vermeylen, 451–517; S. Sekine, *Die Tritojesajanische Sammlung (Jes 56–66) redaktionsgeschichtlich untersucht* (BZAW 175; Berlin and New York, 1989) (with a useful extensive summary of previous research on pp. 3–23); and K. Koenen, *Ethik und Eschatologie im Tritojesajabuch: Eine literarkritische und redaktionsgeschichtliche Studie* (WMANT 62; Neukirchen-Vluyn, 1990).

Isaiah, and to that extent his suggestion need have no more effect upon the present discussion than other studies of Trito-Isaiah. But in the earliest stage of this development, which he isolates in 60: 1–9, 13–16; 61: 1–11 (supplemented by 60: 10–11; 62: 1–7), he finds no significant trace of influence from 1–39, and so concludes that this first phase was a *Fortschreibung* of 40–55 *before* it was joined to an earlier form of Proto-Isaiah. Were this aspect of his theory to be upheld without modification, it would run directly counter to any suggestion that Deutero-Isaiah himself built directly on the (edited) work of Proto-Isaiah. Steck's view at this point is certainly strongly influenced by his understanding of 62: 10–12 (which he dates later) as being an integral part of the redactional phase which he thinks was first responsible for the joining of Proto- and Deutero-Isaiah into a single work, and accordingly this will be examined in Chapter 8 below.

With rather less confidence, a fundamental presupposition of the following discussion must be made clear. Until comparatively recent times, there has been general agreement that in chapters 40–55 we have before us the work of a single prophet, conventionally named Deutero-Isaiah. Apart from a few minor glosses and additions, these chapters have been regarded as a unity. Indeed, this still seems to be the majority opinion, and some recent work has in fact tended to strengthen it with regard to two sets of passages which have often been thought to constitute an exception to the general rule, namely the anti-idol polemical material, especially in 40: 19–20; 41: 5–7; and 44: 9–20, and the four so-called servant songs in 42: 1–4; 49: 1–6; 50: 4–9; and 52: 13–53: 12. Against the earlier view that these two sets of passages constituted later insertions into the work of Deutero-Isaiah, a number of voices have been raised urging that they must be regarded as integral, and indeed indispensable, parts of their present literary contexts.[4]

[4] For the servant songs, see in particular T. N. D. Mettinger, *A Farewell to the Servant Songs: A Critical Examination of an Exegetical Axiom* (Lund, 1983); P. Wilcox and D. Paton-Williams, 'The Servant Songs in Deutero-Isaiah', *JSOT* 42 (1988), 79–102, and F. Matheus, *Singt dem Herrn ein neues Lied: Die Hymnen Deuterojesajas* (SBS 141; Stuttgart, 1990); for the anti-idol passages, see e.g. H. D. Preuß, *Verspottung fremder Religionen im Alten Testament* (BWANT 92; Stuttgart, 1971), 192–237; H. C. Spykerboer, *The Structure and Composition of Deutero-Isaiah, with Special Reference to the Polemics against Idolatry* (Meppel, 1976); R. J. Clifford, 'The Function of Idol Passages in Second Isaiah', *CBQ* 42 (1980), 450–64, and F. Matheus, 'Jesaja xliv 9–20: Das Spottgedicht gegen die Götzen und seine Stellung im Kontext', *VT* 37 (1987), 312–26.

Of potentially more far-reaching significance for a discussion of the unity of Deutero-Isaiah, however, is a series of studies which finds within these chapters one or more pervasive levels of redaction, and that to such a degree that the usual understanding of Isaiah 40–55 as conveying essentially the thought of a single mind ought to be abandoned. In his helpful survey and discussion of this new line of approach, Hermisson singles out in particular the work of Kiesow, Merendino, and Vermeylen,[5] and in doing so makes some apposite general remarks of a cautionary nature. He observes, for instance, that linguistic style is unlikely to prove decisive either way, both because Deutero-Isaiah himself made extensive though creative use of the language of the Psalms and because he himself had a number of later imitators; doublets too are unreliable as a criterion, since the message of comfort demanded much repetition; and tensions in the text may be of help in distinguishing between one level and another, but even here there are the twin dangers of oversimplifying thereby what may have been quite complex theological conceptions and of overlooking the poetic nature of the material by forcing it all into rigid constraints which may be more appropriate to a piece of prose.

Hermisson is thus himself far more reserved than the scholars he is primarily interacting with, and in this he reflects what still seems to be the consensus of opinion.[6] Nevertheless, he also points out that, because Isaiah 40–55 is not orientated towards the person of the prophet, there are particular problems to be faced on the other

[5] H.-J. Hermisson, 'Einheit und Komplexität Deuterojesajas: Probleme der Redaktionsgeschichte von Jes 40–55', in Vermeylen (ed.), *The Book of Isaiah*, 287–312; K. Kiesow, *Exodustexte im Jesajabuch: Literarkritische und motivgeschichtliche Analysen* (OBO 24; Fribourg and Göttingen, 1979); R. P. Merendino, *Der Erste und der Letzte: Eine Untersuchung von Jes 40–48* (SVT 31; Leiden, 1981); J. Vermeylen, 'Le Motif de la création dans le Deutéro-Isaïe', in P. Beauchamp (ed.), *La Création dans l'Orient Ancien* (LecD 127; Paris, 1987), 183–240; and 'L'Unité du livre d'Isaïe', to which should now be added R. G. Kratz, *Kyros im Deuterojesaja-Buch* (Forschungen zum Alten Testament, 1; Tübingen, 1991). This recent approach is to be distinguished from the earlier view of K. Elliger that Isaiah 40–55 underwent a major redaction at the hand of Trito-Isaiah, who himself added chapters 47, 54, 55, and the fourth servant song, on which see further H.-C. Schmitt, 'Prophetie und Schultheologie im Deuterojesajabuch: Beobachtungen zur Redaktionsgeschichte von Jes 40–55', *ZAW* 91 (1979), 43–61.

[6] See e.g. Matheus, *Singt dem Herrn ein neues Lied*, for a recent defence of the unity of Deutero-Isaiah. B. Lindars has gone so far as to write, 'I have to say that I find Merendino's analysis arbitrary and lacking in respect for the text' ('Good Tidings to Zion: Interpreting Deutero-Isaiah Today', *BJRL* 68 (1985–6), 473–97 (481) ).

side. It is not possible, for instance, to arrive at an agreed basis for isolating the *ipsissima verba* of the prophet, nor is it legitimate to appeal to development in his thought as a means for explaining differences of emphasis within the text. With commendable caution, he then proceeds to examine a number of conceptual fields to see whether they are sufficiently coherent both internally and with the rest of the material in these chapters to be allowed to stand as integral parts of the work of Deutero-Isaiah. One other criterion with which he operates is that a prophet is unlikely to 'quote' himself or offer an 'exegesis' of his own oracles; where such devices are found, it is thought more probable that they betray the hand of a later disciple.

The result of Hermisson's examination is to include within Deutero-Isaiah a good deal more material than Kiesow, Merendino, and Vermeylen, but nevertheless to propose that there are some later redactional layers to be discerned. The last major layer (apart from a few isolated later texts) is the anti-idol material, but prior to that he thinks that there was another redactional phase which he provisionally calls 'Die *qarob*-Schicht', to which he tentatively assigns the following verses (see p. 311): 42: 18–25(?); 46: 8, 12–13; 48: 12–16?; 48: 17–19; 49: 7, 8–12, 24–26(?); 50: 3?; 51: 1–2+4–8; 51: 12–14(15–16); 54: 11–17; 55: 6–7. Hermisson's reasons are principally that in this material there is a presupposition that the expected salvation of Deutero-Isaiah has been delayed, since now it is said to be 'near' (*qarob*); that the delay is partly due to Israel's behaviour and that a change is therefore demanded as a condition for salvation, something which does not accord with the message of forgiveness and guilt which has been paid for (when Deutero-Isaiah issues encouragement elsewhere, it is only to accept the offer of salvation, not to change behaviour; see 44: 21–2); that the difference in outlook cannot be explained by appeal to the developing response of the prophet to an ongoing situation, and that the language of these passages suggests a reapplication of Deutero-Isaiah's phraseology to the new outlook.

Clearly, this is not the appropriate place for a full discussion of Hermisson's view, since his is only one of a number of proposals of this sort, the adoption of any one of which would have serious implications for our further study. Nevertheless, because it presents a modest case in a clear and attractive manner, and because it exemplifies some of the methodological difficulties which scholars face in this area, a few comments may be found helpful. I should stress that the following remarks are not intended as a rebuttal of Hermisson's proposals so much as a presentation of other aspects of the case which may help support the conclusion that we are not yet in the position where we can with confidence abandon the usual understanding of Isaiah 40–55 as an essential unity.

First, evaluations will differ over the issue whether the '*qarob*-Schicht' is theologically incompatible with Deutero-Isaiah's main message of forgiveness and salvation. For instance, must the statement that salvation is 'near' imply that it has been delayed by comparison with the immediacy of the announcement elsewhere? At 50: 8 (which Hermisson does not ascribe to this layer) the speaker proclaims that 'he who vindicates me is near' and hence is able to challenge his immediate audience with the words 'who will contend with me? Let us stand up together.' Again, is an announcement of salvation incompatible with a call to a change of direction? At 44: 22, which Hermisson accepts as an authentically Deutero-Isaianic exhortation, the people are encouraged in the very act of accepting the proferred salvation to 'return to me, for I have redeemed you'. There will undoubtedly be some who will believe that these differences of emphasis could as well be explained by the rhetorical requirements of each passage as by a separate and later redaction.

Secondly, in 51: 4–8, from which Hermisson begins his analysis, it may be necessary to draw a clearer distinction than he implies between God's announcement to his own people and that to the gentile nations. Thus, the phrase 'my righteousness is near' (so MT) in 51: 5 seems to refer more to 'the peoples' and 'the coastlands' than to God's own people, and in this case it would not be inappropriate even within Deutero-Isaiah's scheme of things to portray this 'righteousness/deliverance' and 'salvation' (verses 5 and 6) as being still future. By contrast, verses 7–8 have Israel in view ('the people in whose heart is my law'), and here the sentiment is just what we find elsewhere in God's address to them ('fear not . . .'). Finally, because, as is well known, 51: 1–8 forms a well-constructed poem in three stanzas, each with a parallel introduction (verses 1, 4, and 7),[7] Hermisson suggests that the opening

[7] Cf. J. K. Kuntz, 'The Contribution of Rhetorical Criticism to Understanding Isaiah 51: 1–16', in D. J. A. Clines, D. M. Gunn, and A. J. Hauser (eds.), *Art and Meaning: Rhetoric in Biblical Literature* (JSOTS 19; Sheffield, 1982), 140–71.

verses of the chapter must also be applied to his later level; there is no separate reason for this, however, and a question mark must always stand over the need to draw material into a suggested layer of redaction solely on the ground of consequential argumentation without any supporting indications.

Thirdly, while there is truth in Hermisson's point that we cannot argue from a postulated biographical development in Deutero-Isaiah's views, he seems to press this further than is warranted by the text itself.[8] Few would deny that Deutero-Isaiah did not meet with enthusiastic acceptance by his initial audience. This is clearly shown by, for instance, 40: 27, where he cites Jacob/Israel's words that give expression to the people's continuing despondency. Consequently, much of the material in chapters 40–55 is devoted to countering such sentiments in an attempt to stimulate faith; the trial speeches, the disputations, and the oracles of salvation presuppose a situation in which the author is seeking to persuade his readers to accept a series of propositions which at present they are inclined to reject. Deutero-Isaiah's 'disappointment' (if that is the correct word for it) is not, therefore, something which needs to be relegated to his hypothetical old age, but is rather an essential element in his announcement of immediate salvation from the very first. In such a context, the rhetoric of much of the so-called '*qarob*-Schicht' need not be regarded as incompatible with the remainder of the work. In addition, the suggestion that some development in outlook can be detected between, in particular, chapters 40–8 and 49–55 is not dependent on a few isolated passages which might be relegated to a secondary layer within the text, but rather is based on the material as a whole, including much that Hermisson is content to ascribe to Deutero-Isaiah. Significantly, therefore, 49: 1–6, which stands precisely as a hinge between the two halves of the work, itself speaks explicitly about a development in the speaker's task.[9]

[8] Indeed, he himself is not altogether immune from the use of rhetorical exaggeration in this regard; his description of 'den alt gewordenen und enttäuschten Propheten' is something of a straw man.

[9] See H. G. M. Williamson, 'The Concept of Israel in Transition', in R. E. Clements (ed.), *The World of Ancient Israel: Sociological, Anthropological and Political Perspectives* (Cambridge, 1989), 141–61 (especially pp. 144–7). A more far-reaching attempt to trace development in Deutero-Isaiah's thought is proposed by C. Stuhlmueller, 'Deutero-Isaiah: Major Transitions in the Prophet's Theology and in Contemporary Scholarship', *CBQ* 42 (1980), 1–29.

Finally, while we may accept for the moment the proposal that a prophet is unlikely to 'quote' himself, the language of the '*qarob*-Schicht' does not include what would normally be regarded as quotations. Certainly, the language in some of the passages which Hermisson isolates is familiar from elsewhere in chapters 40–55, but the similarities are of the sort which would generally be used to argue for similar, rather than diverse, authorship, and the degree of repetition is no greater, it may be suggested, than is to be found elsewhere within undoubtedly authentic material. Furthermore, some of the similarities are notably due to dependence on the language of the Psalms (see e.g. 48: 13; 51: 6, 13, 15–16), and, as Hermisson elsewhere acknowledges, this makes ascription of authorship either way particularly unreliable in the case of Deutero-Isaiah.

As was stated earlier, the few remarks offered here in response to Hermisson's valuable discussion and stimulating suggestions are not intended to be exhaustive or conclusive. The whole issue of the unity of Isaiah 40–55 has now reached the point where it deserves a full-scale study of its own. Nevertheless, it is hoped that enough has been said to indicate awareness of the problem and to show that what is admitted to be a presupposition in the following discussion is not necessarily to be dismissed as untenable. With the exception of Vermeylen, discussions of the 'unity' of Isaiah in recent years have also generally worked with this presupposition (usually unacknowledged, because it still remains the consensus view), and the present work takes its place among them. Those who are unable to share this point of view will naturally have to make allowances at those places where the passage under discussion is regarded as secondary. Since I shall be drawing on a broad range of material in chapters 40–55, I do not believe that for the most part this will seriously undermine the major conclusions at which I arrive. Moreover, since no common opinion has yet emerged among those who have adopted this newer approach, I have not considered it necessary to draw attention to the matter beyond these few introductory remarks. Unless and until a broader agreement emerges in this area, the relegation of one or another passage to a later redactional level in 40–55 will remain the isolated opinion of individual scholars.[10]

[10] Of course, this conclusion does not rule out the likelihood of occasional later small additions and glosses to the text (e.g. for 48: 22, see below, Ch. 8). But in my

Finally, a word needs to be said about the criteria which will govern the argument in the next three chapters in particular. As was made clear at the end of the first chapter, the initial topic for study is the extent to which, if at all, chapters 40–55 of Isaiah were directly influenced at the point of composition by the form which chapters 1–39 had assumed by that time. That there are some points of connection between the two parts of the book is not in doubt, but there are several different ways in which they might be explained—coincidence and mutual dependence on some separate tradition are only two of the most obvious possibilities that might be considered, alongside that of direct and conscious influence. Once the problem is stated in these terms, the criteria become obvious, though they do not seem generally to have been spelt out or applied in most of the studies which were summarized above.

First, material adduced from chapters 1–39 must naturally be restricted to those passages which can with reasonable probability be ascribed to the book as it existed by the latter part of the exilic period, for, unlike in the case of chapters 40–55, just discussed, there is widespread agreement (which I fully share) that the first part of Isaiah developed over an extended period of time, reaching well down into the post-exilic era. Difficult as it may be to achieve assured results on what these passages are, it is fortunately not as controversial as would be a quest for the *ipsissima verba* of Isaiah himself. Whilst much uncertainty remains about the ascription of a number of passages to Isaiah, many scholars now accept some such view as that a major first collection of material was undertaken before the fall of Jerusalem,[11] and that there are also signs of lighter editorial activity under the impact of that event itself.[12] Disagreement continues with regard to a number of passages concerning which layer of the composition they belong to, but that is not germane to our present concern. Those of a more conservative inclination will naturally have no difficulty in accepting for the purposes of the present discussion material which other scholars

opinion these do not amount to anything like what might be termed a 'redactional layer'.

[11] So e.g. H. Barth, *Die Jesaja-Worte in der Josiazeit: Israel und Assur als Thema einer produktiven Neuinterpretation der Jesajaüberlieferung* (WMANT 48; Neukirchen-Vluyn, 1977), and Vermeylen.

[12] e.g. Clements, 'The Prophecies of Isaiah and the Fall of Jerusalem in 587 B.C.'. In his commentary, Clements also accepts many of Barth's conclusions, so that it serves as a useful summary of this whole approach to the study of Isaiah 1–39.

date rather later. A problem will arise only in cases where there is serious dispute whether one passage or another should not be dated even later, in the post-exilic period. Where that is so, attention will have to be given to the relevant arguments, though of course I cannot hope to be able to settle the matter decisively. Nevertheless, it should be possible to proceed on the basis of those passages concerning which it would be widely, if not universally, agreed that they were in place by the relevant date. (In the following, this form of the book's development is frequently referred to as 'the literary deposit of First Isaiah'.) Working with this criterion, then, it would be reasonable to make use of chapter 6, for instance, but not chapter 35, since, though the latter has much in common with Deutero-Isaiah, it is most unlikely that it predates him.

Secondly, it is necessary to be aware of the many differences between the two blocks of material which are to be examined. They were written by different authors at different times and in vastly different circumstances, and there is no intention in what follows of covering over the consequences. Thus it follows that 'influence' should not be restricted simply to 'imitation'. We must be alert to the possibility that the later writer may in fact be reversing quite as much as endorsing what was said or written by his predecessor, for that is just as much 'influence' as is continuation.

Thirdly, it is necessary to distinguish clear from possible cases of influence, and that in two senses. (*a*) Is First Isaiah the only or the overwhelmingly probable influence on Deutero-Isaiah in any given particular? Davies[13] has reminded us that material common to them both may also be found elsewhere, so that due account must necessarily be taken of other works from which Deutero-Isaiah might have drawn his inspiration. This possibility will have to be taken into account where appropriate for each item to be examined. It will be argued later, for instance, that Jer. 51: 27 is most unlikely to have been the source of Deutero-Isaiah's talk about 'raising a signal to the peoples' (49: 22), but such a conclusion cannot be presupposed without substantial reasons, and not every case may be so clear-cut.

(*b*) Is an apparent connection between the two bodies of material a real case of influence, or could it be merely a coincidental use of similar and perhaps commonplace language? A decision here will naturally be more subjective. The problem can best be avoided,

[13] Davies, 'The Destiny of the Nations'.

therefore, if the discussion is restricted to the most reasonably assured cases. If such cases can be established in sufficient number, then less certain cases may also be admitted, not as evidence to establish the case in the first place, but as likely further examples of influence in the light of the 'fact', as we should then be able to say, that Deutero-Isaiah was influenced by the written deposit of First Isaiah. Though some examples of the latter sort will be mentioned in the course of the following chapters (e.g. at the end of Chapters 3 and 4), they will not be taken up in any detail. It is imperative at this stage of research to restrict the main line of argument to clear-cut cases.

A final point should also be made here. Part of the force of the argument which follows is its cumulative nature. This has a negative value as well as the positive one of merely making the case increasingly strong. In theory, evidence might be presented to suggest that one or other item being considered reached Deutero-Isaiah from some other quarter, such as Jeremiah 50–1. But the more cases can be seen with equal or greater probability to derive from the literary deposit of First Isaiah, and especially the more they relate to different and diverse topics, so the greater the likelihood that disputed ones are influenced by him as well. Unless another book, passage, or tradition circle could be found that also embraced all the data to be considered, the most economical hypothesis would be to ascribe all possible examples of influence to First Isaiah.

# 3

# Isaiah Chapter 6

THE account of Isaiah's vision and commissioning in chapter 6 provides a convenient starting-point for our investigation, both because it is widely agreed that it comes substantially from the earliest literary layer in the book, and because there are many echoes of it in the later chapters. It should, therefore, repay detailed examination to lay a foundation for the broader discussion which will follow in the next chapter.

Isaiah 6 recounts Isaiah's vision and subsequent commissioning in the first-person singular. It thus appears to be closely associated with the first-person material in chapter 8, whose authenticity is likewise widely accepted. It displays a number of links (some of which will be discussed later on) with other passages generally agreed to come from the eighth-century prophet, and it fits well from a traditio-historical point of view with what could be expected of Isaiah.[1] Most scholars are, therefore, more than content to take the bulk of the chapter at face value as a report by Isaiah himself.

The number of those who have questioned an early date for this passage in its entirety is consequently extremely small, and their arguments do not appear to have convinced many. Whitley,[2] for instance, has drawn attention to some grammatical, linguistic, and theological features of the text which he thinks point to a post-exilic date.

First, he maintains that the use of the *wāw*-consecutive in *wā'er'eh* ('(and) I saw') in verse 1 is strange following the date formula, that it therefore originally stood at the start of a sentence, and that the date formula, 'irrespective of the niceties of grammar', has therefore probably replaced an introductory section detailing

[1] See Wildberger, 234–42.

[2] C. F. Whitley, 'The Call and Mission of Isaiah', *JNES* 18 (1959), 38–48.

the time and place of the description of a vision current in the writer's own later day. This replacement allowed the account of the vision to be attributed instead to the eighth-century Isaiah. He compares Ezek. 1: 1 as a parallel to the kind of introduction he thinks originally stood here. Apart from the highly speculative nature of this argument from silence, however, Whitley's initial grammatical objection is without foundation, as Vermeylen (p. 189) has pointed out. The use of the *wāw*-consecutive after various expressions of time is not at all uncommon (cf. GK §111*b* for examples),[3] whereas the use of the perfect tense in such a position (which is apparently what Whitley would have expected) is said to be found 'only in late books or passages' (again with examples).

Secondly, Whitley's linguistic argument turns out to be no more than a comparison of the phrase 'high and lifted up' (*rām wᵉniśśā'*) in verse 1 with its use in a number of other texts which he judges to be of late date. This phrase will be dealt with more fully later in this chapter, so that it is sufficient to observe here that Whitley fails to take account of the very close parallels to be found in Isaiah 2 (whose authenticity he does not appear to doubt), and that he does not consider the possibility that the later passages may themselves be dependent on Isa. 6: 1. Indeed, since most of his examples are from the book of Isaiah itself, this conclusion will be the more probable if further examination can demonstrate that they are only part of a wider phenomenon, attested in a variety of other passages.[4] His other examples all come from the Psalms. On the one hand, these are less exact, since they include only the word *rām* and related forms, whereas it is the combination of the two words that is the distinctive feature of the passage in Isaiah, and, on the other hand, if they are dated late (which is not universally agreed), it is usually precisely on the ground that they have borrowed such phrases as this from the later chapters of Isaiah.[5]

Thirdly, Whitley maintains that a number of the chapter's theological themes, such as the holiness, the glory, and the kingship of

[3] See further S. R. Driver, *A Treatise on the Use of the Tenses in Hebrew* (Oxford, 1892³), §127*b*, and C. Brockelmann, *Hebräische Syntax* (Neukirchen, 1956), §123*f*.

[4] See too R. Knierim, 'The Vocation of Isaiah', *VT* 18 (1968), 47–68 (47 n. 1).

[5] Note, however, the strong case which has recently been made out for regarding the use of *rām* in Ps. 99: 2 as being dependent on Isaiah 6 itself; see R. Scoralick, *Trishagion und Gottesherrschaft: Psalm 99 als Neuinterpretation von Tora und Propheten* (SBS 138; Stuttgart, 1989).

God, or the uncleanness of the prophet and the people, must be of post-exilic origin. In particular, he draws attention to parallels with the vision of Ezekiel and maintains that the latter must precede Isaiah 6. These suggestions have convinced no one, however, both because they are drawn with so broad and yet selective a brush, and because they fail to take account of the pervasive influence of the Jerusalem cult tradition whence a number of these elements must derive (cf. Wildberger, 239). The form of Isaiah's vision is quite as close to that of Micaiah ben Imlah in 1 Kings 22 as to that of Ezekiel, and, following Zimmerli's detailed traditio-historical analysis, it is preferable to regard Isaiah 6 as standing midway between these two.[6]

More recently, Kaiser too has sought to defend the view that 'we must give up the notion . . . that in this chapter we can hear directly the voice of the prophet Isaiah' (p. 123 = ET 121). His reasons for this are less specifically framed than those of Whitley just examined, and they also relate to his whole understanding of the composition and interpretation of Isaiah 1–39, so that a full examination of his case would go far beyond the needs and confines of the present discussion. Nevertheless, there are a few points which can be made which will help to clarify why Kaiser has not yet attracted much support for his position.

First, central to his argument regarding chapter 6 is his insistence that the hardening saying of verses 9–10 cannot have been known by the prophet from the start of his ministry, while at the same time no prophet who had undergone such an experience as that described in chapter 6 would have allowed himself to alter the wording of his commission in the light of his subsequent experience, as many commentators have assumed. Therefore, since the saying in fact refers more to the effects of the prophet's mission than to its content, it must be viewed in its entirety as later, written up in the light of the catastrophe which eventually overtook the nation.

To this reasoning, however, it must be questioned whether Kaiser has not too quickly cut the Gordian knot of verses 9–10. No one will deny that the passage is theologically harsh, but it is not clear that it is made any easier from that standpoint simply by

[6] W. Zimmerli, *Ezechiel* (BKAT 13/1; Neukirchen-Vluyn, 1969), 16–21 = ET *Ezekiel 1* (Philadelphia, 1979), 97–100; cf. O. H. Steck, 'Bemerkungen zu Jesaja 6', *BZ* N.F. 16 (1972), 188–206, with further literature.

dating it later. It is noteworthy that Kaiser argues that it is a mistake to interpret the passage in psychological or biographical terms. Yet these are the very terms by which he denies that Isaiah could have known the saying in the first place. If in the end the passage is 'meant to be understood theologically' (which there is no reason to deny), then the problem might just as well be faced with Isaiah as with an editor two centuries later. An attempt along these lines has in fact recently been undertaken by Evans,[7] who advances a number of useful considerations. While it may not be possible to follow him in every respect, he has certainly made a start in the right direction.

Secondly, Kaiser argues that the so-called Isaiah Memoir is framed around the nucleus of 7: 1–9 in its original form. Chapter 6 is added to it, as is the first-person account in chapter 8. In particular, he concludes from this that there is a great arc stretching from the prophet's question 'how long?' in 6: 11 to the confession of hope in 8: 17, so revealing that the real concern of the author of these chapters is 'to restore trust in Yahweh's power and thus hope for his help and for their own future to the people of the remnant who have been handed over to the world power' (p. 118 = ET 115).

The issues raised by the widespread assumption that Isaiah 6–8 should be regarded as an Isaiah Memoir cannot be dealt with here, but, even without that assumption, Kaiser's observation, which is based on comparison of the first-person material alone, is not without significance. If his analysis of the literary structure and its consequences for interpretation are correct, it could equally well be held that he has cut off one of the planks (i.e. the unqualified nature of the hardening saying) on which his case for denying Isaianic authorship of chapter 6 rests. It is, of course, in any case widely assumed that at the very earliest chapter 6 was not committed to writing until after the events of chapter 7 had taken place.

[7] C. A. Evans, *To See and Not Perceive: Isaiah 6.9–10 in Early Jewish and Christian Interpretation* (JSOTS 64; Sheffield, 1989), 17–52; note also the arguments of those who think that Isaiah 6 does not refer to the initial call of the prophet, but to the commissioning of the prophet for a specific task some time after the commencement of his ministry (M. M. Kaplan, 'Isaiah 6 $_{1-11}$', *JBL* 45 (1926), 251–9; J. Milgrom, 'Did Isaiah Prophesy during the Reign of Uzziah?', *VT* 14 (1964), 164–82), and Steck's attempt ('Bemerkungen zu Jesaja 6') to explain the hardening motif as relating exclusively to the events of the Syro-Ephraimite crisis as detailed in the *Denkschrift* of Isaiah 6–8.

Thirdly, an important step in Kaiser's argument is his conviction that 7: 1–9 has been shaped in accordance with the Deuteronomic understanding of prophecy and can thus have been framed only after the fall of Judah. Since the hardening theme of chapter 6 goes beyond this, it must itself be later. Quite apart from this latter step, the issue of the extent to which there may have been a Deuteronomic redaction of Isaiah is highly controversial, and has been denied completely, for instance, by Brekelmans.[8] We certainly find nothing of the sort of Deuteronomic influence that is so clearly present in Jeremiah, for instance, nor even of the more muted, but convincingly suggested, Deuteronomic redaction of Amos.[9] It is stretching theological categorization too far, in my opinion, to affirm that the prophetic confrontation of the people with a call to a life-or-death decision was unknown before it was given Deuteronomic formulation.

Fourthly, it needs to be remembered that Kaiser's view has important implications for the purpose and dating of other parts of Isaiah 6–8, such as his argument that 8: 1–4 is also not Isaianic. These wider ramifications of his view cannot be discussed here, but it should be noted that they too have been unfavourably received by recent studies,[10] as have some of the other fundamental premisses in his commentary.[11] It remains to be seen whether further research will continue in this critical vein.

Finally, it should be emphasized that a careful distinction needs to be drawn between the composition of a text and how it was read by later generations, for at this latter level Kaiser has much of value to teach us. Indeed, it leads us directly to the next preliminary point which requires attention—namely, whether Isaiah 6 provides evi-

[8] C. H. W. Brekelmans, 'Deuteronomistic Influence in Isaiah 1–12', in Vermeylen (ed.), *The Book of Isaiah*, 167–76. See also the more general comments of H. Ringgren, 'Israelite Prophecy: Fact or Fiction?', in J. A. Emerton (ed.), *Congress Volume: Jerusalem 1986* (SVT 40; Leiden, 1988), 204–10, and of J. R. Porter, 'The Supposed Deuteronomic Redaction of the Prophets: Some Considerations', in R. Albertz, F. W. Golka, and J. Kegler (eds.), *Schöpfung und Befreiung: Für Claus Westermann zum 80. Geburtstag* (Stuttgart, 1989), 69–78.

[9] See W. H. Schmidt, 'Die deuteronomistische Redaktion des Amosbuches', *ZAW* 77 (1965), 168–93.

[10] See e.g. J. Høgenhaven, *Gott und Volk bei Jesaja: Eine Untersuchung zur Biblischen Theologie* (Acta Theologica Danica; Leiden, 1988), 77–113; A. Laato, *Who is Immanuel? The Rise and the Foundering of Isaiah's Messianic Expectations* (Åbo, 1988).

[11] e.g. Barth, *Die Jesaja-Worte in der Josiazeit*, 271–4.

dence for later interpretation. If it does, this may have two important consequences for our present investigation. First, it may provide a *terminus ad quem* for the composition of the core of the chapter (thereby potentially undermining Kaiser's dating); and, secondly, it may require us to conclude that not everything in Isaiah 6 meets the criteria which we laid down in the previous chapter.

Attention here focuses primarily on the concluding two verses of the chapter. First, the last three words, *zeraʿ qōdeš maṣṣabtāh* ('the holy seed is its stump'), are widely regarded as a late gloss on the *maṣṣebet* of the previous line. Despite some who argue to the contrary,[12] the usual view seems almost certainly to be correct. As I have argued elsewhere,[13] the expression 'holy seed', which is found otherwise only in Ezra 9: 2, is there part of a complex passage which manifests a sophisticated hermeneutic by combining a number of Pentateuchal texts in order to present a quite new understanding of the nature of the people of God; indeed, the phrase itself brings together two previously separate lines of thought, and thus shows itself to be a thoroughly integral part of the Ezra passage and of the method of biblical interpretation which it displays. Since this approach can hardly be conceived before the time of Ezra (and certainly not so early as the pre-exilic period), we must conclude that Isa. 6: 13*bβ* derives from that same period at the very earliest. It must, therefore, be discounted from the remainder of our analysis.

Secondly, there is also a considerable measure of agreement among recent studies that Isa. 6: 12–13*abα* has been added secondarily to the core of the chapter.[14] The reasons for this are that in verse 12 the Lord is referred to in the third person in a context where he himself is the speaker, that the passage introduces the idea of exile into a context which is speaking rather of the desola-

[12] See, in addition to the more conservative commentaries, G. F. Hasel, *The Remnant: The History and Theology of the Remnant Idea from Genesis to Isaiah* (Andrews University Monographs, 5; Berrien Springs, Mich., 1972), 240–8; I. Engnell, *The Call of Isaiah: An Exegetical and Comparative Study* (Uppsala Universitets Årsskrift 1949: 4; Uppsala and Leipzig, 1949), 47–53; K. Nielsen, *There is Hope for a Tree: The Tree as Metaphor in Isaiah* (JSOTS 65; Sheffield, 1989), 144–58.

[13] Williamson, *Ezra, Nehemiah*, 131–2.

[14] On the difficult textual problems of verse 13, see the full survey by J. A. Emerton, 'The Translation and Interpretation of Isaiah vi. 13', in J. A. Emerton and S. C. Reif (eds.), *Interpreting the Hebrew Bible: Essays in Honour of E. I. J. Rosenthal* (Cambridge, 1982), 85–118.

tion of the land, and that the metre changes at this point.[15] Taken individually, none of these points is wholly convincing. The last is so weak that many commentators do not even mention it; to the second, it may be said that the shift in perspective is by no means intolerably harsh; and to the first, that God not infrequently appears thus in a passage where he is the speaker,[16] and it is scarcely likely that this always indicates secondary expansion.[17] Nevertheless, the conjunction of factors in this one passage perhaps just tips the balance of probability in favour of the current majority view, and the fact that it thus seems to take its place with other additions of similar import elsewhere in Isaiah 1–39[18] further strengthens the case.

We may note first as a consequence that this conclusion supports the argument for the authenticity of Isa. 6: 1–11.[19] Kaiser, who also accepts that verses 12–13 have been added secondarily, is forced to the less plausible conclusion that the glossator 'felt the lack in v. 11 of a clear reference to the deportation of the people'. In the circumstances in which Kaiser presupposes he was working, it may be wondered why he should have thought that such an addition was necessary.

15 H.-P. Müller, 'Glauben und Bleiben: Zur Denkschrift Jesajas Kapitel vi 1—viii 18', in *Studies on Prophecy: A Collection of Twelve Papers* (SVT 26; Leiden, 1974), 25–54 (31) adds a syntactical argument: the imperfect verb in 11*b* is to be construed as final or consecutive following the perfect verb in 11*a*. It therefore concludes the sentence governed by the initial 'until' (*'ad ᵃšer 'im*). He then makes the interesting observation that the shift from divine speech to a third-person reference to God is paralleled in the closely comparable account of Micaiah ben Imlah; cf. 1 Kgs. 22: 22–3. He thus follows E. Jenni ('Jesajas Berufung in der neueren Forschung', *ThZ* 15 (1959), 321–39 (330)) in suggesting that, although there is a conscious break between verses 11 and 12, verses 12–13*bα* were intended by Isaiah from the start to stand in their present position as his own comment on the preceding vision. While this possibility should be carefully considered, it has to be noted that the link in terms of content is far less explicit than in 1 Kgs. 22: 22–3, having the appearance of development rather than of explanation.

16 E. König (*Stilistik, Rhetorik, Poetik in Bezug auf die biblische Litteratur komparativisch dargestellt* (Leipzig, 1900), 154) lists many passages where the divine name is introduced for emphasis, and a number of these are in contexts where God is speaking in the first person.

17 Note Gray's caution in the present instance: 'it is perhaps hypercritical to claim that men cannot be removed (v.[12]) from an already (v.[11]) desolated country; and the use of Yahweh in words attributed to Yahweh—particularly at some little distance from the beginning of the speech, is hardly sufficient by itself to prove that v.[12] was not the original continuation of v.[11]' (p. 111).

18 Cf. Clements, 'The Prophecies of Isaiah and the Fall of Jerusalem in 587 B.C.'.

19 The suggestion that the final clause of verse 10 ('and turn again, and be healed') is also secondary is much less certain; see Vermeylen, 194–5 (with further bibliography); Nielsen, *There is Hope for a Tree*, 145.

Secondly, however, on the assumption that the verses represent a *relecture* in the light of the fall of Jerusalem and the exile of many of the people of Judah,[20] it is also clear that, with the exception of the final clause of the chapter, the whole was in place before the closing years of the exilic period. We may thus conclude that we are justified in using virtually the whole of Isaiah 6 for our immediate purpose of examining the possible influence of the first part of Isaiah on the later chapters.

We may begin this examination by following the increasing number of scholars who have drawn attention to the parallels between this chapter and the opening of the second main part of the book of Isaiah in chapter 40.[21] Both passages appear to be set in the heavenly court,[22] an observation which does not, and is not intended to, settle the vexed question of whether Isa. 40: 1–8(11) is to be viewed as the account of the prophet's call. Though other prophets recognize the importance of the heavenly council for their role (e.g. Amos 3: 7; Jer. 23: 18, 22), no other prophetic book before the post-exilic period records an actual scene taking place there.[23]

20 There are some who argue rather that the verses represent an isolated fragment by Isaiah himself, reflecting on the fall of Samaria in *c.*722 BC, which has subsequently been interpolated here; see e.g. Nielsen, *There is Hope for a Tree*, 144–57. It is not necessary to follow this minority view further in the present context, since its consequences would be precisely the same for our overall purposes.

21 This is noted briefly by, e.g., F. M. Cross, 'The Council of Yahweh in Second Isaiah', *JNES* 12 (1953), 274–7; Kiesow, *Exodustexte im Jesajabuch*, 30, 43, 66, 161; Vincent, *Studien*, 245–6; N. Habel, 'The Form and Significance of the Call Narratives', *ZAW* 77 (1965), 297–323 (314–16); O. Loretz, 'Die Gattung des Prologs zum Buche Deuterojesaja (Jes $40_{1-11}$)', *ZAW* 96 (1984), 210–20 (220). It has been developed more fully with specific reference to the relationship between the various parts of the book of Isaiah by Melugin, *The Formation of Isaiah 40–55*, 83–4; Ackroyd, 'Isaiah 36–39'; Rendtorff, 'Jesaja 6 im Rahmen der Komposition des Jesajabuches', in Vermeylen (ed.), *The Book of Isaiah*, 73–82; C. R. Seitz, 'The Divine Council: Temporal Transition and New Prophecy in the Book of Isaiah', *JBL* 109 (1990), 229–47; Albertz, 'Das Deuterojesaja-Buch als Fortschreibung der Jesaja-Prophetie'; and Carr, 'Reaching for Unity in Isaiah', 68. For an alternative way of approaching the comparison of these two passages, see A. L. H. M. van Wieringen, 'Jesaja 40, 1–11: Eine drama-linguistische Lesung von Jesaja 6 her', *BN* 49 (1989), 82–93.

22 Cf. H. W. Robinson, 'The Council of Yahweh', *JTS* 45 (1944), 151–7, and E. T. Mullen, *The Divine Council in Canaanite and Early Hebrew Literature* (HSM 24; Chico, Calif., 1980), 207–18. Objections to this view are brushed aside by Seitz, 'The Divine Council'.

23 N. Tidwell ('*Wā'ōmar* (Zech. 3: 5) and the Genre of Zechariah's Fourth Vision', *JBL* 94 (1975), 343–55) draws attention to several of Zechariah's visions, as well as to 1 Kings 22; Job 1 and 2.

At first glance, we might be tempted to suppose that both passages have been independently influenced by the account concerning Micaiah ben Imlah in 1 Kgs. 22: 19–23, but closer examination reveals on the one hand that the connections between that passage and Isa. 40: 1–8 are far less exact than they are with Isaiah 6, whereas on the other hand the two passages in Isaiah share many additional features which cannot be derived from 1 Kings 22. Thus, in both there is a reference to 'a voice calling' (*qôl qôrē'*) (6: 4; 40: 3) and then to 'a voice speaking' (*qôl 'ōmēr*) (6: 8; 40: 6); both the usage, and certainly the combination, appear to be unparalleled elsewhere.[24] In both the prophet responds with initial despair (6: 5; 40: 6); in both there is reference to the removal of sin and iniquity (*ḥṭ't* and *'wn* (6: 7; 40: 2; cf. 1: 4)); and in both there is an emphasis on the glory (*kbwd*) of God (6: 3; 40: 5).[25] Of course, not all these elements are used in the same way. In Isaiah 6, for instance, it is the prophet's sin which is removed, in Isaiah 40 that of the people. Nevertheless, the number of shared elements is certainly striking, especially in view of the facts that they appear in generally comparable contexts and in some cases cannot be paralleled elsewhere. The combination seems difficult to account for other than in terms of direct literary influence.[26]

We may now proceed to build on this initial conclusion by taking account of four other elements in Isaiah 6 which seem to have been influential in the later Isaiah tradition.

(1) In the first verse, Isaiah describes the throne on which the Lord sits as 'high and lifted up' (*rām wᵉniśśā'*).[27] The impact of this on the prophet may be gauged by his repeated use of the phrase (with

[24] Even if *qôl* in 40: 3 is idiomatically to be rendered 'hark!', the unparalleled conjunction of the two words remains noteworthy. The use of *qôl* with *qr'* in such passages as Ps. 3: 5; 27: 7 is syntactically quite different; cf. GK §144*l–m*. It occurs as the subject of *'mr* at 1 Kgs. 19: 13 (and cf. Jer. 33: 11), but in a separate clause; there does not seem to be any connection with our two passages.

[25] Seitz ('The Divine Council', 240) also draws attention to the first-person-plural suffixes in 6: 8 and 40: 3, though it may be held that these are directly consequent upon the setting in the council. Connections between either of these two passages individually and other passages in Isaiah will be taken up later.

[26] The exegetical consequences of this conclusion, particularly with regard to Isaiah 40, are not our present concern; again, they have been followed up in detail by Seitz, 'The Divine Council', and Albertz, 'Das Deuterojesaja-Buch als Fortschreibung der Jesaja-Prophetie'.

[27] It is generally agreed that these words refer to the throne rather than to the Lord himself, although the effect for our purposes is the same.

grammatical modifications where necessary, and with the two words used sometimes in parallelism[28]) in his description of the Day of the Lord in chapter 2: 'For the Lord of hosts has a day against all that is proud and lofty [*rām*], against all that is lifted up [*niśśā'*] and high*' (verse 12). A probable gloss on the next verse describes the cedars of Lebanon as 'high and lifted up' (*hārāmîm wᵉhanniśśā'îm*) (see the Appendix), while in verse 14 the mountains are 'high' (*rāmîm*) and the hills 'lifted up' (*niśśā'ôt*). It seems that any challenge to the Lord's unique exaltation, expressed by this stereotyped pairing, will *ipso facto* be brought low.

This particular combination of words occurs only twice in the Old Testament outside the book of Isaiah. In Prov. 30: 13 (whose date is uncertain), although the reference is again to pride, no other connection with Isaiah is apparent, and, unlike the passages we have looked at so far, the verbs are used in a finite tense. Dan. 11: 12 is certainly too late in date to come in for consideration here, and there is in any case doubt both about the text of this verse and about the meaning of *wᵉniśśā'* in this context.[29] Occurrences of the phrase elsewhere in the book of Isaiah are thus likely to be of significance for our purpose.

The clearest allusion to Isaiah 6 by way of this phrase is found in Trito-Isaiah, at 57: 15: 'For thus says the high and lofty One [*rām wᵉniśśā'*] who inhabits eternity, whose name is Holy.' The absence of the article, which we might have expected, suggests particularly close dependence on the wording of 6: 1. In support of the view that this is a case of conscious dependence, it is noteworthy that earlier in the same chapter there seems to be an allusion to 2: 12*, which we saw was closely related to the same theme (verse 7: 'upon a high and lofty mountain' (*'al har-gābōah wᵉniśśā'*)).

It is difficult not to believe, however, that there has also been influence from the same quarter at 52: 13, where it is said of the Lord's servant that 'he shall be exalted and lifted up, and shall be very high†' (*yārûm wᵉniśśā' wᵉgābah mᵉ'ōd*). Not only do we find here the distinctive combination of the two roots under discussion

[28] For such distribution of fixed pairs over the two halves of poetic lines in parallelism, see E. Z. Melamed, 'Break-up of Stereotype Phrases as an Artistic Device in Biblical Poetry', *ScrH* 8 (1961), 115–53, and S. Talmon, 'Synonymous Readings in the Old Testament', *ScrH* 8 (1961), 335–83; see also the discussion in A. Berlin, *The Dynamics of Biblical Parallelism* (Bloomington, Ind., 1985), 76–80.

[29] See e.g. J. A. Montgomery, *A Critical and Exegetical Commentary on the Book of Daniel* (ICC; Edinburgh, 1927), 437.

from Isa. 6: 1, but in addition there is the introduction of a third verb, *gbh*, whose adjective also occurs in association with our phrase in chapter 2 (verses 12* and 15). In view of what we have seen of the use of these words elsewhere in Isaiah, this puts the exaltation of the servant, presumably following his sufferings which are described later, in a new and striking light.[30]

There are two other passages in Isaiah related to this theme with its distinctive vocabulary. Both come within the first part of the book, but both are widely believed to be much later additions to the Isaianic nucleus. The first is 30: 25, which is undoubtedly reminiscent of 2: 14–15: 'And upon every lofty mountain [*har gābōah*] and every high hill [*gib'â niśśā'â*] there will be brooks running with water, in the day of the great slaughter, when the towers fall.' The fact that in addition to the two phrases which have been singled out, and which clearly echo 2: 14, the concluding reference to 'towers' is paralleled in 2: 15, strongly supports the view that this is a case of direct literary dependence. Although the overwhelming majority of scholars agree that the passage in which this verse occurs (i.e. 19–26) is post-exilic, they differ over its precise date.[31] However, this need not detain us at present. The other passage, 33: 10, again occurs in a context which is universally agreed to be late: 'Now I will arise, says the Lord, now I will lift myself up, now I will be exalted [*'attâ 'ērômām 'attâ 'ennāśē'*]'.

To sum up, it would seem that the description of God in Isa. 6: 1 has exerted an influence on the whole of the Isaianic tradition in a way not generally appreciated previously.[32] We should note as most immediately relevant to our investigation that this includes Deutero-Isaiah, but not overlook as potentially significant later on that Trito-Isaiah also uses the phrase, though more in the form of

30 Other connections between Isaiah 6 and 52: 13–53: 12 are explored by B. Gosse, 'Isaïe 52,13—53,12 et Isaïe 6', *RB* 98 (1991), 537–43. Although they do not satisfy the criteria laid down for the present investigation, they become valuable as supporting evidence once the case as a whole has been established on other grounds. This is also the appropriate point at which to mention Gosse's most recent article on Isaiah 6, in which, however, he suggests on the basis of verbal parallels that the composition of the chapter should be dated late, as part of one of the latest redactional phases in the book's growth: see 'Isaïe vi et la tradition isaïenne', *VT* 42 (1992), 340–9. Needless to say, the present study seeks to explain the direction of dependence differently in most cases.

31 For a representative listing of opinions, see Vermeylen, 418–20, and L. Laberge, 'Is 30, 19–26: A Deuteronomic Text?', *Église et théologie*, 2 (1971), 35–54.

32 See, however, W. L. Holladay, *Isaiah: Scroll of a Prophetic Heritage* (Grand Rapids, Mich., 1978), 17, 151.

direct quotation and so less 'creatively' than Deutero-Isaiah, and that two later passages now included within Isaiah 1–39 also make use of it, though again less woodenly than Trito-Isaiah.

(2) Next, it will be recalled that the Seraphim who stood around the Lord called out 'Holy, holy, holy is the Lord of Hosts', and it is not unreasonable to assume that this is what led Isaiah either to coin, or at least to make peculiarly his own, the title 'The Holy One of Israel' (*qᵉdôš-yiśrā'ēl*).[33] Alternatively, the possibility may be considered that, if the title was already known to Isaiah (see below), it may itself have inspired the words spoken in the vision.

Although this title is found most frequently in the book of Isaiah (twenty-five times in all), it also occurs in several passages elsewhere: 2 Kgs. 19: 22; Jer. 50: 29; 51: 5; Ps. 71: 22; 78: 41; 89: 19. The relationship of these other examples to the book of Isaiah needs clarification if any positive conclusions are to be drawn for our present discussion. The first (2 Kgs. 19: 22) occurs in a speech attributed to Isaiah which has a parallel in the book of Isaiah itself (37: 23). Although the question of dependence between the parallel passages in 2 Kgs. 18–20 and Isaiah 36–9 is disputed,[34] there can be no doubt that the words of Isaiah in 2 Kgs. 19: 20–34 owe a good deal to the Isaiah tradition. It is thus most likely that the occurrence of 'The Holy One of Israel' is simply an example of this and so should not be regarded as having any independent significance from our point of view. The two occurrences in Jeremiah are not dissimilar. Clearly, they cannot be earlier than Isaiah, though they could possibly be early enough theoretically to have influenced Deutero-Isaiah. It is striking, however, that they both come in Jeremiah 50–1, for we have already seen (and will see again) that

[33] So, for instance, besides many commentators, G. Bettenzoli, *Geist der Heiligkeit: Traditionsgeschichtliche Untersuchung des QDŠ-Begriffes im Buch Ezechiel* (Quaderni di Semitistica, 8; Florence, 1979), 25–49; W. J. Kornfeld, 'QDŠ und Gottesrecht im Alten Testament', in J. A. Emerton (ed.), *Congress Volume: Vienna 1980* (SVT 32; Leiden, 1981), 1–9 (3); Høgenhaven, *Gott und Volk bei Jesaja*, 197; and, with some reserve, H. Wildberger, 'Gottesnamen und Gottesepitheta bei Jesaja', in *Jahwe und sein Volk: Gesammelte Aufsätze zum Alten Testament* (ThB 66; Munich, 1979), 219–48 (242). Despite his different approach to this title, A. van Selms accepts that Deutero-Isaiah was 'influenced by the ancient prophet's utterances' ('The Expression "The Holy One of Israel"', in W. C. Delsman *et al.* (eds.), *Von Canaan bis Kerala: Festschrift für Prof. Mag. Dr. J. P. M. van der Ploeg O.P. zur Vollendung des siebzigsten Lebensjahres am 4. Juli 1979* (AOAT 211; Neukirchen-Vluyn, 1982), 257–69 (259)).

[34] See the discussion below, Ch. 8.

these two chapters enjoy a peculiarly close relationship with the Isaiah tradition. Quite what that signifies cannot yet be explained, but it would clearly be precarious to treat these two examples as though they were wholly independent of Isaiah.

It is the three Psalms which refer to 'The Holy One of Israel' which are the most difficult to evaluate. In the first place, their date is by no means certain, but even if they were all comparatively late they might still have drawn the title from some more ancient cult tradition which was independent of Isaiah but which happened not to be attested in other earlier texts. In that case, it would be possible to maintain that Deutero-Isaiah also drew on this rather than on Isaiah of Jerusalem, since it is well known that he makes extensive use of the forms and language of Israel's liturgy as known to us from the Psalms. Of course, if the Psalms are early,[35] the same point could be made even more forcibly.

Let us assume, then, that the title 'was already in the tradition for Isaiah to take over'.[36] This has, indeed, been maintained by Schmidt on the basis of the ascription of holiness to El in the Ugaritic texts. He suggests that it would then probably have been predicated also of El Elyon in the pre-Israelite Jerusalem cult (note the proximity of holiness to Elyon in Ps. 46: 5[4]), whence it would have been transferred to Yahweh sometime after Jerusalem became part of Israel. From here, it would have been but a short step to the development of the fuller title 'The Holy One of Israel', so that, if Isaiah's perception of God as holy in chapter 6 derives from these circles (as other features in this chapter, such as the kingship of Yahweh, make likely), then his adoption of the title may also reflect the influence of the same background.[37]

Does all this mean that the title fails to meet the criteria which we

[35] Note in particular the arguments for an early date for Psalm 78 in J. Day, 'Pre-Deuteronomic Allusions to the Covenant in Hosea and Psalm lxxviii', *VT* 36 (1986), 1–12, with reference to 'The Holy One of Israel' on p. 10 n. 23.

[36] W. H. Schmidt, *Alttestamentliche Glaube und seine Umwelt: Zur Geschichte des alttestamentlichen Gottesverständnisses* (Neukirchen-Vluyn, 1968), 138 = ET *The Faith of the Old Testament: A History* (Oxford, 1983), 155. See also van Selms, 'The Expression "The Holy One of Israel"'.

[37] W. H. Schmidt, 'Wo hat die Aussage: Jahwe "der Heilige" ihren Ursprung?', *ZAW* 74 (1962), 62–6. Scoralick (*Trishagion und Gottesherrschaft*), however, has argued that the threefold use of 'holy' in Psalm 99 is dependent on Isaiah 6, not the other way round. Gammie (*Holiness in Israel*, 75) suggests rather that Isaiah has been influenced by the expression 'the Holy One in your midst' in Hos. 11: 9.

laid down in the previous chapter for securing reasonably certain evidence of the influence of one part of the book of Isaiah on another? Not necessarily, and that for at least three reasons. First, Schmidt himself has pointed out that Isaiah appears to have used the title in a distinctive manner, for in his work it occurs 'usually in accusations and warnings'.[38] Unlike anything that we find in the Psalms, Isaiah seems to have regarded the holiness of God as something that was threatening to his people, and with this the personal experience of the prophet as recounted in Isaiah 6 coincides.[39] Secondly, Wildberger (p. 23) has made the point that the title must previously have been limited to quite a restricted circle within the Jerusalem cult tradition. Its extremely rare use in the Psalms, which does not appear to have influenced any other of Israel's writers before the time of Isaiah, suggests that the wider use of it which we find both in the Isaiah material and in other passages closely related to it is most likely to be due to the direct influence of the prophet himself. Finally, the unprecedented density of usage of the phrase in the book of Isaiah (twelve times in Isaiah 1–39, eleven times in 40–55, and twice in 56–66) stands out as wholly disproportional by comparison with its use elsewhere, so that any attempt to explain its use in the later chapters without reference to the fact that it is distinctively characteristic of the book as a whole would be perverse. This conclusion, of course, is in no way compromised by the fact that Deutero-Isaiah has developed the phrase in fresh ways in his new 'salvation' context.

There is one last means by which the implications of the title for which we have argued has been challenged, though it does not seem to be one which is likely to enjoy widespread support. In the context of his discussion of the first chapter of Isaiah, Loretz has sought to maintain that the title was never, in fact, used by Isaiah of Jerusalem at all.[40] He suggests that all twelve occurrences in Isaiah

[38] Schmidt, *Alttestamentliche Glaube*, 138–9 = *Faith*, 155; similarly, Bettenzoli (*Heiligkeit*, 43–9) has sought to demonstrate a fresh use of the title by Isaiah in that he first combined it with the more wisdom-like concepts of God as Israel's father and tutor against whose instruction they have rebelled.

[39] Similarly, though not quite so compellingly, Clements finds a new twist in Isaiah's use of the 'Israel' element of the title 'in view of the sharp division between the two kingdoms which had occurred, first with the Syro-Ephraimite conflict and then with the fall of Ephraim to Assyria (733–722). Yahweh still remained the God of the entire people' (p. 31).

[40] O. Loretz, *Der Prolog des Jesaja-Buches (1,1–2,5): Ugaritologische und kolometrische Studien zum Jesaja-Buch* (UBL 1; Altenberge, 1984), 97–110.

1–39 are either in passages which are completely later than Isaiah himself or are in later short additions to genuinely Isaianic texts.

With regard to some of these examples, there would be little dispute today. A representative position which may be cited is that of Wildberger (p. 23), who lists the following examples as either certainly or arguably post-Isaianic: 10: 20; 12: 6; 17: 7; 29: 19; 37: 23. Nevertheless, that still leaves 1: 4; 5: 19, 24; 30: 11, 12, 15; and 31: 1 as being, in Wildberger's opinion, original to Isaiah. In challenging the authenticity of these latter passages, Loretz is able here and there to cite commentators (principally Kaiser and Vermeylen)[41] who agree with his position, though none who follows him in every case.[42]

While we cannot here treat each of the passages in full, we may note by way of a single example that his arguments at 31: 1 are particularly weak. He seeks to maintain that the second two lines of the verse have been added later to the first (whose authenticity, we may note in passing, seems to be assured both by its close association with 30: 1–3[43] and by the development of both its halves in 31: 3; cf. *miṣrayīm-ûmiṣrayīm*; *sûsîm-wᵉsûsêhem*). He bases this conclusion on the use of the *wāw*-consecutive at the start of line *b*, 'colometric' considerations, and the use of the accusative particle *'et* in line *c*. Of these, only the last refers to line *c*, which is the most important from our point of view. His objection, however, that the accusative particle could not have been used in poetry as early as the time of Isaiah is misguided. Not only is some kind of particle expected here, in view of the tight poetic parallelism which these lines display, in order to balance the preposition *'al* in the first half of the line, but it seems that specifically with the verb *drš* the accusative particle was regularly used in eighth-century poetry (including by Isaiah himself), perhaps because it was something of a technical religious term; cf. Isa. 9: 12; Hos. 10: 12; Amos 5: 6.[44] Moreover, even working on the basis of Loretz's own idiosyncratic

[41] With regard to 5: 19, he could now additionally refer to Werner, *Studien zur alttestamentlichen Vorstellung vom Plan Jahwes*, 11–32.

[42] It should further be noted that with regard to 30: 9–17, for instance, both Kaiser and Vermeylen think in terms of early exilic redaction. From the point of view of the present study, the important point still remains, therefore, that it would already have been in place before the time of Deutero-Isaiah.

[43] Though again contrast Werner, *Studien zur alttestamentlichen Vorstellung vom Plan Jahwes*, 85–94.

[44] Cf. F. J. Gonçalves, *L'Expédition de Sennachérib en Palestine dans la littérature hébraïque ancienne* (EB NS 7; Paris, 1986), 162–3.

'colometric' system (i.e. the counting of consonants), there is no objection to be raised against line *c*. By his own count, it is reckoned as 17/13, which compares closely with the 16/12 of line *a*.[45] Moreover, the negative point which line *c* makes, contrasting the Judaeans' dependence on Egypt with their lack of trust in the Lord, seems to be demanded in context by the development of the argument in verse 3,[46] as well as by the parallel thought in 30: 1–5.[47] Whether Loretz's arguments are sufficient to cast doubt on line *b* of this verse as well seems equally improbable to me, but perhaps need not be discussed fully here.[48] For our present purposes it is sufficient to observe that in this one test case (to which others might be added; see below, Chapter 5, on Isaiah 30, for instance) there is no good reason to follow Loretz in denying the use of the title 'The Holy One of Israel' to Isaiah.

We may conclude this discussion, then, by observing that, despite the more complicated situation which this phrase presents, it too is most naturally explained in terms of literary influence of one part of the book of Isaiah on another. Indeed, it is one of the best known of such examples, and has long been paraded as a major argument by those who hold to the authorial unity of the book as a whole. In seeking to evaluate the evidence from within a standpoint of multiple authorship, however, it is preferable to note that we again have an example of the influence of Isaiah of Jerusalem on Deutero- (and Trito-)Isaiah, and further that this influence is also evident in some of the later material now included in Isaiah 1–39.

[45] In arriving at this latter figure, I have discounted the extra-metrical *hôy*, as Loretz does along with most other metrical systems, but I have retained *lᵉʿezrâ*, whose deletion he does not explain or justify.

[46] Cf. F. Huber, *Jahwe, Juda und die anderen Völker beim Propheten Jesaja* (BZAW 137; Berlin, 1976), 122–30.

[47] Cf. B. S. Childs, *Isaiah and the Assyrian Crisis* (SBT 2nd ser. 3; London, 1967), 35.

[48] The poetic parallelism in the line is perfectly satisfactory, and it is doubtful if its slightly greater length from a 'colometric' point of view (15/17) constitutes a real problem; on a conventional metrical analysis, it can be reckoned as 3: 3, like the adjacent lines; cf. H. Donner, *Israel unter den Völkern* (SVT 11; Leiden, 1964), 135, 189. The use of a *wāw*-consecutive at the start of the line is admittedly unusual, but not therefore necessarily inexplicable: see W. Dietrich, *Jesaja und die Politik* (BEvT 74; Munich, 1976), 145 n. 67, and the continuation of the verse in the perfect tense. It is certainly insufficient on its own to argue for a secondary insertion; in view of our continuing uncertainties about many aspects of the Hebrew verbal system, it requires explaining rather than explaining away.

(3) Moving on through Isaiah 6, we come next to the difficult verses 9–10.

> Go, and say to this people:
> 'Hear and hear, but do not understand;
> see and see, but do not perceive'.
> Make the heart of this people fat,
> and their ears heavy,
> and shut their eyes;
> lest they see with their eyes,
> and hear with their ears,
> and understand with their hearts,
> and turn and be healed.

This passage introduces one of the major themes which Clements has dealt with,[49] and we may most conveniently begin by following the line of his argument. First, he sets out three passages in Deutero-Isaiah which relate to this same theme:

> Then I will lead the blind along the road*,
> I will guide them in paths they have not known. (42: 16)

> Hear, you deaf;
> and look, you blind, that you may see!
> Who is blind except my servant,
> or deaf as my messenger whom I send?
> Who is blind as the one with whom I am at peace [or 'who fulfils my purpose']
> or blind as the servant of Yahweh? (42: 18–19; but see the Appendix)

> Bring forth the people who are blind, yet have eyes,
> who are deaf, yet have ears! (43: 8)

Clements stresses in particular the importance of the second of these passages because it makes clear that the blindness is 'spiritual', and because the following verses (42: 21–5) elaborate on the deafness as 'a failure to listen to, and obey, Yahweh's *tôrâ*'.

The next reference comes from the passage on the folly of idolatry (44: 9–20), a practice which is to be seen as a consequence of Israel's blindness and deafness and which Clements thinks may be 'a subsequent elaboration upon the original prophetic text':

[49] Clements, 'Beyond Tradition-History'; see also Matheus, *Singt dem Herrn ein neues Lied*, 165–9.

'They do not know; nor do they understand; for he has covered over their eyes, so that they cannot see, and their hearts, so that they cannot understand' (44: 18). Since this theme in Deutero-Isaiah is used in a way which suggests that it is already known to be the case, Clements has no hesitation in pointing to 6: 9–10 as its source of origin both because of the strikingly similar language and because of the central importance of the call narrative.

Finally, attention is drawn to two passages which reflect similar ideas but which are included among the later additions to Isaiah 1–39:

> Then [in the coming time of salvation] the eyes of the blind shall be opened,
> and the ears of the deaf unstopped. (35: 5)

> On that day the deaf shall hear the words of a book,
> and out of their gloom and darkness
> the eyes of the blind shall see. (29: 18)

On the first of these, Clements comments that we appear to have moved to literal rather than metaphorical blindness and deafness,[50] and on the second that the reference to gloom and darkness implies a linkage of the imagery of 8: 23 with that of blindness. He concludes his discussion by asserting that 'It would seem here that we have a very strong case indeed for regarding the prophetic author of Isa. 42–43 as familiar with the actual words recorded of Isaiah's call in a section which is usually ascribed to the "Isaiah Memoir".'

While I have no quarrel with this conclusion, the steps which lead up to it need both refinement and development. First, it should be recognized that Isaiah of Jerusalem does not himself refer explicitly to blindness or deafness as such; the two key words (*'iwwēr, ḥērēš*) do not occur anywhere in his recorded prophecies. Although several of the passages cited have such words as 'hear' and 'see', 'eyes' and 'ears', in common, it is apparent that Deutero-Isaiah has again shown a considerable degree of freedom in his use and application of this theme. In addition, it is the use of these two key words from Deutero-Isaiah which (among many other things) helps 29: 18 and 35: 5 to stand out within the corpus of chapters 1–39.

50 See further his elaboration on this observation in R. E. Clements, 'Patterns in the Prophetic Canon: Healing the Blind and the Lame', in G. M. Tucker, D. L. Petersen, and R. L. Wilson (eds.), *Canon, Theology, and Old Testament Interpretation: Essays in Honor of Brevard S. Childs* (Philadelphia, 1988), 189–200.

Secondly, it is, perhaps, surprising that Clements does not refer to two other passages in Isaiah 1–39 which manifest a close association with this circle of ideas. At 32: 3 we read:

> Then the eyes of those who see will not be closed*,
> and the ears of those who hear will hearken.

In his commentary (pp. 259–60), Clements follows Barth[51] in ascribing this passage to the Josianic redaction which both scholars believe was an important step in the formation of the book of Isaiah, and in particular he finds here 'a deliberate allusion' to the account of the call of the prophet. He also draws 30: 19–21 into the discussion as reflecting a possible further development of the theme. Whatever conclusion we come to about the possibility of a Josianic redaction, it is certainly striking that 32: 3* stands far closer from a verbal point of view to Isa. 6: 9–10 than do the passages in Deutero-Isaiah. Unlike 29: 18 and 35: 5, it does not refer to the people as 'blind' or 'deaf', whereas on the other hand among several verbal links we may note in particular that it uses the rare word *šʿʿ*, the hiphʿil of which is also found in 6: 10, but which does not occur anywhere in Deutero-Isaiah. So far as it goes, this evidence would favour the view that this passage was in place before the time of Deutero-Isaiah.[52] Secondly, 29: 9–10, generally agreed to be by Isaiah himself, is another passage which clearly reflects a development of the theme of 6: 9–10. It too makes use of the root *šʿʿ*, and it also refers to the 'blinding' (*ʿṣm*) of eyes. These two passages further broaden the scope of influence of 6: 9–10 on the Isaianic tradition and so increase the likelihood of influence on Deutero-Isaiah from this quarter.

Thirdly, there is a related theme running through many of these verses to which Clements makes no reference but which certainly deserves examination as strengthening the overall case considerably. It has been observed by both Watts and Rendtorff[53] that the outcome of the hardening motif is that the people will not 'understand' (*byn*) or 'perceive/know' (*ydʿ*) in 6: 9, and again in 6: 10 that they will not 'understand with their hearts'. In itself this is, of

[51] Barth, *Die Jesaja-Worte in der Josiazeit*, 213–15.

[52] Though opinions are divided, probably a majority of commentators favour a post-exilic date for this passage; see the recent surveys and discussions in Wildberger, 1252–54, and Vermeylen, 424–5.

[53] J. D. W. Watts, *Isaiah* (Word Biblical Themes; Dallas, 1989), 3–10; Rendtorff, 'Jesaja 6 im Rahmen der Komposition des Jesajabuches'.

course, a common enough idea in the Hebrew Bible, as a study of the root *byn* and its derivatives could show. However, its collocation with the ideas of seeing and hearing is distinctively Isaianic. Thus, as an especially striking parallel with 6: 9–10 we should first note 44: 18, which was cited above. There, it is said of the idol-makers that 'they know not, nor do they discern' (*lōʾ yādᵉʿû wᵉlōʾ yābînû*) because God has blinded them, and again in the following verse it is stated that they have no 'knowledge or discernment' (*wᵉlōʾ daʿat wᵉlōʾ-tᵉbûnâ*) (note also the repeated use of *lēb* in the sense of a mind which has been dulled—twice in 6: 10 and twice in 44: 18–19). Again, in the context of 43: 8 which was also referred to above, Israel as God's once blind-and-deaf witness will be brought to the point where they 'know [*tēdᵉʿû*] . . . and understand [*wᵉtābînû*] that I am He' (43: 10).

Moving slightly further afield, the reversal of the judgement of 6: 9–10 as a consequence of God's new salvation is clearly expressed in 41: 20, for whereas formerly the people were told 'see and see, but do not perceive (know)', now the result of what is to happen is precisely that they may 'see and know' (*lᵉmaʿan yirᵉʾû wᵉyēdᵉʿû*). Suggestive too is the effect of the work of the servant on the gentile nations at 52: 15:

> for that which has not been told them they shall see [*rāʾû*],
> and that which they have not heard [*lōʾ-šāmᵉʿû*] they shall understand [*hitbônānû*].

With this may be contrasted the prophet's surprise at Israel's lack of perception heretofore:

> Have you not known? Have you not heard? [*hᵃlôʾ tēdᵉʿû hᵃlôʾ tišmāʿû*]
> Has it not been told you from the beginning?
> Have you not understood . . . [*hᵃlôʾ hᵃbînōtem*] (40: 21)

Similar ideas surface elsewhere in the Isaiah tradition. Indeed, it is given particular prominence by whoever was responsible for positioning 1: 2–3 as the introduction to the book as a whole. Heaven and earth are called upon to 'hear' God's indictment of his people:

> Sons have I reared and brought up,
> but they have rebelled against me.

The ox knows [*yāda'*] its owner,
and the ass its master's crib;
but Israel does not know [*lō' yāda'*],
my people does not understand [*lō' hitbônān*].

Earlier, attention was drawn to the importance of 32: 3 for the theme of those who have eyes and ears but do not see or hear. Now we should add that the following verse continues the reversal of this image in language that is equally strongly reminiscent of 6: 9–10: 'The heart of the hasty shall understand knowledge' (*ûl$^{e}$bab nimhārîm yābîn lādā'at*). Finally, there are echoes of the same circle of ideas in Trito-Isaiah, at 56: 10–11 and 57: 1, and earlier at 29: 23–4 and possibly at 28: 9 and 19.

We may thus conclude that the case which Clements has made for the influence of 6: 9–10 on other parts of the book of Isaiah in terms of blindness and deafness can be considerably strengthened by taking into account the related theme of understanding and knowledge with which it often occurs in close relationship.

A fourth and final point arising from Clements's discussion needs to be addressed—namely, whether Deutero-Isaiah might not have derived his inspiration from some source other than Isaiah of Jerusalem. This is necessary because Davies[54] has contended that 'the "blind and deaf" passages in Deutero-Isaiah are as closely paralleled in Jer 5,21 as they are in Is 6,9–10'. (It may be noted that Davies could also have added Ezek. 12: 2.) If this were true, it would certainly cast doubt on the case that has been made out above. In response, it may readily be admitted that Jer. 5: 21 displays some noteworthy parallels with Isa. 6: 9–10, and indeed it may well be that Jeremiah has himself been influenced by Isaiah:

Hear this, O foolish and senseless people,
who have eyes, but see not,
who have ears, but hear not.

However, this passage does not develop the theme of understanding and knowledge by use of the vocabulary which we have seen to be characteristic both of Isaiah of Jerusalem and of Deutero-Isaiah (it speaks rather of *'am sākāl w$^{e}$'ên lēb*), so that inner-Isaianic influence accounts for the evidence as a whole more satisfactorily than does the possibility of influence from Jeremiah. Moreover, it seems to be less plausible to assume influence from this isolated

54 Davies, 'The Destiny of the Nations', 116 n. 80.

passage than from what we have seen to be a widely used motif within the book of Isaiah itself.[55]

We may observe by way of summary, therefore, that the hardening passage in Isaiah 6 seems to have exerted particular influence on Deutero-Isaiah, but that it also fits into the pattern we have observed earlier of casting its shadow by way of either reaffirmation or reversal on other parts of the book as well.

(4) The fourth section of Isaiah 6 which calls for our attention is verses 11–12.[56] Immediately after Isaiah has been given his difficult assignment, he responds with the question 'How long, O Lord?' The answer is not encouraging:

Until cities lie waste without inhabitant,
  and houses without men,
  and the land is left desolate*,
and the Lord removes men far away
  and the forsaken places are many in the midst of the land.

Once again, Clements[57] has drawn attention to an echo of this passage in 44: 26, where part of the description of God introducing the Cyrus oracle states:

who confirms the word of his servant†,
  and performs the counsel of his messengers,
who says of Jerusalem, 'she shall be inhabited',
  . . . and I will raise up its ruins'*.

There are, of course, some items of vocabulary in common between these two passages (the emphasis on cities and their inhabitants), but Clements is rightly impressed more by the fact that 'both in the terms of the original threat and of the subsequent reversal of it, its centrality to the overall message that is being

55 The expression of similar ideas in the anti-idol polemic of Pss. 115: 3–8 and 135: 15–18 is later than, and probably dependent on, Deutero-Isaiah: see H.-J. Kraus, *Psalmen* (BKAT 15; Neukirchen-Vluyn, 1961²), 788, 897 = ET *Psalms 60–150* (Augsburg, 1989), 380–1, 494; Preuß, *Verspottung fremder Religionen im Alten Testament*, 251–3. The significance of these Psalm passages and of others of similar import for the exegesis of Isa. 6: 9–10 has been explored by G. K. Beale, 'Isaiah vi 9–13: A Retributive Taunt against Idolatry', *VT* 41 (1991), 257–78.

56 See above, pp. 35–7, for a justification for using verse 12 in the context of the present discussion.

57 Clements, 'Beyond Tradition-History', 107–8.

declared is so evident'. Further, he points out that the opening of 44: 26 ('who confirms the word of his servant') may be an allusion to the original threat of Isaiah 6 which has now been fulfilled. (This suggestion furnishes a hitherto unnoticed justification for the otherwise unexpected singular, 'his servant' (*'abdô*).) This contextually attractive suggestion would underline the deliberateness of Deutero-Isaiah's literary allusion here.

Clements includes this example only in his category of 'some further possibilities'. In fact, a study of the wider ramifications of this theme in Isaiah would seem to justify advancing it into the group of the firmly probable. A comparable threat is found among the sayings of Isaiah at 5: 8–10,[58] the first of a series of woes which is universally ascribed to Isaiah:

> Woe to those who join house to house,
>   who add field to field
> until there is no more room,
>   and you are made to dwell† alone in the midst of the land.
> The Lord of hosts has sworn* in my hearing:
>   'Surely many houses shall be desolate,
>   large and beautiful houses without inhabitant.
> For ten acres of vineyard shall yield but one bath,
>   and a homer of seed shall yield but an ephah.'

In addition to the general similarity of theme, we should note the use in both passages of the phrase *mē'ên yôšēb*, ('without inhabitant'), the use in both of the root *šmm* ('to be desolate'), and the fact that both continue by making use of the idea of judgement being expressed in terms of only a tenth remaining or continuing (cf. 5: 10; 6: 13; in the latter passage, even the remaining tenth will be destroyed). It should also be observed that 5: 8 and 44: 26 are the only two passages in the Hebrew Bible where the hoph'al of *yšb*

[58] Recently, it has been maintained by Kaiser and by Werner (*Studien zur alttestamentlichen Vorstellung vom Plan Jahwes*, 12–13, 26) that verses 9–10 are a later redactional expansion of the originally brief oracle in verse 8. This seems to rest, however, (1) on a misapplication of the principles of form-criticism which insists that all examples of a particular genre must conform to a hypothetical original form, without allowing for the possibility that the form itself may have developed in the meantime (in this case already before the time of Isaiah; cf. the use of the 'woe!' form in Amos); and (2) on an apparent presumption that any similarities between one text and another in Isaiah are best explained as imitation or interpretation. In addition, we may note that Werner ascribes the expansion to the exilic period, which would already be sufficiently early for our present purposes, though Kaiser reckons in terms of a much later date.

is found, though admittedly the sense is not quite the same in each case.

Rendtorff[59] also notes the importance of Isa. 6: 11 for our theme, and, although strangely he does not refer to 5: 8–10, he seeks to draw 1: 7 into the discussion because of the twofold use there of the word *šᵉmāmâ* (though it should be mentioned that the second use is often thought to be part of the work of a later glossator; see the Appendix):

> Your country lies desolate,
>   your cities are burned with fire;
> in your very presence
>   aliens devour your land;
> it is desolate, like the overthrow of Sodom*.

Although we are clearly in the realm of similar ideas (and to some extent even of shared vocabulary) here, it should be noted that this passage lacks a reference to the desertion of the land, which serves to link 5: 8–10 and 6: 11–12 so closely together. Indeed, 1: 7 presupposes the continuing habitation of the land ('in your very presence'), which is one of the reasons why it is so often ascribed to the events of 701 BC.[60] The use of *šmm* alone, which appears to be all that Rendtorff considers, is insufficiently specific to carry weight for our purposes without the support of other elements as well. *šmm* also occurs in Isaiah 1–39 at 13: 9; 17: 9; and 24: 12. There are other connections to be noted with our key passages too, but none is as close as 5: 8–10 with 6: 11–13. In addition, a strong case can be made for regarding all three as post-Isaianic, so that they should not be considered in an initial discussion of the possible influence of Isaiah of Jerusalem on Deutero-Isaiah.

When we turn, then, to Deutero-Isaiah with 5: 8–10 and 6: 11–13 in mind, two passages in addition to that referred to by Clements call for examination. Both are mentioned by Rendtorff on the basis of his narrowly based criterion, but in fact there are more points of contact than he observes. First, in 49: 14–21 the Lord reverses Zion's complaint that she has been abandoned and forgotten. In view of what follows, it is possible that this echoes the *hāʿᵃzûbâ* (feminine singular, translated as 'forsaken places') of 6: 12. God promises that the desolate places (*šōmᵉmōtayik*† (verse 19)) will be

[59] Rendtorff, 'Jesaja 6', 79.

[60] Contrast J. H. Hayes and S. A. Irvine, *Isaiah, the Eighth-Century Prophet: His Times and his Preaching* (Nashville, Tenn., 1987), 72–3.

restored (cf. the comparable thought and vocabulary in the last line of 49: 8), and that, whereas in 6: 12 'the Lord removes men far away [*wᵉriḥaq*]', now it is Jerusalem's destroyers who will be 'far away' (*wᵉrāḥᵃqû*) (49: 19). Similarly, in the indictment of 5: 8 there will be no more room in the city because of the property-dealers' avarice, so that appropriately they will end up being left on their own. Eventually, the site will be deserted (5: 9), without inhabitant (5: 9; 6: 11–12). Now, in reversal, there will again be too little room (*tēṣᵉrî miyyôšēb* and *ṣar-lî hammāqôm*), but this time because of the number of those returning who wish to dwell there (*wᵉ'ēšēbâ* (49: 20)). Finally, just as God threatened that the guilty would end up 'on your own' (*lᵉbaddᵉkem*) (5: 8), so now Zion remembers how she had indeed been 'left [*niš'artî*, compare the emended form of the ending of 6: 11] alone [*lᵉbaddî*]' (49: 21).

Secondly, the theme of chapter 54 is comparable with 49: 14–21,[61] and Rendtorff rightly points to the description of Zion as 'desolate' (*šômēmâ*) in verse 1 and to the particularly impressive reversal of the threat in verse 3—*wᵉ'ārîm nᵉšammôt yôšîbû* ('and they will inhabit the desolate cities'). In addition, we should note the theme of numerous inhabitants throughout verses 1–3, another reference to Zion as 'a forsaken wife' (*'iššâ 'ᵃzûbâ*) in verse 6, and further the fact that 'you shall be far [*raḥᵃqî*†] from oppression' (54: 14).

Of course, none of the vocabulary to which we have drawn attention in this section is uncommon, so that the possibility of influence from elsewhere, or of mere coincidence, should theoretically be considered. Kaiser (p. 134 = ET 133), for instance, lists a number of passages, especially in Jeremiah, where the devastation of cities and the loss of inhabitants are mentioned. (This is part of his argument for denying Isaianic authorship of Isaiah 6.) So far as I can see, however, none of these other passages includes the full range of vocabulary parallels which we have seen to characterize the two passages in Proto-Isaiah and the three in Deutero-Isaiah, so that inner-Isaianic influence remains more probable. Moreover, when this is coupled with the centrality of this particular threat in Isaiah (the first of the series of woes and the call narrative) and the

[61] Cf. G. Glaßner, *Vision eines auf Verheißung gegründeten Jerusalem: Textanalytische Studien zu Jesaja 54* (ÖBS 11; Klosterneuburg, 1991), 228; less forcefully, R. Martin-Achard, 'Esaïe liv et la nouvelle Jérusalem', in J. A. Emerton (ed.), *Congress Volume: Vienna 1980* (SVT 32; Leiden, 1981), 238–62.

significance of its reversal for the message of Deutero-Isaiah,[62] that probability becomes all the stronger.

As in the other examples which have been analysed above, there are several possible instances of Trito-Isaiah's dependence upon these passages (e.g. 58: 12; 61: 4; 62: 4; 64: 9; and 65: 21–2). However, because none attests the full range of verbal links, which is what makes the case in Deutero-Isaiah so compelling, these cannot be regarded as particularly strong. The same applies to the possible later use of the theme in non-Isaianic parts of Isaiah 1–39 alluded to above. Whereas in the light of the other more certain examples noted earlier these too should be regarded as possible, they are not in themselves sufficiently striking to act as independent evidence in their own right.

To sum up this fourth main point: there seems to be clear evidence for the development by way of reversal in Deutero-Isaiah of the theme of Isa. 6: 11–13 and the closely related passage 5: 8–10. In particular, it is attractive to believe with Clements that it even includes a reference to the work of the earlier prophet in this regard with the otherwise unexpected singular 'his servant' in 44: 26. The use of the theme elsewhere in the Isaianic tradition is only a possibility, however. In this, it differs from most of the other evidence considered in this chapter.

We have now examined the connections between the overall form of Isaiah 6 and Isa. 40: 1–8 and between four important elements in the chapter and their recurrence elsewhere in the book. Even if there is room for disagreement about individual details here and there, the cumulative effect of all this material seems irrefutably to point to the direct literary influence of this chapter on the Isaianic tradition as a whole and on Deutero-Isaiah in particular. There are, of course, other points of contact between Isaiah 6 and Deutero-Isaiah, such as the reference to God as King (6: 5; cf. 41: 21; 43: 15; 44: 6; 52: 7; note also 24: 23; 33: 22), and the contrast between the enthroned Lord (6: 1; cf. 40: 22) and the fate of Babylon (47: 1). These have not been dealt with here, however, because they are not unique to the Isaianic tradition,[63] and so cannot, on the basis of

[62] Cf. J. F. A. Sawyer, 'Daughter of Zion and Servant of the Lord: A Comparison', *JSOT* 44 (1989), 89–107; see also C. A. Franke, 'The Function of the Satiric Lament over Babylon in Second Isaiah (xlvii)', *VT* 41 (1991), 408–18.

[63] Though Wildberger (p. 245), points out that the other prophets before Deutero-Isaiah are singularly reticent about referring to God as King.

the criteria we have laid down, be used as positive evidence for our case. Naturally, once that case is established, the likelihood that they too are part of the same process becomes more probable.[64]

With regard to the nature of this influence, the questions 'how?' and 'why?' have not yet been addressed, and without adequate answers to these our understanding of the process of composition of the book of Isaiah remains unsatisfactory. But before we can move on to take up those questions, the case which we have begun to develop in this chapter needs to be broadened to see whether the situation with regard to chapter 6 is also true of the remaining material which can be ascribed to the eighth-century Isaiah.

64 See also the comments on Gosse, 'Isaïe 52,13—53,12 et Isaïe 6', above, n. 30.

# 4

## Further Examples of Isaianic Influence

HAVING established in the previous chapter that, on the basis of the evidence from Isaiah 6, there is a prima-facie case for the influence of the literary deposit of Isaiah of Jerusalem on the remainder of the Isaianic tradition as a whole, we shall proceed in this chapter to examine some further examples of this phenomenon from elsewhere in Isaiah 1–39. Reference will naturally again be made to the criteria for this investigation laid down in Chapter 2. It will be found that the cases adduced vary in their cogency, as is only to be expected. In particular, scholars are far from agreed about the 'authenticity' of some of the passages that we shall be dealing with. While I have attempted to use only material over which a general consensus may be said to exist in this regard, and equally to exclude cases whose secondary nature is widely agreed, it would be too much to hope for complete agreement. Nevertheless, the cumulative force of the collection of a number of examples should be sufficient to nullify the effect of disagreement in any single case, or even several particular cases.

The only exception to this will be those few scholars whose understanding of the growth of the book of Isaiah differs radically from the consensus view. For them, any similarity with later material is taken *ipso facto* to endorse the opinion that what we may call the 'base passage' in Isaiah 1–39 is late as well. While I cannot expect my few contrary remarks in what follows to overthrow such a presupposition, it should perhaps be observed that, the more this extreme line of thinking is pursued, the more difficult it becomes to present an alternative hypothesis to account for the growth of the Isaianic tradition in the first place. Indeed, one of the underlying attractions of the argument of this book as a whole will be seen to be the simplicity of its explanation for what appears to be otherwise such a bewilderingly complex composition as Isaiah has often been thought to be.

The examples which follow make no claim to be comprehensive, though it is hoped that at least all the major ones have been referred to. It should be noted, however, that one group has been reserved for the following chapter because it contains the clue which may help to explain the process as a whole, thus moving the argument on from observation to explanation. The order in which the examples are presented is of no particular significance.

(1) Isa. 29: 15–16 is the third of a group of three short, independent sayings (29: 9–10,[1] 13–14, 15–16) which condemn Judah. The 'woe!' saying of verse 15 condemns the leaders for their secretive political intrigues which they seek to hide even from the Lord; most commentators link this with the similar condemnation in 30: 1–5, a passage which probably once immediately followed 29: 15–16, since 17–24 is generally thought to have been added later. Then in verse 16, after a textually obscure introduction (perhaps an exclamation, 'Your perversity!'; see GK §147*c* and Wildberger), we read:

> Shall the potter be regarded as the clay;
> that the thing made should say of its maker,
> 'He did not make me';
> or the thing formed say of him who formed it,
> 'He has no understanding'?

The point of this developed metaphor comes, of course, with the last line. It is absurd to suppose that one can hide one's plans from the 'maker'. This is expressed in characteristic Isaianic style by use of the verb 'he does not understand' (*lō' hēbîn*), which pairs nicely with the concluding words of verse 15, 'Who sees us? Who knows us?' (*mî rō'ēnû ûmî yôdeʿēnû*). As we saw in the previous chapter, these three verbs are closely associated in Isaiah's writing (cf. especially 6: 9–10). Thus verse 16 is not so much a general statement about creation and its creator as an argument (in the form of a brief disputation) which builds on the commonly accepted belief in God as creator in order to reinforce the conclusion that God must understand, and hence see and know, all that the politicians of Judah naïvely suppose they can do in secret.

The close connections of this verse with Isa. 45: 9 are obvious:

[1] Isa. 29: 11–12, which is in prose, is widely regarded as secondary, though this is hardly significant for our present purposes.

Woe to him who strives with his Maker,
  a potsherd among the potsherds of the earth!
Does the clay say to him who fashions it,
  'What are you making'?
or 'Your work has no skill'?†

Both take the form of a 'woe!' oracle followed by a rhetorical question in order to reinforce the condemnation being advanced, and both share the same general imagery and its attendant vocabulary. It is difficult to suppose that two such similar verses were composed in complete isolation from one another. Nevertheless, it should also be observed that both are closely integrated into their present contexts,[2] and that this helps account in particular for the way in which the two verses conclude. The element which we noted as the climax and goal of 29: 16 is lacking from 45: 9, where the concerns for which the image is employed are different.

Before we can conclude that these verses support our overall thesis, however, two matters call for comment.[3] First, could Deutero-Isaiah perhaps have been influenced by Jeremiah 18 rather than Isa. 29: 16, since it too shares some of the same vocabulary and at first sight seems to deal with a similar theme?[4] The answer

[2] For Isa. 45: 9, see the several points of contact with verses 10–12 immediately following as well as the more general development of the argument of the end of the preceding paragraph at 45: 7; cf. B. D. Naidoff, 'The Two-Fold Structure of Isaiah xlv 9–13', *VT* 31 (1981), 180–5.

[3] A third issue that should be mentioned is the fact that several scholars have suggested that Isa. 45: 9–10 is a secondary addition to Deutero-Isaiah; see e.g. Westermann; Merendino, *Der Erste und der Letzte*, 425–42; and Hermisson. Their authenticity is defended, however, by, e.g., A. Schoors, *I am God your Saviour: A Form-Critical Study of the Main Genres in Is. xl–lv* (SVT 24; Leiden, 1973), 259–67; J. L. Koole, 'Zu Jesaja 45,9ff.', in M. S. H. G. Heerma van Voss *et al.* (eds.), *Travels in the World of the Old Testament: Studies Presented to Professor M. A. Beek on the Occasion of his 65th Birthday* (Assen, 1974), 170–5; and Naidoff, 'The Two-Fold Structure of Isaiah xlv 9–13'. It may suffice to notice here that the occurrence of *hôy* in these two verses but nowhere else in Deutero-Isaiah may be explained precisely by the influence of 29: 15–16 and further, as Koole points out, that such questioning of God's ways with reference to Cyrus was no longer an issue in the post-exilic period. In Deutero-Isaiah, the messenger formula (verse 11) need not necessarily indicate the start of a completely new unit; see e.g. 49: 22 and 25, both within the unquestionably single poem of 49: 14–26.

[4] We should note in passing that no other biblical parallels come into question. Isa. 64: 7[8] is often compared, but even if, as I have suggested elsewhere, it is part of an exilic liturgy on the ruined site of the Jerusalem temple (see H. G. M. Williamson, 'Isaiah 63,7–64,11: Exilic Lament or Post-Exilic Protest?', *ZAW* 102 (1990), 48–58), it is unlikely to have been known by Deutero-Isaiah in Babylon, and in any case it lacks the application of the image by way of rhetorical questions which form such a striking connection between the other two passages.

is—almost certainly not. One of the distinctive features of the two Isaianic passages is the absurdity of the clay talking back to the potter (*kî-yō'mar maʿ$^{a}$śeh l$^{e}$ʿōśēhû/h$^{a}$yō'mar ḥōmer l$^{e}$yōṣ$^{e}$rô*), and indeed this is central to the polemic in each case. This, however, is lacking in Jeremiah 18, a passage whose function turns out on closer examination to be somewhat different.

Secondly, it is more difficult to be sure that Isa. 29: 16 was in place prior to the time of Deutero-Isaiah. Opinion has been divided on this question during the present century, the authenticity of the verse being challenged by, for instance, Duhm, Marti, Huber,[5] and Vermeylen (pp. 406–7), whereas it has been defended by such scholars as Procksch, Donner,[6] Wildberger, Fohrer, Kaiser, Dietrich,[7] and Høgenhaven.[8] Clements seems to be undecided,[9] while Barth, without discussion, labels the verse as a later addition and yet indicates that it was already in place by the time of his Assyrian redaction.[10]

The connection between verses 15 and 16 outlined above strongly supports the authenticity of the latter.[11] This argument may now be strengthened by the observation that all three of the short units which originally made up this section (i.e. 29: 9–10, 13–14, and 15–16) reflect in some measure the vocabulary and ideas of 6: 9–10. This is widely recognized in the case of verses 9–10, in particular because of the otherwise almost unparalleled use of the verb *śʿʿ* (see above, p. 48), but also because of the statement that God has 'closed your eyes'. In the second unit (verses 13–14) the same passage is faintly echoed in the statement that 'Their hearts are far from me' and finds a more considered reflection in the concluding climax, where part of God's own judgement of the

5 Huber, *Jahwe, Juda und die anderen Völker beim Propheten Jesaja*, 134–5.

6 Donner, *Israel unter den Völkern*, 155–7.

7 Dietrich, *Jesaja und die Politik*, 170.

8 Høgenhaven, *Gott und Volk bei Jesaja*, 212–13.

9 He comments on Vermeylen's position that 'This may indeed be so, although there is nothing that decisively precludes the acceptance of v. 16 as Isaiah's own comment.'

10 Barth, *Die Jesaja-Worte in der Josiazeit*, 280 n. 20, 332.

11 This appears to have been noted previously only by Dietrich, whose presentation bears repetition: 'Man erwartet in V.16b*b* analog dem vorangehenden Satz ein *lō' yāṣarnî*. Stattdessen erfolgt ein überraschender Wechsel in ein anderes Wortfeld—aber nicht in irgendeines, sondern in ein vorher schon verwendetes: *bîn* steht nahe neben *r'h* und *ydʿ* (V.15). Dies dürfte ein hinreichend starkes Argument für die Zusammengehörigkeit von V.15 und V.16 sein' (p. 170 n. 206).

people is that 'the discernment of their discerning men shall be hid' (*ûbînat nᵉbōnāw tistattār*). It is, therefore, fully in keeping with this overall context to find that verses 15 and 16 together should draw on the same circle of ideas with their attendant vocabulary. In similar vein, Fohrer[12] has observed that these three short paragraphs are united thematically, associating 'whose deeds are in the dark' (verse 15) with the idea of blinding in the previous units. Finally, we should note that verses 15–16 are closely linked with the previous paragraph on the basis of inverted catchwords: the last word of verse 14 (*tistattār*) is picked up in the first line of verse 15 (*lastīr*) and the penultimate phrase (*ûbînat nᵉbōnāw*) in the last line of verse 16 (*lō' hēbîn*).

Returning to the specific association of verse 16 with verse 15, there again seems to be every reason to regard them as belonging originally together. Form-critically, a 'woe!' oracle concluded by a rhetorical question in place of the more usually expected condemnation finds a precise parallel in 10: 5–15, as observed already by Childs[13] (note also Amos 5: 18–20; 6: 1–3; and, less exactly, Isa. 10: 1–4), and this is undoubtedly a more satisfactory construal of the passage than such wholly hypothetical proposals as that the expected element of condemnation had become illegible and so was replaced by verses 16–24 (Duhm) or that for some unknown reason it was omitted (Marti). Equally, once it is observed that the possibly proverbial saying[14] in verse 16 is adopted and adapted in order to lead up to its concluding statement, it may be seen that it serves admirably to show up the self-destructive folly of those who say 'Who sees us? Who knows us?'

In the light of these observations, we must consider finally some of the principal objections which have been raised against the authenticity of verse 16. Several, for instance, maintain that nowhere else in the authentic sayings of Isaiah do we find such a reference to the theme of creation. That, however, is to misconstrue the verse. It implies no more of a theology of creation than

[12] G. Fohrer, 'Entstehung, Komposition und Überlieferung von Jesaja 1–39', in *Studien zur alttestamentlichen Prophetie (1949–1965)* (BZAW 99; Berlin, 1967), 113–47 (130).

[13] Childs, *Isaiah and the Assyrian Crisis*, 43; see also W. Janzen, *Mourning Cry and Woe Oracle* (BZAW 125; Berlin, 1972), 56. A number of scholars, such as Wildberger, and Barth (*Die Jesaja-Worte in der Josiazeit*, 23), regard the second half of 10: 15 as secondary, but this does not affect the present argument. Similarly, there is no need to consider here the possibility of other additions elsewhere in 10: 5–15.

[14] See J. W. Whedbee, *Isaiah and Wisdom* (Nashville and New York, 1971), 73–5.

does 10: 15*a*, and its understanding of the nature of God is not far removed in principle from the depiction of him as a wise farmer in 28: 23–9. As noted already, it is possible that Isaiah was here drawing on some proverbial saying, where such a theology would not be at all out of place, but the important point is that he has turned it for his own particular purpose regarding the omniscience of God in this passage rather than dwelling on the idea of creation itself. Furthermore, as Høgenhaven has observed, the emphasis is more on the overthrow of the divine order (*hpk*) than on creation as such, and of this idea he finds a number of other examples in Isaiah.[15] Again, both Duhm and Marti assert that Isaiah did not enter into such theological arguments with those who took a different political view from himself. Rather, he castigates them as 'rebels' (cf. 30: 1), and deals with them in their own terms. This argument is unwittingly rebutted by Huber, who himself rejects the authenticity of verse 16. He quotes Duhm's form of this argument, though he mistakenly supposes that Duhm was using it to challenge the authenticity of verse 15. But, since Huber wishes to defend verse 15 (as, in fact, did Duhm himself), he points out (quite reasonably) that for Isaiah it was the theological argument that was always decisive. He thus unknowingly saws off part of the branch on which he himself is sitting.

As Vermeylen (pp. 406–7) is the most recent representative of this line of thought, but upholds it partly on different grounds, it may be worth looking at each of the points he raises in turn. First, he maintains on form-critical grounds that a 'woe!' oracle in Isaiah's time was never completed by a rhetorical question, and that verse 15 may be regarded as complete in itself. I have already observed, however, that 10: 5–15 supplies the parallel which Vermeylen finds lacking. Vermeylen, however, asserts that the whole of 10: 15 is secondary. On examination of his reasons for this conclusion on pp. 258–9, it transpires that they are almost wholly dependent on the secondary nature of 29: 16 together with the links with 45: 9. This is patently, therefore, a case of circular argumentation.[16] Secondly, Vermeylen points out that 29: 16 is conceptually

[15] Høgenhaven, *Gott und Volk bei Jesaja*, 212–13.

[16] Vermeylen's only independent argument relates to 10: 15*b* alone, a line which we have already noted has been considered secondary by several other scholars without that fact affecting our present discussion.

close to other texts, all of which he considers late: Isa. 10: 15; 45: 9; 64: 7; and Jer. 18: 1–6. The force of this argument has already been blunted by what has been said above. Isa. 10: 15*a* provides, not only form-critically but also from the point of view of its thought, a significant argument *in favour* of the authenticity of 29: 16; the parallel with Jer. 18: 1–6 has been seen to be inexact; and the links with passages later in the book of Isaiah are equally well explained in terms of the total hypothesis that I am advancing in this book. Thirdly, Vermeylen finds two verbal links between Isa. 29: 16 and the verses which follow it, which are generally considered to be late. This argument too, however, is not convincing. He agrees with Donner[17] that there is a distinct break between verses 16 and 17–24, and the verbal links are not of real substance but are rather of the sort that may themselves account for the later redactional placing here of verses 17–24. One of the words he mentions is *mʿśh*, which comes in both verses 15 and 16 as well as at 23. Not much can be made of so distant a connection, but for what it is worth we may counter that verse 23 could be said to be drawing on 15–16, not just 16 alone. The other word is *yēḥāšēb* (verses 16 and 17). If anything, this looks like a catchword between two originally separate units. If so, it would favour the view that verse 16 was in place before the addition of 17–24, providing a peg, so to speak, on which the remainder could subsequently be hung.

The upshot of this discussion is that there are good formal and thematic grounds for regarding the connection of verse 16 with verse 15 as original. The authenticity of the latter is universally upheld both on internal grounds and because of its close association with the equally authentic preceding two paragraphs, 29: 9–10 and 13–14. We may be confident, therefore, in ascribing verse 16 to Isaiah, and the arguments which have been advanced to the contrary have been shown to be weak, and to rest in large part on a misunderstanding of the function of the verse in context. I therefore conclude that Isa. 29: 16 and 45: 9 may be regarded as a firm example of the literary influence of the earlier part of Isaiah on the later.

(2) We turn next to the theme of God raising a signal (*nēs*) to the

[17] Donner, *Israel unter den Völkern*, 155–8.

nations.[18] The word *nēs* occurs quite frequently in Isaiah, ten times in all,[19] and also in Jeremiah (five times).[20] Some of the passages in the two books have certain similarities (e.g. at both Isa. 18: 3 and Jer. 51: 27 *nāśā' nēs* occurs in parallel with *tāqa' šôpār*), and the threefold occurrence of the word in Jeremiah 50–1 is noteworthy in view of the particular connections between these chapters and the Isaiah tradition which we have observed elsewhere. Indeed, Davies (p. 116) refers to these occurrences in order to blunt the evidential value of this theme for our purposes.

Our concern here, however, is not just with the use of the word on its own, but with the more particular and striking theme of God himself (in either the first or the third person) raising a signal to the nations in order to summon them for some special purpose. This theme is restricted to only three passages, all of them in Isaiah—5: 26; 11: 12; 49: 22.

With good reason, 5: 26 is universally ascribed to the prophet Isaiah himself,[21] though its present setting is another matter to which we must return later. It comes as part of what appears to have been originally an extended poem with a refrain ('For all this his anger is not turned away and his hand is stretched out still') which has now been separated at 5: 25–9 (30) and 9: 8–21 (or 10: 4).[22] An additional argument in favour of the authenticity of our verse in particular comes from the use of the verb *šrq* ('to whistle'), in connection with God summoning a nation as his agent of judgement. The only other occurrence of this colourful image is at 7: 18, and although this passage, and perhaps even this verse, has been subsequently expanded, this particular point seems generally also

18 This theme is noted briefly by Clements, 'Beyond Tradition-History', 108–9. For the discussion by Davies, 'The Destiny of the Nations', see below.

19 Isa. 5: 26; 11: 10, 12; 13: 2; 18: 3; 30: 17; 31: 9; 33: 23; 49: 22; 62: 10. At 33: 23 the word is generally thought to have the meaning 'sail', and the part of the verse in which it occurs may in any case have been misplaced.

20 Jer. 4: 6, 21; 50: 2; 51: 12, 27. The few occurrences of *nēs* elsewhere in the Hebrew Bible do not seem to be of any relevance for our discussion; cf. Exod. 17: 15; Num. 21: 8, 9; 26: 10; Ezek. 27: 7 (cf. Isa. 33: 23); Ps. 60: 6.

21 Kaiser seems to be a lone exception when he speaks of the author as 'a theologian of history from the fifth century, in the guise of the prophet, speaking of the annihilating blow of the Babylonians against the kingdom of Judah' (p. 116 = ET 112).

22 The speculative reordering of this material into what is thought to have been its original sequence is irrelevant at this stage of our discussion, though we may note that the undertaking has recently been criticized as fundamentally misguided by W. P. Brown, 'The So-Called Refrain in Isaiah 5: 25–30 and 9: 7–10: 4', *CBQ* 52 (1990), 432–43.

to be ascribed to Isaiah.[23] We may thus be reasonably confident that the reference to God summoning a nation (or nations[24]) to judge his people by way of 'raising a signal' was present in the work of Isaiah as known to Deutero-Isaiah.

In Isa. 49: 22 we find the use of the same imagery, though this time with a different purpose:

> Thus says the Lord God:
> 'Behold, I will lift up my hand to the nations,
> and raise my signal to the peoples;
> and they shall bring your sons in their bosom,
> and your daughters shall be carried on their shoulders.

Here again, God acts to summon the nations, but this time to aid in the restoration of his people rather than their judgement. It is a good example of apparent influence on Deutero-Isaiah by way of reversal, appropriate to the new salvation context out of which he speaks.

A further possible indication of the fact that there has been such influence here rather than that this is a coincidental usage of what might have been a widely known image is observed by Davies. He points out that 'each continues with a reference to "prey" which can only with great difficulty be rescued from a strong enemy'. After citing the relevant passages (5: 29 and 49: 24–5), he continues: 'The words for "prey" are different (*ṭerep*, *malqôaḥ*), but this may be only a sign of the freshness of Deutero-Isaiah's poetry, even where he is dependent on older materials.'[25] (Note may also be taken of the appearance of the same theme at 42: 22, which further shares the expression 'and there is none to rescue' (*w*$^{e}$*'ên maṣṣîl*) with 5: 29.) Here, then, is a further pointer, in addition to the more significant fact that God is the subject of the action (a fact not observed by Davies), which draws these two passages together and away from the possible influence of Jeremiah.

[23] See e.g. among recent writers, Fohrer; Wildberger; Dietrich, *Jesaja und die Politik*, 121–2; Huber, *Jahwe, Juda und die anderen Völker beim Propheten Jesaja*, 161–2; Barth, *Die Jesaja-Worte in der Josiazeit*, 199–200; Clements; Høgenhaven, *Gott und Volk bei Jesaja*, 98–9. Vermeylen (p. 222) is not explicit about authorship, but dates the verse still within the Assyrian period.

[24] See below, Ch. 6, for discussion of this textual point.

[25] Davies, 'The Destiny of the Nations', 115.

There is another point of the kind which Davies makes to which attention should also be drawn. In 49: 22 the reference to God raising a signal to the peoples is paralleled by the preceding statement that he will lift up his hand to the nations. This, too, is not found in any of the passages mentioned in Jeremiah, but significantly it does occur (twice, in fact) in Isa. 5: 25 (though without reference to the nations), which comes immediately before the phrase which we have been examining. We thus have three elements in 49: 22–5 which follow one another in the same order as is found in 5: 25–9. The effect of this similarity is to draw 5: 26 and 49: 22 even closer together.[26] We need have no hesitation, therefore, in affirming that this example too may be regarded as firm evidence for our overall purpose.

Finally, we should consider the third example of this theme, Isa. 11: 12. Although the wording of the phrase in question is exactly the same as 5: 26 ('He will raise a signal to the nations' (*wᵉnāśā'-nēs laggôyı̄m*)), it is used in the positive manner of 49: 22, as the continuation of the verse makes clear ('and will assemble the outcasts of Israel, and gather the dispersed of Judah from the four corners of the earth'). In view of the widely held, and certainly correct, opinion that this part, at least, of Isaiah 11 is from a date much later than Isaiah of Jerusalem (see below, Chapter 6), there need be no doubt in affirming that this verse manifests a knowledge of both the other two passages discussed above. It thus furnishes another example of the kind of back-influence from Deutero-Isaiah on the later redactional activity attested throughout Isaiah 1–39 which we began to take note of in the previous chapter. The fact that in using the language of 5: 26 it refers to 'the nations' in the plural suggests the possibility that it was composed no earlier than the time of the redactional ordering of the ending of chapter 5, and that it could even be the work of the same hand.[27] We might also

[26] It is further worth speculating whether the description of the army in 5: 27 may not have been in the back of Deutero-Isaiah's mind in his encouragement to the weary in 40: 28–31; note especially the use of *kšl* and the *'yp/y'p* word-play, while the army in which 'none is weary . . . none slumbers or sleeps' is not unlike the God of 40: 28 who 'does not faint or grow weary' and his devotees who in verse 31 'shall run and not be weary, they shall walk and not faint'. This cannot, of course, be included in the category of firm examples, but, in view of the obvious influence of 5: 25–9 elsewhere on Deutero-Isaiah, the similarities are suggestive.

[27] As we shall see below, Ch. 6, it is probable that the originally singular *gwy* at 5: 26 was made plural as part of the work of the redactor who gave 5: 24–30 its present setting.

note in passing that 11: 10 is likely to have been added even later, an editor seeking to explain in anticipation that the signal to which reference is made in verse 12 is none other than the 'root of Jesse' of 11: 1 (cf. Clements). He thus connects the two parts of the chapter together, even though he shows a measure of independent thought in adding that the nations will 'seek him' rather than merely assisting in the regathering of Israel.

(3) The next passage for consideration, 8: 23*b* [9: 1] and to a lesser extent the verses immediately following, differs somewhat from those considered so far in at least two respects. On the one hand, assuming that it pre-dates Deutero-Isaiah, its influence appears to have been more pervasive than possibly any other, even though, so far as I am aware, it has hitherto gone completely unnoticed in discussions of the 'unity' of Isaiah.

On the other hand, its authenticity is much more controversial, so that it is unlikely to carry conviction with all readers on the basis of one of the major criteria with which we are operating. Discussion of this issue in the present century has gone through several phases.[28] Earlier scholars tended to deny 8: 23*b*–9: 6 [9: 1–7] to Isaiah of Jerusalem because they maintained that it expressed the eschatological hopes of the post-exilic community.[29] The 1950 study of A. Alt,[30] however, reversed this situation, and persuaded many that the passage could best be understood against the politico-historical and cultural background of the time of Isaiah[31] or of Josiah.[32] Despite this, not all have been convinced,[33] and recently several voices have been raised which have sought to return the passage to the post-exilic period,[34] even though this must still be

[28] For fuller surveys of the secondary literature than is necessary here, see J. Vollmer, 'Zur Sprache von Jesaja $9_{1-6}$', *ZAW* 80 (1968), 343–50; Wildberger; Vermeylen, 232–45; Barth, *Die Jesaja-Worte in der Josiazeit*, 141–77.

[29] e.g. Marti and Gray.

[30] A. Alt, 'Jesaja 8,23–9,6: Befreiungsnacht und Krönungstag', in *Festschrift Alfred Bertholet, zum 80. Geburtstag gewidmet* (Tübingen, 1950), 29–49 = *Kleine Schriften zur Geschichte des Volkes Israel*, ii (Munich, 1953), 206–25.

[31] e.g. Wildberger and Clements.

[32] e.g. Barth and Vermeylen.

[33] e.g. Fohrer.

[34] See Vollmer, 'Zur Sprache von Jesaja $9_{1-6}$'; W. Werner, *Eschatologische Texte in Jesaja 1–39: Messias, Heiliger Rest, Völker* (Forschung zur Bibel, 46; Würzburg, 1982), 20–46; R. Kilian, *Jesaja 1–39* (Erträge der Forschung, 200; Darmstadt, 1983), 5–10.

judged to be a minority opinion. A further complicating factor is the issue whether in any case 8: 23*b* is an original part of the passage or whether it is a secondary redactional join between what precedes and what follows.[35]

In view of this uncertainty, our procedure here will be slightly different. The connections between 8: 23*b* and Deutero-Isaiah will first be outlined, working on the assumption that the majority view, which regards the passage as being in place at least by the time of the exile, is reasonable. Only then shall we return to a brief consideration, in the light of our findings, of the issue of authenticity. Needless to say, it will not be possible in the present context to do full justice to all the many issues of dating and interpretation which have been raised in the course of so protracted and intense a debate.

The translation of 8: 23*b* is itself a controversial matter. The *RSV* (9: 1*b*) represents one widely-held approach: 'In the former time he brought into contempt the land of Zebulun and the land of Naphtali, but in the latter time he will make glorious the way of the sea, the land beyond the Jordan, Galilee of the nations.' As has been demonstrated by Emerton,[36] this translation slides over several difficulties, including the facts that the two verbs in the verse, *hql* and *hkbyd*, are in the perfect tense, whereas *RSV* translates the first as perfect and the second as future, and that *ʿēt* ('time') is normally a feminine noun,[37] whereas it is construed by *RSV* as being complemented by two masculine adjectives, *hāriʾšôn* and *hāʾaḥᵃrôn* ('the former' and 'the latter'), and additionally that an ellipse of *kāʿēt* has awkwardly to be presupposed before the second adjective, 'and (in) the latter (time)'. After a thorough study of these and other problems, together with a discussion of the historical background presupposed in the verse, he offers the following translation 'with a certain freedom intended to bring out the suggested meaning': 'Now has everyone, from first to last, treated with contempt and harshness the land of Zebulun and the land of Naphtali, the way of the sea, the region beyond Jordan, Galilee of the nations.'

35 See most recently D. Vieweger, '"Das Volk, das durch das Dunkel zieht . . ." Neue Überlegungen zu Jes (8,23aβb) 9,1–6', *BZ* N.F. 36 (1992), 77–86.

36 J. A. Emerton, 'Some Linguistic and Historical Problems in Isaiah viii. 23', *JSS* 14 (1969), 151–75.

37 Though see P. D. Wegner, 'Another Look at Isaiah viii 23B', *VT* 41 (1991), 481–4.

Whatever we decide about the correct translation of the verse,[38] it is clearly divided into two halves by the contrasting pair *hāri'šôn* and *hā'aḥ*^a^*rôn* ('the first and the last', or 'the former and the latter'), and whether correctly or not this has frequently been taken as referring to contrasting periods of time, one characterized by 'contempt' and the other by 'glory'. No doubt, this reading has been influenced by the verse's position between the gloomy conclusion of chapter 8 and the bright future envisaged at the start of chapter 9 (a point which may have been appreciated as early as the inclusion of the redactional join in 8: 23*a* [9: 1*a*]: 'But there will be no gloom for her that was in anguish', if that is the right interpretation of an admittedly obscure text). Once the matter is expressed in these terms, several points of connection with the work of Deutero-Isaiah suggest themselves.

First, God himself is described as 'the first and the last' at 44: 6 and 48: 12 ('I am the first and I am the last'), using the very two words which divide 8: 23*b* into two halves. Isa. 41: 4 is similar: 'I, the Lord, am the first; and with the last [*w*^e^*'et-'aḥ*^a^*rōnîm*] I am He.' This title for God appears to be without parallel; it is distinctive to Deutero-Isaiah. The possibility should, therefore, be considered that he took the relevant words in 8: 23*b* as titles for God—that it was 'the First' (with a capital 'F') who brought the land into contempt and 'the Last' (with a capital 'L') who would eventually glorify it again.[39] It will then have been this understanding which led him to coin his distinctive title. It is noteworthy that, so far as I can see, no commentator has proposed any other possible influence on Deutero-Isaiah as regards this title,[40] and that in this respect it

38 Emerton has been followed by, e.g., Clements, and to a considerable extent by Hayes and Irvine, *Isaiah, the Eighth-Century Prophet*, 176–9. Alternative interpretations, which at least refer to his article even if not all of them do full justice to the points he raises, have been advanced by, e.g., Wildberger; Barth, *Die Jesaja-Worte in der Josiazeit*, 143–5; J. Høgenhaven, 'On the Structure and Meaning of Isaiah viii 23b', *VT* 37 (1987), 218–21; Oswalt, 231; H. Eschel, 'Isaiah viii 23: An Historical-Geographical Analogy', *VT* 40 (1990), 104–9, and N. Na'aman, 'Literary and Topographical Notes on the Battle of Kishon (Judges iv–v)', *VT* 40 (1990), 423–36 (434–6).

39 If so, he must have taken *kā'ēt* as an independent adverb, meaning 'now', which Emerton has shown is certainly possible, and in addition he may have regarded the use of *hāri'šôn* and *hā'aḥ*^a^*rôn* as an example of what we would now call the break-up of stereotyped phrases in poetry; cf. above, Ch. 3 n. 28.

40 Volz (p. 16) and Bonnard (p. 109 n. 4) refer to 'the first and the last' as a description of (Ahura) Mazda in the *Gathas* (31: 8), but it is hardly possible to speak of influence at this stage, even by way of polemic.

differs markedly from all the other divine titles which the prophet uses. Since the title appears in passages where the form of the argument suggests that he is appealing to an accepted characteristic of God in order to build his new revelation upon it, it would be surprising if the prophet had here introduced a wholly novel title which might have invited a challenge from his hearers or readers.

Secondly, therefore, and in development of this last point, we should note that at 44: 6 the title occurs in a short paragraph (verses 6–8) which introduces a very characteristic theme in this prophet and one which, moreover, seems certainly to have been developed in association with it. This is the theme of the contrast between the former (or first) things and the new things that are yet to come, referred to within the context of the ability to prophesy, which makes up an important element in the prophet's anti-idol polemic.

> Who has announced from of old things to come*,
> Let them tell him what is yet to be. (44: 7*b*)

Only the God who is himself 'the first and the last' is able to do such a thing. The occurrence of the title at 48: 12 is in a context which is making a similar point, while at 41: 4 the closely related issue is broached of God's control of history both in the remote past ('calling the generations from the beginning') and in the present ('Who has performed and done this?'), with reference to the rise of Cyrus.[41]

In these expressions of Deutero-Isaiah's familiar theme, the vocabulary with which we are here primarily concerned is used for God himself, and alternative forms of wording are used for the sharp division of history into distinctive periods. Elsewhere, however, where God is not referred to in these terms, the same ideas are expressed by using the language of 8: 23*b* in a manner which suggests that the various forms of wording are virtually interchangeable. We may compare the following examples:

> Tell us the former things [*hāri'šōnôt*], what they are,
> that we may consider them;

[41] From the Targum to C. C. Torrey, 'Isaiah 41', *HTR* 44 (1951), 121–36, there have been those who have referred Isa. 41: 2–4 to Abraham alone. This is unconvincing, however; at best, Abraham is alluded to as a 'type' of Cyrus, as suggested by G. H. Jones, 'Abraham and Cyrus: Type and Anti-Type?', *VT* 22 (1972), 304–19, with further literature.

or declare to us the things to come [*habbā'ôt*],
so that we may know their outcome [*'aḥ^a rîtān*]*.
Tell us what is to come [*hā'ōtiyyôt*] hereafter,
that we may know that you are gods. (41: 22*b-c*, 23*a*)

Behold, the former things [*hāri'šōnôt*] have come to pass,
and new things [*waḥ^a dāšôt*] I now declare;
before they spring forth
I tell you of them. (42: 9)

Oh that even one of them would declare this
and that they would show us the former things† [*w^e ri'šōnôt*]. (43: 9*b*)

Who told this long ago [*miqqedem*]?
Who declared it of old [*mē'āz*]? (45: 21*b*)

Similar ideas and vocabulary are found throughout the extended passage 48: 3–16, starting with 'The former things I declared of old' (*hari'šōnôt mē'āz higgadtî*), especially in verses 5, 6, 7, 8, 12, 14, and 16, and at 41: 26.[42]

Thirdly, this polemical theme is closely associated with the related message of encouragement to the exiles to forget the former things because now God is doing something quite new:

Remember not the former things [*ri'šōnôt*],
nor consider the things of old [*w^e qadmōniyyôt*].
Behold, I am doing a new thing [*ḥ^a dāšâ*];
now it springs forth, do you not perceive it? (43: 18–19*a*)[43]

Equally, it is turned to good use in refuting those who query God's propriety in raising up Cyrus as his agent of deliverance, and the continuation of the passage to be cited makes clear that this is the

[42] The use of *hā'ōtiyyôt* at 45: 11 is almost certainly the result of textual corruption, however; see the Appendix.

[43] The details of this message and its distinctive vocabulary have, of course, been frequently analysed from within the standpoint of study of Deutero-Isaiah himself; in addition to the commentaries, see North, 'The "Former Things" and the "New Things" in Deutero-Isaiah'; M. Haran, 'The Literary Structure and Chronological Framework of the Prophecies in Is. xl–xlviii', *Congress Volume: Bonn 1962* (SVT 9; Leiden, 1963), 127–55; A. Schoors, 'Les Choses antérieures et les choses nouvelles dans les oracles deutéro-Isaïens', *ETL* 40 (1964), 19–47 (including a full bibliography of many earlier discussions); C. Stuhlmueller, '"First and Last" and "Yahweh-Creator" in Deutero-Isaiah', *CBQ* 29 (1967), 495–511; Childs, *Introduction to the Old Testament as Scripture*, 328–30; H. Leene, *De vroegere en de nieuwe dingen bij Deuterojesaja* (Amsterdam, 1987 [not available to me]); Matheus, *Singt dem Herrn ein neues Lied*, 133–42.

reverse side of the message of encouragement that the prophet is striving to get across to his recalcitrant audience:

Remember this and consider,
  recall it to mind, you transgressors,
  remember the former things of old [*ri'šōnôt mē'ôlām*];
for I am God, and there is no other;
  I am God, and there is none like me,
declaring the end from the beginning [*maggîd mērē'šît 'aḥ^a rît*]
  and from ancient times things not yet done. (46: 8–10*a*, and cf. 12–13)

Now, it is important to notice that all three usages are closely related to one another and that sometimes they appear to overlap within a single passage (e.g. at 42: 8–9; 44: 6–8; 46: 9–11, and in chapter 48).[44] Moreover, Deutero-Isaiah uses a wide range of vocabulary to express what is basically the same thought (for the first half of the pair *r'šnwt*; *qdmnywt*, qualified sometimes by *mr'š*; *mlpnym*; *m'wlm*; *mr'šyt*; *m'z*; *mqdm*; and for the second half of the pair *hb'wt*; *h'tywt*; *ḥdšwt*; *'šr tb'nh*). We should note, however, that, in addition to reflecting three times the specific vocabulary of 8: 23*b* in descriptions of God, he also comes very close to it on two other occasions in these wider contexts—at 41: 22 (*hr'šnwt . . . 'ḥrytn*) and 46: 10 (*'ḥryt mr'šyt*).

In the light of all this material, it may now be suggested that Deutero-Isaiah could have reflected on and been influenced by Isa. 8: 23*b* in at least three ways.[45] First, whether or not Emerton is right about the verse's original meaning, it is probable that Deutero-Isaiah read it in his new historical context more along the lines suggested by *RSV*.[46] Specifically, he may have been encouraged in this direction (as many others since have been) by the general tenor of the verses immediately preceding and following with their apparent switch from a period of gloom to one of hope. Thus, for instance, Isa. 9: 1[2],

The people who walked in darkness [*baḥōšek*]
  have seen a great light [*'ôr*];

[44] It is also of interest to note the probable overlap with concerns introduced under reflection on Isaiah 6, as outlined in the previous chapter; see e.g. 43: 8–10, 48: 6–8, 41: 22–3, etc.

[45] In addition, it may be noted that W. H. Schmidt has suggested that the form of 9: 1–6 may be regarded as a 'Vorform' of Deutero-Isaiah's hymns of praise: see 'Die Ohnmacht des Messias', *Kerygma und Dogma*, 15 (1969), 18–34 (19 n. 3).

[46] It is worth observing here in particular that 'make glorious' is securely attested as a possible meaning for *hkbyd* by Jer. 30: 19.

those who dwelt in a land of deep darkness,
on them has light shined,

will have been taken by him as referring forward to his own day, when those in the 'darkness' of exile would now be led back into the bright 'light' of God's salvation:

And I will lead the blind in the way*,
in paths that they have not known I will guide them.
I will turn the darkness [*maḥšāk*] before them into light [*lā'ôr*],
the rough places into level ground. (42: 16)

Of course, the use of such common words as 'light' and 'darkness' could not in themselves serve as evidence for Deutero-Isaiah's use of earlier Isaianic material, but, if the case can be established that 8: 23–9: 6 was of particular significance for him in the framing of his theology of the turning of the tide from judgement to salvation, then the allusion gains weight as a supporting argument. There can certainly be no doubt that he made frequent use of 'light' as an image of salvation (usually, though not always, in association with its converse 'darkness'); see (in addition to 42: 16) 42: 6–7 (and cf. 49: 9); 45: 7; 49: 6; 50: 10; and 51: 4.[47] Similarly, the emphasis in 9: 2[3] on 'joy' (the root *śmḥ* is there used three times and *gyl** twice) is also found several times in Deutero-Isaiah as an appropriate response to what is happening (see 41: 16; 49: 13; 51: 3, 11; 55: 12; and the comparable uses with *rnn* at 42: 11; 44: 23; 48: 20; 52: 8, 9; 54: 1). Other links between this passage and Deutero-Isaiah include the expression *ḥlq šll* ('to divide spoil'), which is found only at 9: 2 and 53: 12 in the prophetic literature; the emphasis at the end that 'the zeal of the Lord of hosts will do this [*ta'ᵃśeh-zō't*]' may be compared with the similar expression at 41: 20 (and cf. 42: 16), though it occurs also at Amos 9: 12; while the idea of fire consuming the oppressor (9: 4[5]) may be reflected at 47: 14 and 50: 11. Thus, seeing the contrast between judgement and salvation in 8: 23–9: 6 as a whole, he was led to see it also in what he took to be the contrasting halves of 8: 23*b* itself.

Secondly, reflection on this contrast may have influenced him to adopt his sharp and characteristic juxtaposing of 'the former things'

47 Additionally, a strong case can be made out for the restoration of the reading *yir'eh 'ôr* in 53: 11; it is attested by both 1QIsa[a] and [b] and is further supported by the Septuagint.

and 'the new things' in different contexts precisely on the basis of *hāri'šôn* and *hā'aḥ$^a$rôn* in 8: 23, and we have seen that amongst the variety of expressions that he uses for this idea there is evidence for the specific reflection of the language of the verse itself.

Finally, as already noted, 8: 23*b* provides the only possible source for one of his characteristic titles for God in a context where we expect him to be appealing to common ground between himself and his audience rather than coining some wholly novel designation.

In the light of this discussion, we may conclude that a connection between Isa. 8: 23*b* and the various passages in Deutero-Isaiah seems to be very probable. Certainly, no other text can be adduced which could serve as an independent source of influence in this regard. Attention has sometimes been drawn, for instance, to Jer. 50: 17 (we note again the occurrence within Jeremiah 50–1), where 'First [*hāri'šôn*] the king of Assyria devoured him, and now at last [*w$^e$zeh hā'aḥ$^a$rôn*] Nebuchadrezzar king of Babylon has gnawed his bones'. Several considerations rule out this possibility, however. First, the date of Jer. 50: 17 is uncertain, many commentators arguing that it is later than Deutero-Isaiah. This problem is only heightened by the observation that verses 17*b*–18 appear to be a prose addition to their poetic context. Secondly, it is equally uncertain whether the adjectives are to be construed as adverbial accusatives of time, as is generally done, or as personal adjectives; this latter possibility is entertained by S. R. Driver: 'The first one (who) devoured him was the king of A.; and this, the last one (who) gnawed his bones, was, etc.'[48] Finally and decisively, however, this verse in Jeremiah lacks the very features of Deutero-Isaiah's interpretation of Isa. 8: 23*b* which have been singled out above as being most significant and characteristic. Whereas Jer. 50: 17 may attest the later influence of Isa. 8: 23 very much along the lines proposed by Emerton (i.e. wholly negative) and reinterpreted in the light of the Babylonian conquest, Deutero-Isaiah appears to have developed a quite different interpretation in the light of his new historical situation. His contrasting of a period of oppression with a following period of deliverance is not found in Jer. 50: 17, and, when the passage in Jeremiah goes on in verses 18–19 to speak of a future hope, it does so in a quite different way. It may thus be concluded that Jer. 50: 17 cannot have served as the inspiration for

[48] See S. R. Driver, *The Book of the Prophet Jeremiah* (London, 1906), 370.

those features of Deutero-Isaiah's thought and style which have been examined above.

If this conclusion is sound, we may suggest that it sheds new light on the question of authenticity which we left to one side at the start of our analysis. Naturally, this procedure could be charged with arguing in a circle—from the assumption of authenticity to its establishment. Despite this, however, it seems reasonable to frame the issue in another way: if there is a literary connection between two bodies of literature, which can be more easily explained as dependent? The connection may be observed without recourse to any assumption about priority, and the question of dependency may then be resolved on its own merits. In terms of the present example, we should then seek to establish whether the connection fits in with other examples where Deutero-Isaiah seems to be drawing on earlier material or whether it is another example of the kind of retrojection from Deutero-Isaiah on to the redaction of the earlier chapters which we have noted elsewhere. Since both processes appear to be abundantly attested, either could in theory provide an explanation for this particular instance.

In my judgement, even discounting the specific manner in which the evidence has been set out above, the material can be more easily explained in terms of Deutero-Isaiah being the one who is dependent than the reverse. We have seen that he uses the theme and its associated vocabulary in several slightly different ways, and that there is considerable uncertainty as to whether any of these exactly represents the meaning of 8: 23. It is thus easier to think that he has been led to reread the material in the light of his changed circumstances than that an editor has picked up several distinct, though related, themes in his work, brought them together, and incorporated them in a single passage in Isaiah 1–39 in a manner which does not accurately reflect any one of them in particular or all three of them together. We have already noted examples where Deutero-Isaiah works creatively with the material he has inherited, and his presumed manner of procedure here fits in well with this.

Of course, if an irrefutable case had been made out for the post-exilic origin of 8: 23*b*–9: 6[9: 1–7], then we should be obliged to seek other ways of understanding the method of composition here. In the light of recent discussions, however, it may be questioned whether this is so—and in saying that, it is not necessary to decide whether Isaiah himself wrote the passage, or whether, as Barth and Vermeylen have maintained, it is to be attributed to a Josianic redactor; for our present purposes, either position would be sufficient to account for the evidence we have unearthed. The strongest counter-argument that could be produced would be the presence of linguistic features that could only be explained as deriving from the period of late biblical Hebrew, but there are none such. The old suggestion that *s'wn* (9: 4) refers to a specifically Macedonian sandal[49] has long since been refuted; it is to be compared with Akkadian *šēnû(m)* ('sandal, shoe'),[50] Aramaic *s'n* and Ugaritic *š'an*,[51] as is recognized even by those who appeal to other aspects of the passage's language to favour a late date,[52] and thus cannot be used to settle the issue either way. The manner in which other linguistic evidence has been used in this debate is generally unsatisfactory from the point of view of method: in particular, because some words or phrases are elsewhere used only in passages which are generally thought to be late, this cannot settle the issue of whether those words or phrases must themselves be regarded as late. As Hurvitz has shown,[53] this line of argument should be admitted only when it is demonstrated that the postulated later element has consistently replaced some earlier alternative; otherwise, the whole thing turns into a weak argument from silence whose dubious nature is made the greater by the heavily restricted quantity of comparative data available to us.[54] This necessary second step in the argument has not, however, been undertaken by proponents of a late date. Indeed, it is striking that even Vermeylen, who is generally by no means averse to this type of argument, does not find the evidence at all compelling in this particular example (p. 240). Conversely, of course, the fact that much of the vocabulary of

[49] R. H. Kennett, 'The Prophecy in Isaiah ix 1–7', *JTS* 7 (1906), 321–42.

[50] C. F. Burney, 'The "Boot" in Isaiah ix 4', *JTS* 11 (1910), 438–43; and see now *AHw* 1213.

[51] Cf. Ahiqar, line 206; *DISO* 287; J. M. Lindenberger, *The Aramaic Proverbs of Ahiqar* (Baltimore and London, 1983), 205, 273–4; I. Kottsieper, *Die Sprache der Ahiqarsprüche* (BZAW 194; Berlin, 1990), 233; and D. Pardee, 'Troisième réassemblage de RS 1.019', *Syria*, 65 (1988), 173–91 (187).

[52] See Vollmer, 'Zur Sprache von Jesaja $9_{1-6}$', 345–6.

[53] See A. Hurvitz, *The Transition Period in Biblical Hebrew: A Study in Post-Exilic Hebrew and its Implications for the Dating of Psalms* (Hebrew; Jerusalem, 1972), 20–4.

[54] See C. Hardmeier, 'Jesajaforschung im Umbruch', *Verkündigung und Forschung*, 31 (1986), 3–31, who is followed in particular by Laato, *Who is Immanuel?*, 21–3, 182.

the passage has parallels elsewhere in the writing of Isaiah of Jerusalem cannot be used to support Isaianic authorship (see Wildberger). The most it can do is to demonstrate Isaianic authorship as a possibility. In short, the evidence from language cannot settle the issue either way.

Other arguments for a late date are equally indecisive, and have all been either discounted or alternatively explained by recent studies.[55] This being so, the new evidence which has been set out above may be allowed its prima-facie force; the dependence of Deutero-Isaiah on 8: 23*b* is the best explanation of the data. Thus, while it has already been admitted that this is a less straightforward case than some others we have examined, it appears to me still to be admissible. If that be granted, then we may conclude that it is of peculiar importance in view of both its widespread use by Deutero-Isaiah and its centrality to one of his most characteristic themes.

(4) Isa. 28: 1–4 is almost unanimously ascribed to Isaiah of Jerusalem; the only exception appears to be Kaiser, whose arguments have been examined in some detail and rejected by Vermeylen (pp. 385–8). Vermeylen himself, however, tentatively suggests that verse 2 may be a much later addition to the oracle, being part of an anti-Samaritan redaction of which he finds traces elsewhere in the book, but even this may not be necessary. The early Samaritan community was centred on Shechem, not Samaria; the storm imagery may be compared with Isaiah's use of similarly colourful metaphors for Assyria elsewhere (e.g. at 8: 7–8; at 5: 29 they are likened to a lion seizing prey, and so on); and the verse satisfactorily introduces God's agent of judgement, whose work is then applied in verses 3–4 by way of two further metaphors to the twofold symbolism of the garland–flower motif of verse 1.[56]

Part of the picture of Ephraim which Isaiah presents here is that

[55] It is, for instance, noteworthy that Werner (*Eschatologische Texte in Jesaja 1–39*, 45–6) relies heavily on the argument from vocabulary and then concedes that 'Einzeln genommen mögen die Argumente, die dem Text die Herkunft von Jesaja absprechen und ihn in die nachexilische Zeit datieren, nicht durchschlagen'. Thereafter, he concentrates more on seeking to establish that Wildberger has not convincingly proved Isaianic authorship than on presenting positive arguments for his own alternative view. Naturally, his assumption that 9: 1 is dependent upon Deutero-Isaiah begs the question raised by our discussion above.

[56] 'The double use of the image of a garland of flowers, as a sign of a reveller's rejoicing and as a portrayal of the capital Samaria set at the head of a fertile valley' (Clements); cf. Høgenhaven, *Gott und Volk bei Jesaja*, 108.

of what should be an attractive garland, but whose 'glorious beauty' is now but a 'fading flower' (*ṣîṣ nōbēl*) (in the resumptive verse 4, this is expressed by the slightly altered form *ṣîṣat nōbēl*, which may be no more than an example of 'gender-matched parallelism'[57]). This picture serves well to show up the misplaced pride of the inhabitants of Ephraim, a theme which we have seen to be central to Isaiah's theological position.

It may be no accident, therefore, that a comparison can be drawn both with the topic and with the vocabulary of 40: 6–8. First and most striking, the phrase *nābēl ṣîṣ* occurs there twice†, but nowhere else in the Hebrew Bible. This, therefore, immediately satisfies the criteria laid down in Chapter 2 for this investigation. Beyond that, however, the phrase is used in a manner which may be seen to have developed from consideration of the context of 28: 1–4. Deutero-Isaiah has universalized the line of thought applied originally only to the inhabitants of Ephraim. The meaning of *ḥasdô* in 40: 6 is, of course, disputed, and even the text is not always thought to be sound (see the discussion in the Appendix). The LXX rendered it with 'glory', which if correct would bring it very close to 28: 1 and 4, but, even if the meaning is something more like constancy or strength, the thought is not far removed: some aspect of man's character on which he might normally be expected to rely (and hence be tempted to boast about) is to become 'like the flower of the field' (*kᵉṣîṣ haśśādeh*). More remotely, God's 'mighty and strong' (*ḥāzāq wᵉ'ammiṣ*) agent in 28: 2 may perhaps be compared, again by way of a certain universalization, with his commanding of the stars to do his will in 40: 26 (*'ammîṣ kōaḥ*, though note Amos 2: 14 and 16), while the valley (*gê'*) of 28: 1 and 4 ties in with the development of thought in 40: 4 noted below, pp. 246–7.

Seitz, too, has noted the connection between 28: 1–4 and 40: 6–7, and he adds to it some other interesting observations about the linguistic contacts with 37: 26–7.[58] This passage, of course, cannot be appealed to for our immediate purposes, because there can be no guarantee that Isaiah 36–9 was put into position before the time of Deutero-Isaiah; it may well reflect rather the reverse process of influence which seems to accompany so many of these elements

57 See W. H. Irwin, *Isaiah 28–33. Translation with Philological Notes* (Biblica et Orientalia, 30; Rome, 1977), 10; for a general description of this feature, with further bibliography, see W. G. E. Watson, *Classical Hebrew Poetry: A Guide to its Techniques* (JSOTS 26; Sheffield, 1984), 123–8.

58 Seitz, 'The Divine Council', 242–3.

that the various parts of the book of Isaiah share in common. We can, however, now go one step further than Seitz does with regard to 28: 1–4. He writes cautiously, 'From a redactional perspective, references to the "flower of the field" and the "fading flower" at 40: 6–7 are coordinated with language typical of the judgment proclamation Isaiah was commissioned to deliver in Isa 6: 9–13 and which finds expression at 28: 1–4'. In the light of our examination of this same material, we need not stop at the level of redaction; it appears rather to be a case of direct influence from the literary deposit of Isaiah of Jerusalem on Deutero-Isaiah.

(5) We come next to two details concerning the manner in which reference is made to the fact that an oracle is said to be the word of the Lord. A matter of such detail might be thought at first to be too insignificant to carry any weight in the present argument. In fact, however, the reverse is the case. In the literature of the Old Testament, and not least in the prophets, it is extremely common for an oracle to be introduced with the words 'Thus says the Lord' or concluded with 'Oracle of the Lord' and so on. If, therefore, in the light of so many stereotyped expressions, we come across an alternative method of making the same point, it stands out as highly distinctive from a stylistic point of view.

One such example is the use of the phrase *yō'mar yhwh* ('says the Lord') as an independent clause with either present or past reference. Despite the use of the imperfect tense, it certainly does not refer in context to the future. What appears to be the phrase's exact equivalent from a semantic point of view but with the verb in the perfect tense—*'āmar yhwh*—is found frequently enough; the distribution of usages with the imperfect, however, is restricted, either entirely or almost entirely, to the book of Isaiah, where it occurs no less than eight times (1: 11, 18; 33: 10; 40: 1, 25; 41: 21 (twice); 66: 9;[59] this point was noted by several earlier commentators; cf. König, 330).

The only other occurrence of this usage in the Masoretic Text is at Ps. 12: 6, where, however, *Seb* has the more usual perfect *'āmar*. The issue is complicated by the fact that there is an obvious

[59] In several of these examples, *yhwh* is replaced by an alternative title for God; this does not, of course, affect the substantive point under discussion. Thus we find *'ᵉlōhêkem* at 40: 1; *qādôš* at 40: 25; and *melek yaᵃqōb* for one of the occurrences at 41: 21. For a recent discussion of such discourse markers, see S. A. Meier, *Speaking of Speaking: Marking Direct Discourse in the Hebrew Bible* (SVT 46; Leiden, 1992).

connection between this verse and Isa. 33: 10. The possibility should, therefore, be considered that an original perfect tense in Ps. 12: 6 has been replaced with an imperfect by contamination from Isa. 33: 10. In view of the facts that this usage is otherwise restricted to the book of Isaiah and that Isaiah 33 is generally regarded as late, the reverse process seems less likely. However, even if that alternative solution were entertained for Isa. 33: 10, the late date of the chapter means that it is not significant for our present purposes.

The other two occurrences of our phrase in Isaiah 1–39 both come in the first chapter. It is still the opinion of the overwhelming majority of commentators that the bulk of this chapter (including the two verses in question) stems from the prophet Isaiah himself, even though the oracles may have been subsequently gathered from elsewhere in his work and given their present position as the result of a redactor's desire to provide a suitable introduction to the book as a whole. It is true that more recently a number of voices have been raised to explore the possibility that much of the chapter should be ascribed to the Deuteronomistic circles of the exilic and post-exilic periods.[60] Fortunately in this case prolonged discussion is not necessary, because Sweeney has recently devoted a thorough study to the matter.[61] He draws the important distinction between origin and redaction: because of tensions between several of the units within the chapter, they cannot all derive from the same situation or be regarded as parts of a single composition. It is, therefore, necessary to distinguish carefully between the original date and purpose of each unit and the new use to which a later redactor may have put them. In this way, it is possible to accommodate many of the observations of recent scholars who find the appeal of this chapter as it now stands to be most appropriate to a late (probably post-exilic) setting, while at the same time doing justice to the evident thematic and historical connections between many of the chapter's individual units and the thought and times of Isaiah himself. While not necessarily agreeing with every detail of Sweeney's analysis, I concur completely with his general approach and method. It therefore suffices here to refer to his work for further details and to conclude on this basis that the two verses with

60 Notably Vermeylen, 42–111 (though he accepts the probable authenticity of verses 10–17; cf. 57, 65, and 109), and Kaiser; Werner (*Eschatologische Texte in Jesaja 1–39*, 118–33) adopts a similar position.

61 Sweeney, *Isaiah 1–4*, 101–33.

which we are primarily concerned should not be dated as late as the time of Deutero-Isaiah (or even later).

There is one further potential source of difficulty to which reference must be made before we can include the use of this phrase in the category of firm examples. It has been observed by several scholars that there are a number of links between Isaiah 1 and 65–6, suggesting that part of the concern of the chapter's final redactor was to balance the opening and the close of the book as a whole in the form of what might loosely be called a massive *inclusio*.[62] Since our phrase occurs in 66: 9, it might be possible to argue that it has found its way into Isaiah 1 under the influence of that passage. In general, however, the influence is thought to go the other way, since the concluding chapters of the book draw on other parts of the Isaiah tradition as well.[63] This potential challenge to our argument may, therefore, be rejected, and, in view of the highly distinctive nature of this phrase by comparison with the rest of the Old Testament, we may conclude that Deutero-Isaiah must have been influenced by Proto-Isaiah in this regard.

The same conclusion can probably be drawn with regard to another way of referring to God's speech, 'for the mouth of the Lord has spoken it' (*kî pî yhwh dibbēr*). This precise form of wording is found only at Isa. 1: 20; 40: 5; and 58: 14 (and we may also note *kî yhwh dibbēr* at 1: 2; 22: 25; and 25: 8; the same phrase occurs at 21: 17, with the addition of *'ᵉlōhê-yiśrā'ēl*[64]), though a very similar expression occurs at Mic. 4: 4, with merely the addition of *ṣᵉbā'ôt* to the divine name. It may not be without significance that this comes at the conclusion of the passage which Micah shares in common with Isa. 2: 2–4. Though the matter remains controversial, many commentators believe (rightly, in my opinion) that this passage cannot be dated before the late exilic or early post-exilic period at the earliest.[65] If that is true, the significance of our phrase's occurrence there will be blunted in the context of the present discussion.

62 See in particular the works of Liebreich, Lack, and Sweeney, as summarized above, Ch. 1 sect. 5.

63 See in particular Vermeylen, 492–503, and Beuken, 'Isaiah Chapters lxv–lxvi'. It is also pertinent to observe that according to Vermeylen, 505–8, Isa. 1: 2–2: 5 has exerted influence on the whole of Isaiah 56–66.

64 As an independent summarizing clause, this phrase occurs elsewhere at 1 Kgs. 14: 11; Jer. 13: 15; Joel 4: 8; and Obad. 18.

65 See the discussion below, Ch. 6.

More seriously, there is a considerable weight of opinion which maintains that, even if Isa. 1: 18 is Isaianic, verses 19–20 are Deuteronomic, in particular because of the way in which 'they specifically tie faithfulness to YHWH with reward and rebellion with punishment'.[66] Since these verses come at the conclusion of a major section in the chapter, the suggestion that they function as a redactional application to a later situation of the whole of the foregoing passage is undoubtedly attractive. On the other hand, not all scholars are persuaded by such arguments. In particular, Brekelmans has examined our passage with this very question in mind, and found that neither its theology nor its language is to be associated with the Deuteronomic movement.[67] Discussion of this issue therefore seems to have reached something of an *impasse*.

Since this comes down to a matter of individual judgement about probabilities, it is unlikely to be resolved here. Two comments are in order, however. One is that, even if the passage was originally formulated within the Deuteronomic school, that does not in itself necessarily imply a post-exilic date, even though this is frequently assumed. This point is recognized by Vermeylen (pp. 693–709), who dates our passage to the period immediately following the fall of Jerusalem in 587/6 BC. On this view, Isa. 1: 20 would still have been in the form of the book which Deutero-Isaiah would have known.

Secondly, this may be another passage where it is necessary to distinguish between original composition and subsequent redactional placement. As Brekelmans has shown, Isa. 1: 19–20 does not manifest any features which can be said to be truly characteristic of Deuteronomic style, a fact to which due weight must be given in view of the highly stereotypical nature of Deuteronomic compositions elsewhere. It may be that a redactor who shared the outlook of the Deuteronomists was drawn to place this passage at this point because it suited his intention in the arrangement of the chapter as

[66] See Sweeney, *Isaiah 1–4*, 129.

[67] Brekelmans, 'Deuteronomistic Influence in Isaiah 1–12'. One point of detail relevant to our discussion may be added to his observations. Sweeney (*Isaiah 1–4*, 129 n. 78) claims on the basis of Vermeylen's work that the phrase 'for the mouth of the Lord has spoken it' is 'frequently used in Deuteronomistic literature'. In fact, this is not so; Vermeylen (p. 60) refers only to the expression 'the mouth of the Lord' (*pî yhwh*), and rightly points out that the phrase in its entirety occurs only in the book of Isaiah.

a whole, but the evidence that he also wrote it *de novo* for this purpose turns out to be slender indeed.

The conclusion of this discussion must, therefore, be that the formula for divine speech which is found at the end of 1: 20 is the most probable source of influence on Deutero-Isaiah at 40: 5 (and the absence of the phrase from Isaiah 65–6 removes any possibility that it has entered chapter 1 from that source). In view of the uncertainties surrounding the composition of 1: 19–20, however, it must be recognized that this example will not be regarded as acceptable by all scholars.

(6) The next example may not be of great significance in itself, but in a cumulative argument of this nature it may be allowed to carry some slight weight. At Isa. 30: 7 there is a reference to the mythical creature Rahab, a sea-monster of chaos[68] whom God defeated in a primeval battle. In this verse, however, Rahab is used as a colourful picture for Egypt:

> For Egypt's help is worthless and empty,
> therefore I have called her
> 'Rahab that is stilled*.'

The preceding context speaks of an embassy making its way through the Negeb desert in an effort to entice Egypt by means of gifts to come to the help of the people of Judah. For whatever reason they have chosen this dangerous route in preference to the normally safer coastal road, they will meet there a number of dangerous animals which already begin to give the impression of a progression towards the surreal, if not mythical: lioness, lion, viper, and flying serpent. It is thus an effectively dramatic denouement to suggest that, when they eventually reach the hoped-for source of aid, they will find that she is none other than Rahab! But, if the usually accepted slight emendation of the Masoretic Text is adopted, she is totally ineffective: 'Rahab that is stilled.'

There is virtual unanimity in ascribing this passage to Isaiah of Jerusalem, writing during the period 705–701 BC. It is true that

[68] The name is thought to be connected with the root *rhb*, meaning 'be boisterous, agitated', but the further suggestion that it is a loan-word from Akkadian is rejected by J. Day (*God's Conflict with the Dragon and the Sea: Echoes of a Canaanite Myth in the Old Testament* (Cambridge, 1985), 6). He accepts, however, that Hebrew *rhb* is cognate with Akkadian *ra'ābu* ('storm at [of raging waters]') (personal communication).

Huber[69] has attempted to revive the suggestion of Marti that the concluding part of verse 7 is a later gloss, but this has been widely rejected, particularly by those who have recently advocated that verse 8 belongs with verses 6–7 rather than marking the start of a new and independent section.[70] If they are right, then the reference to 'Rahab that is stilled' is demanded as an antecedent to the feminine-singular suffixes in verse 8: it provides the text of what Isaiah was commanded to write on a tablet. Even without that, however, we have seen how the reference to Rahab is well integrated into its immediate context. Huber's other arguments are equally weak. He maintains that the use of mythological names for historical peoples developed only later, which merely begs the question, and also that *lāzō't* must refer back to *miṣrayim* ('Egypt') earlier in the verse, a word which he also considers to be a later gloss. This latter point is itself uncertain, of course, but, even if it were to be accepted, Huber's consequence would not necessarily follow: *lāzō't* could be construed as an example of the use of the feminine for abstract (GK §122*q*).

In Isa. 51: 9 there is another reference to Rahab in a way which, by its clear allusion to the deliverance of the Israelites at the Red Sea, identifies the mythical monster with Egypt:

> Awake, awake, put on strength,
>   O arm of the Lord;
> awake, as in days of old,
>   the generations of long ago.
> Was it not thou that didst cut Rahab in pieces,
>   that didst pierce the dragon?
> Was it not thou that didst dry up the sea,
>   the waters of the great deep;
> that didst make the depths of the sea a way
>   for the redeemed to pass over? (Isa. 51: 9–10)[71]

Here, then, there appears to be a point of connection between the two parts of the book of Isaiah.

[69] Huber, *Jahwe, Juda und die anderen Völker beim Propheten Jesaja*, 119–20.

[70] e.g. Auvray; K.-D. Schunck, 'Jes $30_{6-8}$ und die Deutung der Rahab im Alten Testament', *ZAW* 78 (1966), 48–56; Vermeylen, 410–11; Gonçalves, *L'Expédition de Sennachérib*, 145–51; see earlier Delitzsch; Kaiser appears to be undecided. Dietrich (*Jesaja und die Politik*, 141–4) argues that a new section begins at 30: 7*b* and continues through the following verses.

[71] Rahab in these verses is identified with Egypt by e.g. Bonnard and Westermann.

The question arises, however, whether this is an example of direct literary influence or whether both are not drawing independently on a common tradition. At first, this might seem to be clear from Psalm 87: 4:

> Among those who know me I mention Rahab and Babylon;
> behold, Philistia and Tyre, with Ethiopia . . .

Without question, Rahab here too is used as a sobriquet for Egypt. Moreover, since Psalm 87 is one of the Psalms of Zion which most scholars date in the pre-exilic period and which are often thought to have exerted particular influence on Isaiah of Jerusalem himself,[72] this passage might appear to rule out the evidence of Rahab for our purposes altogether. However, this initial appearance is deceptive. Psalm 87 itself is certainly late, whatever conclusion we hold regarding the Psalms of Zion as a whole. The continuation of verse 4 cited above together with verse 5 refers to a number of nations whose precise function is disputed. 'There is uncertainty amongst scholars . . . whether Egypt and the other nations alluded to here form part of an eschatological vision of Zion as the world centre of Yahweh's worship, or whether the reference is to proselytes who had come to the festival cult in Jerusalem, perhaps symbolic of the future eschaton, or whether the Jews of the Diaspora are in mind.'[73] Whichever interpretation is adopted, however, the situation which is presupposed can hardly have obtained in the pre-exilic period. In view of the close connections between this group of Psalms and the Isaiah tradition as a whole, it seems entirely reasonable to conclude that the reference to Rahab in Psalm 87 could be dependent on Isaiah.

A stronger case for influence from the Psalms on Deutero-Isaiah at this point comes from the reference to Rahab at Ps. 89: 11[10]. Day has drawn attention to the number of verbal parallels between this verse and Isa. 51: 9, while Eissfeldt has listed at length the connections between Psalm 89 as a whole and Deutero-Isaiah.[74]

[72] See most recently J. Day, *Psalms* (Sheffield, 1990).

[73] Day, *God's Conflict*, 90–1. He notes that Weiser favours the second position, and Kraus the third, but, with Kirkpatrick, thinks that the first is the most likely. 'It is surely improbable that Jews who were merely in exile in Egypt would themselves be referred to by the name of the defeated sea monster Rahab, and much more natural to suppose that actual Egyptians are in mind' (p. 91).

[74] See Day, *God's Conflict*, 92, and O. Eissfeldt, 'The Promises of Grace to David in Isaiah 55: 1–5', in B. W. Anderson and W. Harrelson (eds.), *Israel's Prophetic Heritage: Essays in Honor of James Muilenburg* (New York, 1962), 196–207.

Nevertheless, in view of the continuation of the passage in Isa. 51: 10, it seems most probable that in verse 9 Rahab is used as a reference to Egypt at the time of the Exodus. Thus, while it may readily be accepted that the prophet has made use of the Psalm here, his interpretation of its imagery still appears to indicate reflection on the application of Rahab to Egypt in Isa. 30: 7.

A related point concerns the use of a different mythical monster, *tannîn* (usually translated as 'the dragon' or 'the serpent'), at Ezek. 29: 3 and 32: 2[75] (and cf. Ps. 74: 13, which, according to Kraus, is to be dated to the same period, though some would date it later). In these passages in Ezekiel, Pharaoh, the king of Egypt, is either equated or compared with the dragon, while in Isa. 51: 9 *tannîn* stands in parallel with Rahab. We thus appear to be moving in the circle of closely associated ideas. The possibility must, therefore, be allowed that the equation of Rahab with Egypt was in wider circulation and that the fact that before the time of Deutero-Isaiah it occurs only in Isa. 30: 7 is a matter of coincidence. Looking at the evidence in another way, however, it might be more accurate to conclude that the use of this imagery is first attested by, and quite probably was first coined by, Isaiah of Jerusalem,[76] that it may have been developed in a slightly different, because personalized, way by Ezekiel, and thus that the use of it by Deutero-Isaiah is most likely to have been inspired by his reading of the earlier work of Isaiah.

Although in formal terms this example satisfies the criteria with which we are working, it clearly cannot be put in the same firm category as most of the others that we have discussed. Nevertheless, in the light of the overall case that we have sought to build up, it adds a certain corroborative weight to the argument as a whole.

(7) We have just noted that opinions are divided as to whether Isa. 30: 8 belongs with the verses which precede or follow it. Similarly, scholars are not agreed about the extent of the next unit in the chapter. Childs, for instance, confidently asserts that 30: 8–17 'is clear and straightforward from a form critical perspective',[77] but

75 For the textual uncertainty in both passages, see Zimmerli's commentary, *ad loc.*, and *BHS*.

76 So too Schunk, 'Jes $30_{6-8}$ und die Deutung der Rahab im Alten Testament'.

77 Childs, *Isaiah and the Assyrian Crisis*, 36; similarly Duhm; Marti; Donner, *Israel unter den Völkern*, 159–62 (with hesitations); J. Jensen, *The Use of* tôrâ *by Isaiah: His Debate with the Wisdom Tradition* (CBQMS 3; Washington, 1973), 112–13; Høgenhaven, *Gott und Volk bei Jesaja*, 204–7.

merely the listing of alternative suggestions is enough to demonstrate that there remains room for doubt: verses 8–11,[78] 8–14,[79] 8–18,[80] 9–17,[81] 7*b*–11,[82] 9–26,[83] and 9–14.[84] Not surprisingly in view of so much uncertainty, it has also been proposed that 'the impression is created of various short sayings from Isaiah, all to be linked with the situation of 701, which have been coupled together by a redactor'.[85]

While some aspects of this material will be examined more closely in the next chapter, we may focus for the present on verse 9. Regardless of the precise extent of the literary unit to which this verse is thought to belong, it is almost universally ascribed to Isaiah. Doubts appear first to have been raised by Kaiser, who suggested that the passage might be a reflection by Isaiah's 'trustees' on the catastrophe of the year 587 BC. He does not offer any specific evidence for this, however; it seems to arise more from his general approach whereby, if material can be found to have relevance to a later situation, it is probably to be dated then as well. In the present instance, it is equally suitable to the time of Isaiah, as all previous commentators have observed. Once again, therefore, it may be acknowledged that Kaiser has contributed valuable observations in terms of the growing awareness of the need to consider how the prophet's words were understood and so re-applied by later generations without finding any need to follow him in his conclusions concerning the text's origin.

An attempt to underpin Kaiser's position with more specific arguments, however, has been made by Vermeylen. Some of his points refer to the later verses and so perhaps need not be considered here. With regard to verse 9, his principal observation is

78 R. Fey, *Amos und Jesaja: Abhängigkeit und Eigenständigkeit des Jesaja* (WMANT 12; Neukirchen-Vluyn, 1963), 115–20; Wildberger, who appears to have been misled by the layout of Auvray's commentary into thinking that he too favoured this division; G. Stansell, *Micah and Isaiah: A Form and Tradition Historical Comparison* (SBLDS 85; Atlanta, 1988), 96–8.

79 Fohrer; Huber, *Jahwe, Juda und die anderen Völker beim Propheten Jesaja*, 136–7.

80 Procksch.

81 Eichrodt; Vermeylen, 411–16.

82 Dietrich, *Jesaja und die Politik*, 141–5.

83 Auvray.

84 Gonçalves, *L'Expédition de Sennachérib*, 220–4.

85 Clements; this solution is also entertained as a possibility by Kaiser, though he develops it rather differently.

that its phraseology is 'tout entière' Deuteronomic.[86] In support, he lists four words or phrases and notes their occurrences in Deuteronomy or other supposedly Deuteronomic literature. The dangers inherent in such a line of argument have been repeatedly rehearsed, and some are fully evident here. 'Rebellion' (*m*ᵉ*rî*), for instance, is by no means confined to Deuteronomic texts, the more so if, as Vermeylen does, we extend the discussion to include the verb *mrh* as well. Similarly, 'lying' (*kḥš*) is a *hapax legomenon*, and so should not be used as evidence at all. Vermeylen seeks to avoid the problem by dealing with the common verb from the same root, but again a glance at the concordance quickly reveals that it is by no means a characteristically 'Deuteronomic' word, for it occurs in a wide variety of sources. The other two phrases which he lists will be investigated from a rather different point of view below, and it will be shown there that the occurrences in Isaiah have certain distinctive features which set them apart from initially similar-looking expressions in the Deuteronomic corpus. In view of connections between this verse and other material in Isaiah (cf. Wildberger), we may conclude that Vermeylen has failed to make out his case, and that the usual view which regards 30: 9 as deriving from the hand of the prophet Isaiah himself is correct.

In the second half of the verse, the people are described as 'sons who will not hear the instruction of the Lord'. There are three matters here which require more detailed comment. The first is the use of the word *tôrâ*, translated 'instruction' by the *RSV*. It has long been noticed that Isaiah uses this word in a somewhat distinctive manner, and the whole matter has been the subject of a thorough investigation by Jensen.[87] It is clear in this passage and at 8: 16, to go no further, that *tôrâ* cannot have its most familiar meaning of 'law', and equally that it is not to be associated with the notion of priestly instruction either. Rather, in both these passages the word is associated in the closest possible manner with God's message to his

86 A further argument, which does not strictly concern verse 9 though Vermeylen includes it in his discussion, is that verses 9–11 may be compared with Amos 2: 11–12 and verses 16–17 with Amos 2: 13–16. Since he believes that the Amos passage has been subjected to Deuteronomic redaction, he concludes that the same is true of Isa. 30: 9–17. This is a precarious argument, however, since there are other possible ways of explaining similarities between Isaiah and Amos (cf. Fey, *Amos und Jesaja*). From the point of view of method, it should first be established independently that both passages are Deuteronomic before conclusions are drawn on that basis about their composition and redaction.

87 Jensen, *The Use of* tôrâ *by Isaiah.*

people as mediated through the prophet. Jensen seeks to refine this further by denying that it is ever legitimate to speak of 'prophetic *torah*' and seeing here instead the idea of wise instruction as attested in particular in the book of Proverbs. He believes that this reflects ancient usage and that Isaiah made use of it because of his debate with wisdom circles in Jerusalem. Whether or not this is so, the significant point for our present purpose, and one which commands general agreement, is that Isaiah uses the term in a manner which is not found in other prophets of his period, and that later prophets too scarcely, if at all, followed him in this.[88]

Deutero-Isaiah refers to *tôrâ* on five occasions (42: 4, 21, 24; 51: 4, 7). Attention has been drawn to two of these by Clements in the context of the present discussion. After a reference to 8: 16, he writes:

> In 42.4 and 21 the term *tôrâ* = 'teaching' is used in a very unusual fashion, since it can hardly be intended as a reference to Yahweh's 'law' in the later sense. Rather it appears to refer to Yahweh's 'purpose', which is shortly to be realized and which has been declared beforehand by the prophets . . . a connection with the earlier prophetic usage serves greatly towards a better understanding of its significance in ch. 42.[89]

It is not entirely clear why Clements limits his comments to only these two occurrences. Isa. 51: 4 in particular seems to be closely associated with 42: 4. Moreover, when these passages are viewed in the context of the whole of Deutero-Isaiah's ministry, Jensen's attempt (p. 23) to divorce the meaning here from anything resembling that found in Isa. 8: 16 and 30: 9 seems unduly restricted, especially since later on (p. 132) he maintains in connection with other aspects of his study that 'Deutero-Isaiah reflects in a general way some of the elements of Isaiah's teaching that we have investigated'. Deutero-Isaiah's distinctive use of *tôrâ* is thus best understood as carrying forward into his new situation the equally distinctive terminology of his eighth-century predecessor.

Secondly, in 30: 9 the people are accused of not having been

[88] There is some question about one or two passages in Jeremiah, discussed by Jensen on pp. 19–22.

[89] Clements, 'Beyond Tradition-History', 107; note also Whybray's comment on *tôrâ* in 42: 4: 'not the "Law" in the Deuteronomic or later legal sense, but the will of the sovereign God announced by the prophet'.

willing to listen to (*lōʾ-ʾābû šᵉmôaʿ*) the Lord's instruction; Isa. 28: 12 ('yet they were unwilling to listen') and 30: 15 ('but you were not willing') are closely comparable. This seems to be directly reflected at 42: 24*c*: 'neither were they willing to walk in his ways, nor to listen to his instruction.'[90] The verb *ʾbh* ('to be willing') is not, of course, uncommon, but the way in which it is used in these verses sets it apart from other occurrences. It is otherwise used in connection with Israel's unwillingness to listen to God only at Lev. 26: 21; Ezek. 3: 7; 20: 8; and Ps. 81: 12 (and note the unparalleled positive use at Isa. 1: 19), which at once means that it cannot be regarded as Deuteronomic, as Vermeylen curiously claims. Within this more limited circle of texts, however, the group in Isaiah is further distinguished by the fact that in them alone is the verb followed by a simple infinitive. Everywhere else it is followed by the preposition *l* and the infinitive (לשמע (*lišmōaʿ*)).[91] This may seem to be a small point, but it probably conceals something rather more. At 42: 24 the infinitive governed by *ʾbh* is certainly the infinitive absolute, הלוך (*hālôk*). Now, it is striking that at 30: 9 and 28: 12, although the infinitive is pointed by the Masoretes as an infinitive construct, it is on both occasions unusually spelt *plene*: שמוע (*šᵉmôaʿ*). The question of when such *plene* spelling came into use and of its significance is, of course, debatable,[92] but the possibility may certainly be entertained that on this occasion it has preserved an alternative way of understanding 28: 12 and 30: 9 to that which was finally settled upon by the Masoretes. At any rate, the *plene* spelling of the infinitive construct qal after *ʾbh* is not found anywhere else, so far as I can see. It may thus be suggested that Deutero-Isaiah understood the infinitives at 28: 12 and 30: 9 to be infinitives absolute, and that this influenced him in the use of the same construction at 42: 24.

Thirdly, 30: 9 and 42: 24 are further drawn together by the fact that the object of the verb 'to listen' (*šmʿ*) is in each case the *tôrâ* of the Lord. Despite what one might suppose, this is remarkably

[90] The changes in person throughout 42: 18–25 (cf. Bonnard, 136) mean that it is precarious to argue that parts of this verse are a later addition, as a number of commentators have suggested.

[91] Elsewhere, the infinitive without *l* is used after *ʾbh* at Deut. 10: 10; 29: 19 (where, however, SP has *l*); 1 Sam. 15: 9; 2 Kgs. 13: 23; Job 39: 9. The verbs which are governed by *ʾbh* in these verses are in no way related to the ideas with which we are concerned. We may further note that, whenever the infinitive used in these verses is qal, it is always spelt defectively.

[92] See J. Barr, *The Variable Spellings of the Hebrew Bible* (Oxford, 1989).

rare.[93] It is found at Zech. 7: 12 and Neh. 13: 3. Both these passages are too late to be of relevance for our discussion, and furthermore it may well be that Zechariah also reflects the influence of Isaiah at this point.[94] It also occurs at Prov. 28: 9, whose date is uncertain. Jensen uses this reference as part of his argument that Isaiah was particularly influenced by the use of *tôrâ* in wisdom circles. Even if that be true, however, we should note that it is used in an absolute sense in Proverbs, and that Isaiah has developed this by making it explicitly the Lord's instruction. Since this is also the case at 42: 24, Deutero-Isaiah's usage is better explained as deriving from Isaiah rather than directly from wisdom sources. Finally, the plural form of *tôrâ* occurs as the object of 'to listen' at Ezek. 44: 5, but both the general context and the use of the plural make clear that this is quite unrelated to the expression in Isaiah.

It thus appears that Isa. 30: 9 has exerted a general influence on Deutero-Isaiah with regard to his use of the word *tôrâ*, and that in association with this there has been particular influence of a pronounced nature on the phraseology of 42: 24.

In both the last chapter and the present one, a number of passages have been explored which indicate that Deutero-Isaiah was influenced at the literary level by the form that the book of Isaiah may be presumed to have reached by his time. One further important piece of evidence remains to be examined in the next chapter. This discussion has not exhausted every possible example, because the attempt has been made to keep strictly to the criteria which were laid down in Chapter 2. This is necessary if the case is to advance from the category of the possible to the highly probable ('proof' would seem an inappropriate term to use).

Once the case is accepted, then, of course, much other material could be drawn into the discussion. In formal terms, this may not satisfy all the criteria, but if the fact of influence is already agreed, then it becomes by far the most likely explanation in these cases too. Reference was made in Chapter 1, for instance, to several themes which other scholars have believed serve in some sense to 'unite' the two major parts of the book; the concentration on Zion

93 Vermeylen thus again rather misses the point when he draws attention to the common use of the *tôrâ* of the Lord in Deuteronomic literature. On the one hand, as we have seen, the word *tôrâ* is used in a quite different sense in Isaiah, and on the other it does not occur as the object of 'to listen' in the Deuteronomic corpus.

94 See Jensen, *The Use of* tôrâ *by Isaiah*, 24.

and Jerusalem is a good case in point, while reference has also been made in passing to the emphasis in Deutero-Isaiah on the kingship of God and to the theme of God's 'plan' (*'ēṣâ*). Other, smaller examples, too, might come in for consideration, such as the references to God destroying his enemies like stubble in the fire at Isa. 5: 24 and 47: 14 (but Ps. 83: 14–15 means that this cannot come in the category of firm examples); the not dissimilar theme of the dispersal of Israel's enemies like chaff before the storm wind at 17: 13; 29: 5; and 41: 15–16 (but there are doubts about the authenticity of the passages in Proto-Isaiah); the image of God's agent of judgement as a bird of prey (*'ayiṭ*) at 18: 6 and 46: 11 (but cf. Jer. 12: 9); the several connections between 11: 1–5 and such passages as 40: 24; 42: 1–4 and others noted by Jensen[95] (but there are doubts about the authenticity of Isaiah 11, even though the matter is by no means certain and many still hold to Isaianic authorship); the expression *śym mšpṭ* at 28: 17 and 42: 4; the links between 8: 10 and 40: 8, 44: 26, and 46: 10 (but again some doubt the authenticity of 8: 10); the similarities between 1: 25 and 48: 10; the (probably) ancient divine title *'ᵃbîr yiśrā'ēl/yaᵃqōb*, used only at 1: 24, 49: 26, and 60: 16 in the prophets; the possible association of the 'fear not' oracles as explored by Conrad;[96] the thematic similarity of 31: 2 with such verses as 44: 25–6; 45: 7, 23; and 55: 11 (but a number of commentators think that 31: 2 has been added later), and Clifford's suggestion that 45: 8–13 may be a 'citation' of 10: 5–19.[97] It is worth remembering in this connection that, even when a verse or passage in Isaiah 1–39 is judged to be secondary, it may nevertheless have been added before the time of Deutero-Isaiah.

These and other examples which could doubtless be added are suggestive even though not in themselves compelling. At best, they contribute to the argument some indication of the extent to which Deutero-Isaiah may have been dependent on the earlier material. Even without them, however, the conclusion is surely justified in answer to one of the questions which was raised following the survey of research in Chapter 1 that we may legitimately speak of direct literary influence by Proto-Isaiah on Deutero-Isaiah. The evidence cannot be satisfactorily explained merely in terms of

95 See ibid. 132.

96 See E. W. Conrad, 'The Royal Narratives and the Structure of the Book of Isaiah', *JSOT* 41 (1988), 67–81.

97 R. J. Clifford, 'The Unity of the Book of Isaiah and its Cosmogonic Language', *CBQ* 55 (1993), 1–17.

mutual influence from some alternative source. Deutero-Isaiah must have read an earlier form of the work and been influenced by it sufficiently to adopt a considerable number of its themes and modes of expression. The question which then arises is, why? So far as I can see, contributors to the modern discussion of the 'unity' of Isaiah have stopped short at this point, leaving the impression that it is somehow 'just one of those things'. This is unsatisfactory. We have reached our present position as the result of many decades of application to the text of Isaiah of the historical-critical method, and that method itself demands that we seek to press on to explain the phenomena in 'historical' terms so far as is possible. It is the first step towards such an explanation that will be attempted in the next chapter.

# 5

## On Writing and Witnesses

As a result of the evidence set out in the two preceding chapters, we have arrived at the conclusion that the nature of the influence of Proto-Isaiah on Deutero-Isaiah is quite different from anything that can be ascribed to their common adherence to a single school or stream of tradition. Indeed, the marked differences between them in just these respects tell strongly against such an explanation. Deutero-Isaiah's appeal to the patriarchal and Exodus traditions,[1] as well as his distinctive handling of the Davidic theme (see 55: 3), are only the most prominent points that need be noted. Because of the focus of our discussion, these have perforce been left on one side for the present. Nevertheless, they serve to highlight the conclusion that the evidence can only be explained on the assumption that the influence is primarily of a literary nature. That is to say, however unfashionable such a view may be, we must reckon with the likelihood that Deutero-Isaiah was familiar with an early form of the book of Isaiah and that both consciously and sometimes also, no doubt, unconsciously he took up various of its themes, images, and modes of expression in the course of his own ministry, and that he did so in a way that is not true to anything like the same extent of his use of any other single body of earlier Old Testament literature. His reasons for doing so will be the primary focus of attention in this chapter, though it should be appreciated that a secondary result of the investigation will be to add further material to buttress the results which have already been achieved.

Since our interest here begins to move towards an understanding of the process of composition, the easiest way to start will be to look

[1] Cf. below, Ch. 6 n. 15. Clifford ('The Unity of the Book of Isaiah') has recently argued that Deutero-Isaiah's three 'new' themes of Exodus, creation, and Cyrus as Yahweh's king, while not themselves found in First Isaiah, are nevertheless presented in Isaiah 40–55 in such a way that they are used to develop, and 'are in fact deeply continuous with', the Isaian tradition.

at three passages in Isaiah 1–39, all widely believed to go back to Isaiah of Jerusalem himself, in which he refers to the writing down of certain parts of his message.[2]

The first example of this motif is in Isa. 8: 1–4.[3] In this passage, Isaiah is commanded by God to take a large tablet of some kind[4] and to write on it 'Belonging to[5] Maher-shalal-hash-baz'. He then records that he got two reliable witnesses, who are named, to certify the document.[6] The continuation of the paragraph then goes on to speak of the conception, birth, and naming of Maher-shalal-hash-baz, and the significance of the name within the historical context of the Syro-Ephraimite war. It seems probable both that the phrase which was written down at the first was already intended to serve as a (highly unconventional) proper name,[7] in view of the introductory preposition *l*, and also that its significance, as explained in verse 4, was known to Isaiah from the start, even though in the economic style of the paragraph as a whole this is recorded only once at the end, where it achieves maximum effect in the present form of the text.[8]

[2] For a study of these passages with different, though to some extent complementary, concerns, see C. Hardmeier, 'Verkündigung und Schrift bei Jesaja: Zur Entstehung der Schriftprophetie als Oppositionsliteratur im alten Israel', *TGl* 73 (1983), 119–34.

[3] So far as I am aware, only Kaiser has challenged the view that this paragraph derives from Isaiah himself. His observations are almost entirely concerned with the links between this passage and chapter 7 and so depend on the cogency of Kaiser's arguments against the historical nature of that chapter as well. At the same time, account should also be taken of the differences, principally that 8: 1–4 is a first-person narrative whereas chapter 7 is third person, and that there is no overt mention of the royal house in 8: 1–4 whereas this was the primary focus of chapter 7. In my view, these differences point to separate origins, so that links between them relate only to the level of redaction, not composition. See further Høgenhaven, *Gott und Volk bei Jesaja*, 81.

[4] The precise nature of the enigmatic *gillāyôn* is not of importance in the present context, though it has been much debated; see Wildberger, who underlines in particular the weaknesses in the textual conjectures of K. Galling, 'Ein Stück judäischen Bodenrechts in Jesaia 8', *ZDPV* 56 (1933), 209–18.

[5] In view of the common use of *l* before personal names on seals, *RSV* seems to follow the most probable interpretation here.

[6] The hiph'il of *'wd* followed by the cognate accusative *'ēdîm* occurs three times in Jeremiah 32 with the meaning 'take as witness'; as here, the context concerns the certifying of a document.

[7] *Pace* Hayes and Irvine, *Isaiah, the Eighth-Century Prophet*, 143.

[8] See Donner, *Israel unter den Völkern*, 21.

Although not explicitly stated, it is likely that the tablet was intended for public display. This is suggested by the description of the tablet as 'large', and perhaps also by the description of the writing itself as being done *bᵉḥereṭ ʾᵉnôš*. The meaning of this phrase is disputed, and so not too much weight should be put upon it. *RSV* follows one widely held view with its 'in common characters', taking *ʾᵉnôš* as 'a poetical synonym for איש, so that on the analogy of אמת איש, *an ordinary cubit* (Dt $3^{11}$), חרט אנוש should mean *an ordinary stylus*' (Gray). Gray further argues that 'stylus' could by extension refer to the 'style' or character of the writing, and concludes that 'the command is to use the ordinary alphabet with which every one was familiar'.[9] Finally, the fact that Isaiah later gave his son the name that was inscribed on the tablet supports the view that it was intended to be known openly.[10] Hab. 2: 2 is often cited as a parallel.

If, then, the tablet was not to be kept secret, why was there a need for witnesses?[11] It is usually, and reasonably, explained that they were needed to certify that Isaiah had indeed written his message in advance of the fulfilment of the events which it predicted. 'The role of the witnesses is to affirm at what time the prophet disclosed the name so that later, when the message it bore had proved true, they would be in a position to uphold the prophet's claim to have foretold the defeat of Syria and Ephraim' (Clements; so too, for instance, Wildberger and Watts). There is an element of 'belt and braces' about this explanation, but, in view of the crucial importance of guaranteeing that Isaiah was not manipulating the situation after the event, this was not, perhaps, unreasonable. In addition, however, Donner has advanced a further valuable suggestion—namely, the need to attest that it was indeed Isaiah who wrote on the tablet, since otherwise it could not serve to validate his ministry, and also that the summoning of

[9] Alternative suggestions are listed by Wildberger, who himself favours revocalizing the second word as *ʾānûš*, so rendering 'mit einem Unheilsgriffel'.

[10] Jones ('The Traditio of the Oracles of Isaiah of Jerusalem', 231) accepts this general conclusion. It is thus not clear to me why he then seems drawn to the possibility that the document was also sealed and put away until the fulfilment of the prediction. That apart, I am in close sympathy with Jones's position.

[11] The fact that there were two witnesses corresponds, of course, to legal requirement; cf. Deut. 17: 6; 19: 15. Furthermore, it is often assumed that they did not come from the immediate circle of Isaiah's putative supporters. They appear to have been individuals of high standing in society (for Uriah the priest, see 2 Kgs. 16: 10–16; Zechariah may have been Hezekiah's maternal grandfather, mentioned in 2 Kgs. 18: 2, but this cannot be certain) whose position would have made them 'reliable' witnesses in the eyes of the people at large.

witnesses would add to the general publicity surrounding the event.[12]

We may thus conclude from this passage that the purpose of Isaiah's writing was to record his message in advance of the events to which it related and that he went to some considerable effort to guarantee the integrity of the operation. Though this is not stated in the text, it is a reasonable inference that Isaiah did not expect the message of hope for Judah which the name, as explained in verse 4, contains to be accepted and acted upon by his contemporaries. It would thus testify against them in future days.[13] We should note, too, that the whole episode is played out in public, and that it relates in its entirety to events that need not have spanned more than two or three years from start to finish.

The second passage which requires examination is the well-known episode recorded later in the same chapter. It is translated by *RSV* as follows:

> Bind up the testimony, seal the teaching among my disciples. I will wait for the Lord, who is hiding his face from the house of Jacob, and I will hope in him. Behold, I and the children whom the Lord has given me are signs and portents in Israel from the Lord of hosts, who dwells on Mount Zion. (Isa. 8: 16–18)

This passage raises several questions which have been endlessly debated. First, are the two verbs in verse 16 to be construed as imperatives, as the MT vocalization implies and as translated by the *RSV*, or should they rather be taken as infinitives absolute, giving expression to Isaiah's own intention ('I will bind up . . .')? It is regarded as axiomatic by many commentators that the continuation in verse 17 demands this slight change, but this is to go too far. The infinitive absolute itself can, of course, be used for the divine imperative, while, if Isaiah himself is speaking in the imperative in verse 16, then the continuation in the first person in verse 17 is not a problem. The lack of any certainty about what, if anything, originally preceded the passage makes it difficult to come to a firm decision. Nevertheless, on balance, the context following favours

[12] Donner, *Israel unter den Völkern*, 20.

[13] Note that O. H. Steck ('Beiträge zum Verständnis von Jesaja 7,10–17 und 8,1–4', *ThZ* 29 (1973), 161–78 (174–8)) suggests that the text has been framed specifically to illustrate the 'hardening' of the people (6: 9–10) and their consequent judgement (8: 6–8*a*).

the view that Isaiah himself is speaking in verse 16, but whether in the imperative or as a statement of intent is not clear. Our understanding of the passage is not seriously affected by this uncertainty, since on either rendering Isaiah's purpose and ultimate initiative in whatever is being done comes equally to expression.

Secondly, there are two related problems which focus on the interpretation of the preposition *b*$^{e}$ before *limmudāy*. Is the tying-up and sealing to be taken literally, presupposing that an actual written document had previously been drawn up, or is it rather to be understood metaphorically? In the latter case, the preposition can retain its commonest meaning, 'in', in the sense of 'in the hearts of my disciples'. Isaiah did not actually write anything down, but committed his teaching to the circle of his disciples; 'die Jünger sind lebendige Zeugnisse' (Procksch); compare Jer. 31: 33*b*: 'I will put my law within them, and I will write it upon their hearts.' If the sealing is of a literal document, however, then the preposition has presumably to be taken to mean something like 'in the presence of' or *RSV*'s 'among'.[14]

Despite the considerable number of those favouring the metaphorical approach, it seems to strain the use of language too far; of what could 'tie up' and 'seal' be a metaphor? Dillmann pointed this out long ago (for those who have followed him more recently, see below), and when Gray, for instance, refers to his comments, it is striking that he is unable to offer any arguments to contradict them, even though he himself follows the alternative line. Two further points may be added to Dillmann's argument. If Isaiah were indeed speaking metaphorically, we might have expected him to make the point clearer by using a less ambiguous preposition than *b*. The idea of 'writing on the heart' would have been new and strange to his audience, and we may well wonder whether they would have been given sufficient indication from the text as it stands to appreciate the point. It is noteworthy that the verse from Jeremiah 31 just cited uses unambiguous prepositional phrases, as if to ensure that so novel an idea should not be misunderstood: *b*$^{e}$*qirbām w*$^{e}$*'al-libbām*. This type of argument is often directed against those

[14] There does not seem to be anything to favour the speculative attempt to cut the gordian knot by deleting *b*$^{e}$*limmudāy* as an addition or serious corruption of some other unknown word; cf. Fohrer, 132–3, and 'Entstehung, Komposition und Überlieferung von Jesaja 1–39', 141–2; Müller, 'Glauben und Bleiben', 53.

who understand Isa. 8: 16 literally; it is said that on that view Isaiah should have used *b^etôk*, *lipnê* or the like (see Duhm). This line of reasoning seems inverted, however. The preposition itself is neutral; having a wide range of meanings, it can theoretically fit either approach,[15] so that it is the overall context which must decide the issue, not the other way round. In that case, the earlier words in the verse should be taken at their face value unless there are strong indications to the contrary. There are none such, however; the whole case has been based upon the preposition, which as we have seen is not strong enough by itself to sustain the weight which has been put upon it. We may, therefore, conclude that Isaiah is speaking of a literal tying-up and sealing. The fact that there is no direct reference to the document itself is no reason for rejecting this view,[16] since its existence is an obvious and legitimate inference from the actions described.

The other point to be added in support of Dillmann's position is the occurrence of *tôrâ* and *t^eʿûdâ* in verse 20. Although there are a number of obscurities in this verse, it is generally agreed at least that these words are here being used in the sense of a written document (see Wildberger). In view of the rarity of *t^eʿûdâ* (elsewhere only at Ruth 4: 7) and the fact that as in verse 16 it occurs in parallel with *tôrâ*, there can be no doubt that they are intended to refer to the same thing in each of the two verses. It is probable that verses 19–20 are a later expansion of the original text of Isaiah, but they nevertheless stand as impressive early evidence for a non-metaphorical interpretation of verse 16. Of particular importance for the present discussion is the conclusion that this, at any rate, is how the verse appears to have been understood around the time of Deutero-Isaiah.

A third introductory question concerning this passage relates to the mood of verse 17. It has generally been assumed that Isaiah's 'waiting' and 'hoping' are directed towards a more positive future, after the expected judgement has passed. A few,[17] on the other hand, have suggested that Isaiah is here waiting only for the judgement of God to fall. This alternative interpretation, however, does not do justice to the force of *qwh*, which elsewhere seems nearly

15 For *b* = 'among' (i.e. 'of presence in the midst of a multitude'), see BDB 88*a*, 2.

16 *Contra* Fohrer, 'Entstehung, Komposition und Überlieferung von Jesaja 1–39', 142–3.

17 e.g. Fohrer; Steck, 'Bemerkungen zu Jesaja 6', 201 n. 33.

always to have the sense of 'to wait eagerly/expectantly for', especially when it is used, as here, with God as its object.[18] By itself, *ḥqh* could be taken either way, though it too is more usually used of waiting in hopeful expectation. Of course, there are other elements in verse 17 which are indicative of judgement in the short term, but they need not rule out the possibility that Isaiah held to a more positive expectation thereafter. We may conclude that the usual interpretation of verse 17 is the correct one.

It follows first from these introductory remarks that our understanding of 8: 16 should incline towards those who take fullest account of the quasi-legal language of the verse.[19] While *ṣrr* (or *ṣwr*; so Wildberger) cannot help us here, *ḥtm* ('to seal up'), when used in connection with a document, is suggestive of a formal act of securing the scroll so that its authorship is guaranteed, its contents are safeguarded from alteration, and its opening is reserved only for one who is authorized; cf. Jer. 32: 9–15, 44; Dan. 12: 4, 9; Est. 3: 13; 8: 8; Neh. 10: 1[9: 38], etc.[20] This has, of course, been amply illustrated by the finds of papyri from Elephantine and of bullae from Jerusalem and elsewhere.[21] As a matter of course, this was done in the presence of witnesses, and we must assume that the 'disciples' are mentioned in 8: 16 partly in order to fulfil this role.

The use of the rare word *t*$^{e}$*ʿûdâ* is also suggestive in this connection. Its only occurrence outside this passage is at Ruth 4: 7, a verse which is an editorial aside in the narrative to explain a legal custom which might otherwise not have been understood by the reader. It appears there to be a technical term, referring to a custom which gave visible expression to an agreement that had been reached. Because of the word's etymology and the references in the context to witnesses (cf. Ruth 4: 9 and 11), it has been reasonably explained as an 'attestation custom'.[22] It is not difficult to see how this same general sense might be transferred to a document which also can

[18] See the discussions in Wildberger; Th. Lescow, 'Jesajas Denkschrift aus der Zeit des syrisch-ephraimitischen Krieges', *ZAW* 85 (1973), 315–31 (326); D. W. Van Winkle, 'The Relationship of the Nations to Yahweh and to Israel in Isaiah xl–lv', *VT* 35 (1985), 446–58 (448); and G. Waschke, 'קוה', *TWAT* vi, cols. 1225–34.

[19] See especially Jones, 'The Traditio of the Oracles of Isaiah of Jerusalem'; Kaiser; Barth, *Die Jesaja Worte in der Josiazeit*, 278–9.

[20] Cf. S. Moscati, 'I sigilli nell'Antico Testamento', *Biblica*, 30 (1949), 314–38.

[21] See e.g. Y. Shiloh and D. Tarler, 'Bullae from the City of David: A Hoard of Seal Impressions from the Israelite Period', *BA* 49 (1986), 196–209.

[22] See R. L. Hubbard, *The Book of Ruth* (NICOT; Grand Rapids, Mich., 1988), 251–2.

act as a witness or attestation to the statements contained within it. Jones in particular has drawn attention to the similar function of the related word *'ēdût*. Isaiah's scroll, therefore, served as an independent attestation to his teaching for purposes and with consequences which are not unlike those noted in connection with Isa. 8: 1–2 above.

Clements has taken the similarity with 8: 1–4 a step further and sought thereby to specify in greater detail what is meant by 'my disciples' in 8: 16. He believes that 8: 16–18 originally formed the immediate continuation of verse 4 and therefore that the 'testimony' and the 'instruction' referred only to the name Maher-shalal-hash-baz. Its extension to cover the whole of the so-called Isaiah Memoir is the consequence of later editorial activity. Consequently, he writes:

> 'my disciples' must then refer to the two witnesses to the inscribing of the name mentioned in 8: 2, Uriah and Zechariah. Almost certainly, therefore, the translation of *AV* and *RSV* as 'disciples' is too strong a rendering, since these were not disciples in the normally understood sense of that term. 'Those I have instructed' better captures the sense of the Hebrew.

Quite apart from the question whether 8: 16 once followed 8: 4 immediately (a case can be made for the alternative view that 8: 5, and so part of the material which follows it, was written for its present position from the start), there are several difficulties for Clements's position. Isa. 8: 18 refers to 'the children whom the Lord has given me', suggesting that the document of 8: 16 contained more than just the name Maher-shalal-hash-baz. The verbs in 8: 16 ('tie up' and 'seal') do not seem to be appropriate for the kind of writing material mentioned in 8: 1. Although, as already noted, there is some uncertainty as to the precise nature of the *gillāyôn gādôl*, Clements himself thinks that it was 'most probably of clay, less probably of wood, and may have been disc shaped', and he appears to reject Galling's proposal (which involves textual emendation) that it was a sheet of papyrus. Furthermore, in 8: 2 Uriah and Zechariah are explicitly called 'witnesses', and we noted above the probability that they were not called to act because of any close personal association with Isaiah but because of their public position. It is thus not clear why now, at a secondary stage, they should need to be instructed by Isaiah; people in their position would have known what being a witness entailed, and 8: 2 shows that they were already able to fulfil that role. Finally, 'those I have instructed' implies a closer association with Isaiah than these two witnesses were likely to have had; 'the sense of the Hebrew', to which Clements appeals, includes prominently the teacher–pupil relationship, something which it is possible to slide over with the wider-ranging English word 'instruct', and it is unlikely that Uriah, in particular, would have come into that category in view of what we learn about him from 2 Kgs. 16: 10–16.

We may thus conclude that the 'disciples' of 8: 16 refer to some group other than the two individuals named in verse 2. As we shall see later, the word is comparatively rare in the Hebrew Bible, and this has led Jensen[23] to suggest that it was deliberately adopted by Isaiah from the wisdom schools as a further means of indicating the opposition of his 'instruction' to that of the political advisers of King Ahaz. The specificity of this suggestion naturally has an element of the hypothetical about it, but it serves well to draw attention to the fact that included in the term is the implication that these people looked to Isaiah as their teacher. Recent sociological studies of Israelite prophecy have commented on the fact that the prophets must have had support groups if they and their teaching were to survive,[24] and it is not necessary for our present purposes to define the precise nature of this group in greater detail. Suffice it to say that they were closely associated with the prophet, and so were in a position to act as witnesses of the tying and sealing of the document alluded to in 8: 16.

This leads us naturally to consider next the contents of this document. We have already noted that it must have been more extensive than the text of 8: 1, and indeed the majority of scholars consider that it comprised the whole of the original form of the Isaiah Memoir (i.e. 6: 1–8: 18 or 9: 6[7], minus later, secondary additions). There is no way, of course, to prove, or even properly to test, this hypothesis. In the first place, it depends upon the supposition that there ever was such an extensive Memoir. This has become the common view since the work of Budde,[25] but in my opinion it raises a number of difficulties which require that the hypothesis should at the very least be substantially modified. (I

23 Jensen, *The Use of* tôrâ *by Isaiah*, 110–11.

24 See R. R. Wilson, *Prophecy and Society in Ancient Israel* (Philadelphia, 1980); D. L. Petersen, *The Roles of Israel's Prophets* (JSOTS 17; Sheffield, 1981).

25 K. Budde, *Jesajas Erleben: Eine gemeinverständliche Auslegung der Denkschrift des Propheten* (Gotha, 1928).

hope to be able to deal with this issue more fully on another occasion.) Fortunately, however, it is not necessary to settle this question at present. The document might have contained no more than the names of Isaiah's children (8: 18), or it might have contained as much as a full summary of all Isaiah's teaching to date, rather as in the case of Jeremiah's scroll (cf. Jer. 36: 2, 4, 28). We shall never know. What does matter is that Isaiah secured its contents in a formal manner as he 'settled down' to wait.

The period of waiting is not specified, and indeed seems to be open ended, thus implying a further development over the situation envisaged in 8: 1–4. The need to wait, as to undertake the elaborate procedure of 8: 16, was caused by the fact that God was 'hiding his face from the house of Jacob'. It is to be assumed that this was the consequence of the rejection of Isaiah's teaching at the time of the Syro-Ephraimite crisis (hence his withdrawal from the public arena). This rejection would lead to disastrous consequences in the short term, but, when the people had reaped the bitter fruit of their decisions, there would be written testimony to the fact that all that had happened was but a vindication of what God had said through his prophet. Isaiah apparently anticipated that this would be still within his own lifetime,[26] and that therefore he would see the day when he would be able to unseal the document and thereby contribute to the establishment of a truer faith, with all the positive potential which that would entail (this being the implication of the hopeful nature of the verbs in verse 17).

The third passage in Isaiah 1–39 in which there is a reference to the writing down of the prophet's message is 30: 8.

> And now, go, write it before them on a tablet,
>   and inscribe it in a book,
> that it may be for the time to come as a witness* for ever.

Once again, there are a number of obscurities in this text which are

[26] Contrast 30: 8, discussed below. It is perhaps worth noting in passing that the passages under discussion in this chapter testify to a development in certain aspects of Isaiah's thinking about the future. This should serve as a caution against a number of recent attempts to impose a uniform view about this on Isaiah (usually completely negative), and then to delete as secondary any passage which does not fit with this view. Even on the basis of material which can certainly be ascribed to Isaiah, it now seems clear that such consistency is not to be expected. The 'parable of the farmer' in 28: 23–9 (if indeed it comes from Isaiah!) may testify to his consciousness that he could be accused of apparent inconsistency in just this regard.

unlikely to be resolved to everyone's satisfaction in the present state of our knowledge. In particular, the combinations of verb and noun in the first two lines are puzzling. We might have expected 'book' (*sēper*) to be the object of 'write', and 'tablet' (*lûaḥ*) to be the object of 'inscribe' (*ḥqq*). Although various suggestions have been made to help ease this difficulty,[27] the problem is not too serious for the present discussion. All are at least agreed that Isaiah was commanded to write in some form or another.

Equal uncertainty confronts attempts to determine precisely what Isaiah was supposed to write. Opinions vary from a collection of all the genuinely Isaianic material in chapters 28–31 (e.g. Duhm) or at least a selection from those chapters,[28] to a short passage such as verse 9 alone (Fohrer) or the name 'Rahab that is stilled*' in verse 7.[29] An important step towards resolving this issue would be a determination of whether verse 8 belonged from the start as an integral part of verses 6–7 or whether it begins a new, and originally independent, section, but as we saw in the previous chapter (above, p. 87) this in itself is by no means clear. Given such a variety of opinions, it is probably best to conclude that we do not know, and to content ourselves with the observation that whether in extensive or cryptic form Isaiah recorded a summary of his stance during the fateful events of 705–701 BC. So far as we can judge, he consistently argued against political intrigue against Assyria, especially by way of alliance with Egypt (see 30: 1–5; 31: 1–3), and urged rather an attitude of quiet trust in the Lord, which 30: 15 is usually thought to encapsulate. Though a single sentence can hardly be said to do justice to an issue over which so much has been written in recent

[27] For instance, Duhm conjecturally proposes that the words *'al-lûaḥ 'ittām* should be deleted as a secondary imitation of 8: 1, Fohrer ('Entstehung, Komposition und Überlieferung von Jesaja 1–39', 143–4) argues that *sēper* here means 'an inscription', and Wildberger appeals to Akkadian *siparru* to support the translation 'Erz' (copper or bronze). Galling ('Ein Stück judäischen Bodenrechts in Jesaia 8', 213 n. 3) conjecturally proposes the far more radical emendation of the words *'tm w'l-spr hqh* to *'tm m'ly rhqym* ('you are those who are far from me'), which he thinks was the content of what was recorded in writing, but this seems too speculative to warrant further consideration. Of course, a number of commentators also attempt to retain the MT and to justify the kind of rendering represented by the *RSV* cited above. On the apparent parallel in Job 19: 23, see D. J. A. Clines, *Job 1–20* (WBC 17; Dallas, 1989), 432.

[28] e.g. Barth, *Die Jesaja-Worte in der Josiazeit*, 280; Procksch would limit this further to the Isaianic material in the following sections of chapters 30–1 alone.

[29] e.g. Schunk, 'Jes 30 $_{6-8}$ und die Deutung der Rahab im Alten Testament'; Dietrich, *Jesaja und die Politik*, 142; Vermeylen, 411.

years,[30] this summary would seem to cover the substance of what most commentators think that Isaiah was commanded to write, whether in brief or full form.

The reason why it was necessary for Isaiah to write is explicitly stated in verse 9:

> For they are a rebellious people,
> lying sons,
> sons who will not hear
> the instruction of the Lord;

and this is developed in verse 10 by the accusation that they have forbidden the prophets to preach against them, favouring rather to listen only to 'smooth things'. We may confidently assume that Isaiah is here reflecting on his own experience during the time of crisis.[31] This being the case, God's word through the prophet is to be recorded in writing so that it can stand as a witness for those who in future may be more willing to listen to it.[32] It will then demonstrate that Judah's judgement was a sign not of God's weakness, but rather of the execution of his will (Fohrer). Although a decision about whether the document explicitly included words of hope as well as judgement will depend on the unresolved question discussed above, we may agree that such a notion is implicit in the action itself. The phraseology of verse 8 presupposes that the text will be read in some unspecified future time, and, if it is to function then as a witness, it must imply a circle of readers who are more sympathetic to its contents than the present generation.

A difference from chapter 8 now becomes apparent, however, for unlike on that earlier occasion it looks as though Isaiah no longer expected himself to be personally involved in that future day (see Procksch). The text's function as a witness is cast into the indefinite future—*lᵉyôm 'aḥᵃrôn* (see further below)—and the likelihood that this will be remote from Isaiah's lifetime is suggested by the further qualification 'for ever'.

30 Mention need be made of only the massive study by Gonçalves, *L'Expédition de Sennachérib en Palestine*.

31 For a defence of Isaianic authorship against Vermeylen's attempt to find the hand of the Deuteronomists in this passage, see above, pp. 87–8.

32 We should note that the feminine verb *wthy* (verse 8*b*) must have the substance of what was written as its subject (note the feminine suffixes in the first part of the verse), and not the 'tablet' or the 'book' *per se* (both masculine).

To sum up the three passages discussed so far, we may say that they all reflect a common purpose and reason for the writing-down of parts of Isaiah's message, though to start with it is only implicit. The essential elements are the rejection of the prophetic word by Isaiah's contemporaries leading to the writing-down of his words under secure conditions so that they may act as a witness in future, more hopeful days. Until that time, however, his words remain a closed book, as we might say.[33] The theme of witness is common to all three passages, though expressed in slightly different ways, and in two of them the prophet's teaching is referred to somewhat unusually as *tôrâ* (8: 16; 30: 9), a term on which we have already had some occasion to comment (see above, pp. 88–91). A development in Isaiah's stance has been detected, however, with regard to his own position; whereas in chapter 8 he appears to believe that the period of waiting will be relatively short and (8: 17) that he will live to see its completion, by the time of 30: 8 he has abandoned such hope. This was doubtless due not only to the fact that he himself was much older by this time, but more importantly to the growing realization that the people's attitude of rejection was so deep-rooted that no change could be anticipated without some fundamental reorientation. Isaiah saw no prospect of this in the present circumstances (see 22: 14), and he therefore cast his hope into the more remote and indefinite future.[34]

In the light of these considerations, I wish now to proceed to suggest that these passages exerted a profound influence on Deutero-Isaiah in his understanding of his ministry within the unfolding purposes of God. Naturally, we must also bear in mind

[33] Note the recurrence of this theme in 29: 11–12 and 18, though these verses are widely thought to derive from a time long after Isaiah.

[34] This will doubtless raise in some minds the question of how such development can be reconciled with the 'hardening' message of 6: 9–10. Should Isaiah not have realized that his mission was doomed to 'fail' from the start? This question, of course, raises many related issues, but we may suggest for the time being that Isaiah may have been led by circumstances to a more developed understanding of his commission. Assuming that the verses in question were in their present form from an early stage in Isaiah's career, he may initially have anticipated that they were about to be fulfilled in the events of the Syro-Ephraimite war (their particular connection with the record of that war in Isaiah 6–8 has been explored by O. H. Steck). Only later, under the impact of the events of 705–701 BC, did he come to appreciate that the hardening was applicable in an even more radical sense than had at first appeared. Whether this might be sufficient to account for the addition of 6: 12–13*ab* cannot be decided here.

that he would not have approached them in the analytical manner of a modern commentator; it may be assumed that he would readily have associated them with other related material in the work of Proto-Isaiah and would probably have taken the references to writing to apply to the whole of the Isaianic literary deposit which he inherited.

As the period of divine judgement by means of the exile wore on, it may be proposed that Deutero-Isaiah came to appreciate that now was the time of which Isaiah had written when the sealed document was to be opened and a new message of salvation, to which the earlier prophet had alluded, was to be proclaimed. As we shall see, this comes to expression in a number of ways, but it is most clearly articulated in 50: 4–9,[35] and so we may conveniently begin there.

This passage has long been labelled the third servant song. It should be noted, however, that within the passage as usually delimited (50: 4–9) there is no reference to the servant (though verse 10 immediately following testifies to an early interpretation in this direction). Moreover, it differs from the first and fourth of the so-called songs by being cast in the first-person singular. As Whybray has commented, 'in the prophetical books generally the subject of speeches in the first person singular, when it is not Yahweh and not otherwise indicated, is normally the prophet himself' (p. 135). Furthermore, there has been a marked tendency in recent writing to move away from an interpretation of these passages in isolation from their present literary context.[36] Pursuing this line, Wilcox and Paton-Williams comment on 50: 4–9 that 'there is a prevailing identification of the servant with the prophet in chs. 49–55, and given that the words of this song are in any case inappropriate to Israel, this further combination of circumstances makes it very likely that the prophet is indeed the subject of these verses'.[37]

In this passage, the speaker claims to be one who faithfully listens

[35] See, independently, R. J. Clifford, *Fair Spoken and Persuading: An Interpretation of Second Isaiah* (New York, 1984), 161–3.

[36] See above, Ch. 2 n. 4; a comprehensive survey of work on the servant passages in Deutero-Isaiah has been compiled by H. Haag, *Der Gottesknecht bei Deuterojesaja* (Erträge der Forschung, 233; Darmstadt, 1985).

[37] See Wilcox and Paton-Williams, 'The Servant Songs in Deutero-Isaiah', 94. Note that even North concedes that 'the passage almost certainly embodies something of the Prophet's experience' (p. 202).

to what God has to say. Unlike the earlier generation, whose ears were made heavy so that they could not hear (6: 10), this prophet has his ears opened daily to hear (50: 4*b*-5*a*).[38]

Moreover, he both hears 'like those who are taught' (*kallimmûdîm*) and has 'the tongue of those who are taught' (*l*ᵉ*šôn limmûdîm*) (verse 4; see the Appendix). This, of course, is precisely the word which is used in 8: 16, where it is often translated 'disciples'. It occurs only six times in the Hebrew Bible, twice in Jeremiah and four times in Isaiah. The two occurrences in Jeremiah are entirely different from those in Isaiah and they seem to be irrelevant to our subject. In Jer. 2: 24[39] it refers to a wild ass who is 'used to' the desert, while in 13: 23 it is used in the construct plural to describe those who are 'accustomed to do evil' (*limmudê hārēaʿ*). The occurrences in Isaiah, by contrast, seem to be closely associated with each other. They all use the word in the plural, and they all have the positive meaning of those who are instructed by God, either directly or through his prophet. We have already taken note of Isa. 8: 16 and 50: 4 (twice). The fourth occurrence is at 54: 13, where the prophet looks forward to the day when 'all your sons shall be taught by the Lord [*limmûdê yhwh*]'. It must be regarded as highly probable that all three occurrences in Deutero-Isaiah reflect the influence of 8: 16–17. At 50: 4, Deutero-Isaiah consciously includes himself among the group of those who witnessed the sealing of the prophetic teaching; indeed, it is not impossible that, like Jerome and some more modern commentators such as Dillmann, he took the imperatives of 8: 16 as having been spoken by God himself (i.e. simply continuing the divine speech of verses 11–15), so that 'my disciples' will mean disciples of God, precisely his own role at 50: 4. Even without that, however, the parallel is striking, and his emphasis on the word implies that he is one of those who is 'qualified ' to unseal the document. Again, at 54: 13, the reference to 'all your sons' being taught by the Lord suggests a reversal of 30:

38 It is sometimes suggested that verse 5*a* is an accidental repetition of parts of verse 4. This is not entirely accurate, since the verb *pt*ḥ (to open) does not occur there. Alternatively, Westermann suggests that half a line may have dropped out following 5*a*. Even if 5*a* is to be deleted, the important point for our present purposes is adequately stated in verse 4. More radical still are the proposals of G. Schwartz ('Jesaja $50_{4-5a}$: Eine Emendation', *ZAW* 85 (1973), 356–7), but even so they do not affect the main points at issue in the present analysis.

39 Assuming that the MT is correct; cf. W. McKane, *A Critical and Exegetical Commentary on Jeremiah*, i (ICC; Edinburgh, 1986), 43–7; W. L. Holladay, *Jeremiah 1* (Philadelphia, 1986), 53, 100–1.

9; it further implies that Deutero-Isaiah looked forward to the day when his own faithfulness would be adopted by the whole of the new community. In this, there is a striking similarity to the use of the plural 'servants of the Lord' a few verses later in 54: 17, where again there is the suggestion that the role of the servant figure is here (for the only time in Deutero-Isaiah) being transferred to all the members of the community.[40]

A further point of contact with one of the key passages in Proto-Isaiah comes at 50: 5*b*. Whereas the earlier generation was characterized as 'a rebellious people [*'am m^e rî*] . . . who will not hear [*lō'-'ābû š^e môa'*] the instruction of the Lord' (30: 9), so that Isaiah was obliged to commit his teaching to writing, this figure associates his listening (*lišmōa'* (verse 4)) to God's word with the statement that 'I was not rebellious' (*w^e 'ānōkî lō' mārîtî*). These are the only two places where the root *mrh* occurs in Isaiah 1–55. Along similar lines, Clifford[41] has additionally drawn attention to the links between 30: 12 and 50: 10, namely the paired verbs 'trust' and 'rely upon' (*š'n 'l/b* (niph.) and *bṭḥ b*). While this is suggestive, it should be noted that it does not refer directly to the speaker in 50: 4–9, so that, while the possibility of influence in a general way may certainly be entertained (especially in view of the fact that they are part of a more extended set of similarities between two passages), these parallels cannot contribute to the specific interpretation of the role of Deutero-Isaiah himself which we are here suggesting.

Finally, it may be of significance that, whereas the Lord 'hides his face from the house of Jacob' because they refuse to listen to him (8: 17), this prophet states that 'I did not hide my face from shame and spitting' (50: 6) when openness to God's word leads in turn to his rejection. All in all, therefore, we may conclude that in his own person Deutero-Isaiah meets the conditions necessary to open the long-sealed book which bespeaks the end of God's judgement, and that he has deliberately portrayed himself in that role. Furthermore, he looks forward to the day when this will be true too of all Zion's children (54: 13).

If reflection on these key passages from Proto-Isaiah was of

[40] See K. Jeppesen, 'From "You, My Servant" to "The Hand of the Lord is with my Servants"', *SJOT* (1990/1), 113–29; and cf. W. A. M. Beuken, 'The Main Theme of Trito-Isaiah: "The Servants of YHWH"', *JSOT* 47 (1990), 67–87.

[41] See Clifford, *Fair Spoken and Persuading*, 162.

such significance for Deutero-Isaiah's understanding of his own ministry, we should expect them to be referred to in other parts of his work as well, and this indeed proves to be the case.

First, the unusual use of *tôrâ* to describe the prophet's teaching occurs in two of them, and in Chapter 4 we noted that this was also a characteristic of Deutero-Isaiah.

Secondly, we also observed that Deutero-Isaiah uses similar language to that found in 30: 9 to explain the reason for the judgement of the exile.

Thirdly, similar concerns lie behind the phrasing of the lament which the exiles are portrayed as uttering in 40: 27:

> Why do you say, O Jacob,
> and speak, O Israel,
> 'My way is hid [*nist*ᵉ*râ*] from the Lord,
> and my right is disregarded by my God'?

Although this may be a citation of an actual lament uttered by the exiles (so Westermann), it is noteworthy that it expresses just the sentiment which might be expected from 'the house of Jacob' from whom, according to 8: 17, God was 'hiding his face'. The combination of addressee and sentiment suggest that Deutero-Isaiah had the earlier passage in mind as he shaped this key passage. The reference to *mišpāṭî*, translated 'my right' by *RSV*, introduces one of the major themes in Deutero-Isaiah's work,[42] and so confirms that he selected this particular lament with care; it expresses concisely the depressed condition of those to whom he was to deliver his new word of salvation.

Fourthly, in both passages there is a contrast between the rejected house of Jacob and those who derive their strength from 'waiting' (*qwh*) on the Lord (8: 17 and 40: 31; see also 49: 23).

Fifthly, it is likely[43] that 8: 17 is consciously picked up and then reversed at 54: 8:

> In overflowing wrath for a moment
> I hid my face from you,
> but with everlasting love I will have compassion on you,
> says the Lord, your redeemer.

Sixthly, it is noteworthy that at 30: 8 Isaiah stated that the

42 Cf. W. A. M. Beuken, '*Mišpāṭ*: The First Servant Song and its Context', *VT* 22 (1972), 1–30.

43 See Matheus, *Singt dem Herrn ein neues Lied*, 164.

written text should serve as a witness 'for the time to come' (*l^eyôm 'aḥ^arôn*). In our discussion of 8: 23 in Chapter 4 above we saw how this kind of language was taken up by Deutero-Isaiah in the formulation of his understanding about the new situation in which he lived by contrast with the former times which were now passed. It is thus of considerable significance that the group of passages which we have been examining in this chapter is also tied in to this fundamental theme of his.

Finally, we should certainly follow Clements[44] in picking up the theme of 'witness' in Deutero-Isaiah. We have already seen that this is central to all three of the passages discussed in Proto-Isaiah. Because the people had rejected the prophet's message, it had to be committed to writing, initially in the presence of witnesses (8: 2), but later (8: 16; 30: 8*) in order that the document itself might function as a witness for the time to come. Deutero-Isaiah believed himself to be living at that time, however, and in consequence he envisages a development of this theme. The most important passage for consideration is 43: 8–13. In this trial-speech, the exiles are summoned to act as witnesses (verses 10 and 12) to the identity of the true God, even though on the face of it they are singularly unsuited to this role:

> Bring forth the people who are blind, yet have eyes,
> who are deaf, yet have ears!

There can be little doubt that the use of this striking language (whose connections with Isaiah 6 we have already examined in Chapter 3 above) is intended to refer back to 42: 18–20, where the same paradox is expressed. There, however, it introduces one of the key passages explaining why the exiles were suffering God's judgement (42: 18–25):

> Hear, you deaf;
> and look, you blind, that you may see!
> Who is blind but my servant,
> or deaf as my messenger whom I send?
> . . . . . . . . . . .
> He sees many things, but does not observe them;
> his ears are open, but he does not hear. (see the Appendix)

In the present form of the text, it can hardly be coincidental that

[44] Clements, 'Beyond Tradition-History', 107.

between this summoning of the blind and the deaf who in the first paragraph are so culpable but in the second so valuable as witnesses there comes a powerful oracle of salvation in 43: 1–7, which assures the exiles of God's care, redemption, and gathering of the dispersion. That, and that alone, is the reason why they can now act as his witnesses. Precisely because of their helplessness, they testify to the fact that God, and no other, is saviour (43: 11–13).

It would seem, then, that Deutero-Isaiah is developing several lines of thought here with an internal consistency. In the earlier, pre-exilic situation, God's word written served as a witness to Israel, testifying to the fact that their judgement was his intended work and not a sign of weakness on his part. Now, however, their salvation has as part of its purpose a function in his wider dispute with the nations and their idols. In line with this, it is Israel herself who takes over the role of witness. Rather in the manner of the development of the ideas of 'disciples' and 'servants' in 54: 13 and 17, so too here; in the scheme of God's wider purposes, all the people of Israel adopt collectively the function which previously had been assumed by only an individual or small group in its relation to the people as a whole.

Similar thoughts lie behind the other references to the people as God's witnesses. According to 44: 8, it is precisely because God has 'declared it beforehand' that they can now serve as his witnesses. In other words, because of their new experiences they will be in a position to replace the sealed book as witnesses to God's faithful word. Isa. 55: 4 is not so clear in all its details, but seems to fit with the main pattern of thinking which we have detected. There, the prophet reminds his readers that David was 'a witness to the peoples', but since in the previous verse he has already declared that God is in some sense transferring the terms of the Davidic covenant to 'you' (plural), it is not surprising to find that in verse 5 he can go on to declare that 'you shall call nations that you know not, and nations that knew you not shall run to you'. The label 'democratization' has often been applied to this treatment of the Davidic theme by Deutero-Isaiah;[45] our survey suggests that this would not be an inappropriate term to apply to several other parts of his understanding of Israel's new role as well.

If my reasoning up to this point is generally sound, then it seems to

[45] Reference is frequently made to Eissfeldt, 'The Promises of Grace to David in Isaiah 55: 1–5', though so far as I can see he does not himself use the expression.

me that we can no longer rest content with talking merely about the influence of First Isaiah on Second. The manner in which Deutero-Isaiah makes use of the theme of 'the former things', the way in which he interprets his ministry as an opening of a book long sealed up, and the cumulative effect of minor allusions to a body of earlier material, such as that noted at 44: 26, together demand that from the outset he deliberately included the earlier work in his own. I have already argued at length that he did not develop his work in isolation from the literary deposit of First Isaiah, as earlier scholars supposed. More recently, we have noted that several have come to the conclusion that in some way he expected his new message to be read alongside the earlier work. In particular, of course, this view fits well with an understanding of some of his uses of 'the former things' as including a reference to earlier prophecy,[46] among which it is almost inevitable that we should see an allusion principally to the literary deposit of First Isaiah, especially in view of the contrasting mention in 30: 8 of the *yôm 'aḥ$^{a}$rôn*, loosely translated by *RSV* as 'the time to come'.

What I am here proposing is that we should take the next logical step by doing justice to the internal dynamic of his argument and maintain that he regarded his own work as an integral continuation of the work of Isaiah, or, which comes to the same thing, that he bound the version of Isaiah's book into his own as the necessary precursor to what he was now announcing to his compatriots in exile. If important aspects of his own work were never meant to be understood apart from their connection with the earlier material, it seems only reasonable to suggest that he included that material along with his own fresh contribution.

Analogies on a smaller scale from other prophetic books readily suggest themselves. To take one example, it has long been found

[46] Others who see a reference to First Isaiah in these passages include Jones, 'The Traditio of the Oracles of Isaiah of Jerusalem'; Becker, *Isaias—der Prophet und sein Buch*, 37–8; Childs, *Introduction to the Old Testament as Scripture*, 328–40; Meade, *Pseudonymity and Canon*, 35–7; Albertz, 'Das Deuterojesaja-Buch als Fortschreibung der Jesaja-Prophetie', 251–3; and C. R. Seitz, *Zion's Final Destiny: The Development of the Book of Isaiah: A Reassessment of Isaiah 36–39* (Minneapolis, 1991), 199–202. An additional argument in favour of this approach, which does not seem to have been noted previously, is that, when Isa. 65: 16*b*–17 refers to this aspect of Deutero-Isaiah's thought, it clearly relates 'the former things' to the time of Israel's judgement. It should, perhaps, be emphasized that there is no suggestion that this interpretation should be applied to every occurrence of 'the former things'; 43: 18, for instance, seems most probably to refer to the Exodus.

difficult to ascribe the closing verses of the book of Amos to the eighth-century prophet. More recently, however, it has been observed that these verses cannot have been conceived in isolation and then tacked on to the book of Amos as part of the wider process by which, following the historical vindication of their warnings, the prophets of judgement became, paradoxically, to be interpreted as messengers of hope.[47] Rather, these verses so clearly pick up vocabulary and themes from elsewhere in Amos that they must have been composed specifically for their present setting;[48] as it is now presented to us, the book of Amos is expected by its editor or redactor to be read as a complete whole.

Of course, what I am proposing in connection with the book of Isaiah is on a much larger scale than this small example from the book of Amos. Furthermore, it demands as an important consequence that Deutero-Isaiah was involved in the process of composition from the very start of his ministry. It has often been thought that his ministry was oral, and that the setting of his words in writing was the work of subsequent disciples or collectors.[49] It is, of course, entirely probable that he exercised a spoken ministry amongst the exiles in Babylon, but that does not rule out a self-awareness of his unique association with the work of his Judaean predecessor or an intention to present his work in literary form from the start. Indeed, the whole orientation of his recorded words seems to demand that he did.[50]

There is a further possible consequence of this understanding of the work of Deutero-Isaiah. If indeed he associated the written presentation of his oracles with the literary deposit of Proto-Isaiah from the start as part and parcel of the same 'book', did he in fact contribute anything to what we now find in Isaiah 1–39? On the face of it, we might expect that he would have subjected the work of his

[47] Cf. R. E. Clements, 'Patterns in the Prophetic Canon', in G. W. Coats and B. O. Long (eds.), *Canon and Authority: Essays in Old Testament Religion and Theology* (Philadelphia, 1977), 42–55.

[48] See J. W. Groves (*Actualization and Interpretation in the Old Testament* (SBLDS 86; Atlanta, 1987), 179–91), who concludes that 'the sum total of the parallels forms a significant network of literary allusions' (p. 189).

[49] For a survey of opinions with discussion, see Y. Gitay, 'Deutero-Isaiah: Oral or Written?', *JBL* 99 (1980), 185–97.

[50] For a quite different line of argument, but one which also sees an internal association of prophecy and the written word, this time in the case of Deutero-Isaiah's slightly earlier predecessor in the exile, Ezekiel, see E. F. Davis, *Swallowing the Scroll: Textuality and the Dynamics of Discourse in Ezekiel's Prophecy* (JSOTS 78; Sheffield, 1989).

predecessor to some kind of redaction in order to integrate his own substantial addition at the end more closely. Assuming that there were recognizable sections within the material which he inherited, for instance, it would not have been inconsistent of him to add at their conclusion pointers towards the kind of resolution which he was ultimately going to furnish for the work as a whole. In the next chapter, we shall turn to examine whether or not there is any solid evidence for the work of Deutero-Isaiah himself within Isaiah 1–39.

# 6

## Deutero-Isaiah and Isaiah 2–12

AT the end of the previous chapter the question was raised whether any evidence could be found for the work of Deutero-Isaiah within the present form of chapters 1–39. As is well known, for instance, a few commentators have maintained that chapter 35 should be ascribed to the later prophet,[1] and have included it in their commentaries on the latter part of the work. If they are right (a question to which naturally we must return), it would furnish a good example of the sort of evidence we are looking for, since it rounds off the whole section of the poetic material in 1–39, and thus might well be thought to be part of Deutero-Isaiah's redactional activity. The commentators just referred to are at a loss to explain how this chapter came to its present position; McKenzie, for instance, can do no more than surmise 'that this poem was detached from the other poems of Second Isaiah and by some roundabout way reached the collection of First Isaiah independently' (p. 12). The merit of our fresh way of regarding the development of the book of Isaiah is that it would provide a clear explanation for both why and how this happened.

In fact, the evidence to be presented in this and the following two chapters can never be said to amount to proof of the position being maintained. Whereas the case which has been developed up to this point seems to me to reach a high degree of probability, it should be frankly admitted that we move now into the realm of what might best be termed plausible hypothesis. There are two main reasons for this. In the first place, the amount of text is much more restricted than the two large blocks of material which have formed the basis of the examination so far. Consequently, it will seldom be

[1] e.g. Torrey and McKenzie; McKenzie also includes chapter 34, though he is less certain about its precise authorship.

possible to provide more than a few points of contact on which to form a judgement. Secondly, even in the places where a strong prima-facie argument exists for detecting the hand of Deutero-Isaiah, the possibility of secondary imitation needs always to be borne in mind. The situation is not unlike that which is found in parts of Trito-Isaiah. There too (e.g. in 60–2) the similarities are such that some scholars would actually ascribe them to Deutero-Isaiah himself,[2] whereas others prefer to think only of strong influence and conscious imitation. It is, therefore, perhaps worth adding the comment that even if the precise form of the case to be made out below does not prove acceptable, the evidence presented may still retain some independent value as testifying to an important redactional level in the composition of Isaiah 1–39.

This all being readily conceded, the persuasive force of the argument has naturally to depend to some extent upon its inherent simplicity and consequent attractiveness as a plausible way of accounting for an important phase in the growth of the book. It is clear to anyone familiar with the modern literature on the book of Isaiah that many theories about how it developed are almost self-defeating because of the number and complexities of the redactional layers which are postulated. While we do not know anything like as much as we could wish about the way in which books developed in antiquity, there still comes a point where unduly complicated hypotheses strain credulity to breaking-point. If, on the other hand, we have managed to establish that a particular author (in this case, Deutero-Isaiah) incorporated an earlier work into his own, rather like a source, then it becomes reasonable to allow that to influence our judgement to some extent in regarding possible examples of his handling of that 'source' as in fact probable.

Although the nature of the literature is quite different, a certain analogy might be drawn with the Chronicler's treatment of the books of Samuel and Kings. There, where we have both the source and the completed text available for comparison, we can see how he regularly 'tops and tails' the material which he has inherited—for example, by the addition of editorial comment at the end of his

[2] e.g. N. H. Snaith, 'Isaiah 40–66: A Study of the Teaching of the Second Isaiah and its Consequences', in H. M. Orlinsky and N. H. Snaith, *Studies on the Second Part of the Book of Isaiah* (SVT 14; Leiden, 1977[2]), 139–46.

account of the death of Saul in 1 Chron. 10: 13–14 or his new introduction to the account of the transfer of the ark to Jerusalem in 1 Chron. 13: 1–5. Of course, there are many other smaller changes which it would probably be impossible to detect did we not have his *Vorlage* present in front of us, and similarly there can be no likelihood that we would be able to detect all the details of Deutero-Isaiah's redaction of chapters 1–39, but that need not prevent us from at least attempting to isolate some of the more obvious examples. One other point that we might learn from this crude analogy is that redactors not only compose material from scratch as a means of setting older material in a new interpretative framework; they also sometimes rearrange existing material in a new order to achieve the same effect (see, for example, 1 Chronicles 14 or 2 Chronicles 1). If we come across evidence that what once may have been a connected passage has been subsequently rearranged, it will be worth asking whether this, too, is to be ascribed to conscious redaction rather than accidental transposition or careless handling.

With these introductory remarks in mind, it would seem most orderly to take the three major blocks of Isaiah 1–39 (i.e. 1–12; 13–27; 28–39) in order, devoting a separate chapter to each. Within each chapter, however, we shall not necessarily keep to the present arrangement of the text, but rather work in the order which enables us to present the case with the greatest clarity.

It is widely agreed that the psalm-like passage in Isaiah 12 marks a major break in the book. It is followed by a fresh heading in 13: 1 which introduces the lengthy section of 'oracles against the nations' in 13–23, and it has a number of connections with the preceding chapters which suggest that it has been shaped to function as a conscious conclusion. The allusions to the exodus in verses 2 and 5 by way of an echo of Exod. 15: 2 and 1 respectively (as well as the possibility that verse 3 may be intended as a reference to the story of water from the rock; see Schoors) have long been noted as connecting closely with the closing verses of chapter 11.[3] Further afield, the reference to God's anger (verse 1) may look back to 5: 25; 9: 11[12], 16[17], 20[21]; 10: 4, 5, and 25, the theme of the exaltation of God's name in verse 4 picks up the language of 2: 11 and 17, and the presence of the Lord in Zion (verse 6) occurs in

[3] So already Skinner; Marti; Gray.

several earlier passages, not least in 2: 2–4.[4] Vermeylen's development of a suggestion of Schulz[5] that the chapter looks forward in providing part of a framework for the oracles against the nations thus seems misguided. His principal argument is that he finds some parallels with chapters 25–6, but if correct these can equally well be explained as an editor rounding off two sections in a similar manner; a literary parallel need not automatically be an *inclusio*.

There have often been doubts expressed as to the unity of the chapter. There seems to be a second introduction in verse 4, and there are changes in person between singular and plural between verses 2 and 3 and 5 and 6. More recently, however, it has been observed that these two criteria do not dovetail with each other, so that there is doubt as to whether the division should come after verse 2 or verse 3; consequently, it is now regarded as more likely that the chapter is a unity, but comprised of two parts with different, though related, content; the first concentrates on praise for God's salvation, while the second moves on to proclaim this universally and so to summon the whole earth to join in worship.[6] Form-critically, the chapter is thus something of a mixture, but, since even within its constituent parts it combines more than one form,[7] that in itself is no argument against compositional unity.

There are several reasons for suspecting that this chapter could well have been written as part of Deutero-Isaiah's redaction of Isaiah 1–39. First, it shows similarity of general form with the so-called 'eschatological hymns of praise' as isolated and described by Westermann.[8] Although the praise relates to events that still lie in the future, the substantiation is cast in the past tense.[9] As he puts it,

[4] Cf. L. Alonso-Schökel, 'Is 12: De duabis methodis pericopam explicandi', *VD* 34 (1956), 154–60; Auvray; Ackroyd, 'Isaiah i–xii', 37–8.

[5] H. Schulz, *Das Buch Nahum: Eine redaktionskritische Untersuchung* (BZAW 129; Berlin, 1973), 118; Vermeylen, 280–2.

[6] So Wildberger; Auvray; Ackroyd, 'Isaiah i–xii', 36–7; Werner, *Eschatologische Texte in Jesaja 1–39*, 165–7.

[7] See the careful discussion by Wildberger, and cf. F. Crüsemann, *Studien zur Formgeschichte von Hymnus und Danklied in Israel* (WMANT 32; Neukirchen-Vluyn, 1969), 55–65.

[8] C. Westermann, 'Sprache und Struktur der Prophetie Deuterojesajas', in *Forschung am Alten Testament* (ThB 24; Munich, 1964), 92–170, with reference to 42: 10–13; 44: 23; 45: 8; 48: 20–1; 49: 13; 51: 3(?); 52: 9–10; 54: 1–2.

[9] So clearly in verses 2, 4, and 5, and by probable emendation in verse 1 (see the Appendix). The recasting of the verbs at the end of verse 1 as jussives has parallels at 42: 6 and 51: 2, and is to be explained as 'a dogmatic emendation [*sc.* by the Masoretes] . . . in order to represent historical statements as promises', no doubt because of what was perceived as a problem of non-fulfilment; cf GK §107*b* n. 2.

'faith in his message is expressed by raising of cries of exultation at God's act of deliverance, conceived as already accomplished, even although there is no visible evidence to prove it.'[10] If Westermann is right in his claim that 'this is a form of psalm found only in the prophecy of Deutero-Isaiah and is the product of his prophecy',[11] then its occurrence also in Isaiah 12 must point firmly in the direction of his authorship. Of course, the introductory 'You will say in that day' is not found in chapters 40–55, but it is a logical addition within the context of the first part of the book (see also 25: 9; 26: 1; 27: 2); by the time of the later chapters, 'that day' is presented as having now arrived.

Secondly, Westermann has also argued that these eschatological hymns of praise are sometimes used as major structural markers in Deutero-Isaiah, because he thinks that they serve to mark the conclusions of the major sections of the book. This proposal has now been developed by Matheus, whose careful and comprehensive study argues that this is in fact true of all the hymns of praise in Deutero-Isaiah and indeed that they are so carefully related by theme and vocabulary with the sections which they round off or introduce that they must have been integral parts of the literary composition of Isaiah 40–55 from the start. While not all would agree with this suggestion in every case, not least because of the difficulties of knowing quite how the major sections of Deutero-Isaiah are to be determined, there are some cases at least which would command widespread agreement; 44: 23 and 48: 20–1 are good examples. It is noteworthy that, as we have seen, Isaiah 12 functions in exactly the same way.

Thirdly, and more importantly, the major themes of the chapter are very much of a piece with those of Deutero-Isaiah, and in some cases this is underlined by the use of characteristic vocabulary. The psalm envisages three main phases in God's dealings with his people: a time of suffering God's anger (verse 1), a change to the experience of his salvation with accompanying joy (verses 1*c*–3, 6), and a proclamation of this to the nations, who in turn are summoned to join in the praise (verses 4–5).

[10] Westermann, 20 = ET 20.

[11] Westermann, 166 = ET 205. For a full discussion of the form and structure of Deutero-Isaiah's hymns, see now Matheus, *Singt dem Herrn ein neues Lied*, esp. 30–55; he accepts that there are novel aspects to Deutero-Isaiah's mode of expression in these passages, but denies that they amount to a new *Gattung*: 'wohl ist dies ein neuer, eigener Ausdruck, nicht jedoch eine Gattung' (p. 53).

This corresponds to the letter with Deutero-Isaiah's thought. He too speaks of the exile as a period when Israel experienced God's anger; see 42: 25 and 48: 9 (in both of which *'ap* is used, as in 12: 1); 47: 6; 51: 17, 20, 22; 54: 8–9.

The time of salvation is then initially described by the verb 'thou didst comfort me' (*wtnḥmny**). This verb is highly characteristic of Deutero-Isaiah;[12] it is not only emphasized by repetition in the opening words of his work (40: 1), but it recurs in a number of other places as well: 49: 13; 51: 3, 12, 19; 52: 9; 54: 11. It may well have been that Deutero-Isaiah intended it especially to reverse the mournful refrain of Lamentations 1 that 'there is none to comfort her' (and equivalents); cf. Lam. 1: 2, 9, 16, 17, 21. If so, it would reinforce the impression that it entered the book of Isaiah through him. In view of its use in chapter 12, it is perhaps particularly striking that on two occasions at least in 40–55 it also occurs as part of the substantiation in the past tense in an eschatological hymn of praise; see 49: 13; 52: 9.[13]

For the era of salvation in Isaiah 12, furthermore, the noun *yᵉšûʿâ* is used three times, twice in verse 2 and once in verse 3. This noun, which does not occur in any of the genuine oracles of Isaiah of Jerusalem, is also characteristic of Deutero-Isaiah; see 49: 6, 8; 51: 6, 8; 52: 7, 10.[14]

Similarly, the implication of chapter 12 that the new time of salvation will be reminiscent of the first exodus is a well-known feature of Deutero-Isaiah,[15] but again forms no part of the written deposit of Isaiah of Jerusalem. If it is correct, in view of this

[12] As noted too by Rendtorff, 'Zur Komposition des Buches Jesaja', 298–300.

[13] Additionally, 51: 3 is a fragment of such a hymn according to Westermann and Matheus, but this is by no means certain; Whybray, for instance, emphatically rejects the suggestion.

[14] The situation is not materially different if all derivatives of the root *yšʿ* are taken into account; cf. Ackroyd, 'Isaiah i–xii', 38–9.

[15] Cf. B. W. Anderson, 'Exodus Typology in Second Isaiah', in B. W. Anderson and W. Harrelson (eds.), *Israel's Prophetic Heritage: Essays in Honor of James Muilenburg* (New York, 1962), 177–95; and 'Exodus and Covenant in Second Isaiah and Prophetic Tradition', in F. M. Cross, W. E. Lemke, and P. D. Miller (eds.), *Magnalia Dei, The Mighty Acts of God: Essays on the Bible and Archaeology in Memory of G. Ernest Wright* (Garden City, NY, 1976), 339–60; W. Zimmerli, 'Der "neue Exodus" in der Verkündigung der beiden grossen Exilspropheten', in *Gottes Offenbarung: Gesammelte Aufsätze zum Alten Testament* (ThB 19; Munich, 1963), 192–204; and D. Baltzer, *Ezechiel und Deuterojesaja: Berührungen in der Heilserwartung der beiden großen Exilspropheten* (BZAW 121; Berlin, 1971), 12–24, *pace* H. M. Barstad, *A Way in the Wilderness* (*JSS* monograph, 12; Manchester, 1989).

connection, to regard verse 3 as in part, at least, a recollection of the time when the Israelites were provided with water in the wilderness, then it will provide a further point of association with Deutero-Isaiah's expectation of the return from exile; see 41: 17–18 (note especially the use of *ma'yān* in 12: 3 and 41: 18); 43: 19–20; 44: 3–4; 48: 21; 49: 10.

In a general way, the joy that will accompany the experience of salvation is prominent in Deutero-Isaiah (see the references above, p. 73) and it is reflected too in 12: 3 and 6. Beyond that, however, a particularly impressive point of contact is provided by the use of *ṣahᵃlî wārōnnî* in verse 6. These two verbs are also found together, again as feminine singular imperatives addressed to Zion, at 54: 1. A further small indicator comes from the form of this address to Zion: the use of the feminine singular participle *yôšebet* as a collective or even personification for 'the inhabitants of' Zion[16] is comparable with the *mᵉbaśśeret ṣiyyôn* of 40: 9. The only other use of this construction with *ṣiyyôn* is at Jer. 51: 35, where again we find *yôšebet ṣiyyôn*. The association of Jeremiah 50–1 with themes common to Proto- and Deutero-Isaiah has been repeatedly noted in the previous chapters, and thus need cause no surprise here.

Turning to the proclamation of God's deeds among the nations and the summons to 'all the earth' to join in praising him, we again find ourselves in a world of ideas which is familiar from Deutero-Isaiah and which scarcely needs full documentation. Nor is it necessary to take sides on the issue whether he is to be regarded as a 'nationalist' or a 'universalist', because precisely the same dispute could be said to confront the interpretation of chapter 12. The vocabulary of 12: 4–5 is not sufficiently specific to provide striking points of comparison. However, there are a number of similarities; limiting ourselves for the sake of convenience to the eschatological hymns of praise, we may note as examples the call for 'praise from the end of the earth' in 42: 10, the proclamation 'to the end of the earth' in 48: 20, and statements that God has acted 'before the eyes of all the nations' and that 'all the ends of the earth shall see the salvation of our God' in 52: 10. Additionally, the absolute use of *kî-'āśâ yhwh* ('for the Lord has done it') at 44: 23 is not unlike the *kî gē'ût 'āśâ* ('for he has done gloriously') of 12: 5.

These three phases of God's dealings with his people according to Isaiah 12—his anger, his salvation, and his revelation to the

[16] Cf. GK §112*s*; Joüon §134*o*.

nations—may thus all be seen to relate this chapter closely to the world of Deutero-Isaiah. Finally, we should draw attention to three features of the chapter which further suggest its close association with the Isaiah tradition as a whole. These do not, of course, direct us exclusively to Deutero-Isaiah, but they at least add weight to the contention that this chapter was composed from within that tradition, so making an ascription to Deutero-Isaiah that much more reasonable. First, there is the characteristic divine title, 'the Holy One of Israel', at the climax of the passage. Secondly, there is the similarly climactic reference to the presence of God in Zion. And, thirdly, it has been suggested that the threefold use of *yᵉšûʿâ* ('salvation'), noted above, may have been consciously employed because of its association with the name Isaiah itself.[17]

In the light of all this evidence, it would seem reasonable to conclude that Isaiah 12 could well have been written by Deutero-Isaiah, and that he set it in its present position as a conclusion to one of the main parts of the work which he was including in his book. The only element which would be out of place in chapters 40–55 is the introductory phrase 'You will say in that day', but as we have seen this is fully intelligible as a device to help work such material into chapters 1–39 in a proleptic fashion. Apart from that, the chapter functions just like the eschatological hymns of praise in 40–55.[18]

This conclusion sets the chapter a little earlier than has been suggested by most other scholars, who generally date it in the post-exilic, rather than the exilic, period. We must, therefore, ask whether their reasons for so doing are sufficiently strong to overturn our proposal. The fact of the connection with the end of chapter 11 points only to a date as late as that passage, not necessarily later, as seems often to be supposed, since the possibility must be allowed that the two passages come from the same author. We shall be considering chapter 11 shortly, and we will see that it supports, rather than detracts from, our case. Part of Werner's reason for a later date comes from his observation (in dependence on Fohrer) that the chapter testifies to a belief in a time of salvation following chronologically after the time of judgement, something

[17] Cf. Procksch, who even wonders whether 'the wells of salvation' might not be a veiled reference to the book of Isaiah; Alonso-Schökel, 'Is 12', 158; Auvray; Schoors; Ackroyd, 'Isaiah i–xii', 38–9.

[18] See also Matheus, *Singt dem Herrn ein neues Lied*, 159–64. He, however, ascribes Isaiah 12 to the redaction of the book of Isaiah as a whole (p. 164).

which he believes is never the case with the pre-exilic Isaiah.[19] This, however, as we have sought to lay out in some detail, by no means demands a date later than Deutero-Isaiah, since he himself clearly adheres to this same point of view. Similarly, when Kaiser refers to the chapter's character and thought as late, the same point can be made in reply.

The chief argument, however, which goes back at least to the time of Duhm, comes from the connections between the chapter and other passages in the Old Testament, principally Exodus 15 and various Psalms, all thought to be late. In the case of Exodus 15, however, it is precarious in the extreme to base any such conclusion on a passage which the overwhelming majority of commentators regard as pre-exilic at the very least.[20] Among the Psalms, the closest points of comparison are of verse 4 with Pss. 105: 1 and 148: 13. Several difficulties stand in the way of using such material for absolute dating, however. In the first place, it hardly needs saying that the dates of the Psalms themselves are highly uncertain in most cases. Secondly, the kind of phrases in question may often have had a general currency in the cult before they were taken up by the particular psalmists whose compositions we now have. In fact, our chapter has a striking example of this fact: verse 2*b* in its entirety is almost identical with Ps. 118: 14; we might well have been tempted to think that it must therefore be dependent on the Psalm—were it not for the fact that exactly the same line also occurs in Exod. 15: 2! Either, or both, of these points could account for the parallel with Ps. 105: 1. It may not be later than the exilic period, but even if it were, the opening call to praise, which is all that we are concerned with, is of just that general nature which could well have enjoyed

[19] Cf. Werner, *Eschatologische Texte in Jesaja 1–39*, 167.

[20] This date, it should be noted, is by no means necessarily dependent on the linguistic evidence which has sometimes been advanced in favour of an extremely early (pre-monarchic) date for this passage (on which cf. D. A. Robertson, *Linguistic Evidence in Dating Early Hebrew Poetry* (SBLDS 3; Missoula, Mont., 1972)), but which others regard as too speculative for certainty; cf. Day (*God's Conflict*, 97–101), who argues that the tenth century must be regarded as the *terminus a quo*, but who sees no objection to a 'relatively early' date, and T. N. D. Mettinger (*The Dethronement of Sabaoth: Studies in the Shem and Kabod Theologies* (ConB, OT Ser., 18; Lund, 1982), 75–6), who dates it to the time of Josiah. (He notes that there appears to be a direct reference to Exod. 15: 16 at Isa. 43: 21.) The recent monograph of M. L. Brenner (*The Song of the Sea: Ex 15: 1–21* (BZAW 195; Berlin, 1991)) includes a useful survey of research on pp. 3–18. His own attempt to uphold a post-exilic date, however, is problematic; see J. Day, Review of Brenner, *The Song of the Sea*, in *ExpT* 103 (1991), 82.

wider circulation. In the case of Ps. 148: 13, there is a further point to take into consideration. The relevant phrase in Isa. 12: 4 reads *kî niśgāb š*$^{e}$*mô*, and this reminds us to some extent of the refrain in Isa. 2: 11 and 17: *w*$^{e}$*niśgab yhwh l*$^{e}$*baddô*. When we observe that Ps. 148: 13*b* reads *kî-niśgāb š*$^{e}$*mô l*$^{e}$*baddô*, we might more reasonably conclude that the psalmist has conflated the thought of these two passages in Isaiah and so is dependent upon them rather than the other way round. In that case, we cannot draw any conclusion about the date of Isaiah 12 from this example.

In sum, we may confidently conclude that none of the arguments which have been advanced concerning the late date of Isaiah 12 demands that it be set later than Deutero-Isaiah. We may, therefore, allow our new proposal about its authorship, purpose, and time of inclusion in the book of Isaiah to stand.

The next passage which we must consider is the one immediately preceding chapter 12, namely 11: 11–16.[21] It will be necessary, however, also to draw 5: 25–30 and 8: 21–2 into this discussion before it is finished, so that what follows will inevitably be somewhat more involved than the analysis of chapter 12. The final conclusion, however, will be seen to be an equally simple and clear-cut process of composition and redaction, and I shall endeavour to make this plain in the summary.

We may start by noting the most obvious connections between 11: 11–16 and the work of Deutero-Isaiah. The opening of verse 12, with its reference to God raising a standard to the nations in order to regather those of Israel and Judah in the dispersion, is, as we have seen, closely parallel with 49: 22. The point may be underlined that not only is the same vocabulary used, but also that the passages are brought closely together by the fact that here God's action in summoning the nations is for a positive purpose, unlike the judgemental use of the same theme elsewhere.

The continuation of verse 12 has close conceptual parallels in a number of places in Isaiah 40–55. That God will regather the dispersed exiles is mentioned at 40: 11; 49: 5–6, 18; and 54: 7 (besides 49: 22), and in particular, the use of masculine and feminine forms alongside each other (*nid*$^{e}$*ḥê yiśrā'ēl* and *n*$^{e}$*puṣôt y*$^{e}$*hûdâ* ('the outcasts of Israel' and 'the dispersed of Judah')) resembles the 'your sons' and 'your daughters' of 49: 22 (and cf.

[21] For the even later addition of 11: 10, see above, p. 67.

43: 6; 60: 4, etc.), as observed by Duhm and Gray, amongst others. No doubt in all cases these are examples of the use of the masculine and feminine together to express entirety; cf. GK §122*v*. *qbṣ*, in terms of God gathering the people of Israel, recurs at 40: 11; 43: 5; 49: 18; and 54: 7, and *'sp* at 49: 5* and 52: 12. Finally, the regathering from 'the four corners of the earth' is similar to 43: 5–6 and 49: 12*. Although the exact wording of 11: 12 is not used here, these two passages spell out the four points of the compass instead, and so come to much the same thing.

In verse 11 (on which see more fully below), it is said that the Lord will 'recover' (*liqnôt*) the remnant of his people. This verb is not used with this sense in Isaiah 40–55,[22] but it does occur in Exod. 15: 16 in a context which suggests the idea of redemption. Similarly, at Ps. 74: 2 it stands in parallel with *g'l*. Redemption is a common image for the release from exile in Deutero-Isaiah (e.g. 43: 1; 44: 22, 23; 48: 20; 52: 9, together with the frequent divine title *gô'ēl*), and the implications of 'purchase' which the verb *qnh* usually conveys are certainly prominent in 43: 3*b*–4.

In verses 15–16 the return of Israel from exile is explicitly compared with the exodus from Egypt. We have already noted that this is widely recognized as characteristic of Deutero-Isaiah (see above, n. 15). Specific points of contact with these two verses include the idea of drying up the sea at 50: 2 and 51: 10 (and this will be expressed in the same language if the widely proposed emendation of *wᵉheḥᵉrîb* for *wᵉheḥᵉrîm* in 11: 15 is adopted); the returning dryshod where once there were rivers may be compared with 42: 15; 43: 16; 44: 27; and 51: 10; the use of God's wind as a destructive agent is found at 40: 7 and 41: 16; and the preparation of a 'highway' (*mᵉsillâ*) for the returning exiles is mentioned twice in Deutero-Isaiah, at 40: 3[23] and 49: 11. The word is not used anywhere else with precisely this nuance, though some other passages in Isaiah clearly develop it and are no doubt dependent on Deutero-Isaiah's usage (e.g. 19: 23; 62: 10). Outside the book of Isaiah, the nearest parallel is Jer. 31: 21, where it refers to the way *into* exile, back along which Jeremiah hopes that Israel will return. Possibly, Deutero-Isaiah consciously developed the fulfilment of

22 Wildberger (p. 466) compares 43: 24, but its use there is quite different.

23 The 'highway for our God' in this context is clearly the highway by which God will accompany his people on their homeward journey; cf. verses 9–11, and Westermann, 35 = ET 38; Elliger, 18: 'die Strasse . . ., auf der der König Jahwe mit seinem Volk nach Jerusalem ziehen wird.'

this hope. Finally, the curious collocation of Assyria with Egypt (see also verse 11) is closely paralleled in 52: 4. This is found elsewhere only rarely—at 19: 24–5, for instance, which is probably no earlier than the Persian period (see Wildberger), and at Zech. 10: 10–11, which I shall shortly try to show is dependent on Isaiah.

We may thus conclude that Isa. 11: 11–16 displays many similarities with the thought and diction of Deutero-Isaiah, and that some of these are limited to this passage and Deutero-Isaiah alone. It is striking that Auvray, who does not write from within the hypothesis which I am here seeking to defend, comments that 'il semble que l'on soit à peu près dans le même contexte que la seconde partie du livre d'Isaïe' (p. 148).

As was the case with chapter 12, we need next to examine the strength of the arguments for dating 11: 11–16 in the post-exilic rather than the exilic period.[24] Once again, a good deal of the discussion has been directed towards establishing that this passage could not come from Isaiah of Jerusalem, and with this, of course, we fully concur.[25] Beyond that, some commentators, such as Wildberger, seem to assume that the resemblances with Deutero-Isaiah point to a date later than his ministry, but in our view that is an illegitimate inference. Moreover, the very late (Maccabean) date proposed by earlier scholars such as Duhm and Marti on the basis of verses 13–14 is generally discounted.[26] Apart from the problems of dating any substantial part of the book so late in view of the finds from Qumran, there is the further difficulty that even at that time Judah and Ephraim did not act in concert against their neighbouring enemies (so already Procksch); indeed, it is probably the very period when the Samaritan schism developed to a point that was beyond recall.[27] Whereas it would be possible to understand the mention of Egypt and Assyria in verses 11 and 15–16 as referring to the Ptolemies and the Seleucids respectively had the passage been

[24] For the following, see, in addition to the commentaries, Werner, *Eschatologische Texte in Jesaja 1–39*, 102–9.

[25] For recent attempts to defend the Isaianic authorship of 11: 11–16, see B. Otzen, *Studien über Deuterosacharja* (Acta Theologica Danica, 6; Copenhagen, 1964), 44; S. Erlandsson, 'Jesaja 11: 10–16 och dess historike bakgrund', *SEÅ* 36 (1971), 24–44; Oswalt.

[26] Though cf. U. Kellermann, *Messias und Gesetz: Grundlinien einer alttestamentlichen Heilserwartung: Eine traditionsgeschichtliche Einführung* (BSt 61; Neukirchen-Vluyn, 1971), 52–3.

[27] Cf. J. D. Purvis, *The Samaritan Pentateuch and the Origin of the Samaritan Sect* (HSM 2; Cambridge, Mass., 1968).

written as late as that, this by itself does not demand such an interpretation; the similar references at 52: 4, already noted, show that there is no objection to the mention of these two powers together in the exilic period. Furthermore, the fact that the LXX has apparently reread some of the place names in verses 11 and 14 in terms that approximate closer to the conditions of the second century BC implies that the Hebrew text with which it was working was itself somewhat earlier.[28]

There are three more substantial arguments which we should now examine. First, verses 13–14[29] speak of a reuniting of Judah and Ephraim and their joint conquest of some of their neighbouring peoples. Since from a historical point of view this never happened at any time from Isaiah's day on, the passage must be expressing a prophetic hope for the future, and some commentators believe that this was only entertained in the post-exilic period. In fact, however, the hope that the formerly divided people will be reunited is clearly attested shortly before Deutero-Isaiah's time—in Ezek. 37: 15–28[30] and in parts of Jeremiah 30–1 (whose date, however, is disputed) —so that in principle there is no problem with a date for its occurrence in Isaiah 11 as early as the late exilic period. It might be objected that such a hope never comes to expression in Isaiah 40–55, but an explanation lies ready to hand. In those chapters the prophet is directly addressing the Judaean exiles in Babylon, and in the context of what he has to say there such sentiments would have been out of place. In working over the literary deposit of Isaiah of Jerusalem, however, there was a good deal in the chapters preceding our passage which would have brought it to the forefront of his mind, and, since we have already seen (and will see again below) that in drawing up this redactional conclusion to the first major section of the book he took careful account of some of its dominant

28 See I. L. Seeligmann, *The Septuagint Version of Isaiah: A Discussion of its Problems* (Leiden, 1948), 78–9, 86–7; A. van der Kooij, *Die alten Textzeugen des Jesajabuches: Ein Beitrag zur Textgeschichte des Alten Testaments* (OBO 35; Freiburg and Göttingen, 1981), 37–8. It is not necessary to come to a decision here over the debated issue of whether the list of places at the end of verse 11 is an original part of the text or has been added secondarily. While many favour this latter position, it is noteworthy that Deutero-Isaiah already mentions a considerable number of places in which the dispersed Jews of his time were to be found; see 43: 5–6; 49: 12.

29 Again, it is not important for our present purposes whether 13*b* is to be regarded as a later expansion.

30 For the many points of contact between Ezekiel and Deutero-Isaiah, see Baltzer, *Ezechiel und Deuterojesaja*.

themes, it is fully intelligible that he should have worked in such a reference here as well. The history of the Syro-Ephraimite war in chapters 7–8, together with its reflection elsewhere in such passages as 9: 21, the recollection of the trauma of the division of the monarchy in 7: 17, the joint condemnation of both houses of Israel in 5: 1–7 and of the northern kingdom in 9: 8–12,[31] and the hope for a brighter future for the north (as we have argued he understood it) in 8: 23[9: 1]–9: 6[7], combine to suggest that a reference to the healing of this division would have been appropriate in a redactional conclusion to this section whose purpose is clearly to point to a time when past wrongs will be put right. There is certainly no need to believe that it could not have been written before the divisions of the post-exilic period surfaced: the immediately preceding context furnishes sufficient motivation for Deutero-Isaiah to have echoed Ezekiel's hopes here. That the restored people would triumph over their enemies is widely attested in Deutero-Isaiah (e.g. 41: 11–16; 49: 7, 23–6; 51: 22–3; 55: 5), and all he has done in the present context is to transfer this expectation to a stereotypical list of Israel's hostile neighbours (note how, for instance, the same four nations are brought together in Ezekiel 25) in a manner which is consistent with the setting for which he is here writing.

The second argument for a post-exilic date for Isa. 11: 11–16 arises from the observation that it has a close parallel in Zech. 10: 3–12, and verses 10–11 in particular:

> I will bring them home from the land of Egypt,
> and gather them from Assyria;
> and I will bring them to the land of Gilead and to Lebanon,
> till there is no room for them.
> They shall pass through the sea of Egypt,
> and the waves of the sea shall be smitten,
> and all the depths of the Nile dried up.
> The pride of Assyria shall be laid low,
> and the sceptre of Egypt shall depart. (*RSV*)[32]

Fohrer (who thinks that this passage served as a *Vorlage* for Isa. 11:

[31] These references, at least, are explicit. There may be others, such as 2: 6–22 and 9: 13–17, but there is dispute as to who is being addressed here.

[32] The textual issues raised by these verses do not affect the following discussion; see W. Rudolph, *Haggai—Sacharja 1–8—Sacharja 9–14—Maleachi* (KAT 13/4; Gütersloh, 1976), 194.

11–16) and Werner (who thinks rather in terms of a general parallel of ideas) in particular have argued that this points to a date for our passage as late as that in Zechariah. Closer inspection reveals, however, that there are contacts with other passages in Isaiah as well. The use of the verb *śrq* ('to whistle') with the sense of God signalling to a nation (verse 8) occurs elsewhere only at Isa. 5: 26 and 7: 18, and there can be little doubt that this colourful imagery is directly dependent on Isaiah; the expression *hûrad g*ᵉ*'ôn* (verse 11) is only found otherwise at Isa. 14: 11[33] (and of course *g*ᵉ*'ôn* is one of Isaiah's 'favourite' words); the statement 'for I am the Lord their God and I will answer them' (verse 6) looks as though it may have been based on Isa. 41: 17: 'I am the Lord (who) will answer them'; although both passages refer to God 'smiting' (*ḥkh*) the sea (Zech. 10: 11; Isa. 11: 15), the reference to the 'drying up' (*hōbîšû*) of the depths of the Nile (which does not occur in Isaiah 11) seems rather to reflect such passages as Isa. 19: 5–7; 42: 15; and especially 44: 27, where the *hapax legomenon ṣûlâ* is no doubt reflected in the commoner *m*ᵉ*ṣûlâ* (pl.) of Zech. 10: 11; the theme of the returning exiles being so numerous that there is not sufficient room for them (*lō' yimmāṣē' lāhem* (verse 10)) may be compared with Isa. 49: 19–21 and 54: 1–3; and so on. There is no need to continue multiplying examples, since the main point seems to be securely established that Zechariah 10 draws on many passages in Isaiah, of which 11: 11–16 is only one, although admittedly a prominent one. In this, it is not unlike other parts of Deutero-Zechariah, one of whose features is a liberal use of earlier prophetic material.[34] This being the case, it is unsatisfactory from the point of view of method to isolate one point of comparison and to treat it in separation. In the light of all the evidence, it becomes obvious that Zech. 10: 10–11 is dependent upon Isa. 11: 11–16 (among other passages), and therefore can provide no more than a *terminus ad quem* for the date of the latter's composition. It cannot legitimately be used to argue that Isa. 11: 11–16 could not have been written during the exilic period.

The third, and probably most influential, argument for a post-

[33] And only once elsewhere with any part of the verb *yrd*, namely at Ezek. 30: 6, where it is in the qal.

[34] See B. Stade, 'Deuterozacharja: Eine kritische Studie', *ZAW* 1 (1881), 1–96 (esp. 41–96); M. Delcor, 'Les Sources du Deutéro-Zacharie et ses procédés d'emprunt', *RB* 59 (1952), 385–411, and J. Day, 'Prophecy', in D. A. Carson and H. G. M. Williamson (eds.), *It is Written: Scripture Citing Scripture: Essays in Honour of Barnabas Lindars, SSF* (Cambridge, 1988), 39–55 (48–9).

exilic date for our passage is based upon the first part of verse 11: 'In that day the Lord will again extend* his hand to recover the remnant which is left of his people.'[35] Two main ways of understanding this have generally been advanced. One group of commentators thinks that there is a reference to the first exodus; God is about to move again as he did on that previous occasion.[36] If that is correct, then, of course, no conclusion could be drawn about the date and setting of the writer. Others, however, suggest that the reference is to the first return from exile in the time of Cyrus, with which also the returns at the time of Ezra and Nehemiah may have been associated.[37] On this view, the writer must be dated later than the first return, and it is usually thought that his location in Palestine is presupposed. It is common to both these approaches, however, that what God is about to do again is to 'recover the remnant of his people'.

I wish to propose an entirely different way of interpreting this passage. It has been suggested, only then to be rejected, by Vermeylen, but it seems that his initial insight can be expanded and developed into a convincing hypothesis.[38] We start by noting that, from a grammatical point of view, what the Lord may be doing again, according to 11: 11, is not so much recovering his people as raising or extending his hand. If we then ask when he extended his hand for the first time, we are led to consider the fact that, in the chapters to which this passage provides a conclusion, there is a repeated refrain to the effect that 'for all this his anger is not turned

[35] As noted in the Appendix, there is doubt about the original reading here; the rendering given above follows the widely adopted proposal to emend *šēnît* to *ś$^{e}$'ēt*. This uncertainty does not, however, seriously affect the present discussion, since the central plank of the argument, the idea of repetition, is already inherent in the use of *yôsîp*.

[36] So, e.g., Delitzsch; Gray; Auvray. We may also note here Procksch's suggestion that it refers back to verse 10 immediately preceding. I have already indicated, however, that verse 10 was added later, as a link between verses 1–9 and 11–16.

[37] So, e.g., Duhm; Marti; Fohrer; Wildberger; Kaiser.

[38] Vermeylen (pp. 278–9) prefers to associate our verse with 10: 32, which he thinks the redactor would have understood as a reference to God waving his hand in protection of Zion, rather than as an attacker 'shaking his fist' in enmity at the city. Consequently, Vermeylen proposes to read *hēnîp* or *y$^{e}$nōpēp* instead of *yôsîp* in 11: 11 (cf. 11: 15 and 10: 32 respectively), and to leave *šēnît* unchanged. Both steps in this argument are problematic. No good reason is given why the redactor should have misinterpreted 10: 32 in a manner which runs so contrary to the clear sense of the context (the change in subject to the Lord acting in judgement on the enemy is emphatically marked at the start of 10: 33), while the proposed emendation of 11: 11 is entirely conjectural.

away, and his hand is stretched out still' (5: 25; 9: 11[12], 16[17], 20[21]; 10: 4). We have already seen that 11: 11–16 picks up a number of themes from these chapters, so that the possibility that this is a further example of the same process is attractive. As with the raising of a signal, there would be a shift in perspective implied: at the first, God raised his hand in judgement of his people, but now he will raise it to initiate their salvation.

The case becomes more than merely an attractive possibility, however, when we look particularly at the passage introduced by 5: 25, for there, exactly as at 11: 12, there follows in verse 26 the statement that God will 'raise an ensign to the nations' (the identical words, *wᵉnāśā' nēs laggôyim*, are used in each passage), and then a reference to the fact that they will come 'from afar . . . from the ends of the earth' in 5: 26 and 'from the four corners of the earth' in 11: 12. With three elements occurring in the same order in the two passages (God's hand; the ensign; from afar), it is hard to escape the conclusion that the one has been framed with an eye on the other.

Pursuing these observations further, we should remember next that 5: 25–9(30) is generally thought to have been relocated from an original literary setting somewhere between 9: 7[8] and 10: 4, where it seems to belong because of the refrain already cited. Exactly where it might have come in that passage is a matter of continuing debate amongst the commentators, and one which need not detain us here.[39] It is sufficient to observe that the case for some such transposition is strong.[40] How and why the passage was transposed, however, has been less satisfactorily answered. Usually it is thought to have been the result of some error in transmission, so that a number of commentaries, and even one translation of the Bible (*NEB*), rearrange the material into what they consider to

[39] In addition to the commentaries, see Fey, *Amos und Jesaja*, 83–8; Donner, *Israel unter den Völkern*, 66–75; J. Vollmer, *Geschichtliche Rückblicke und Motive in der Prophetie des Amos, Hosea und Jesaja* (BZAW 119; Berlin, 1971), 130–44; Barth, *Die Jesaja-Worte in der Josiazeit*, 109–12; Vermeylen, 177–86; C. E. L'Heureux, 'The Redactional History of Isaiah 5.1–10.4', in W. B. Barrick and J. R. Spencer (eds.), *In the Shelter of Elyon: Essays on Ancient Palestinian Life and Literature in Honor of G. W. Ahlström* (JSOTS 31; Sheffield, 1984), 99–119.

[40] For an attempt to defend the originality of the present order of the MT, see Dietrich, *Jesaja und die Politik*, 186–7; R. B. Chisholm, 'Structure, Style, and the Prophetic Message: An Analysis of Isaiah 5: 8–30', *BibSac* 143 (1986), 46–60; Brown, 'The So-Called Refrain in Isaiah 5: 25–30 and 9: 7–10: 4'; see also Y. Gitay, *Isaiah and his Audience: The Structure and Meaning of Isaiah 1–12* (SSN 30; Assen, 1991), 87–116.

have been the original, correct order. Our observations point to a different solution, for it should not escape notice that 5: 25–30 comes at the very end of another major section in the book. It is thus highly satisfying from the point of view of redaction criticism to find that two concluding sections are introduced by closely parallel material, the one referring to God's judgement, following the lengthy and varied invective of 2: 6–5: 24,[41] and the other, referring to God's salvation, following the material in 6: 1–11: 9, which in the present form of the book, at least, includes a good deal of more hopeful material.[42]

There is good reason to believe, therefore, that the transposition of 5: 25–9(30) to its present position was consciously undertaken by the same redactor who composed 11: 11–12: 6, who in our view was Deutero-Isaiah himself. What is more, his procedure, which on the face of things appears in two respects to be rather clumsy, now receives adequate explanation.

First, there is the oddity that the passage which seems to have been removed from its original setting begins with an unattached 'therefore'. Although in a general way this can, of course, be read in the present form of the text as referring to the material which precedes it, it is nevertheless awkward in that verse 24 itself rounds off the section with its own introductory 'therefore'. If, however, the redactor was attempting to locate material here which could serve as a balance to his conclusion of the following main section in 11: 11–16, then his choice becomes intelligible. Not only did he need, of course, to begin this passage with a reference to God's outstretched hand which the refrain provided, but he has drawn particular attention to this element by choosing the one and only example of the refrain which is itself immediately preceded by another reference to this same point: 'Therefore the anger of the Lord was kindled against his people, and he stretched out his hand against them and smote them' (5: 25*a*). This element is not found in any of the other examples of the refrain in chapters 9–10. It is thus clear that the redactor chose to move precisely this material

41 As we shall see below, 4: 2–6 is later, so that originally the whole of the earlier form of 2: 6–5: 24 comprised invective.

42 Of course, some of this may not originally have been so, but may have been reread as hopeful subsequently (see e.g. the discussion of 8: 23*b* above, Ch. 4). More importantly, however, the threatening material in this section is included within a wider context which uses it as a backdrop for an overall hopeful message; see e.g. 10: 5–19 following 9: 7–10: 4.

from its original setting because it was particularly suited by repetition of the crucial element for the wider purposes on which he was engaged. Furthermore, the double reference to the anger of the Lord in the first and last lines of the verse also suited his intention in the final rounding off passage, chapter 12 (see 12: 1).

Secondly, commentators have often drawn attention to the fact that in 5: 26 there is a curious reference to the plural 'nations' in a context which obviously referred originally to only a single nation (cf. the singular *lô* in the next clause and the singular verb *yābô'* immediately after that); they therefore propose emending the plural *laggôyim* to the singular *l^egôy*, explaining the error as due to a mistaken division of the words: the final *mem* should be attached to the following word, which is then to be read as *mimmerḥāq*; cf. Jer. 5: 15. There is no reason to doubt that this, or something very like it, was what Isaiah himself would have written when this verse stood in its original position, but comparison with 11: 12 as well as with 49: 22 indicates that the alteration was not caused by scribal error, nor even, as Gray suggests, by 'a scribe who wished to assimilate to 11$^{12}$', but rather by the deliberate activity of the redactor who was forging a link between this passage and his composition in 11: 11–16. He thereby involves the nations at large in the judgement of his people just as he envisages the time when they will all assist in their restoration.

It is worth recalling at this point that in the discussion of 49: 22 in Chapter 4 above we observed that 5: 25–9 was one which seems to have been particularly influential on Deutero-Isaiah. In addition to the several points of similarity which we have seen are shared by 5: 25–6, 11: 11–12, and 49: 22, the further point was noted there, following Davies, that 5: 29 and 49: 24–5 have in common the idea of a tyrant's captives being compared to a wild animal's prey. In addition, we drew attention to the possible influence of 5: 27 on 40: 28–31. If I have been right in my suggestion that Deutero-Isaiah was the one responsible for relocating 5: 25–9 to its present position as part of his redactional work on the earlier Isaiah material, then it is not surprising that we should find an especially marked influence from it on his own composition.

So far, our discussion of 5: 25–30 has only gone so far as to suggest that the redactor was responsible for giving it its new and present setting in the book. With one slight alteration (the substitution of the plural for the originally singular 'nation'), it seems that his purpose was adequately achieved by using inherited material in a new setting. It could now serve to round off the condemnations of the first section in the book, and he used it as a basis for constructing a new parallel conclusion to what he took to be the second, more hopeful, section at 11: 11–16. The question naturally arises next whether in the process he may not himself have added anything on his own account to this inherited material.

In answering this question, attention quickly falls on the concluding verse of the passage, 5: 30:

> They will growl over it on that day,
> like the roaring of the sea.
> And if we look* to the land,
> behold, darkness closing in;
> and the light is darkened by its clouds.

This verse is widely regarded as an addition to the previous paragraph.[43] Attention is drawn to the tell-tale phrase 'on that day', to the development in a new direction of the catchword 'growl' (*w$^e$yinhōm*) (verses 29 and 30), and to the widening of the scope of the prophecy from a military defeat in verses 26–9 to a more mythologically expressed universal catastrophe in verse 30. In addition, verse 29 gives the strong impression of being itself a conclusion that expects no continuation.

Differences of opinion arise, however, when we turn to the interpretation of the first line: who is growling over whom? A considerable number of commentators think that the glossator has sought to reverse the gloom of the previous paragraph—either God or some unnamed subject is now going to growl over Assyria (*'ālāw*), so that eventually there will be unrelieved darkness for the country which once oppressed Israel.[44] Against this, however, it must be observed that the first word of the verse—*w$^e$yinhōm* ('and

[43] It is not at all clear why Clements limits the addition to the second half of the verse only, especially in view of the fact that two of the main reasons for detecting an addition here in the first place come in the first half of the verse. He gives no reason for his position, and indeed offers no comment on the first half of the verse. Nor is the suggestion of Procksch convincing; he thinks that the verse originally belonged with 25*a*. He bases this on metrical considerations in large part, but is only able to do so following radical surgery on verse 30. Among the casualties of this operation is the phrase 'on that day', but there is no evidence whatsoever for deleting it, and it is itself one of the markers of the secondary nature of the verse.

[44] So, e.g., Duhm; Marti; Becker, *Isaias—der Prophet und sein Buch*, 50–1; Kaiser; Barth, *Die Jesaja-Worte in der Josiazeit*, 193; Vermeylen, 185; Gray seems to be unable to decide.

he will growl')—exactly repeats the same word from verse 29, and, since there is no indication of a change of subject, it is more natural to suppose that the one responsible for the addition picked it up with the intention of developing the meaning which it has there rather than of using it in some completely different way. On this view, the lion of verse 29, representing Assyria, remains the subject, and the object over which he growls remains the prey, representing Israel.[45] However, as we have already noted, the effects are now drawn in an even more terrifying manner by the suggestion that this will mark a return to the conditions of the primeval chaos. Clements may thus well be right to see here a reflection of the disaster of 587 BC, and so to conclude that 'the note must have been added during the exilic age'.

There is thus every reason to regard 5: 30 as a redactional addition, and no objection to ascribing it to the same redactor as the one responsible for moving 5: 25–9 to its present position. It serves to strengthen the note of judgement with which he rounded off the passage on the prophetic indictment of Israel. If that is so, then *ex hypothesi* its author will have been Deutero-Isaiah, and this is by no means an unreasonable conclusion to draw. On 'the roaring of the sea', compare Isa. 51: 15, and, for the sea as an image of chaos, compare 51: 10 (and 50: 2?); on 'look to (the) earth', see immediately below; and on darkness without light as an image of a time of oppression or exile, see the discussion of 8: 23–9: 5[9: 1–6] in Chapter 4 (and note in addition that 50: 3 has a similarly gloomy atmosphere).

The similarity of this verse with 8: 22 has often been noted,[46] and with good reason:

> And they will look to the earth,
> but behold, distress and darkness,

[45] So, e.g., Delitzsch; Eichrodt; and in part Wildberger. Barth's objection to this interpretation (that 'eine Fortsetzung der Unheilsaussage im Blick auf den 5,26–29 Angegriffenen über V29 hinaus nur einen Rückschritt und eine Abschwächung bedeuten könnte') would only be applicable if this were all part of a single composition. In the case of an appendage, such a 'Rückschritt' poses no problem, while the development of the image through the rest of verse 30 can hardly be called an 'Abschwächung'.

[46] First, apparently, by the LXX (cf. J. Ziegler, *Untersuchungen zur Septuaginta des Buches Isaias* (Münster, 1934), 138–9), and most recently by B. W. Anderson, '"God with Us"—In Judgment and in Mercy: The Editorial Structure of Isaiah 5–10 (11)', in G. M. Tucker, D. L. Petersen, and R. R. Wilson (eds.), *Canon, Theology, and Old Testament Interpretation: Essays in Honor of Brevard S. Childs* (Philadelphia, 1988), 230–45.

the gloom of anguish;
and they will be thrust into thick darkness.[47]

The first phrase, *wᵉʾel-ʾereṣ yabbîṭ wᵉhinnēh*, is just like the start of 5: 30*b*, *wᵉnibbaṭ lāʾāreṣ wᵉhinnēh*. The expression *hbyṭ l/ʾl (h)ʾrṣ* occurs only six times in the Hebrew Bible, three times with God as subject (Pss. 102: 20; 104: 32; Job 28: 24), and three times with a human subject—in the two passages under consideration and (*mirabile dictu*!) at Isa. 51: 6. Our two usages are alone, however, in being followed in each case by *wᵉhinnēh*. In addition, both passages go on to speak of a time of oppression under the image of deep darkness, *ḥōšek ṣar* in 5: 30 and *ṣārâ waḥᵃšēkâ* in 8: 22. There can thus be no doubt that there is a close association between them.

It seems, furthermore, that 8: 21–2 has also been added into its present context by a redactor. Although a few scholars have sought to defend the unity of 19–22,[48] the majority hold firmly to the view that 21–2 should be taken independently. (The brief remarks of Gray (p. 157) are usually considered decisive; see further below.) That observation does not, however, settle the question of authorship, on which opinions are divided. While the majority find here an Isaianic fragment,[49] not a few others think of a later exilic[50] or post-exilic[51] composition.

Naturally, in the case of so short a passage it is difficult to reach an absolutely firm decision on the matter, but such evidence as there is favours the case for authenticity, while the arguments to the contrary are weak. Wildberger adduces three positive arguments: metre and style, the reference to 'their king' in verse 21, which should apply to the pre-exilic period, and vocabulary; although most of the vocabulary of the passage is general (having parallels

[47] *Or* 'gloom with no brightness', if the proposal to emend *mᵉnuddāḥ* to *minnōgah* is adopted; cf. Amos 5: 20.

[48] e.g. G. R. Driver, 'Isaianic Problems', in G. Wiessner (ed.), *Festschrift für Wilhelm Eilers* (Wiesbaden, 1967), 43–57 (43–9); C. F. Whitley, 'The Language and Exegesis of Isaiah 8 $_{16-23}$', *ZAW* 90 (1978), 28–43; Vermeylen, 229–30.

[49] e.g. Duhm; Marti; Procksch; Alt, 'Jesaja 8,23–9,6'; Fohrer; Wildberger; K. Jeppesen, 'Call and Frustration: A New Understanding of Isaiah viii 21–22', *VT* 32 (1982), 145–57; Høgenhaven, *Gott und Volk bei Jesaja*, 103–5; Laato, *Who is Immanuel?*, 188–9; Gray is again undecided.

[50] e.g. Barth, *Die Jesaja-Worte in der Josiazeit*, 153–4; Vermeylen, 228–30; Clements.

[51] e.g. Kaiser.

both in Isaiah and elsewhere), he is particularly struck by the similarity of *bᵉʾereṣ ṣārâ wᵉṣûqâ* (‘through a land of trouble and anguish’) in 30: 6 with our passage, the more so in view of the fact that *ṣûqâ* occurs elsewhere only at Prov. 1: 27. Negatively, Wildberger also makes the point (along with many others) that there is nothing to prevent Isaianic authorship.

Of these arguments, the second is undoubtedly the strongest; it is difficult to see what sense could be made of the verse once the monarchy had ceased to exist.[52] The argument from vocabulary adds some weight to the case, but of course the possibility of later imitation means that it cannot be decisive. As to the negative argument, this is certainly true as far as it goes. Clements, for instance, dates the fragment late simply on the ground that verses 19–20 are an addition; therefore, he assumes, 21–2 must have been added after that.[53] But the conclusion does not follow from the observation. If 19–20 are indeed an addition (a matter which we need not decide here), it does not follow that 21–2 could not already have been in place before they were added. The position of 19–20 was no doubt governed by the link between ‘the teaching and the testimony’ in verses 20 and 16. Similarly, Barth’s reasons for dating 21–2 to the exilic period rest merely on the similarity between the description of the time of distress, such as hunger, with the conditions attested by Jeremiah and Lamentations for the time of the fall of Jerusalem. This argument, too, is insignificant; such conditions were common at any time of military catastrophe, and they would have been known—even from first-hand experience—long before the final downfall of Jerusalem.[54] On balance, then, the case in favour of the authenticity of this passage, or at the very least for a pre-exilic origin, seems to be the stronger.

At this point, a further argument needs to be brought into the discussion. As already noted, most commentators believe that

[52] G. C. Heider’s proposal to emend *bᵉmalkô* to *bᵉmōlek* is unconvincing: see *The Cult of Molek: A Reassessment* (JSOTS 43; Sheffield, 1985), 328–32. In joining verses 19–20 and 21–2, he fails to explain the switch to singular verbs in the latter, has to assume the unexpressed ‘Sheol’ as the antecedent for *bāh*, and conjecturally deletes the suffix on *bᵉmalkô*.

[53] Clements; see also his ‘The Prophecies of Isaiah and the Fall of Jerusalem in 587 B.C.’, 427.

[54] This is not to deny, of course, that later readers may have understood these verses in the way that Barth and Clements suggest.

these two verses are fragmentary. This is because the first word of the passage, the verb *'br* ('to pass over/through'), lacks a subject, and the suffix on the second word, *bāh* ('(through) it' (feminine singular)) lacks an antecedent.[55] That being the case, it is difficult to believe that these verses were written specifically for their present context. Even someone writing an addition could be expected to make his composition fit the context and not to introduce unattached verbs and suffixes. Nor is there any evidence that something has dropped out from the start of the passage, as implied by Wildberger's row of dots at the start of his translation. The obvious conclusion is that these words have been secondarily transferred to their present position from their original context, which was presumably at some other point in the early form of the collection of Isaianic material.

Barth seeks to evade this conclusion with three arguments, but they are not all convincing. First, he maintains that appeals to fragment hypotheses should be a last resort. In these early chapters of Isaiah, however, there are so many well-attested examples of material being rearranged for later redactional purposes that even as a last resort such a hypothesis is by no means unlikely. Secondly, with an appeal to GK §144*d*, he proposes that the verb may be construed as having an indefinite personal subject, 'one' or 'they' (cf. *RSV*); that is certainly a reasonable possibility. Thirdly, to explain the unattached feminine singular suffix on *bāh*, he draws attention to an apparently similar phenomenon at 3: 25–6 and 5: 14; since in these two cases Jerusalem is the implied point of reference, he suggests that the same may be true here. Unfortunately, however, he does not observe that the two passages which he refers to are not so straightforward as he implies. Isa. 3: 25–6 must certainly once have been the direct continuation of 3: 16–17 before the addition of the prose insertion in verses 18–23. The feminine singular suffixes in 25–6 (both second and third person) then relate easily enough to the mention of Zion in 16–17. At 5: 14 there is also evidence that the feminine singular suffixes may once have had an explicit antecedent. The verse's introductory 'therefore' sits uneasily after the 'therefore' of verse 13 and suggests, as many have recognized, that this verse has been given its present

[55] Against Vermeylen's attempt to overcome this, see Høgenhaven, *Gott und Volk bei Jesaja*, 104.

position as part of the redactional compilation of the 'woe!' cycle in 5: 8–24.[56] It is, therefore, probable that this verse too once stood in a context where the suffix's antecedent was made clear. Barth's case against the fragmentary nature of 8: 21–2 thus fails, and accordingly I conclude that at this point some words of Isaiah have been relocated from elsewhere by a later redactor.[57]

Following 8: 21–2, there is a short addition (8: 23*a*[9: 1*a*]) which has clearly been introduced to link what precedes with what follows. Although there are a number of uncertainties about the text of this line, the use of the words *mûʿāp* and *mûṣāq* are obviously intended to pick up on 8: 22. Similarly, on the assumption that the negative *lōʾ* of the MT is sound (which then implies that the introductory *kî* should be understood as an adversative), there is also a connection with the following passage: those who have walked in darkness (as in 8: 22) will not do so for ever, for light and joy will follow (9: 1–2[2–3]). The addition may also, therefore, testify to an understanding of the first part of the passage (8: 23*b*[9: 1*b*]) as contrasting a 'former time' of oppression followed by a 'latter time' of glory.

It appears, therefore, in the light of this discussion, that 8: 21–3[9: 1]*a* has been compiled along exactly the same lines as those we suggested for 5: 25–30. A fragment of Isaianic material has been put in a new setting, and it has been followed by a brief addition which links up with the fragment by means of verbal association. It was suggested that Deutero-Isaiah was responsible for this at the end of chapter 5, and accordingly I now propose that he was also respon-

56 See J. A. Emerton, 'The Textual Problems of Isaiah v 14', *VT* 17 (1967), 135–42, and Vermeylen, 172, for references. Anderson ('"God with us"—In Judgment and in Mercy', 234–45) acutely observes that there are several 'double therefores' in Isaiah, and suggests that this may be a mark of the work's redaction. He is careful to draw a distinction between this and original composition, however ('These rhetorical uses of the "double therefore" do not necessarily indicate that the present text of Isa. 5: 13, 14 is original.'). It is highly suggestive to observe that there is an example of this feature in Isa. 50: 7, where it does seem to be part of the original writer's work. Since we have already noted that a further instance was created by the addition of 5: 25–30, which I have attributed to the redactional activity of Deutero-Isaiah, I am tempted to suggest that this may be an indicator of his hand. It may not be coincidental that 5: 14 'mythologizes' the judgement of the people, just as 5: 30 does.

57 It is unnecessary, and in any case extremely speculative, to go further by suggesting where these words might have once stood or what exactly their point of reference may have been. For a suggestion about the former, see P. W. Skehan, 'Some Textual Problems in Isaia', *CBQ* 22 (1960), 47–55 (48–51), and about the latter, see Høgenhaven, *Gott und Volk bei Jesaja*, 105.

sible for the present shape of the close of chapter 8. Furthermore, since we have seen that 8: 22 was part of the material which he relocated from elsewhere in Isaiah's work rather than that he wrote it himself, it follows that the similarities between this verse and 5: 30, described above, are to be explained by his imitating at 5: 30 the kind of sentiments and expressions which he learnt from 8: 22. That he should have been influenced by earlier Isaianic material in this way is, of course, no surprise in view of the whole thesis of this book, and that he should have modelled one of his redactional compositions (5: 30) on Isaianic material which he relocated as part of his editorial activity (8: 22) is equally intelligible.

Finally, although 8: 23[9: 1]*a* is far too short to supply material to compare with Deutero-Isaiah's language and style elsewhere (and in any case its significant vocabulary is drawn straight from 8: 22, as we have seen), nevertheless it reflects closely his point of view. The change from oppression to salvation under the imagery of light and darkness was noted in our discussion of 8: 23–9: 5[9: 1–6] in Chapter 4 above, and there is no need to repeat it here. Moreover, it fits well with what seems to have been his understanding of the major thrust of chapters 6–11 as a whole, namely predominantly a movement towards salvation following the judgement of the opening chapters of the book, each mood being reflected in the summing-up which he supplied for the two sections at 5: 25–30 and 11: 11–16 (plus chapter 12).

At the start of this whole analysis (p. 125), I indicated that the problems of 11: 11–16 could not be treated in isolation, but would require discussion of 5: 25–30 and 8: 21–2 as well. Now that that has been done, I must try to keep my promise of drawing the whole matter together in a clear and straightforward summary.

(1) Deutero-Isaiah composed 11: 11–16 to round off chapters 6–11. There are several elements of both language and thought which strongly support this conclusion, and the remainder can be understood on the hypothesis that he was deliberately writing with an eye on the previous chapters. Despite the inclusion of a good deal of 'judgement' material in these chapters, there are also a number of passages which are more hopeful in content and some which may have been read so by him even if that was not their original intention.

(2) There are such close parallels between 5: 25–6 and 11: 11–12

that a connection must be postulated. Since the passage in chapter 5 seems to have been drawn from elsewhere in Isaiah (note the refrain in 5: 25 which recurs in a series in chapters 9–10), one must assume that 11: 11–12 has been modelled upon it (and that the 'again' of 11: 11 therefore refers to the former stretching out of God's hand in 5: 25).

(3) Isa. 5: 25–30 serves a redactional function as a summary to the condemnatory section which precedes it. In view of the facts that it neatly balances 11: 11–16, that there is a literary connection between these two passages, and that 5: 25–9 was particularly influential on other parts of Deutero-Isaiah's work, it seems reasonable to suggest that it was he who moved this passage to its present position. As part of this process, he would have introduced the plural 'nations' for the originally singular form in verse 26.

(4) Isa. 5: 30 was not part of the material transferred from elsewhere in Isaiah, but was written as an addition for its present position (cf. the catchword 'growl'). Its purpose is to heighten the judgement from simply military disaster to a threat of the return of the primeval chaos. It fits the redactional aims of whoever relocated 5: 25–9, and there is no reason why it should not have been written by the same person at the same time. Its language and imagery are fully compatible with authorship by Deutero-Isaiah.

(5) Isa. 5: 30 is too close to 8: 22 not to be related in some manner. Development of this clue led us to discover that the same redactional process has been followed in 8: 21–3*a* as in 5: 25–30—that is to say, the movement of a short passage from somewhere else in the book to this new setting, followed by an addition which is attached by catchword. The inevitable supposition that the same hand was at work in both places was strengthened by the observation that here again some of Deutero-Isaiah's favourite themes were being drawn out, and that part of the purpose of this brief passage was to emphasize the interpretation of 8: 23*b*–9: 5[9: 1–6] which he took and which we know independently was a major influence on his work. (It also followed that from a literary point of view Deutero-Isaiah drew on his prior knowledge of 8: 22 at 5: 30.)

(6) Isa. 5: 25–30 and 11: 11–16 serve to define major sections of the book, so that the similarities between them are appropriate. At the same time, each of them uses both the similar material and the material peculiar to each to reflect the general atmosphere of its section as understood by the redactor (judgement and salvation

respectively). This somewhat schematized presentation of two distinct eras in God's dealings with his people is exactly what we should expect from Deutero-Isaiah in view of his message in Isaiah 40–55. While 8: 21–3*a* does not serve in this major structuring way, it is noteworthy that in itself it indicates a similar transition from one era to the other, that it is used to introduce the very passage which we suggested in Chapter 4 was most influential on Deutero-Isaiah in his development of this line of thought, and that it comes at the end of what is clearly a discrete literary section in the book (6: 1–8: 18).

Working backwards from the end of Isaiah 5, I do not find any major indications of the redactional process described above until we reach the start of chapter 2. This is not to deny that there may be some slight activity (the possibility has already been raised that 5: 14 may owe its present position to this redactor), but the evidence is too slight to detect it with any confidence. Furthermore, it must be remembered that much of the material in these chapters could have been understood just as it is in terms of the judgement of the fall of Jerusalem to the Babylonians. It therefore served the needs of the redactor without significant intervention on his part.

The question might be raised whether 4: 2–6 should be ascribed to this redactor. It is widely agreed that it has been added at some time considerably later than Isaiah's own day, so making chapters 2–4 into a section of its own. In verses 5–6 it alludes to the exodus, or more precisely to the wilderness-wanderings theme, and this, together with its generally hopeful message, might be thought to point in the direction of the circle of ideas found in 11: 11–16 and in Deutero-Isaiah generally. In addition, Sweeney points out that 'the use of creation language, such as *bārā*' in v. 5, is characteristic of Deutero-Isaiah'.[58]

Despite this, however, the passage lacks any of the kind of specific links with Deutero-Isaiah with which we have become familiar by now, and, as Sweeney further observes (pp. 179–80), there are several elements which positively point in a different direction. The imagery and terminology used to describe the purification of Jerusalem are distinctly priestly, as is the concept of the presence of the Lord in his sanctuary being made visible by cloud, smoke, and fire. The idea of names of the members of the

[58] Sweeney, *Isaiah 1–4*, 179.

community being recorded in writing (verse 3) seems also to have been a late development. For these and other reasons,[59] a post-exilic date seems to be demanded for this passage (the further question, whether the passage is itself a unity or whether it was developed in stages, need not be considered here), making its insertion later than the major redaction for which I am arguing. A result of this conclusion which deserves mention is that at that earlier stage 2: 6–5: 24 will have been wholly taken up with words of condemnation and threat, and this fits well with the conclusion which 5: 25–30 provides.

We must now turn to consider the opening of chapter 2 in greater detail. Verse 1 is a heading of the kind usually found at the start of prophetic books, verses 2–4 (which have a close parallel in Mic. 4: 1–3) are a somewhat visionary description of the future place of the temple in Zion as the place of God's universal instruction and judgement, and verse 5 is an appeal to the house of Jacob to 'walk in the light of the Lord'.

Verse 5 presents the simplest point of entry into consideration of this passage. Unlike the preceding verses, it has no parallel in Micah 4. It has sometimes been suggested (e.g. by Marti) that it is directly related to Mic. 4: 5:

> For all the peoples walk
> each in the name of its god,
> but we will walk in the name of the Lord our God
> for ever and ever.

Gray has a characteristically judicious discussion of this issue, which can hardly be improved upon. He accepts that 'Mic. asserts what Is. exhorts to', but then proceeds to observe that they could well be independent comments on the poem by different editors. 'The house of Jacob' in Isa. 2: 5 is clearly derived independently from its context (cf. verse 6), while the verbal similarities between the two passages all derive from the poem itself (cf. verse 3). In other respects, the two verses differ (e.g. the reference to 'light' in Isa. 2: 5). Thus, while Gray himself is prepared to leave the question open, his observations point rather firmly towards the independent origin of Isa. 2: 5.

As already indicated, the verse has verbal links both with what

[59] In addition to Sweeney's discussion, see Wildberger; Clements; Vermeylen, 152–7; and Werner, *Eschatologische Texte in Jesaja 1–39*, 91–100.

precedes and with what follows. The phrase 'house of Jacob' occurs in the next line (verse 6), but it is also reminiscent of 'the house of the God of Jacob' in verse 3. Of course, the word 'house' is used in different senses in verses 3 and 5, but the verbal echo remains. In addition, 'come, let us walk' (*lᵉkû wᵉnēlᵉkâ*) in verse 5 is undoubtedly modelled on 'come, let us go up' (*lᵉkû wᵉnaʿᵃleh*) in verse 3. We may, therefore, without hesitation accept the well-nigh universal agreement among commentators that verse 5 has been added to its present context to form a bridge between the positive statements of verses 2–4 and the negative tone of the material which follows.

It is interesting to observe that the editor encourages the house of Jacob to walk 'in the light of the Lord', because there is no immediate trigger for this expression in the poem itself; 'light' seems to be his way of understanding the 'ways', 'paths', 'law', and 'word of the Lord' of verse 3. The imagery of light (and its converse, darkness) was prominent, of course, in the two short passages which were ascribed to the redactor in 5: 30 and 8: 23[9: 1]*a* above. Since there appears to be no other motivation for its introduction in 2: 5, it is tempting to suppose that he may have been responsible for it here too. If that is right, we should *ex hypothesi* expect the verse to reflect closely the concerns of Deutero-Isaiah. While certainty cannot be attained in the case of so short a verse, such evidence as there is strongly supports this conclusion.

First, 'Jacob' is one of Deutero-Isaiah's favourite names for the exiled Israelites whom he is addressing. He uses it some twenty times to refer to the people, and among these 'the house of Jacob' occurs at 46: 3 and 48: 1. Secondly, he generally uses Jacob for the empirical Israel of his day—that is to say, for the people in their dispirited and depressed condition rather than as the Israel full of faith which the prophet holds out before them and towards which he encourages them to move. The exhortation to 'the house of Jacob' to walk in the light of the Lord would thus fit his general attitude well. Thirdly, an understanding of God's self-revelation as 'light' is prominent in Deutero-Isaiah. We have already noted his use of light and darkness in general terms; this particular application of the image occurs at 42: 6; 49: 6; 50: 10–11; and 51: 4. Fourthly, Clifford has suggested with reason that there is a direct association between 2: 5 and 50: 10–11.[60] He does not amplify his comment, and the exegetical problems which these two verses pose

[60] Clifford, *Fair Spoken and Persuading*, 158 n. 6.

bar the way to a complete understanding of how the imagery is being used here,[61] but there are certainly striking reminiscences. Those who 'walked in darkness, without brightness' (verse 10) could well be the same group as those now exhorted to 'walk in the light of the Lord', whereas the ironical appeal to the persecutors in verse 11 to 'walk by the light/in the flame of [*lᵉkû bᵉʾûr*] your own fire' seems to be a play on the words of 2: 5. Finally, the movement from a universalistic vision in 2: 2–4 to an exhortation to the house of Jacob to set an example of godly living in 2: 5 also reflects the outlook of Deutero-Isaiah. In general terms it may be said that throughout his work he too holds out an ideal for the future which includes an important position for the nations but that the way to this is repeatedly frustrated by the faithlessness of Jacob/Israel. In consequence, he has to devote a good deal of attention to the correction of the faults, such as lack of faith, which he finds among his own people.[62] In such a context, the application of 2: 2–4 by verse 5 makes good sense.

It may, therefore, be concluded that Isa. 2: 5 serves as an editorial bridge between verses 2–4 and 6–21, that its use of catchwords and of the theme of 'light' suggests that it functions in a similar way to one group of other short redactional insertions in Isaiah 1–12, and that thematically there is much to be said for attributing it too to the hand of Deutero-Isaiah.

This conclusion, if correct, already has certain implications for the vexed question of the date of 2: 2–4. The parallels with the redactional procedures at 5: 25–30 and 8: 21–3[9: 1]*a* suggest that 2: 2–4 was known to Deutero-Isaiah, that it was a passage which influenced him in his own composition, and possibly that he was responsible for putting it in its present setting. None of this is self-

[61] See W. A. M. Beuken, 'Jes 50 $_{10-11}$: Eine kultische Paränese zur dritten Ebedprophetie', *ZAW* 85 (1973), 168–82, and the major commentaries for discussion. In particular, it appears that the two verses are addressed to different audiences.

[62] For a detailed treatment of this theme, see R. E. Watts, 'Consolation or Confrontation? Isaiah 40–55 and the Delay of the New Exodus', *TynB* 41 (1990), 31–59. I have deliberately expressed this summary in vague and general terms because I do not wish to be side-tracked into discussion of the problems of nationalism and universalism and related matters which a full exposition of this theme in Isaiah 40–55 would require. For myself, I would adopt a position closely comparable with that of Van Winkle, 'The Relationship of the Nations to Yahweh and to Israel in Isaiah xl–lv'. For discussion of how this approach relates to the servant theme, see Wilcox and Paton-Williams, 'The Servant Songs in Deutero-Isaiah', and Williamson, 'The Concept of Israel in Transition'.

evident or universally accepted, however, so that a careful examination of the passage with these questions in mind cannot be avoided.

We may set the scene by observing the variety of opinions which are currently held about the origins of the passage.[63] First, there are those who still defend Isaianic authorship. The most sustained defence of this position is that of Wildberger, and those who have followed him have added little to his arguments.[64] Secondly, there is a group of scholars who, for different reasons, believe that the passage is later than Isaiah but that it should nevertheless still be dated within the pre-exilic period, perhaps during the reign of Josiah.[65] Thirdly, some have argued for a date in the early post-exilic period, perhaps even as early as the closing years of the reign of Cyrus, or at any rate soon after that,[66] while others, fourthly, argue for a somewhat later date within the post-exilic period, though there is no agreement as to exactly when.[67] Finally, a two-stage theory of the development of the passage has been advanced by Cazelles.[68] He thinks that a genuine oracle of Isaiah, originally directed towards the northern kingdom, has been redacted into its present state by Deutero-Isaiah.

The first, second, and fifth positions all have in common that

63 Some older views are now so outmoded and universally discredited that there seems little point in cataloguing them again here; for a survey of research, see H. Wildberger, 'Die Völkerwallfahrt zum Zion: Jes. ii 1–5', *VT* 7 (1957), 62–81, and his commentary, *ad loc.*; Vermeylen, 114–17; and Sweeney, *Isaiah 1–4*, 164–9.

64 e.g. Jensen, *The Use of* tôrâ *by Isaiah*, 85–9, and, in respect of authenticity, at least, Høgenhaven, *Gott und Volk bei Jesaja*, 109–11. A brief attempt to defend an early date on rhetorical grounds is offered by Gitay, *Isaiah and his Audience*, 39–41.

65 Auvray; Vermeylen, 114–33; B. Wiklander, *Prophecy as Literature: A Text-Linguistic and Rhetorical Approach to Isaiah 2–4* (ConB, OT Ser., 22; Uppsala, 1984). Wiklander's position is deduced from the fact that he regards Isaiah 2–4 as a unity which he dates to the period 734–622 BC (p. 181). So far as I can see, he does not discuss the date of 2: 2–4 as a separate issue, nor does he relate his discussion of this passage to the usual arguments which are employed to determine its date.

66 e.g. O. H. Steck, *Friedensvorstellungen im alten Jerusalem* (ThSt 111; Zurich, 1972), 69–71; H. W. Wolff, *Micah: A Commentary* (Minneapolis, 1990), 117–18 (= *Dodekapropheton 4: Micha* (BKAT 14/4; Neukirchen-Vluyn, 1982), 87–9); cf. 'Schwerter zu Pflugscharen—Missbrauch eines Prophetenwortes?', *EvTh* 44 (1984), 280–92 = *Studien zur Prophetie: Probleme und Erträge* (Munich, 1987), 93–108; Werner, *Eschatologische Texte in Jesaja 1–39*, 151–63; Sweeney, *Isaiah 1–4*, 164–74.

67 See e.g. Kaiser; Clements.

68 H. Cazelles, 'Qui aurait visé, à l'origine, Isaïe ii 2–5?', *VT* 30 (1980), 409–20. Høgenhaven (*Gott und Volk bei Jesaja*, 109–11) is in broad agreement with him so far as the 'first edition' is concerned.

they ascribe the passage in its original form to the pre-exilic period, and this would fit well with the redactional process which we have unearthed elsewhere. Tempting though it thus appears to be to adopt one or other of these positions here, the problems for so early a date preclude such a simple solution.[69] The principal difficulty stems from the presentation of the nations coming voluntarily to Jerusalem in order to seek God's instruction. Wildberger in particular has sought to overcome this by showing how closely related the passage is to a number of the Psalms (especially 46, 48, and 76) in which both Zion and the nations play a prominent role. However, while the themes, and sometimes even the vocabulary, are found in both sets of passages, so that some kind of link seems to be assured, they are handled in totally different ways. In Isa. 2: 2–4, in complete contrast with the Psalms, the nations come in peace and of their own accord, not in order to attack Jerusalem; they will themselves destroy their weapons, not be forcibly disarmed by God; and they come to learn from God, rather than being submitted to him in fear. It is this total reversal in the overall atmosphere of the Zion Psalms which makes it so difficult to date the passage as early as the time of Isaiah, for, although the prophet was undoubtedly capable of making creative use of the traditions which he may have inherited, there is no parallel for this particular reversal in other passages which can confidently be ascribed to him, nor does it seem that such ideas were picked up or developed by anyone else at the time or in the decades immediately following.[70]

The general theme and outlook of Isa. 2: 2–4 first find their closest parallels in Isaiah 40–55; 56: 6–8; 60; 66: 18–21; Jer. 3: 17; Hag. 2: 7–9; Zech. 2: 14–16 and 8: 20–3. That is why a very early post-exilic date is favoured by a number of the most recent studies of the passage. At the same time, however, it is recognized that some aspects of Isa. 2: 2–4 give it a place all of its own within this group. It makes no reference, for instance, to the idea that the nations are to be joined with Israel, nor does it show any interest in

[69] In addition to the matters discussed immediately below, there are some specific criticisms of Vermeylen's arguments in Werner's analysis of this passage, and of Wiklander's thesis, in Sweeney, *Isaiah 1–4*, 134–5 n. 88.

[70] For fuller discussion, leading to the same conclusion, see the works of Werner and Sweeney cited above. In addition, we should note that the argument from vocabulary is inconclusive, and should probably not be cited on either side of the discussion; cf. E. Cannawurf, 'The Authenticity of Micah iv 1–4', *VT* 11 (1961), 26–33; the data are presented by Wildberger, 'Völkerwallfahrt', 72–5, and Vermeylen.

their bringing of gifts and sacrifices, even though both these ideas are prominent in the texts which are of definitely post-exilic origin. Prudence demands, therefore, that we ought to examine the possibility that Isa. 2: 2–4 was the earliest passage amongst this group (after all, someone must have had the original idea!), and that the others were developed from it. The following points combine to support this hypothesis.

First, there is an especially close connection with Zech. 8: 20–3. Renaud[71] has pointed out that the expressions *'ammîm rabbîm* and *gôyim 'ₐṣûmîm* occur together only in Zech. 8: 22 and Mic. 4: 3 as part of the Micah parallel to the Isaian passage (and many scholars believe that from a textual point of view the version in Micah has been preserved better than that in Isaiah. This, of course, is a separate issue from that of origin.). The peoples' desire to 'entreat the favour of the Lord' and to 'seek' him are like their stated desire to be taught by him in Isaiah 2, and in addition the word *nēlᵉkâ* is prominent in both passages. When Zech. 8: 23 finishes with the peoples' confession that 'God is with you', however, it looks very much as though account is being taken of Isa. 7: 14; 8: 8, 10. In that case, Zechariah must be dependent on the prior Isaiah tradition rather than the other way round (Rudolph comments that Zech. 8: 20–2 is written 'in unverkennbaren Anschluß an Jes 2, 2–4'[72]). It is not impossible that the *'ōd* ('yet' or 'again') of Zech. 8: 20 is a conscious acknowledgement of this fact.

Secondly, the raising up of Mount Zion is also found in Ezek. 40: 2.[73] Zimmerli comments on this verse that 'The idea that in the eschaton an elevation above all other mountains is expected for this particular mountain finds its clearest expression in Is 2: 2. This elevation of the temple mount in Jerusalem to the form of the mythical divine mountain is doubtless also presupposed here.'[74]

[71] B. Renaud, *Structure et attaches littéraires de Miché iv–v* (Cahiers de la *RB* 2; Paris, 1964), 73; cf. D. L. Petersen, *Haggai and Zechariah 1–8: A Commentary* (OTL; London,1984), 317.

[72] Rudolph, *Haggai—Sacharja 1–8*, 152. We may note too G. von Rad's conclusion which points in a similar direction: '*Isa.* lx stands almost exactly half-way between *Isa.* ii and *Hag.* ii' ('The City on the Hill', in *The Problem of the Hexateuch and other Essays* (Edinburgh and London, 1966) 232–42 (241) = 'Die Stadt auf dem Berge', *EvTh* 8 (1948–9), 439–47 (447) = *Gesammelte Studien zum Alten Testament* (ThB 8; Munich, 1958), 214–24 (223)). By a different route, M. Fishbane reaches the same conclusion; see *Biblical Interpretation in Ancient Israel* (Oxford, 1985), 498.

[73] This seems to have been overlooked by Cannawurf, 'The Authenticity of Micah iv 1–4', 32–3, where he implies that this is only attested in post-exilic times.

[74] W. Zimmerli, *Ezekiel 2* (Philadelphia, 1983), 347 = *Ezechiel*, 997.

Thirdly, comment is required on the connections between Isa. 2: 2–4 and Deutero-Isaiah. That there are general similarities is widely recognized. The centrality of Zion in God's self-revelation,[75] the transformation of the natural order that will accompany the realization of this hope, and the change in the attitude of the nations from the hostility which characterized the pre-exilic period—these are the kind of features which lead to such general observations as that 'The spirit of the whole and some of the particular ideas . . . leave the impression of a passage that was written nearer to the time of chs. 40–55 and Ezek. than of Isaiah', and that 'The standpoint is substantially that of chs. 40–55'.[76] More specifically, the pilgrimage of the nations is sometimes compared with 45: 14–23, their desire for his 'law' (*tôrâ*) is mentioned in 42: 4, the 'establishment' (*kwn*) of Zion (verse 2) is reaffirmed in 54: 14, and her position as the site of God's self-revelation is presupposed at 51: 3–4 (and cf. 40: 9). In particular, however, there is a clear verbal allusion to 2: 3 at 51: 4, 'for a law will go forth from me [*kî tôrâ mēʾittî tēṣēʾ*] and my justice for a light to the peoples'; cf. *kî miṣṣiyyôn tēṣēʾ tôrâ* at 2: 3. While this has been noted before,[77] it has not been observed that there is a further allusion in the continuation of this passage where we read that 'my arms will rule/judge [*špṭ*] the peoples'; cf. 2: 4. Under normal circumstances, therefore, we should suppose that Deutero-Isaiah is dependent on Isa. 2: 2–4, and this is the conclusion which some have been prepared to draw.[78]

Why, then, do some scholars who recognize many of the connections mentioned above nevertheless prefer to see Isa. 2: 2–4 as testifying to a development of Isaiah 40–55 rather than as lying behind it? Sweeney's arguments (p. 173) may be taken as representative. First, he observes that in 51: 4 *tôrâ* is paired with *mišpāṭ*, but in 2: 3 with *dᵉbar-yhwh*. This is true, but is of no significance for determining chronological priority.

Secondly, he points out that in 51: 4 the Torah will go forth directly from the Lord, but in 2: 3 from Jerusalem. Since in 40–55 it is to Jerusalem that the Lord is returning, whereas 2: 2–4 presup-

[75] Cf. Dumbrell, 'The Purpose of the Book of Isaiah'.

[76] Gray, 43–4, 46.

[77] e.g. by Cazelles, 'Qui aurait visé, à l'origine, Isaïe ii 2–5', 418; Werner, *Eschatologische Texte in Jesaja 1–39*, 158; Sweeney, *Isaiah 1–4*, 172–3.

[78] Clifford (*Fair Spoken and Persuading*, 46 n. 8), e.g., speaks of 2: 1–5 as 'a text mined more than once by Second Isaiah'.

poses that he is already there, the latter text must be of later origin. This represents something of an oversimplification of the case. On the one hand, it fails to take into account the different settings of the two passages. Naturally, 40–55 emphasizes to the people in exile that the Lord will return to Jerusalem with them, but that does not mean that the prophet is incapable of projecting himself forward into the time when that has been accomplished; see, for instance, 40: 9; 49: 14–18; 52: 1–2; and 54. Indeed, for a few scholars this feature is sufficiently strong for them to suggest that Deutero-Isaiah should himself be located in Jerusalem.[79] In 40–55 there is to be observed a broad development (after the prologue of 40: 1–11) from the exhortations to Jacob/Israel in 40–8 to the greater emphasis on Zion/Jerusalem in 49–55. While this cannot be made into a hard and fast distinction, there is certainly enough material in 49–55 to indicate that even from his setting in the Babylonian exile Deutero-Isaiah was capable of speaking also about the situation which he envisaged immediately after the return about which he was so confident. On the other hand, the point about the Torah going forth from the Lord or from Jerusalem appears to be a distinction without a difference. Although, as Sweeney says, 'Isa 51, 4 does not mention Jerusalem at all', verse 3 does. Isa. 51: 1–8 is a tightly constructed passage (note, for instance, the three introductions in verses 1, 4, and 7),[80] so that it is precarious to imply that the prophet could not have been thinking of verse 3 as providing the setting from which the Lord will send forth his Torah. It is, moreover, difficult to believe that a word from the Lord must necessarily be earlier in date than a word from Jerusalem.

Thirdly, Sweeney makes a point which others too have seized upon, namely that Deutero-Isaiah says little about a pilgrimage of the nations to Jerusalem: 'The only context in which the nations come to Jerusalem in Deutero-Isaiah portrays them as bringing the exiles back and submitting to them (49, 22–23).' This may overlook 44: 5 and 45: 14–17. More significantly, however, we have difficulty in holding together the ideas of the nations bringing the

[79] See most recently Barstad, *A Way in the Wilderness*; on p. 6 n. 9 Barstad refers to others who have held this minority opinion.

[80] See also Kuntz, 'The Contribution of Rhetorical Criticism to Understanding Isaiah 51: 1–16'.

exiles home, their submission to Israel, and their eager embrace of the Lord's ways as revealed to Israel. Such a combination seems to offend our modern liberal inclinations. We therefore postulate a development of thought from the 'lower' sentiments of Isa. 49: 22–3 to the 'higher' ideals of 2: 2–4. It is not at all certain that the ancients were bothered by this, however. The ideas which Sweeney suggests must be kept apart are found inextricably united, for instance, in Isa. 14: 1–2, and they also occur in close proximity in Isaiah 60. Once again, therefore, we seem here to be in the presence of a bundle of ideas which cannot be neatly unpacked in terms of development from one to the other, and which the prophet could either handle together or treat only in part according to the rhetorical dictates of the particular context.

Finally, Sweeney distinguishes between the presentation in Deutero-Isaiah of the servant taking God's justice and Torah out to the nations (e.g. 42: 4) and the picture of the nations coming in person to Jerusalem for instruction. But here again, as 2: 3 itself makes clear, the two ideas are complementary and do not imply development from the one to the other. In explanation for why the nations will come to Jerusalem in the first place, 2: 3*b* states that it is because (*kî*) God's Torah and word will 'go forth' (*tēṣē'*) from Zion and Jerusalem (note the use of the same verb at 51: 4 and of its hiph'il in 42: 1 and 3). Once more, therefore, there is nothing here to indicate that someone who knew 2: 2–4 could not have dwelt mainly on the servant's or Israel's responsibilities in this matter as a first step towards the realization of the vision.

In sum, the points of distinction which Sweeney draws between 2: 2–4 and 51: 4 cannot be explained in terms of development. The thought and language of the two passages are too close to admit such an approach, and it is preferable to seek an explanation by way of closer attention to the purpose to which this circle of ideas is put on each occasion. The evidence already presented in favour of the view that 2: 2–4 is roughly contemporaneous with Deutero-Isaiah may therefore be allowed to stand. Equally, we have seen that the most natural conclusion to draw from the manner in which the two passages relate to one another is that 40–55 has drawn on 2: 2–4 rather than the other way round.

The next point which we must consider both reinforces this conclusion and takes us a step further in penetrating the redactional procedure which has resulted in the present form of 2: 2–5.

At the end of the material which Micah 4 and Isaiah 2 share in common, Mic. 4: 4 includes a couple of additional lines:

> but they shall sit every man under his vine
> and under his fig tree, with none to make them afraid;
> for the mouth of the Lord of hosts has spoken.

A strong case can be made on both strophic[81] and thematic[82] grounds for regarding these lines as an integral and original part of the passage. What is more, if we did not know where they came from, we should probably conclude that they were written from within the Isaiah tradition. The last line, as we saw in an earlier chapter, occurs elsewhere only at Isa. 1: 20 (and cf. 1: 2); 40: 5; and 58: 14. Moreover, whereas the first part of the verse reproduces a stereotypical vision of peace, the additional words 'with none to make them afraid' (*w*$^{e}$*'ên maḥ*$^{a}$*rîd*) recur at Isa. 17: 2 (and elsewhere too, admittedly), but never in Micah. Again, the divine title 'Lord of hosts' (*yhwh ṣ*$^{e}$*bā'ôt*) comes nowhere else in the book of Micah, but it is very common in Isaiah. Needless to say, the focus on Zion throughout the passage is, as we have seen, very much at home in the Isaiah tradition.

This suggests the possibility not only that Isa. 2: 2–4 was known to Deutero-Isaiah, but that it reached him in an 'Isaianic' context in which the extra lines of Mic. 4: 4 were still present. Such a conclusion opens up the probability that he has acted here in the same way that we proposed for his intervention at 5: 25–30 and 8: 21–3*a*. He moved the material which he inherited to its present position and included a brief addition of his own (2: 5) in order to underline the purpose for which he included the material in its new position. It was at this stage that the material now found in Mic. 4: 4 was dropped.

If we then ask why he should have wished to relocate this passage to its present setting, a consideration of 2: 1 readily provides an answer. The presence of this heading indicates that at one time a form of the book of Isaiah started here. In view of the fact that Isaiah 1 seems to have been compiled with the whole of the book of

[81] See Marti and Gray, *pace* Wolff.

[82] See Wildberger, 'Völkerwallfahrt', 75–6; W. Rudolph, *Micha—Nahum—Habakuk—Zephanja* (KAT 13/3; Gütersloh, 1975), 80–1; Kaiser (hesitantly).

Isaiah in mind,[83] it may be proposed that it was the earlier form of the work as compiled by Deutero-Isaiah that began at 2: 1.[84] Verses 2–4 furnish an admirable introductory vision for such a work, and as we have seen he returns to its themes with increasing frequency towards the end of his work in chapters 49–55. Moreover, its influence is apparent at other climactic points which we have ascribed to his redaction, such as 12: 6 and 40: 1–11.

Despite the lengthy discussions which this chapter has necessitated, our conclusions concerning possible Deutero-Isaianic redaction in Isaiah 1–12 may be briefly summarized. At 2: 2–4; 5: 25–9; and 8: 21–2 he has relocated material which he inherited from an earlier version of the Isaiah tradition and in each case added a short passage to them (2: 5; 5: 30; 8: 23[9: 1]*a*) with the use of catchwords. At 11: 11–16 he composed a passage to serve a redactional purpose which should balance 5: 25–30. Finally, he supplied chapter 12 as a conclusion to the whole section. The understanding of the overall shape of the material which emerges from this analysis is of 2: 2–4 providing a vision of how things should be but one from which the house of Jacob has fallen dramatically short. The initial statement of condemnation and judgement is concluded at 5: 25–30, after which there follows material which he seems to have taken as leading towards a more hopeful outcome, and this he summarizes in a similar passage at the end of chapter 11. Chapter 12

83 The view that Isaiah 1 was consciously compiled as an introduction to some form of the work is accepted with varying emphases by many commentators and was given its classical formulation by G. Fohrer, 'Jesaja 1 als Zusammenfassung der Verkündigung Jesajas', *ZAW* 74 (1962), 251–68 = *Studien zur alttestamentlichen Prophetie (1949–1965)* (BZAW 99; Berlin, 1967), 148–66. For the connections between chapter 1 and the later parts of the book, including especially chapters 65–6, see Liebreich, 'The Compilation of the Book of Isaiah'; Becker, *Isaias—der Prophet und sein Buch*, 45–7; Lack, *La Symbolique du Livre d'Isaïe*, 139–41; Sweeney, *Isaiah 1–4*, 21–4; and Tomasino, 'Isaiah 1. 1–2. 4 and 63–66'.

84 I am not persuaded by the attempt of P. R. Ackroyd, 'A Note on Isaiah $2_1$', *ZAW* 75 (1963), 320–1, reiterated in 'Isaiah i–xii', 32–4, to argue that 2: 1 was added only to claim Isaianic authorship for 2: 2–4 in view of its presence also in the book of Micah, with the consequence that 2: 2–4 was once the direct continuation of chapter 1. In addition to the solid arguments of Wildberger, 77, and Sweeney, *Isaiah 1–4*, 134 n. 87, it may further be noted that if Isaiah 1 was added at the last stage in the composition of the book as a whole, arguments from the suitability of chapter 2 as its continuation can be equally well explained on the assumption that the compiler of chapter 1 was aware that his collection would be followed by chapter 2 and so did not feel himself obliged to complete his own collection with an oracle of hope.

then supplies an eschatological hymn of praise with which he rounded off other sections of his work, and it concludes with a recall of the introductory focus on Zion and the involvement of all the nations.

In terms of method, we have noted a certain consistency both in that he has intervened primarily at the start and finish of sections and in that he has usually employed similar procedures of combining older materials with his own composition. The only exception to this comes at the end of the passage as a whole, no doubt because there was not available from the earlier form of the work the kind of 'second-exodus' passage which he wanted to use in view of the evident importance to him of this theme. Instead, he modelled the shape of the start of this passage on the inherited 5: 25–6. Finally, as might be expected, he made particular use of the themes and vocabulary of these passages in the course of his own more extended composition in chapters 40–55.

# 7

# Deutero-Isaiah and Isaiah 13–27

THE second major section of the book of Isaiah comprises chapters 13–27, in which are found an extensive collection of 'oracles against the nations' in chapters 13–23 (together with some different but not unrelated material in chapters 20 and 22) and the so-called 'Isaiah Apocalypse' in chapters 24–7, whose connection with the preceding collection by way of a generalizing or universalizing tendency is widely recognized.

The origins and development of this section have been, and continue to be, the subjects of debate. In very broad terms, however, there is agreement that some parts of chapters 13–23 derive from Isaiah of Jerusalem, whereas the whole of 24–7 is later. It is explicitly stated at 16: 13–14, furthermore, that one of the oracles against the nations was reapplied to a new historical situation over the course of time, and many other examples of this procedure have been suggested to explain various parts of these chapters. In addition, the use of *maśśā'* ('oracle') to introduce many, though not all, of the oracles, points to a degree of conscious compilation at some stage in the formation of these chapters. The disagreements among scholars are thus concerned not so much with general principle as with the detail of which passage or section is to be ascribed to which stage of composition or redaction.[1]

All this suggests the possibility that there may be a number of places where the hand of Deutero-Isaiah might be detected either as author or as redactor. It is not difficult to imagine, for instance, that chapter 21 would have been of particular interest to him. Verses 1–10 appear to look forward to an attack on Babylon which will result in its downfall, and they are usually dated to the exilic

[1] For a recent, helpful introduction to these chapters, see A. K. Jenkins, 'The Development of the Isaiah Tradition in Isaiah 13–23', in Vermeylen (ed.), *The Book of Isaiah*, 237–51.

period.[2] In particular, in verse 9 the announcement of the fall of Babylon (whose double use of the verb *nāpᵉlâ* is reminiscent of Deutero-Isaiah's style; cf. 40: 1; 51: 9, 12, 17; 52: 1, 11[3]) is followed by a reference to the overthrow of her idol gods, which 'accords with the polemic against idolatrous worship in Deutero-Isaiah'.[4] Again, the chapter ends with a probable addition in verses 16–17 (note the close affinity with 16: 13–14, referred to above), whose conclusion, 'For the Lord, the God of Israel, has spoken', is reminiscent of one of the formulae discussed earlier in Chapter 4.

Details such as these, however, are at best 'straws in the wind', and it is clearly not possible to mount even a tentative argument upon them. Like other pieces of evidence we have purposely noted without examining, they become of possible significance only if the case in question is regarded as sufficiently strong to be entertained as a working hypothesis. Rather than piling up what many might consider to be dubious arguments of this kind, I shall therefore confine myself in this chapter to only two passages which offer the possibility of establishing somewhat firmer ground beneath our feet.

The first is the opening, and longest, of the oracles against the nations, that against Babylon in 13: 1–14: 23. In the case of the development of this passage, it is possible to speak of something of a consensus among the commentators, although recently some further refinements have been suggested to which I shall refer after describing what still appears to be the 'usual' view.

2 An alternative hypothesis has been advanced by A. A. Macintosh (*Isaiah XXI: A Palimpsest* (Cambridge, 1980)), who proposes that an originally eighth-century oracle has been reread and partially rewritten to apply now to the sixth century. His arguments against the more usual view have been rejected, however, by J. Day, Review of Macintosh, *Isaiah xxi*, in *JTS* NS 34 (1983), 212–15.

3 Cf. L. Köhler, *Deuterojesaja (Jesaja 40–55) stilkritisch untersucht* (BZAW 37; Giessen, 1923), 99.

4 Jenkins, 'The Development of the Isaiah Tradition', 245. B. Gosse (*Isaïe 13,1–14,23 dans la tradition littéraire du livre d'Isaïe et dans la tradition des oracles contre les nations* (OBO 78; Freiburg and Göttingen, 1988), 43–67) also notes some points of contact between Isa. 21: 1–10 and Deutero-Isaiah, but argues rather for an early post-exilic date. His main argument is the evident connection between verse 6 and parts of Isaiah 60–2, esp. 62: 6. It is of interest to observe, however, that the watchman of 21: 6 has, so to speak, become plural in 62: 6, a feature of Trito-Isaiah's reuse of earlier Isaianic themes which we noted earlier; see above, p. 109. Since in addition the role of the watchmen is different in each passage, it seems preferable to regard 62: 6 as a reflection upon an earlier passage rather than as coming from the same hand or circle.

Following the heading in 13: 1, which is clearly editorial, the lengthy composition of 13: 2–22 is generally regarded as a unity. Its description of the coming day of the Lord in judgement upon Babylon is mostly devoid of specific historical allusion, but verses 17 and 19 provide two clues which have been thought to point to a date in the (probably late) exilic period. The reference to God stirring up the Medes (verse 17) and the comparison of the fall of Babylon to the overthrow of Sodom and Gomorrah (verse 19) is sufficiently different from the true course of history in 539 BC, when Cyrus the Persian was welcomed into Babylon as a liberator, as to make it unlikely that this was written as a *post eventum* prophecy. On the other hand, prior to the demise of the Assyrian empire at the end of the seventh century BC the Medes were generally in alliance with Babylon against Assyria, so that a date as early as the Assyrian period is equally unlikely.[5] A date shortly before the rise of Cyrus is thus generally favoured for this poem.

Isa. 14: 4*b*–21 is an extended, mocking lament over the fall of an oppressive tyrant. He is not identified in the poem itself, and this has allowed scholars to speculate that he may have been an Assyrian, such as Sargon or Sennacherib, or a Babylonian, such as Nebuchadnezzar or Nabonidus; there is thus even a possibility that the poem may come ultimately from Isaiah himself.

Disagreement on this detail, however, cannot overshadow the universal consensus that these two lengthy poems have been redactionally joined (and the second explicitly associated with the king of Babylon) by the editorial material in 14: 1–4*a* and 22–3. In 14: 1–4*a*, in a style which differs sharply from the surrounding material, the fall of Babylon in chapter 13 is made the ground for the imminent reversal in Israel's fortunes (note the connective *kî* at the start of this passage), and this then becomes the context in which the taunt-song is set. Verses 22–3, at the end of the passage, also serve to link the poem with Babylon, and in doing so to move beyond the death of a single king to the fall of the city as a whole. This conclusion thus links back to the end of chapter 13, and so functions as an effective summary to the oracle against Babylon as a whole. Within this consensus, we may note that there are

[5] This is one of the main reasons why the sustained attempt of S. Erlandsson (*The Burden of Babylon: A Study of Isaiah 13: 2–14: 23* (ConB, OT Ser. 4; Lund, 1970)) to defend Isaianic authorship has not found wide acceptance.

differences of opinion as to whether this redactional activity (i.e. 13: 1; 14: 1–4*a*, 22–3) is to be ascribed to a single writer or several.

In recent years two new approaches to these chapters have been outlined. The first, which is of less significance for our present purposes, challenges the unity of 13: 2–22. Clements, for instance, finds here five prophetic utterances. The first two, verses 2–3 and 4–5, which may 'represent only fragments of longer prophecies in which the historical context was originally made clear' (p. 133), are to be taken in a positive sense towards Babylon; she is being raised up as an instrument of God's judgement. The first could even go back to Isaiah himself, while the second, which is wider in scope, comes from the time when Babylon was replacing Assyria as the new world-ruler. The third prophecy, in verses 6–8, is also in historical order, since it is thought to reflect the fall of Jerusalem in 587 BC, while the fifth (verses 17–22), with its references to the Medes and the overthrow of Babylon, comes from the end of the exilic period. Only the fourth prophecy, verses 9–16, is thus out of chronological order, being a much later, because heightened eschatological, reflection on the day of the Lord, a theme which had been introduced in less extravagant terms in the preceding paragraph.

The difficulty with this interesting fresh analysis of Isaiah 13 seems to be that we are given no indication in the text that the attitude towards Babylon changes as the passage progresses. It seems to me that the language of the opening verses in the chapter, which has suggested to Clements that Babylon is being addressed in a positive manner, can equally well be explained by the procedure attested elsewhere in which material once spoken in condemnation of Judah is now reused in condemnation of the world power; Hab. 2: 6–20 is generally recognized to contain some clear examples of this, while the reuse of Jer. 6: 22–4 at 50: 41–3 is quite explicit.[6] Whereas it is possible, therefore, that parts of Isa. 13: 2–5 have been influenced by earlier material of a different outlook, that does not enable us to affirm that they were ever composed as they stand to serve that purpose. The consistently anti-Babylonian stance of chapter 13 is a major reason why most scholars have regarded it as a unity.

An alternative division of Isaiah 13 has been proposed by

[6] Cf. Gosse, *Isaïe 13,1–14,23 dans la tradition littéraire du livre d'Isaïe*, 122–3.

Jeppesen,[7] who maintains that 13: 2–16 is an original 'Day of Yahweh text'. Comparison of Isaiah 2 with this passage leads him to suggest that it might go back to Isaiah, in which case it was probably directed against the Assyrians. Whether or not this is so, 'Isa. 13: 2–16 is a text which could be accepted as Isaianic by the exiles. These "Isaiah-words" reveal themselves to be a prophecy concerning that Babylon, which had subjugated the people who ought by nature to live in Jerusalem around Zion without fear' (p. 69). Isa. 13: 17–22, by contrast, is one of the oracles against the nations proper, and Jeppesen accepts its late exilic date, finding in it several connections with the thought-world of Deutero-Isaiah. Thus, although he finds separate origins for the two parts in this chapter, his principal concern is to point out how the chapter would have been read by the exiles. As we shall have occasion to observe below, his approach to these chapters comes very close indeed to that being explored here, and to that extent the possibility of an originally independent composition in 13: 2–16 is less significant than the role which it plays in the present, exilic form of the text.

The second recent trend in study of these chapters is to date their composition either in whole or in large measure to the post-exilic period.[8] While the reasons advanced for this later dating differ from one scholar to another, as do the precise dates they assign to these chapters, they all have in common an emphasis on the development of Babylon as a symbol of the oppressive opponents of the people of God; this enables them to play down the significance of the apparently historical references in 13: 17 and 19. If they are right, then clearly there is no value in pursuing a study of Isaiah 13–14 in the present context; any search for connections with the work of Deutero-Isaiah would *ex hypothesi* be ruled out of court. While noting this here as an 'early warning', I shall nevertheless continue with the procedure adopted in the previous chapter—namely, to undertake first a positive presentation of the case for Deutero-Isaianic influence in these chapters before returning to examine

[7] K. Jeppesen, 'The *maśśā*' *Bābel* in Isaiah 13–14', *PIBA* 9 (1985), 63–80.

[8] See explicitly Kaiser (who allows that parts of chapter 13 may be earlier); Vermeylen, 285–96; and Gosse, *Isaïe 13,1–14,23 dans la tradition littéraire du livre d'Isaïe*. Though not quite so clear, this seems also to be the implication of the study of R. Martin-Achard, 'Esaïe 47 et la tradition prophétique sur Babylone', in J. A. Emerton (ed.), *Prophecy: Essays Presented to Georg Fohrer on his Sixty-Fifth Birthday 6 September 1980* (BZAW 150; Berlin, 1980), 83–105.

more closely the recent arguments which would ascribe all this material to a later date. As a starting-point, therefore, I shall go along with the consensus view outlined above which finds evidence for an exilic dating for chapter 13[9] and probably for the present use, at least, of 14: 4*b*–21, and for the work of one or more editors in 13: 1; 14: 1–4*a* and 22–3.

The first matter which requires more attention than it has generally received from the hand of the commentators is the setting of these chapters at the start of the long passage of oracles against the nations in 13–23. At the most elementary level, it is, of course, striking that so much material concerning Babylon should have been collected here, especially in view of the fact that there is in any case a separate oracle against Babylon in 21: 1–10. If this prominence by both position and quantity is indicative of the passage's particular significance to the compiler, as might be supposed, then we should naturally look to the period when Babylon impinged most severely and negatively upon the community, and this must surely point to the period of the Babylonian exile. Following the shift in power to the Persian empire, Babylon continued to be a prominent centre of Jewish life, but as a political force in its own right it no longer played the threatening role which it had previously. Of course, it is true that thereafter Babylon began to be regarded as symbolic of all that was evil, but this can only have been because it had already become prominent, thereby demanding that its central role in the texts be reinterpreted; it does not necessarily explain its prominence in the first place. Similarly, whereas Gosse suggests that it may have been positioned first by analogy with the Behistun inscription, in which Darius I proclaimed his subjugation of the numerous rebellions which marked the start of his reign, beginning with Babylon (522–520 BC), this analogy could only be potentially illuminating if it were first established that this was the time of the chapters' composition; it does not in itself seem at all strong as an argument for such a dating. Even before we begin to look for specific points of contact with Deutero-Isaiah, therefore, it would be reasonable to suppose, in view of the importance of the fall of Babylon in his work, that there

[9] In a private communication, J. Day has written that 'the reference to the Medes suggests a date prior to 550 BC, and the picture of an all-conquering Babylonian king indicates a date in the reign of Nebuchadnezzar, prior to 562 BC'. As will be seen, this refinement of what I have called 'the usual view' is fully compatible with the suggestions I advance below.

is a strong prima-facie case for suggesting that he would at the least have been sympathetic towards the redactional placement of this material in its present setting.[10]

More particularly, there is some evidence, which has not been recognized hitherto, to suggest that the positioning of this passage may have been undertaken separately from the main work of collecting the oracles against the nations in Isaiah. At 14: 28 there is a new heading: 'In the year that King Ahaz died came this oracle.' We do not find any other heading quite like this in chapters 13–23, but it is, of course, closely comparable with 6: 1 ('In the year that King Uzziah died'), which on any analysis introduces a new section in the work. It is natural, therefore, to ask if it once did the same here.

To answer this, we need to look at the material which precedes it, for at present it looks rather like 'just another' heading within the collection of oracles against the nations, even if an unparalleled one. Isa. 14: 24–7 is a brief passage concerning Assyria, whose downfall is portrayed as a prefigurement of God's 'purpose that is purposed concerning the whole earth'. These few verses have evoked more than their fair share of discussion, and there is no agreement about their unity, date, or original setting.[11] It is clear, however, that they show an uncommon degree of connection with material in Isaiah 9–10, so much so that many scholars have argued that they once belonged with those chapters, whether as part of an original Isaianic composition or as part of the later redaction of his work during the reign of Josiah. In this connection, it may be significant that the paragraph lacks one of the headings which regularly precede the oracles against the nations in the following chapters.

In view of these cursory observations, it is possible to imagine

[10] Cf. C. T. Begg, 'Babylon in the Book of Isaiah', in Vermeylen (ed.), *The Book of Isaiah*, 121–5.

[11] In addition to the commentaries, cf. Skehan, 'Some Textual Problems in Isaia'; Donner, *Israel unter den Völkern*, 145–6; Childs, *Isaiah and the Assyrian Crisis*, 38–9; Huber, *Jahwe, Juda und die anderen Völker beim Propheten Jesaja*, 41–50; Dietrich, *Jesaja und die Politik*, 120–1; Barth, *Die Jesaja-Worte in der Josiazeit*, 103–19; Vermeylen, 252–62 and 296–7; Høgenhaven, *Gott und Volk bei Jesaja*, 126–7; Gonçalves, *L'Expédition de Sennachérib en Palestine*, 307–9; Werner, *Studien zur alttestamentlichen Vorstellung vom Plan Jahwes*, 33–6; R. E. Clements, 'Isaiah 14,22–27: A Central Passage Reconsidered', in Vermeylen (ed.), *The Book of Isaiah*, 253–62; Gosse, 'Isaïe 14, 24–27 et les oracles contre les nations du livre d'Isaïe', *BN* 56 (1991), 17–21.

two ways by which 14: 24–7 might have reached its present position, and it is not necessary for us to distinguish between them at this stage of our investigation. Despite the distance which now separates 14: 24–7 from chapter 10, much of the intervening material is clearly to be dated to the exilic period or later, as we have already argued for the second half of chapter 11, for chapter 12, and as we accept with most commentators for chapters 13 and 14: 1–23 as well. It is therefore possible, as Vermeylen maintains, that the present position of 14: 24–7 is the result of accident rather than design, a separation between two connected bodies of writing which may have started with only a modest addition and which then grew by subsequent accretions to its present extent. Alternatively, this material may have been deliberately moved to its present position as part of a conscious redactional shaping of this part of the work, in which case, of course, it would have to have been no earlier than (though it could conceivably be contemporaneous with) the inclusion of 13: 1–14: 23. Either way, the paragraph has to be accounted for without recourse to the theory that it was included in its present position because it was deemed to be one of the oracles against the nations.

Prior to 14: 24–7, we find, of course, the oracle against Babylon, with which we are here principally concerned. As noted above, there is already an oracle concerned with Babylon included amongst the regular oracles against the nations at 21: 1–10. In addition, we have seen that 13: 1–14: 23 differs in both its length and more involved composition from the other oracles against the nations. The conclusion naturally follows that this passage is to be distinguished from the bulk of the collection which follows, and this enables us to propose that at an earlier stage in the compilation of the book 14: 28 was indeed a major heading—the heading, in fact, to the section of oracles against the nations as a whole, together with, presumably, the early material now included in chapters 28–32. The parallel with 6: 1 will have been deliberate, marking a significant shift from a focus on events following the death of Uzziah (i.e. during the reign of Ahaz) which we find in the section introduced by chapter 6, to the period of Hezekiah when, as we know from the later chapters of the book, Isaiah so bitterly opposed the anti-Assyrian alliances in which Judah became embroiled. It does not, of course, necessarily follow from this that all the oracles which follow 14: 28—even the authentically Isaianic ones—must therefore date to the reign of Hezekiah (though in fact many of them probably do). The compiler's intention may not in every case have reflected accurately the circumstances of Isaiah's delivery of his oracles. Nevertheless, the reasoning behind his ordering of the early form of Isaiah's work can be appreciated.

The reason why this conclusion has generally been overlooked is because 13: 1 has a heading of its own which at first sight seems to include 13: 1–14: 23 in the main collection of oracles against the nations. Its opening words, 'An oracle concerning Babylon', are of the same type which introduce many of the later oracles; cf. 15: 1; 17: 1; 19: 1; 21: 1, 11, 13; 22: 1; 23: 1. However, 13: 1 differs from these other examples in that it continues 'which Isaiah the son of Amoz saw', a clause which is identical with part of the heading in 2: 1. I suggested in the previous chapter that 2: 1 may have marked the start of the book of Isaiah as Deutero-Isaiah shaped it, and it would be wholly consistent with this approach if 13: 1 were to be regarded as a heading introduced at the same time. His use of *maśśā'* in this verse would not be surprising if he were adding a new introductory passage to a section which already used this word as a regular form of heading.

To sum up our main conclusions so far, we may now distinguish two major forms of heading in this part of the book of Isaiah. In the earliest version of the book to which we have access, and hence the one which Deutero-Isaiah will have inherited, we find the form 'In the year that King X died' at 6: 1 and 14: 28, and this was intended to distinguish between the two main periods in which Isaiah himself was active. Subsequently, as part of the process by which the book was reworked in the exilic period, the form 'which Isaiah the son of Amoz saw' was introduced at 2: 1 and 13: 1 to mark the new main divisions in the work. It was argued in the previous chapter that Isaiah 12 was intended at this stage of the book's redaction to function as the conclusion of a major section; appropriately, therefore, 13: 1 was used to introduce the next main section.

So far, we have established only that the oracles against Babylon in 13: 1–14: 23 have been given their present setting later than the early ordering of the work of Isaiah of Jerusalem, and that a probable time for this was the period of the exile. In order to reach more specific conclusions, we need to turn to consider the contents of this passage more closely. Naturally, our primary interest will focus on the work of the redactor, whose hand is agreed by all to be found in 13: 1; 14: 1–4*a*, and 22–3. Sufficient comment having already been made for the time being about 13: 1, we turn first to the opening of chapter 14.

Jeppesen has written of verses 1–2 that 'if there are Deutero-Isaianic interpolations in Isa. 1–39, this text is one of the most obvious examples' (p. 71). The reasons for this confident assertion are not difficult to see, and there are even more points of connection than Jeppesen himself briefly mentions. In the first line of 14: 1, as he rightly points out, the designation of the people as Jacob in parallel with Israel is rare in Isaiah 1–39 (and then generally refers to the northern kingdom) but extremely frequent in Isaiah 40–9, precisely that portion of Deutero-Isaiah's work which also deals with Babylon.[12] It is never used in Trito-Isaiah. Similarly, Isaiah himself nowhere says that the Lord 'will have compassion on' (*yᵉraḥēm*) his people,[13] but the thought is common in Deutero-Isaiah; cf. 49: 10, 13, (15); 54: 8, 10; 55: 7.[14] The situation is similar with regard to God 'choosing' (*bḥr*) his people. The verb does occur in 1: 29, but the subject there is the people, and gardens are the object. In addition, it is uncertain whether this verse should be ascribed to Isaiah. The use of the infinitive in 7: 15–16 also has a different subject and object. In Deutero-Isaiah, by contrast, the thought is prominent; cf. 41: 8 (object: Jacob–Israel), 9; 43: 10; 44: 1 (object: Jacob–Israel), 2; 48: 10; 49: 7. Although the verb occurs a number of times in Trito-Isaiah, never once is it used of God choosing his people. It is, therefore, misleading when Gosse (p. 202) lists all the uses in Isaiah without drawing this distinction, for it is clear that the thought being expressed in 14: 1 is paralleled only in Deutero-Isaiah. Finally, attention should be drawn to the introductory *kî* ('for, because'), which joins this passage to chapter 13.[15] It serves to underline the fact that in the redactor's thinking the fall of Babylon is inextricably linked with the salvation of Israel. This is precisely Deutero-Isaiah's perspective, as is clear from his first mention of Babylon in 43: 14 ('For your sake I will send to

[12] Cf. 40: 27; 41: 8, 14; 42: 24; 43: 1, 22, 28; 44: 1, 5, 21, 23; 45: 4; 46: 3; 48: 1, 12; 49: 5–6. Jeppesen's list contains some minor inaccuracies.

[13] The verb occurs only once in Isaiah's work, but then in a negative sense–9: 16. The occurrences at 13: 18; 27: 11; and 30: 18 are all agreed to be later.

[14] It is perhaps worth mentioning that this verb occurs only once in Trito-Isaiah, at 60: 10.

[15] Cf. G. Quell, 'Jesaja 14, 1–23', in J. Herrmann (ed.), *Festschrift Friedrich Baumgärtel zum 70. Geburtstag, 14. Januar 1958* (Erlanger Forschungen, Reihe A, 10; Erlangen, 1959), 131–57 (esp. 134–5), on the importance in context of this particle.

Babylon') as well as from the combination of the two themes in chapters 46–7 and in the closing part of chapter 48[16] (and cf. 45: 1–4). It is thus evident that both in its specific vocabulary and in its thought as a whole the first line of 14: 1 is distinctively Deutero-Isaianic.

The second half of the verse goes on to speak of God restoring his people to their land and of aliens joining them. This is the first explicit indication that the redactor is writing from the standpoint of exile, and it is for that very reason revealing: he simply assumes that this is the context within which chapter 13 should be read. The thought of foreigners joining the returning exiles is not, as we saw in an earlier chapter, exclusive to Deutero-Isaiah, but equally it is not absent from his work either; cf. 44: 5, where the idea of belonging specifically to the people known as Jacob occurs; 45: 14; 49: 7; 55: 5. The vocabulary of this part of the verse reveals little about its origin, since it is generally uncommon in the book of Isaiah; the root *lwh* occurs in (24: 2 and) 56: 3 and 6, but that does not give us much to go on, since, in common with Trito-Isaiah's frequent practice, it could as well be a reflection of this verse as an indication of contemporaneity. Since *gēr* seems already to have developed the meaning of proselyte in a few texts in Ezekiel,[17] it is not justified to conclude that this usage must of necessity point to the post-exilic period.

Verse 2 gives greater precision to the role of the foreign nations in the return of Israel to their land and to their status in the renewed community: 'And the peoples will take them and bring them to their place, and the house of Israel will possess them in the Lord's land as male and female slaves; they will take captive those who were their captives, and rule over those who oppressed them.' With a number of other commentators, Jeppesen observes how close this is to the thought of 49: 22–3, a passage which we have already seen was particularly influential in the redaction of Isaiah 1–12. It too speaks of the 'peoples' (*'ammîm*) who will 'bring' (hiph. of *bw'*) the people of Israel home (see also 43: 6), and then immediately continues by describing the subservient status of their leaders (both male and female; cf. the discussion of 11: 12, above, Chapter 6 ) in terms which are even stronger than the 'male and

[16] For the links between these three chapters, see Franke, 'The Function of the Satiric Lament over Babylon in Second Isaiah (xlvii)'.

[17] Cf. D. Kellermann, 'גּוּר', *TWAT* i, col. 989.

female slaves' of 14: 2.[18] The role-reversal mentioned in the last line of the verse is also characteristic of Deutero-Isaiah; cf. 41: 11–16; 49: 7, 23, 25–6; 51: 22–3; 52: 13–15; 54: 15–17. Again, the vocabulary of the second half of this verse is not particularly distinctive,[19] and it is thus strange that Gosse (p. 204) compares its general thought only with three passages in Trito-Isaiah without mentioning the equally close parallels in Isaiah 40–55.

At 14: 3–4*a*, the address switches to the second person singular in order to prepare the way for the introduction of the taunt which follows. There can be no certainty whether this passage is to be ascribed to the same author as verses 1–2 or whether it was already attached to the following passage when the author of 1–2 took it over. Either way, it coincides with the outlook of Deutero-Isaiah in looking forward to the end of 'your pain and turmoil and the hard service with which you were made to serve'; see especially 40: 2.

Our analysis of Isa. 14: 1–4*a* has revealed that the thought of the passage is throughout closely comparable with that of Deutero-Isaiah and furthermore that in some places the vocabulary, and indeed the specific manner in which that vocabulary is used, is identical with his. Elsewhere, however, the vocabulary is not particularly characteristic of his style. This latter circumstance, which might appear to argue against his authorship, can be partly explained, however, by the observation that some of these elements appear to have been drawn from the surrounding material which this passage was framed to weld together.[20] Thus *rdh* (verse 2) occurs in 14: 6, *ngś* in 14: 4*b*, and *rgz* in 14: 9 (and cf. 13: 13; 14: 16). In addition, the root *nwḥ* (verses 1 and 3) recurs in 14: 7, though the phrase *hnyḥ ʿl-ʾdmh* seems to be stereotypical; cf. Jer. 27: 11;

[18] This parallel, together with the considerations advanced in connection with the discussion of Isa. 2: 2–5 above, Ch. 6, render unnecessary Wildberger's proposal to regard this part of 14: 2 as a later addition. He himself admits that the switches in subject are not sufficient to challenge the unity of the verse; the intended referent is clear throughout from the context. His argument thus rests entirely on what he considers 'eine fast unerträgliche Wendung des Gedankens' (p. 525), but it appears that what is intolerable for a modern commentator was not considered a problem to the author(s) of the passages listed above, p. 152. For a defence of the unity of the opening verses of Isaiah 14, see further Quell, 'Jesaja 14, 1–23'.

[19] Though for *nhl*, see 49: 8; with *šbh* cf. *šby* of 46: 2; 49: 24, 25; 52: 2; for *rdh*, cf. 41: 2; 45: 1 (?); and for *ngś*, cf. 53: 7.

[20] A further explanatory consideration is that the last clause of 14: 3 seems to be closely modelled on Exod. 1: 14; cf. Erlandsson, *The Burden of Babylon*, 121. The use of exodus typology by Deutero-Isaiah is well known, and has been referred to several times in the previous chapter.

Ezek. 37: 14. This habit, it will be recalled, was found to be a prominent characteristic of his method in the redactional portions of Isaiah 2–12 which were discussed in Chapter 6 above, so that its recurrence here not only explains the apparent anomaly in 14: 1–4*a*, but actually strengthens the impression that the same hand is at work.

The situation in Isa. 14: 22–3 is quite different. There is nothing here to suggest that we have the same editor as the one responsible for the introduction to the chapter. 'Babylon' now refers to the city rather than its king, and the threefold use of the *n*$^{e}$*'um* formula contrasts with its absence elsewhere in the passage. (It may be added that twice this occurs in the form *n*$^{e}$*'um yhwh ṣ*$^{e}$*bā'ôt*, a phrase never once used by Deutero-Isaiah.) It is pure supposition, therefore, on Wildberger's part to associate this passage with the author of 14: 3–4*a*. The question may, therefore, be left open, for our purposes, whether these two verses were added before or after the incorporation of the chapter as a whole into its present setting,[21] and I shall not consider it further in the present context.

If, on the basis of our examination of 13: 1 and 14: 1–4*a*, we may assume that there is a strong prima-facie case for regarding Deutero-Isaiah as the redactor responsible for joining the two previously extant passages 13: 2–22 and 14: 4*b*–21(23) together and for incorporating the passage as a whole in its present setting, we need to ask next whether there is sufficient evidence to conclude that there was already enough in the material which he inherited to attract his attention to it in the first place. At 2: 2–4 and 5: 25–9 we sought to establish that this was so both because of their general themes and because they appeared to have exerted a particular influence on his writing elsewhere. Can the same be said of the two component poems in chapters 13–14?

In terms of the general theme, it may be confidently asserted not only that Deutero-Isaiah would have found the threat of the overthrow of Babylon congenial, but also that he would have agreed closely with the manner in which this is presented and the motivation given for it. This conclusion emerges clearly from the brief study of 'Babylon in the Book of Isaiah' by Begg, whose summary may therefore be cited in full:

[21] See the contrasting analyses of Clements, 'Isaiah 14,22–27', and R. H. O'Connell, 'Isaiah xiv 4B–23: Ironic Reversal through Concentric Structure and Mythic Allusion', *VT* 38 (1988), 407–18.

As to its 'Babylon image', Isaiah 40–48 largely echoes that of Isaiah 13–23 with its references to Babylon's pride (47,7–8, 10) [Begg has earlier found this element at 13: 11; 14: 13–14] and oppressiveness (48,6) [as at 14: 4*b*–6, 12, 16–17] as well as its eventual definitive overthrow by Yahweh (43,14; 47,3.9.11; 48,14) [cf. 13: 19–22; 14: 22–3] in which its former preeminent status is reversed (47,1.5, cf. 13,19; 14,15) and the hope of revival posterity could represent is cut off (47,9, cf. 13,20; 14,22).[22]

In addition, it may not be a coincidence that the element of sarcasm and mockery in the taunt of chapter 14 is echoed in the tone of chapter 47. Indeed, Whybray introduces his commentary on this latter chapter by observing that it combines 'the mocking-song or taunt-song and the funeral-song or dirge over the dead . . . used in an anticipatory way, referring to the expected downfall as if it had already occurred', a description which would be equally apt of chapter 14. (Note also the use in both chapters of the *qinah* rhythm.)

Terminology which may have attracted and even influenced Deutero-Isaiah is also to be found in these chapters, though with one or two exceptions it is not in any sense so marked and striking as other passages which we have examined or as the thematic parallels just summarized. To cite only a few noteworthy examples, 13: 2–5 is strongly reminiscent of 5: 26,[23] whose importance for Deutero-Isaiah and close connections with other parts of his writing have already been fully treated; for the imperative *hārîmû qôl* (13: 2), see the feminine singular form at 40: 9; *mēʾereṣ merḥāq* (13: 5) recurs at 46: 11 (and elsewhere only at Jer. 6: 20 and Prov. 25: 25); God's 'stirring-up' (*mēʿîr*) of the Medes to attack Babylon (13: 17) is echoed in his stirring-up of Cyrus for the same purpose in 41: 2, 25; and 45: 13; and when 13: 17 continues 'who have no regard for silver and do not delight in gold', it is tempting to suppose that the same thought is being expressed in different words in the continuation of 45: 13 with its 'not for price or reward'; in 13: 19 Babylon is described as 'the glory of kingdoms, the splendour and pride of the Chaldeans', and this is not unlike the picture of the city which emerges from the first part of chapter 47 (e.g. 'the

[22] Begg, 'Babylon in the Book of Isaiah', 123. Later on, Begg states that 'Indeed, the only really distinctive feature to the presentation of Babylon in Isaiah 40–48 . . . is its depiction of the city as practitioner of magic arts which, however, are no match for the power of Yahweh' (p. 124). This, of course, may be readily explained against the background of other aspects of Deutero-Isaiah's message.

[23] Cf. Erlandsson, *The Burden of Babylon*, 139.

mistress of kingdoms' (*gᵉberet mamlākût*) (verse 5), and has the extremely rare *ʿōneg* of 13: 22 been picked up in the equally rare related form *ʿᵃnuggâ* in 47: 1?), a picture whose similarity stands out the more by the fact that it is not paralleled in Jeremiah 50–1, with which there are otherwise, of course, so many points of contact.

In the taunt-song of chapter 14 there is one particularly noteworthy detailed parallel with Deutero-Isaiah in verses 7–8. First, the use together of *pṣḥ* and *rnh* ('they break forth into singing') recalls the use of these two words together at 44: 23; 49: 13; 54: 1; and 55: 12, while 52: 9 is similar. The only other place where this combination occurs is at Ps. 98: 4, a Psalm which has some other close links with Deutero-Isaiah's 'eschatological hymns of praise'. Unlike that Psalm, however, Isaiah 14 goes on to speak of how the cypresses and the cedars of Lebanon will also rejoice, and this recalls two of the verses in Deutero-Isaiah just listed, namely 44: 23 ('Break forth into singing, O mountains, O forest, and every tree in it') and 55: 12 ('the mountains and the hills before you shall break forth into singing, and all the trees of the field shall clap their hands'; note too the reference to *bᵉrôš* ('cypress') in the next verse). Finally, Jeppesen has pointed out that there is 'a fine contrast text to 14: 17' at 42: 7 (p. 72).

It should be stressed at this point that there is no intention of 'trying to prove too much' by this cursory presentation of contacts between Isaiah 13–14 and Deutero-Isaiah. There are, for instance, many verbal parallels with Jeremiah 50–1 as well as marked points of contact with other parts of the Isaiah tradition as a whole, and these would all need investigation in a full study of these chapters.[24] Our conclusion, in the light of all the evidence, may be stated as follows. The case for the location of the chapters in their present setting and for the combining of the two main poems by Deutero-

24 See especially the monographs of Erlandsson and Gosse, both of which present substantial collections of data. It is salutary to observe that even then they come to diametrically opposed conclusions! As was stressed earlier, it is not sufficient just to present lists of words; care must be taken, for instance, to examine the particular use of words, to seek to distinguish between cases of coincidence and dependence as well as commonality of authorship, and to take account of alternative sources of influence. Neither of the two monographs is faultless in these respects, and doubtless because of ignorance there will be errors of the same kind in my own work. At the very least, however, one should be aware of the methodological issues involved and so alert to the possible pitfalls.

Isaiah must rest upon the redactional concerns outlined earlier and the evidence for his hand in the editorial passages 13: 1 and especially 14: 1–2. If that conclusion be granted, then (and only then) is it possible to give the benefit of the doubt to the suggestion that he was also influenced by them in his treatment of the Babylon theme in chapters 40–8. There is sufficient indication to conclude that this is perfectly possible, but it would probably not be enough on its own without the strong and independent evidence which 14: 1–2 provides.

Before we can leave Isaiah 13–14, we must undertake a final brief examination of the reasons which have recently been advanced for dating these chapters as a whole in the post-exilic period rather than during the exile, as I, in common with the majority of commentators, have proposed. Since the most sustained defence of this position is presented by Gosse, whose discussion incorporates most of the principal arguments used by others of similar persuasion (see above, n. 8), it will be simplest to concentrate upon his version of the case.

Not all his monograph by any means is relevant to our particular enquiry. His lengthy discussion of the date of Ezek. 32: 17–32, with which he finds a number of connections in Isaiah 14, for instance, cannot help settle the issue, since it is sufficiently early to be accommodated to either view. Similarly, his detailed examination of the vocabulary of Isaiah 13–14 must be judged inconclusive in this regard. He has not, for instance, discovered any words or linguistic forms which must be post-exilic,[25] and we have already had occasion to observe, in connection with Isa. 14: 1, that some of his presentation is misleading either because it is incomplete or because it does not take sufficiently into account the distinctive use of vocabulary in context.

We have noted that his argument from the order in which the nations are mentioned in the Behistun inscription (e.g. pp. 83–4, 267) is not at all persuasive. Another argument which appears weak arises from the literary connections which Gosse, in common with most other commentators, finds between several of the oracles

25 The possibility which Gosse (*Isaïe 13, 1–14, 23 dans la tradition littéraire du livre d'Isaïe*) raises on p. 203 that *hnyh* in 14: 1 may be an Aramaism (itself a questionable opinion) would be no necessary indication of a post-exilic date; see M. Wagner, *Die lexikalischen und grammatikalischen Aramaismen im alttestamentlichen Hebräisch* (BZAW 96; Berlin, 1966), 148–53, and A. Hurvitz, 'The Chronological Significance of "Aramaisms" in Biblical Hebrew', *IEJ* 18 (1968), 234–40.

concerning Babylon in the prophetic books, such as Isaiah 13–14; 21; Deutero-Isaiah; and Jeremiah 50–1. More than once, he raises the question whether so much literary activity could all be squeezed into the late exilic period (e.g. pp. 157, 263). But here, it must be observed in the first place that Gosse accepts that Jeremiah 50–1 is dependent on, and so later than, Isaiah 13–14, or at the least that it reflects a later stage in the development of a common tradition (see p. 163). But in that case, if there is a problem of literary overcrowding, it is likely to affect our judgement about the date of the Jeremiah material rather than that in Isaiah, and indeed this example of dependence is one which has usually been thought to support the earlier date of the substance of Isaiah 13–14. In fact, however, judgements about how much literary activity could be fitted into even as little as a decade (though we could comfortably allow rather longer) are entirely subjective, and the problem of certainty will be aggravated if in fact we should talk of use of a common tradition in these oracles rather than seeking to set up a unilinear literary family tree.[26]

Some of Gosse's arguments are intended to demonstrate that allusions which have generally been thought to point to an exilic date could also derive from the post-exilic period. An important case in point concerns the Medes, who are mentioned in 13: 17. Because of Cyrus' Median connections on his mother's side, and because he became king of Media by conquest at an early stage in his rise to power,[27] a date for this reference around the middle of the sixth century BC seems appropriate; since Cyrus later became better known as the King of Persia, and because his conquest of Babylon was non-violent in nature, it is difficult to imagine that the presentation in the last part of Isaiah 13 could have developed after the latter event had taken place. Gosse accepts that from a historical point of view this passage refers to the late exilic period,[28] but he

[26] The problems of establishing even a relative chronology of the anti-Babylonian oracles are well illustrated by D. J. Reimer, *The Oracles against Babylon in Jeremiah 50–51: A Horror among the Nations* (San Francisco, 1993), 247–88.

[27] See R. N. Frye, *The History of Ancient Iran* (Munich, 1984), 90–2, and I. M. Diakonoff, 'Media', in I. Gershevitch (ed.), *The Cambridge History of Iran*, ii. *The Median and Achaemenian Periods* (Cambridge, 1985), 36–148 (142–8).

[28] It is thus not clear what he means when, in a later summary, he writes: 'Du point de vue historique, on doit alors remarquer que le rôle prêté aux Mèdes n'est guère vraisemblable avant la fin de l'exil' (p. 167). One might suppose that, *a fortiori*, it would be even less likely later on. In fact, a date from the period of the early rise of Cyrus fits perfectly.

thinks that the text itself could be later. Jer. 51: 11 and 28 show that even later the mention of the Medes 'a gardé sa valeur allusive' (p. 157). In other words, if other texts demonstrate that the Medes could be referred to as in some sense a symbolic power in the post-exilic period (as was undoubtedly the case with Babylon), then a reference to them in Isaiah 13 cannot provide a firm criterion for dating the passage. At best, this argument could only demonstrate the possibility of a late date; it does nothing to help establish it. In fact, however, the evidence which Gosse himself adduces points with rather more probability to an earlier date. The 'valeur allusive' of the Medes is not to be put on the same level as that of Babylon. It is striking that the only example which Gosse refers to in support of this point is Jeremiah 51, and yet, as he himself accepts elsewhere, in company with most other commentators, Jeremiah is dependent at this point on our passage in Isaiah.[29] The Medes have thus entered Jeremiah 51 by way of literary dependence, not because both passages are making independent allusion to a widespread tradition in this particular regard, and thus the probability remains as strong as it ever did that the original reference to the Medes, that in Isaiah 13, was due to the writer's perception of the international scene in the middle of the sixth century BC.

Rather stronger are the arguments which several scholars have raised concerning the nature of the description of the Day of the Lord in Isaiah 13. For instance, the fact that this affects 'the whole earth' (verse 5) suggests a late stage in the development of this motif. Before the exile, the prophets applied the negative aspects of the Day of the Lord to Israel, during the exile to the enemies of Israel, and then only later did it move in a more apocalyptic direction: 'le caractère élaboré d'Is. 13 et son ouverture sur l'apocalyptique ne permettent pas d'exclure une date post-exilique' (Gosse, 139). In line with this, verse 10 mentions various cosmic phenomena which are sometimes thought to point in the direction of an apocalyptic development. Here again, Gosse is rightly more guarded than some in the conclusion which he draws from these observations. A post-exilic date cannot be excluded on this basis, as

[29] Note especially the use of *hē'îr*, which should be seen in the wider context of the numerous points of contact between Jeremiah 50–1 and the distinctively Isaianic tradition to which attention has been drawn at several points in the preceding chapters.

he says, but that is not equivalent to demonstrating that it is therefore demanded. The points referred to are also attested in texts of the exilic period, or even earlier, so that no firm conclusions can be drawn either way. Ezek. 32: 7–8, for instance, is sufficient to demonstrate this with regard to the cosmic phenomena (though attention is also drawn by Wildberger, for instance, to Amos 5: 18–20; 8: 9–10; Jer. 4: 23; Zeph. 1: 15; the influence of the tradition of theophanic descriptions should be considered here), while the universal impact of the day is adumbrated in Isa. 2: 12–21; Ezek. 30: 3; 32: 3–4; and Zeph. 1: 17.[30]

Finally,[31] Gosse points to several interesting parallels between Isaiah 13–14 and Zechariah 1–8. Some of these, once more, serve only to show that parts of the Isaiah material could be post-exilic. For instance, Zech. 2: 10–13[6–9] (see pp. 267–8) shows that Babylon was still a place from which the people of God should flee—but, of course, the same theme occurs in Deutero-Isaiah (48: 20; 52: 11–12). Furthermore, there is a reference in this passage to 'the nations who plundered you', which suggests that an oracle against Babylon would serve as a suitable introduction to a whole series of oracles against the nations. But Gosse's summary accurately indicates how indecisive such observations are for the purpose of dating: 'Si ces éléments ne sont pas décisifs pour situer tel ou tel autre oracle contre Babylone à cette époque, tout au moins peut-on dire qu'il est impossible de s'en tenir à la position situant tous les oracles contre Babylone avant 539' (p. 268). Next Gosse suggests that Zech. 6: 1–8 indicates part of the development of Babylon into a symbolic name in the biblical texts, and with this he compares the opening of Isaiah 13, while other scholars have pointed out the striking similarity between part of Isa. 14: 1*a* and Zech. 1: 17*b*. In my opinion, however, these similarities are to be explained in terms of Zechariah grappling with the apparent non-fulfilment of some aspects of earlier prophecies concerning the end

[30] Zeph. 1: 18 refers further to 'the whole earth', though this verse is generally reckoned to be secondary. Its date is thus not certain, and the dangers of circular argumentation in this regard need to be recognized.

[31] A difficulty with treating Gosse's discussion should be mentioned here. He does not have a separate section dealing with the date of Isaiah 13–14, but the various points are scattered throughout his work. When he comes to summarize (e.g. on pp. 271–2), the late date is more or less assumed, and the points mentioned are neither specific nor comprehensive. I cannot, therefore, be sure that I have not overlooked some details of his argument, but I hope that I have not omitted any significant point nor misrepresented his position as a whole.

of the exile. The 'seventy years' of 1: 12 seems to make this clear (cf. Jer. 25: 11; 29: 10), and it is noteworthy that the 'Jacob' and 'Israel' of Isa. 14: 1 (suitable in an address to an exilic audience) have been replaced in Zech. 1: 17 with Zion and Jerusalem, in conformity with Zechariah's concern in this paragraph as a whole (cf. verses 12 and 14). This, together with other possible allusions to earlier texts in Zechariah (e.g. cf. 1: 11 with Isa. 14: 7), suggests that Zechariah is reworking antecedent material rather than that we have here two contemporary writers. Thus the similarities point to an earlier date for Isa. 14: 1, so confirming the date which I have proposed.

In sum, Gosse's work has succeeded in showing that, taken in isolation, many elements in Isaiah 13–14 could as well have been penned in the post-exilic as in the exilic period, but not that they must have been. This does not, however, hold true for the reference to the Medes in 13: 17, while Zechariah 1 is better understood as indicating an earlier date for the redactional passage in Isa. 14: 1–2. Within the book of Isaiah, as Begg has pointed out, the references to Babylon stop abruptly after chapter 48; they seem to be confined deliberately to the exilic period. After that, it is, if anything, Edom which takes over the role of a 'symbolic' power which opposes God's purposes (see 63: 1–6 and our discussion of Isaiah 34 in the next chapter). It may therefore be concluded that the usual date for the bulk of Isaiah 13–14 remains the most probable, and that the simplest explanation for its present setting and redactional shaping (13: 1; 14: 1–4*a*) is provided by our suggestion that this is due to the work of Deutero-Isaiah himself.

Following this discussion of the opening passage in Isaiah 13–27, it is natural that we should turn secondly to the final part of this section, namely the so-called 'Isaiah Apocalypse' in chapters 24–7. There are several reasons why these chapters should superficially attract our attention. First, there is general agreement that they have been given their position as part of a conscious redactional process, both because they serve to round off the oracles against the nations as a whole, and because there is a strong probability that parts of these chapters refer (whether prophetically or in retrospect) to the fall of Babylon. The parallels which have been observed between chapters 13 and 24, for instance, might be thought to point to the presence of similar concerns at the start and close of this part of the book. Secondly, the tendency among recent studies of these chapters has been to date them considerably earlier than was once the majority view,[32] so bringing them within striking distance, so to speak, of the period of Deutero-Isaiah. Finally, Vermeylen and Steck have drawn attention to some similarities between the last two verses of the 'Apocalypse' (27: 12–13) and other significant redactional conclusions in the book of Isaiah, among them 11: 11–16, to which extensive attention was given in the last chapter.[33]

In theory, therefore, it might be possible to combine these observations to frame a hypothesis which would be appealing in the context of the present work. Johnson has presented a sustained, and in many ways attractive, case for the exilic dating of Isaiah 24–7. He suggests that 24: 1–20 is the earliest section, having been written just before, and as a prediction of, the fall of Jerusalem in 587 BC, viewed as a return to chaos. Isa. 24: 21–27: 1 is then an announcement of God's imminent victory when the oppressive city will be overthrown; this was written during the exile, and looks forward to the downfall of Babylon. Finally, 27: 2–13 focuses on the reunification of Israel, somewhat in the manner of Jeremiah and Ezekiel. If to this we add the observations of Vermeylen and Steck, we might propose that Deutero-Isaiah located the bulk of the material in its present position as a conclusion to the oracles against the nations, so paralleling his work at the start of the section in chapters 13–14, and added 27: 12–13 in order to round off the whole with one of his favourite themes which he had already introduced at the conclusion of chapters 2–11. Such a theory would seem to fit well with the redactional methods and concerns which we have sought to uncover elsewhere.

Despite the temptation, therefore, to follow this line on the basis of other scholars' independently argued conclusions, closer

[32] In addition to the more recent commentaries, see e.g. G. W. Anderson, 'Isaiah xxiv–xxvii Reconsidered', *Congress Volume: Bonn, 1962* (SVT 9; Leiden,1963), 118–26; H. Ringgren, 'Some Observations on Style and Structure in the Isaiah Apocalypse', *ASTI* 9 (1973), 107–15; B. Otzen, 'Traditions and Structures of Isaiah xxiv–xxvii', *VT* 24 (1974), 196–206; W. R. Millar, *Isaiah 24–27 and the Origin of Apocalyptic* (HSM 11; Missoula, Mont., 1976); D. G. Johnson, *From Chaos to Restoration: An Integrative Reading of Isaiah 24–27* (JSOTS 61; Sheffield, 1988). These studies also tend to emphasize the unity of these chapters. On both points, of course, there are other scholars who continue to favour the older views.

[33] See Vermeylen, 279–80; 378–9; 381; 446; 749–50; Steck, *Bereitete Heimkehr*, 60–4.

examination precludes such a convenient result. To state the matter simply, I can find no evidence at any point in Isaiah 24–7 for detecting the hand of Deutero-Isaiah. The apparent coincidences of theme and redactional method need to be explained differently, and, as we shall see, an explanation lies readily to hand.

The negative aspect of this conclusion hardly needs to be stated at length; if there is no evidence, little can be said about it! Suffice it to observe, therefore, that so far as I can see the kind of concentration of Deutero-Isaianic themes and phraseology which have been presented in connection with the passages discussed in the last chapter and the first half of the present one does not occur in Isaiah 24–7. Of course, there are occasional words which are found also in Isaiah 40–55, and a convenient list is provided by Lindblom,[34] but these do not appear to be concentrated in a specific passage (contrast, for instance, 14: 1–2), nor do they stand out in any way as different from the instances which Lindblom cites from the other parts of the book of Isaiah. Ringgren's analysis of the data seems apposite: 'it must be admitted that the linguistic affinities are much less significant when [*sic*] the Book of Deutero-Isaiah is concerned. The agreements in vocabulary with Deutero-Isaiah . . . concern isolated words, while the diction and style are different. There are much more agreements with Trito-Isaiah.'[35] In fact, the passage which comes closest to Deutero-Isaiah is 24: 14–16*a*, an abruptly introduced hymn of praise which might be compared with, for instance, 42: 10–12.[36] However, it is noteworthy that the sentiments expressed in the hymn are explicitly rejected as inappropriate by the prophet in the verses immediately following (on some of the textual difficulties, see the Appendix), perhaps modelled on Isaiah's experience as recorded in 22: 1–14. Clearly, therefore, this cannot be ascribed to Deutero-Isaiah, even if it shows a certain influence from his work.[37]

More attention needs to be given to the suggestion that 27: 12–13 is part of the same redactional layer of the book of Isaiah as 11: 11–

[34] See J. Lindblom, *Die Jesaja-Apokalypse: Jes. 24–27* (Lund and Leipzig, 1938), 111–15.

[35] Ringgren, 'Some Observations on Style and Structure', 112.

[36] See e.g. M.-L. Henry, *Glaubenskrise und Glaubensbewährung in den Dichtungen der Jesajaapokalypse* (BWANT 86; Stuttgart, 1967), 50. Henry argues that 24: 14–16*a* is later than Deutero-Isaiah and that it evidences a marked decline in certain respects.

[37] A number of scholars, such as Henry, Anderson, and Otzen refer to the influence of Deutero-Isaiah on the author of 24–7.

16, since I have earlier argued that this latter passage is part of Deutero-Isaiah's redaction.

First, it is probable that these two verses represent separate additions to the text. The repetition of the introductory clause 'And it shall come to pass in that day' is already suspicious,[38] but more significantly verse 13 seems to pick up on the geographical references in verse 12 and yet to make use of them in a quite different way. In verse 12, although the imagery is not entirely clear (see the Appendix), God appears to be dealing with his people *within* the idealized boundaries of the land. 'From the flowing River† to the Brook of Egypt' may be compared in particular with Gen. 15: 18 ('Unto thy seed have I given this land, from the river of Egypt unto the great river, the river Euphrates'; see also 2 Kgs. 24: 7), but it is also reflected in the partial border descriptions at (for the brook of Egypt) Num. 34: 5; Josh. 15: 4, 47; 1 Kgs. 8: 65; Ezek. 47: 19; 48: 28; and at (for the River) Exod. 23: 31; Deut. 1: 7; 11: 24; Josh. 1: 4; 2 Sam. 8: 3, etc.[39] Within this territory, God will either 'beat out' the Israelites like ears of corn or 'beat them off' like olives from a tree, and then collect them together. The idea seems to be that God will separate or refine his people, presumably through judgement, so that they may then be gathered as a purified community. The image is not suitable for exile and restoration; it pictures rather God's activity among the people in their own land (see 17: 5–6 for a partial parallel). Verse 13, by contrast, develops the allusions of verse 12 to Assyria and Egypt in terms of places from which the dispersed exiles will be regathered; they lie outside the land of Israel. While it is certainly not impossible to harmonize the two verses (the land of Egypt is to the west of the brook of Egypt, and Assyria may be thought of as lying to the east of the River), it seems highly improbable that a writer who already had the regathering idea of verse 13 in mind would have used such an extensive description of the land in verse 12. The evidence is much more easily explained in terms of a later supplement.

Despite all this, Steck maintains that these two verses are nevertheless part of the same layer (p. 62 n. 48). His reason is that both verses demonstrate links with 11: 11–16. Quite apart from the

[38] So, e.g., W. Kessler, *Gott geht es um das Ganze: Jesaja 56–66 und Jesaja 24–27* (BAT 19; Stuttgart, 1967²), 170; Wildberger; Clements.

[39] Cf. M. Saebø, 'Grenzbeschreibung und Landideal im Alten Testament mit besonderer Berücksichtigung der min-'ad-Formel', *ZDPV* 90 (1974), 14–37.

circularity of this argument, its cogency may be separately queried with regard to 27: 12. Steck finds a parallel between the idealized border description in this verse and the apparent reference to the extent of the land in David's time in 11: 13–14. The latter is achieved, however, in terms of references to the subject peoples of Philistia, Edom, Moab, and Ammon (in any case not so extensive as 27: 12), while 27: 12 uses an idealized description which is nowhere explicitly referred to in connection with David. Moreover, the purpose of the references is quite different in each case, as we have seen (for 11: 13–14, see above, p. 129). Finally, since none of the significant vocabulary in 27: 12 is present in 11: 11–16, there seems to be no reason whatsoever for associating these two passages.

Our conclusion so far must be that, if we are to equate the redactional activity at the end of Isaiah 24–7 with 11: 11–16, then the case will have to be built on 27: 13 alone. At first sight, there appears to be more evidence to adduce for this. The theme of regathering the dispersed exiles occurs in both places, Assyria and Egypt are mentioned each time, and the use of *hanniddāḥîm* in 27: 13 may be compared with the *nidᵉḥê yiśrā'ēl* of 11: 12. Beside this, however, differences and other considerations must also be weighed. First, the focus of the gathering is quite different in the two passages. Whereas in 11: 11–16 the emphasis is national and political, in 27: 13 the introduction to the verse and its conclusion point firmly towards a gathering for worship. The blowing of a 'great trumpet', used principally in military contexts, came in later times to be used also for summoning religious assemblies (e.g. Joel 2: 15; Ps. 81: 4[3]), and that is clearly its purpose here, as the last line of the verse shows. This particular element does not seem to be attested elsewhere in connection with the return from exile, and it looks very much like an interpretation of the signal (*nēs*) raised to the nations,[40] which we saw was a favourite image of Deutero-Isaiah (5: 26; 11: 12; 49: 22). We should certainly have expected him to retain this image here, if he were also responsible for the addition of this verse.

Secondly, developing this clue that 27: 13 may be a reinterpretation of the earlier promises of a return from exile, it is noteworthy that 'those who were driven out [*hanniddāḥîm*] to the land of

[40] It is of interest to note that the two images are combined at 18: 3, a verse which is almost universally regarded as a later insertion into its present context.

Egypt' stand in parallel with 'those who were lost [*hā'ōbᵉdîm*] in the land of Assyria'. These two words do not occur in parallel elsewhere in Isaiah, but they are so found at Jer. 23: 1; 27: 10, 15; Ezek. 34: 4, and 16. In the light of the characteristic use of quotations of and allusions to other parts of scripture by the author(s) of Isaiah 24–7, to be discussed below, it seems likely that Isa. 11: 12 may be only one among several passages which influenced the author of Isa. 27: 13.

Thirdly, the same argument applies to the paralleled references to Assyria and Egypt. As we have already seen, it was the language of verse 12 which was the major influence in this regard on the author of verse 13, and, as well as (or instead of) 11: 12, he could have had any of Hos. 11: 11,[41] Mic. 7: 12, or Zech. 10: 10–11 in mind.

It may thus be concluded that Isa. 27: 12–13 comprises two separate sayings, verse 13 being a later development of verse 12. Verse 12 shows no connection whatsoever with 11: 11–16, whereas verse 13, inspired primarily, of course, by verse 12, has also been influenced by Isa. 11: 11–16 as well as by other passages. Serving as a conclusion to chapters 24–7, however, it appropriately interprets the return from exile in terms of an assembly for religious worship rather than as a purely political event. This conclusion necessarily implies that 27: 13 is later than 11: 11–16 and so cannot be regarded as part of the same redactional layer as that which we have traced earlier.

Despite this conclusion, the coincidence of two (and perhaps more) sections of the book of Isaiah concluding on a similar note if this is not to be ascribed to the hand of a single redactor remains to be explained. I propose that it be understood as only another among the long list of references and allusions to the writings of other prophets (including the earlier parts of the book of Isaiah) which are a distinctive characteristic of chapters 24–7 as a whole. Although there have been some studies devoted to this phenomenon, it is not, perhaps, as widely recognized as it should be.

The evidence may be presented under two main headings, parallels within the book of Isaiah and parallels in other books. The

41 Note how the way for this usage in Hosea is prepared for by Hos. 7: 11; 8: 9+13; 9: 3; 9: 6; 11: 5. In view of the extensive use of Hosea in Isaiah 24–7, influence from this quarter is not implausible.

first has been the subject of a recent article by Sweeney,[42] and we need only summarize his findings here. He discusses seven such citations or allusions, 'identified by their high lexical correspondence and thematic correlation' (p. 42), namely 24: 13 (17: 6); 24: 16 (21: 2 and 33: 1); 25: 4–5 (4: 5*b*–6 and 32: 1–2[43]); 25: 11*b*–12 (2: 9–17); 26: 5 (2: 6–21); 26: 17–18 (13: 8 and 66: 7–9); and 27: 1–13 (5: 1–7 and 11: 10–16).[44] After a careful comparison of the texts in their respective contexts, he finds that there is a tendency in 24–7 'to universalize the texts that they employ. In many cases, a universal understanding is already apparent in the cited text. But in cases where such an understanding is not already apparent, the writer(s) of Isaiah 24–27 introduces it, often with the aid of other Isaianic texts' (p. 51). This all suggests to Sweeney that chapters 24–7 were not composed in isolation but were specifically written from within the Isaianic tradition for their present setting.

This conclusion is, of course, very much in line with the trend in recent studies of the book of Isaiah. Alongside it, however, needs to be set the evidence for citations from other passages in the Old Testament. The most prominent (and hence generally agreed) include[45] the following: 24: 2 (Hos. 4: 9); 24: 4 (Hos. 4: 3); 24: 7 (Joel 1: 10, 12); 24: 17–18 (Jer. 48: 43–4); 24: 18 (Gen. 7: 11); 24: 20 (Amos 5: 2); in 26: 13–27: 11, Day[46] has claimed that there are no less than eight parallels with Hos. 13: 4–14: 10[9], nearly all occurring in the same order in the two works: 26: 13LXX (Hos. 13: 4);

42 M. A. Sweeney, 'Textual Citations in Isaiah 24–27: Toward an Understanding of the Redactional Function of Chapters 24–27 in the Book of Isaiah', *JBL* 107 (1988), 39–52.

43 See also J. J. M. Roberts, 'The Divine King and the Human Community in Isaiah's Vision of the Future', in H. B. Huffmon *et al.* (eds.), *The Quest for the Kingdom of God: Studies in Honor of George E. Mendenhall* (Winona Lake, Ind., 1983), 127–36 (134).

44 On this last passage, see also Sweeney's more detailed study, 'New Gleanings from an Old Vineyard: Isaiah 27 Reconsidered', in C. A. Evans and W. F. Stinespring (eds.), *Early Jewish and Christian Exegesis: Studies in Memory of William Hugh Brownlee* (Atlanta, 1987), 51–66. Johnson (*From Chaos to Restoration*, 31) finds an equally close relationship between 24: 8–9 and 5: 11–14.

45 It is not necessary for my present purposes to try to unearth every possible allusion. The question of satisfactory criteria would need to be established first, and even then it is unlikely that any one scholar's list would command universal assent. There is a partial such listing in T. K. Cheyne, *Introduction to the Book of Isaiah* (London, 1895), 147–8.

46 J. Day, 'A Case of Inner Scriptural Interpretation: The Dependence of Isaiah xxvi. 13–xxvii. 11 on Hosea xiii. 4–xiv. 10 (Eng. 9) and its Relevance to some Theories of the Redaction of the "Isaiah Apocalypse"', *JTS* NS 31 (1980), 309–19.

26: 17–18 (Hos. 13: 13); 26: 19 (Hos. 13: 14LXX); 27: 8 (Hos. 13: 15); 26: 19 (Hos. 14: 6[5]); 27: 2–6 (Hos. 14: 6–8[5–7]); 27: 9 (Hos. 14: 9[8]); and 27: 11 (Hos. 14: 10[9]).[47]

Several observations are in order about this list. First, some of the examples clearly demonstrate the same universalizing tendency which Sweeney finds in the cases of inner-Isaianic citation. The reuse of Jer. 48: 43–4 at Isa. 24: 17–18 is the most impressive example, since the two passages are verbally identical save that 'O inhabitant of the earth' has been substituted for Jeremiah's 'O inhabitant of Moab', but other passages too fit the same general pattern (e.g. the reuse of Amos 5: 2 at 24: 20, but now with reference to the earth rather than Israel). Secondly, although in some cases there is room for doubt about the direction of the influence (e.g. Joel 1: 10 and 12, in view of the well-known fact that Joel elsewhere quotes extensively from other prophets[48]), in the overwhelming majority of cases Isaiah 24–7 is quite clearly the borrower. Thirdly, two of Day's examples overlap with those of Sweeney (26: 17–18 and 27: 2–6. Unfortunately, Sweeney makes no reference to Day's article). Careful examination suggests the likelihood that in fact references to the other passages have here been combined. The use of the birthpangs imagery at 26: 17–18 was probably suggested by its extensive occurrence elsewhere in the book of Isaiah, but it is certainly given a twist found only in the Hosea passage (no child brought to birth). The allusion to Isa. 5: 1–7 at 27: 2–6 is unmistakeable, but its present setting, which has bothered many commentators, may owe something to the order which Day has uncovered. This manner of citing one passage but interpreting it in the light of another is something which we also suggested at 27: 13.

What conclusions can be drawn from this analysis relevant to our overall discussion? First, it suggests that the occurrence of the same authorial procedure at 27: 13 should be treated in the same way, and not be set apart in a separate category. In other words, 27: 13 is

47 Day draws two consequences from his observations. The first concerns the unity of the composition as a whole, which may be right. Secondly, however, he thinks that his work 'rules out any suggestion that the origins of Isa. xxiv–xxvii should be specifically sought in a distinctive Isaianic school' (p. 319). In the light of the evidence which Sweeney has presented (much of which was previously known if not specifically collected together), this is at best an exaggeration.

48 See G. B. Gray, 'The Parallel Passages in Joel and their Bearing on the Question of Date', *Expositor*, 8 (1893), 208–25.

best understood not as part of the same redaction as that attested in 11: 11–16 but as a further example of the style of composition found throughout 24–7. While of much interest in its own right, it does not have the significance for our general hypothesis which Vermeylen and Steck have suggested.[49] Secondly, the nature and concentration of citations and allusions in these chapters are something which is not to be found to anything like the same extent elsewhere in Isaiah 2–55 (on chapter 35, however, see the next chapter). It is more characteristic of Trito-Isaiah, however, as of the book of Joel (see above, n. 48) and parts of Zechariah. In other words, it is, as might be expected, a relatively late phenomenon, and this is confirmed by the citation of 4: 5–6 at 25: 4–5, since we have already noted that 4: 2–6 seems to be a post-exilic addition to the book. The use of 66: 7–9; Gen. 7: 11, and Jer. 48: 43–4 may also point in the same direction, as probably does the universalizing reading of a number of the texts. This conclusion for the dating of 24–7 as a whole puts these chapters beyond the time of Deutero-Isaiah's activity.[50] It follows that no part of 24–7 can have stood in the book of Isaiah as known (and, in my view, edited) by Deutero-Isaiah.

The many problems which Isaiah 24–7 raises are well known and have been extensively discussed. No attempt has been made here to enter into them; I have sought rather only to advance sufficient evidence to support the contention that they are not relevant for the specific purposes of the present investigation. If I am right, then it is clear that we have not yet arrived at the closure of that section of the work which Deutero-Isaiah introduced with chapters 13–14. To that extent, the next chapter continues in an immediate sense the discussion which has been opened but not concluded in the present chapter.

[49] See also Sweeney ('New Gleanings from an Old Vineyard', 65 n. 48), who, after observing various differences as well as similarities between Isa. 11: 10–16 and 27: 12–13, concludes that 'it therefore seems unlikely that these texts were written by the same author or redactor as Vermeylen maintains'.

[50] I cannot here deal fully with Johnson's alternative and earlier dating. In particular, however, his valiant attempt to date 24: 1–20 to the immediately pre-exilic period because it still looks forward to the fall of Jerusalem would require careful examination. The phrases which he thinks point most strongly to Jerusalem, such as 'the gladness of the earth' (verse 11), while correct in terms of the other passages from which they are drawn, seem most likely to have been subjected to that same universalizing process which we have noted in the case of many of the other citations and allusions.

# 8

## Deutero-Isaiah and Isaiah 28–39

It is widely believed that a new section of the book of Isaiah begins at chapter 28. Following the 'Isaiah Apocalypse' of 24–7, which in the present form of the book serves to round off the oracles against the nations, the bulk of the next few chapters deals once again with political events which can be dated within the lifetime of Isaiah of Jerusalem. Since a number of paragraphs begin with a 'woe!' saying (28: 1; 29: 1, 15; 30: 1; 31: 1; 33: 1), it is thought probable that it was a collection of such sayings which formed the basis of the oldest assemblage. This collection seems to have finished at chapter 31 (though Vermeylen (pp. 429–30) has argued that 33: 1 also belongs to it). Additions of various sorts were made subsequently. The earlier chapters are broken up by a number of more hopeful passages of uncertain date; chapters 32, 33, 34, and 35 are rarely ascribed to Isaiah (though some exceptions to this generalization will be noted later), even though the time of their composition and of their addition to the book of Isaiah is far from agreed, and the narratives of 36–9 are clearly a section apart, whether they were initially developed within the Isaianic tradition or imported wholesale from 2 Kings 18–20.

Amidst much that is uncertain, therefore, a fixed starting-point is the belief in an early collection of authentically Isaian 'woe!' oracles, and, since most of them seem to relate to the events leading up to Sennacherib's invasion of Judah in 701 BC, they are thought to form a digest of Isaiah's teaching during those critical years. In this way, we have a collection from the latter part of Isaiah's ministry to balance the collection relating to the Syro-Ephraimite war, which seems to lie at the heart of the opening part of the book.

Two problems confront this tidy hypothesis, however. First, 28:

1 lacks a heading, even though we saw at the start of the last chapter that headings were regularly used in the first part of the book both for the earliest collections of Isaianic material and for at least one major stage in their subsequent redaction. If 28: 1 were indeed the start of a major new section in the way that is usually supposed, we should certainly have expected it to be marked in the same way that other such sections are.[1]

Secondly, since the collection beginning at 28: 1 is believed to focus on the events of 701 BC, it is odd, to say the least, that the first 'woe!' oracle relates to Ephraim, heartland of the northern kingdom of Israel which had ceased to exist as a political entity some twenty years earlier. The fact that virtually all scholars enthusiastically accept the authenticity of 28: 1–4[2] only reinforces the problem. Earlier commentators do not generally seem to have recognized the difficulty, but the modern interest in the redactional shaping of the prophetic books has tended to highlight it. Fohrer,[3] for instance, suggests that 28: 1–4 originally belonged with chapters 13–23 (his 'Sammlung F') but was removed from there and given its new setting because of its association with the theme of drunkenness in 28: 7–13. Clements suggests that 'the redactor has sought to establish an indictment of "all Israel" by prefacing this threat against Ephraim to a sequence of subsequent threats against Judah during Hezekiah's reign' (p. 224), while earlier Wade had proposed that the passage was 'prefixed to prophecies written more than 20 years later in order to recall the doom of Samaria to the minds of the Judaeans, whose offences resembled those of the ill-fated sister kingdom' (p. 177). Hayes and Irvine avoid the problem altogether by speculatively dating the whole of 28–33 to the last years of Ephraim's existence as a state (a proposal which seems unlikely to attract support), while in equal desperation Watts relates the passage (and indeed the whole section following) to the reign of Josiah: 'The episode fits the beginning of Josiah's reign when he apparently extended his sovereignty over the territory formerly occupied by Northern Israel' (p. 362).[4]

[1] This point was made several times by S. Mowinckel in 'Die Komposition des Jesajabuches Kap. 1–39', *ActOr* 11 (1932–3), 267–92.

[2] Kaiser seems to be a lone exception to whom Wildberger has responded adequately.

[3] Fohrer, 'Entstehung, Komposition und Überlieferung von Jesaja 1–39', 127, tentatively followed by Wildberger.

[4] Apart from other problems with Watts's position, see now the radical re-

These two difficulties for postulating the start of a wholly new section at 28: 1 have been recognized by Vermeylen (pp. 383–4), and in my opinion he points towards the right solution. While acknowledging that 24–7 were added much later to the early nucleus of the book of Isaiah, scholars have been too quick to assume that they were nevertheless added at an appropriate point between two previously self-contained sections. Vermeylen, however, challenges this assumption by arguing that 28: 1–4 and, indeed, the earliest material in the chapters immediately following represent the direct continuation of what we now conventionally call the 'oracles against the nations'. In undertaking a historical reconstruction of the growth of the book of Isaiah, our reading has been too much influenced by the editors who gave it its present shape.[5]

Without chapters 24–7, there is no good reason why 28: 1–4 should not continue the section of the book which we suggested was introduced by the heading in 14: 28.[6] It is true that most of the subsequent oracles are introduced with *maśśā'* ('oracle'), but not all. Indeed, this is not the case with the very first passage, 14: 29, nor with 20: 1, while significantly 18: 1 is introduced with 'woe!', just like 28: 1. Conversely, a *maśśā'* oracle is introduced at 30: 6. No objection can be raised against Vermeylen's proposal on purely formal grounds.

Next, it might be thought that the material in 28: 1–4 is not suitable as a continuation of the earlier chapters. Vermeylen does not broach this issue but it, too, is possibly a response to our attempting to read this section as it is now presented to us, namely as a group of oracles against the nations such as is found in the books of Jeremiah and Ezekiel. In the earliest form of Isaiah, it may be suggested that the section functioned rather more in the manner

appraisal of many aspects of Josiah's reign by N. Na'aman, 'The Kingdom of Judah under Josiah', *Tel Aviv*, 18 (1991), 3–71.

[5] It must be stressed that this is in no way intended as a claim that a reading of the book in its present form is illegitimate; indeed, from most points of view it should be regarded as *more* legitimate than one based on historical speculation. However, the present study happens to be devoted to just such speculation, and in that context the results of enquiry into the literary history of the book must be pursued rigorously. For an attempt to do justice to the present shape of the work at this point, see Sweeney, *Isaiah 1–4*, 54–6, 63; on a smaller but more detailed scale, see also J. C. Exum, 'Isaiah 28–32: A Literary Approach', in P. J. Achtemeier (ed.), *Society of Biblical Literature 1979 Seminar Papers*, ii (Missoula, 1979), 123–51.

[6] Here I differ from Vermeylen, who believes that this section began earlier, with the 'woe!' oracle in 10: 5.

of Amos 1–2. There, it will be recalled, the oracles against the nations serve in part as a rhetorical build-up to the prophet's denunciation of Israel.[7] In view of the several 'woe!' oracles directed against Judah's policies in chapters 29–31, the rhetorical climax of this whole section should be seen just there. In this connection, it is worth noting that Amos's penultimate oracle is directed against Judah (Amos 2: 4–5). Although it is highly probable that the substance of that oracle has been subsequently rewritten under Deuteronomic influence,[8] it is not unreasonable to suppose that some form of oracle against Judah was included from the start. Even if not, its addition is itself sufficient to show the way in which this section came to be understood in Judah, where the oracles of Amos were transmitted after the fall of Samaria. An oracle against the northern kingdom in the corresponding position in Isaiah, the focus of whose invective was, of course, Judah, is thus not surprising. To that extent, we may agree with those scholars, going back at least as far as Hitzig,[9] who have seen that the prefacing of the woes against Judah with one against Israel was for rhetorical effect—to serve as a warning to the southern kingdom. The difference in our way of looking at the situation is that this now becomes merely a part of a larger collection in which the oracle against Ephraim no longer stands as an isolated introduction.[10]

Finally, it will be recalled that the heading in 14: 28 was considered above to suggest that in this earliest form of the book of Isaiah a clear distinction was being drawn between the early and late phases in the ministry of Isaiah. That conclusion receives strong support if the heading was indeed originally intended to introduce a section which reaches its climax in the Isaianic material in 28–31.[11]

[7] Cf. J. Barton, *Amos's Oracles against the Nations: A Study of Amos 1.3–2.5* (SOTSMS 6; Cambridge, 1980), 3–5, 36–8.

[8] Cf. Schmidt, 'Die deuteronomistische Redaktion des Amosbuches'.

[9] Cf. Cheyne, *Introduction to the Book of Isaiah*, 182, and see the comment of Wade, as cited above.

[10] It is worth noting that some of the events referred to in Amos 1–2 may similarly be dated some considerable time before the period with which the prophet himself is concerned; for a balanced discussion of the whole issue, see Barton, *Amos's Oracles against the Nations*, 25–35.

[11] It should perhaps be added that as well as chapters 24–7 there is probably other material in 14–23 and in 28–31 which may have been introduced at a later date; see the commentaries. If so, the shape of the section which I have suggested here will have stood out the more clearly.

The relation of this discussion to our overall purpose should by now be clear enough. In Chapter 6 I argued that, when he incorporated the literary deposit of Isaiah into his new work, Deutero-Isaiah introduced redactional material at the start and conclusion of the sections in Isaiah 2–12 which he inherited. In Chapter 7 we saw that this was true also for the start of the section beginning at chapter 13. No evidence for his hand was found at what is usually considered to be the close of that section—at chapter 23 or 27. It is now clear that this was because for him this was not the end of a section. In the form of the book which he inherited, there was no call for redactional activity there, nor, by extension, at the beginning of chapter 28. Our findings at both places thus fit together most satisfactorily.

In the light of this conclusion, it is natural that we should turn now to the end of this section to see whether it furnishes material that may be held to support our overall case. Here at once, however, we come up against the initially confusing situation that there are no less than three extended passages concerning which in recent years various scholars have independently argued that they serve to unite the two major halves of the book of Isaiah because they refer both backwards to what precedes and forwards to chapters 40–55. The passages in question are chapters 36–9, 35 (with which 34 is often associated), and 33. Clearly, part of our task must, therefore, be to examine these arguments to see which, if any, of these passages serve(s) specifically within the context of our postulated Deutero-Isaianic redaction of the work. This is the more urgent in that, in the case of chapters 33 and 35, at least, the claim has explicitly been that they function to unite forms of the book which already included either the whole or a substantial part of chapters 56–66. If this claim could be upheld, it would, of course, rule these chapters out for our purposes; they would have to have been added at a later stage than that which is our present concern.

One other general point needs also to be borne in mind. The argument of this book has been that the literary deposit of Isaiah of Jerusalem was incorporated into his new work by Deutero-Isaiah from the very first. There was never a time, therefore, when the form of the book with which we are dealing was read apart from its continuation in chapters 40–55. These chapters will thus themselves have functioned (on a much larger scale, of course) in a way similar to what was suggested above for chapter 12. It would be wrong, therefore, to look at this point for a similar 'rounding-off' passage. What we might expect would be a passage which draws together the preceding material and leads the reader on into what follows. Naturally, what we expect and what we actually find may not turn out to coincide—that can only be determined on the basis of the evidence. Nevertheless, it is helpful to have some idea of what we are looking for, since it may save us from embarking down too many blind alleys. Conversely, if our search is successful, it will add a certain corroborating force to the argument as a whole. I shall start with the last of the three passages.

Until recent years, a discussion of Isaiah 36–9 in the present context could have been brief and simple. Since the time of Gesenius early in the last century, the overwhelming consensus of opinion has been that these chapters were extracted with only minor changes from the books of Kings (cf. 2 Kgs. 18: 13, 17–20: 19) and were added to the book of Isaiah by way of a historical appendix.[12] Jeremiah 52 is cited as an analogy, the position there being made clearer by the editorial note which concludes the previous chapter, 'Thus far are the words of Jeremiah.' Under the prevailing view that the various main parts of Isaiah developed initially in isolation from one another, this was thought to show that chapters 1–35 had reached substantially their present shape before the addition was appended. Even if not, the impression given is one of a process which was not particularly closely integrated into the composition of the book as a whole.

In the new climate of the study of Isaiah, however, a fresh approach to these chapters has been developing. This started with observations about their suitability to their present context,[13] developed in terms of redactional intention,[14] and has now reached the point of suggesting that in fact they were written first for their

[12] Some exceptions to this generalization are listed by Gonçalves, *L'Expédition de Sennachérib en Palestine*, 343 n. 60, to which may be added Laato, *Who is Immanuel?*, 271–96.

[13] See in particular Ackroyd, 'Isaiah 36–39', explicitly building on the briefer treatment of Melugin, *The Formation of Isaiah 40–55*, 177–8.

[14] See van der Kooij, *Die alten Textzeugen des Jesajabuches*, 17–18; Sweeney, *Isaiah 1–4*, 12–17, 32–4; Groves, *Actualization and Interpretation in the Old Testament*, 191–201.

setting in Isaiah and were only secondarily copied into the books of Kings, a complete reversal of the usual view.[15] (There is a certain irony in the fact that this marks a return to the pre-critical view and one which has always been favoured by conservative scholars. Perhaps their contributions will not be so marginalized by other scholars in future. For a recent representative, see Oswalt, 699–703.) This theoretically opens up the possibility that they were written by Deutero-Isaiah to serve as a bridge to the main part of his own composition (some suggested links with his style will be noted below). What evidence has led to this volte-face?

We may start by listing the main points summarized by Smelik, who himself builds on the observations of others as well as adding some arguments of his own. (i) The relevant passage in Kings is exceptional in the Deuteronomic History in that it is the only place where a prophet whose sayings are separately recorded in the books of the Latter Prophets is mentioned in the narrative. By contrast, there are narratives elsewhere in the book of Isaiah (notably chapter 7) which are closely comparable with chapters 36–9. (ii) The passage in Kings is further exceptional in that it contains poetic material. (iii) Smelik believes that the account of Hezekiah's illness is 'better composed' in Isaiah 38 than in 2 Kgs. 20: 1–11. (This argument is perhaps weakened by the consequent need to regard Isa. 38: 21–2 as a later addition; see further below.) (iv) 'Most important' is the argument that Isaiah 36–9 serves as an editorial bridge between the two main parts of the book as a whole, and thus functions quite differently from Jeremiah 52. This is an argument which has been developed more fully by others, and the details will be presented in the following paragraphs. (v) Finally, Smelik maintains that the order of some of the material is more logical when viewed within its Isaianic context. In particular, Isa. 38: 6 records God's promise to deliver Hezekiah and Jerusalem from the Assyrians, whereas an account of such a deliverance has

[15] See K. A. D. Smelik, 'Distortion of Old Testament Prophecy: The Purpose of Isaiah xxxvi and xxxvii', *OTS* 24 (1986), 70–93, and now most fully Seitz, *Zion's Final Destiny* (which appeared only after my own work was approaching completion); see also Conrad, 'The Royal Narratives and the Structure of the Book of Isaiah', substantially reproduced in *Reading Isaiah*, 34–51. Conrad's 'reader response' approach means that he is not concerned to discuss the critical issue of how this material reached its present position in the book, but he is concerned to show the integral part that it plays in determining the work's structure; a similar approach is adopted by Webb, 'Zion in Transformation'.

already occurred in the previous chapter. The expected chronological order would entail putting both the account of Hezekiah's illness and the report of the Babylonian embassy which is closely associated with it prior to the story of Jerusalem's deliverance. The present unexpected order can be accounted for, however, because it leads directly to the Babylonian setting presupposed by Isaiah 40. 'We have to conclude that the present arrangement of the Hezekiah-narratives is only understandable from the perspective of the book of Isaiah, not from that of Kings' (p. 74).

As already indicated, Smelik's fourth point in particular has been advanced by several other scholars, and in view of its importance for our overall purposes it needs to be presented in greater detail. In addition, it is perhaps worth pointing out that Smelik, Groves, and Conrad were unaware of each other's work (to judge from absence of citation) and in addition that Groves did not know Ackroyd's 1982 study (whose importance is amply acknowledged by Smelik and Conrad), though he does make extensive use of Ackroyd's earlier work of 1974,[16] in which some of the ideas developed later are adumbrated.

We may begin by noting the main points which connect Isaiah 36–9 with the earlier chapters of the book. First, Conrad (pp. 38–9) lists six points of comparison with Isaiah 7, enabling him to conclude that 'each narrative reflects the same type-scene and contains the same sequence of motifs'. (i) 'Each narrative begins by indicating that an invading army has entered the territory and represents a threat to the city of Jerusalem.' (ii) In both cases, the geographical focus in Jerusalem is the same: 'the conduit of the upper pool on the highway to the Fuller's Field' (Isa. 7: 3; 36: 2). (iii) Both narratives report the great distress of the Judaean king. (iv) Both kings then receive a 'fear not' oracle of assurance (7: 4–9; 37: 6–7). (v) Both kings are offered a sign (*'ôt*) as confirmation of God's word (7: 11; 37: 30). (vi) Both narratives record the sparing of king and city, but this is then followed by a prediction that a worse disaster will follow in the future (7: 15–25; 39: 6–7).

Secondly, Conrad notes also some differences between the two passages which he believes are of significance in themselves and in

[16] P. R. Ackroyd, 'An Interpretation of the Babylonian Exile: A Study of II Kings 20, Isaiah 38–39', *SJT* 27 (1974), 329–52 = *Studies in the Religious Tradition of the Old Testament*, 152–71.

the case of chapters 36–9 develop certain themes already anticipated in the intervening chapters (especially 9 and 10). The result is that the characters of Hezekiah and Sennacherib are far more rounded than those of their counterparts (Ahaz, Rezin, and Pekah) in chapter 7. Examples (only) of the points to which he draws attention on pp. 41–6 are (i) the contrast between the introductions to the two narratives ('but they could not conquer it' (7: 1), and 'and took them' (36: 1)); (ii) the destruction wrought by the Assyrian king as predicted in 7: 14–25 and 8: 6–8; (iii) important aspects of the Rabshakeh's speech which echo the Lord's previous threats (36: 10 and 10: 5–6; 36: 18–20 with 37: 10–13 and 10: 8–11, 13–14); (iv) the anticipation of the eventual downfall of the Assyrian king in 10: 15–19 as reflected at 37: 22–9 and 36–8; (v) Hezekiah's acceptance of and even request for a sign (37: 30; 38: 7, 22), which contrasts with Ahaz's refusal (7: 12); (vi) the contrast between the two kings' relationships with the prophet Isaiah; (vii) the contrast between the two kings in the matter of faithfulness (7: 9 and 38: 3); and (viii) the partial fulfilment of the portrayal of the ideal king in 8: 23–9: 6 in the person of Hezekiah, as emphasized especially by the use of the same clause 'the zeal of the Lord of hosts will do this' in both passages (9: 6; 37: 32).[17]

Thirdly, we should note some other points of connection between Isaiah 36–9 and the earlier Isaianic material to which Conrad does not refer (presumably because they are not relevant to his main purpose) but which have been collected helpfully by Groves. Shebna and Eliakim (36: 3) are the subject of a separate narrative in 22: 15–25. The emphasis on 'trust' (*bṭḥ*) in the Rabshakeh's speech recalls 30: 15. Similarly, his stress on the impotence of Egypt is reminiscent of Isaiah's anti-Egyptian oracles. In addition, the use of the divine title 'The Holy One of Israel' (37: 23) is characteristic of the Isaianic tradition, as we saw in Chapter 3 above, while the inclusion of *ṣᵉbāʾôt* with the divine name in 37: 16, 32, and 39: 5 by contrast with its absence from the parallel passages in 2 Kings also suggests connections with the rest of the book of Isaiah. (It should be noted that both of these latter two points are characteristic of the whole of Isaiah, not just the first part.) To these points, I would add the further observation that 37: 30–2

17 It is important for Conrad's wider discussion that Hezekiah does not, however, fulfil all aspects of the ideal portrait, especially its eternal duration.

seems to show several links with Isaianic themes in addition to those already mentioned above,[18] and in particular that the structure of the first part of verse 32 closely parallels 2: 3*b*.

Finally, throughout his commentary on these chapters Wildberger presents details of similar vocabulary usage elsewhere in the first part of Isaiah. For the most part this is of little significance for our purposes, since the material is not sufficiently specific to enable us to speak of certain dependence. It is noteworthy, however, that the phrase *ḥattû wābōšû* (37: 27) occurs elsewhere in the Old Testament only at 20: 5, and that the verb *š'h* I occurs elsewhere only at 6: 11.

So far, I have presented a summary of only part of the case presented by Ackroyd, Smelik, Groves, Conrad, and others—namely, that there are strong links of a literary nature between Isaiah 36–9 and the earlier chapters in the book. Before proceeding to the remainder of their case, however, it may be helpful to offer a preliminary evaluation of their arguments thus far. Some of the points are undoubtedly weak—valuable, certainly, in a reading of the book of Isaiah as it now stands (which, of course, is Conrad's main purpose), but not strong in a discussion of the historical generation of the text. Isa. 7: 1 and 36: 1, for instance, have parallels in 2 Kgs. 16: 5 and 18: 13; *if* the Deuteronomic version were considered prior (so the usual view until recently), then any intentional contrast between them might be sought at that level, this being then taken over secondarily by those responsible for the book of Isaiah. Similarly, the occurrence of a relatively common word like *bṭḥ* cannot take us very far. Points such as these underline the importance of distinguishing carefully between genuinely probative evidence and observations which may be helpful in reading the texts intelligently, but which are of significance only once the case itself has been established on other, more reliable grounds; in themselves, they prove nothing.

Having said that, however, I am of the firm opinion that some of the points made individually, and then many of them cumulatively, provide strong evidence for the conclusion that these chapters were certainly written by someone who was thoroughly familiar with the

18 See e.g. R. E. Clements, '"A Remnant Chosen by Grace" (Romans 11: 5): The Old Testament Background and Origin of the Remnant Concept', in D. A. Hagner and M. J. Harris (eds.), *Pauline Studies: Essays Presented to Professor F. F. Bruce on his 70th Birthday* (Exeter, 1980), 106–21.

earlier Isaianic tradition (so all the scholars discussed above), and that they were not shaped at the first as part of the narrative of the Deuteronomic History (so Smelik and Seitz[19] in particular); they give every appearance of being incorporated into that work as a source. To avoid misunderstanding, I must emphasize that I am not saying at this stage that they were necessarily written originally for their present position in the book of Isaiah, nor that they were necessarily copied from the book of Isaiah into the books of Kings. Other possibilities still remain open—for instance, that both canonical works were independently drawing on the same separate source, or that the literary order was from an independent source to 2 Kings and thence to Isaiah. Such refinements remain to be examined. Nevertheless, the conclusion that we are dealing with material drafted in some sort of close association with Isaianic circles is an important first step in the investigation.

Next, it is necessary to examine the evidence which is thought to point to links forward to the second half of the book of Isaiah. Here, of course, the main point to which many scholars have called attention is that Isaiah 39 in particular looks forward to the Babylonian exile, itself the setting of chapter 40. This theme is mentioned explicitly in verses 6–7, though Ackroyd in particular has argued further that it lies behind some of the other more allusive language in the chapter, such as the reference to a 'far country' in verse 3 (cf. Jer. 46: 27; Zech. 6: 15; Isa. 43: 6, etc.).[20] This argument is strengthened by those who find no coherent order for the events in the context of 2 Kings 18–20 (where material that is thought historically to precede Sennacherib's invasion is now located after it). Since the present order is suitable as a link with the second half of the book of Isaiah, it is deduced that it is in the Isaianic context that the present order must have been established.[21]

To this main argument, a number of connections between Isaiah

[19] Seitz's view is in fact slightly more complex: he suggests that 36–8 may have been written for both contexts simultaneously (see *Zion's Final Destiny*, 104, 141), and that 39 has its primary home in Kings (pp. 185–90). Nevertheless, the burden of his argument is that 36–8 in particular are to be regarded as thoroughly Isaianic.

[20] See Ackroyd, 'An Interpretation of the Babylonian Exile'.

[21] This argument is far from recent; it was advanced, for instance, by Fischer (p. 228), who maintained that the present order of the chapters was the result of an Isaianic redactor's rearrangement of material which he inherited from Kings, and that the order in Kings was subsequently conformed to that in Isaiah.

36–9 and the work of Deutero-Isaiah are added. The fullest list known to me is that of Groves (pp. 198–9). Most of his examples are drawn from the poem in 37: 23–9.[22] (i) Verse 26 is said to recall Deutero-Isaiah because of its theme, form, and phraseology:

Have you not heard
  that I determined [*ʿāśîtî*, lit. 'I did'] it long ago?
I planned [*wîṣartîhā*, lit. 'and I formed it'] from days of old
  what now I bring to pass,
that you should make fortified cities crash into heaps of ruins.

Such connections have been frequently noted in the past, both at the linguistic level[23] and in terms of the connection of thought (e.g. 40: 21; 41: 4, 26; 44: 7–8; 45: 21; 46: 9–11; 48: 3–5; 51: 9–10). Wildberger points out, however, that there is a difference between the Deutero-Isaianic theme of God announcing his intentions beforehand and the unparalleled thought of the present verse that he has actually performed in this way long ago. Even more damaging to this argument for our overall purpose, however, is the textual status of this verse in Kings (2 Kgs. 19: 25). There, the first half of the verse (i.e. that part which shows closest affinity with Deutero-Isaiah) is absent from what is probably the earliest witness to the Greek translation (Vaticanus; a translation is added later in $boc_2e_2$ and A). It would be a strange coincidence indeed if just this phrase were dropped from the translation or from its Hebrew *Vorlage*. The probability is much stronger that this phrase entered the text in its Isaianic version and that the Kings text was then *secondarily* assimilated to it. There seems to be an example of exactly the same process at 2 Kgs. 20: 19*b* = Isa. 39: 8 (see below). If, then, this half verse was missing from the earliest form of 2 Kgs. 19: 25, this particular piece of evidence can clearly not be used to argue that the Hezekiah narratives as a whole were originally composed for

22 Ackroyd ('Isaiah 36–39', 112) also says that this passage is 'at certain points closely related to Deutero-Isaiah', but he does not elaborate.

23 Groves (*Actualization and Interpretation in the Old Testament*, 198 n. 56) cites the following: *hᵃlôʾ-šāmaʿtâ* (40: 21; 44: 7 (*sic*. Presumably verse 8 is intended, but the association is extremely weak—first-person singular of the hiphʿil of *šmʿ* with second-person singular suffix)); *mîmê qedem* (51: 9); *qedem* (45: 21; 46: 10); *yṣr* (46: 11); hiphʿil of *bwʾ* (46: 11; 48: 3, 5). Of course, these are not unique to Isaiah for the most part.

their present setting in the book of Isaiah.[24] (ii) In verse 25 the Assyrian king boasts that he has 'dried up . . . all the streams of Egypt'. If this is an Exodus allusion, it may be compared with the use of the same verb at 51: 10. It should be noted, however, that Groves omits the words 'with the sole of my foot' from his citation and that these words remove the verse somewhat from the circle of ideas associated with the Exodus. In addition, according to 51: 10 (and other passages) it was 'the sea', not 'the streams [*yᵉ'ōrê*, perhaps the 'Nile-arms' of the Delta] of Egypt' which were dried up at the Exodus. (iii) 'The image of grass as transient and easily blighted in 37: 27 recalls the opening oracle of Deutero-Isaiah in 40: 6–8.' In general terms that may be so, but it does not appear that any direct association is present. The vocabulary links are weak, and as good if not a better comparison may be drawn with Pss. 103: 15–16 and 129: 6, and see especially Isa. 15: 6. By contrast, we noted in Chapter 4 above that 40: 6–8 probably reflects 28: 1–4. (iv) Moving slightly further afield, Groves compares the mention of idols in Hezekiah's prayer (37: 16–20) with the anti-idol polemic of Deutero-Isaiah.[25] Again, however, there is no reason to limit the comparison to these passages; the passage could equally well have been inspired by the comparable material in Isa. 2: 8, 20; note especially 'the work of their/men's hands', a phrase which does not occur in Deutero-Isaiah. (v) Finally, Groves follows Kaiser in linking 37: 35, 'for my own sake and for the sake of my servant David', with the Deutero-Isaianic 'for my own sake' (43: 25; 48: 9;[26] 55: 5) and the Deuteronomic phrase 'for the sake of my servant David' (1 Kgs. 11: 13, 34; 15: 4; 2 Kgs. 8: 9). Since 'for my own sake' occurs nowhere else in the Hebrew Bible, this seems a likely conclusion. The force of this in the context of the present discussion is rendered somewhat ambivalent, however, by the observation that, when the phrase occurs again at 2 Kgs. 20: 6, it is omitted in the Isaiah parallel, 38: 6.

It will already have become clear from my comments on Groves's list that I do not regard this part of his argument and of

[24] See A. H. Konkel, 'The Sources of the Story of Hezekiah in the Book of Isaiah', *VT* 43 (1993), 462–82.

[25] Cf. Ackroyd, 'Isaiah 36–39', 112: 'The prayer is markedly related to psalm passages and to Deutero-Isaiah,' but again he does not discuss the evidence further.

[26] This verse has 'for my name's sake', which is close, but not exact; probably the intended reference is 48: 11, which has an emphatically repeated 'for my own sake'.

those who agree with him as anything like so strong as in the case of the connections with the first part of the book.[27] Two or three of his points are simply wrong, in my opinion, and it must be asked whether the remainder are strong enough to support the case at all. Effectively, only the thematic link between chapters 39 and 40, the phrasing of 37: 26,[28] and possibly the *l*$^{e}$*ma*$^{ʿa}$*nî* of 37: 35 come in for serious consideration. Clearly, so far as style is concerned, this is not enough to indicate the hand of Deutero-Isaiah himself in these chapters (and, of course, it must be remembered that it is not the purpose of the scholars who have been mentioned to suggest that it does), so that from our point of view the issue resolves itself into one of seeking to establish who was responsible for the present order of the material. An immediate consequence of this must be to ask, however, whether these chapters could really have been written in the first place explicitly to serve as a bridge between the two parts of the book of Isaiah. If that were so, we should surely have expected far more association with chapters 40–55. They may now function—and quite effectively—as such a bridge, but it would be surprising if anyone setting out to compose such a bridge would have come up with what we now have. There is simply too much in these chapters which does not contribute to such a purpose for us to entertain the most radical form of the 'bridge hypothesis' as presented by Smelik. As we have seen, he has made a number of useful observations about these chapters with which it is not difficult to agree, but his conclusion that they must therefore have been written for this purpose in the first place is not the only or the necessary explanation for his observations (see further below).

Under the impact of recent studies, the discussion so far has concentrated exclusively on the connections between Isaiah 36–9 and the remainder of the book of Isaiah. In order to progress further it is now time, however, to turn to the other main way into this material, namely a synoptic comparison with 2 Kings 18–20. Naturally, there can be no question of a complete study of this

[27] It may be noted that Seitz too rejects any influence of Deutero-Isaiah on Isaiah 36–9; see *Zion's Final Destiny*, 83–6, 91–2. This is, of course, a necessary step in his argument that 36–9 pre-date Deutero-Isaiah. He does not appear to be aware of Groves's discussion, however, so that his arguments may be viewed as complementary to mine.

[28] Though even this must be discounted as far as the basic composition is concerned if the textual considerations advanced above are correct.

subject here; that would require a monograph to itself.[29] I shall restrict myself to a few particular points which either are, or have been thought to be, of particular relevance to the issue of determining the direction of literary dependence.[30]

In the history of scholarship the most significant point of difference between the two accounts has been that which occurs right at the beginning. Following the introductory verse 2 Kgs. 18: 13 = Isa. 36: 1,[31] the 2 Kings version continues with a short account of Hezekiah's payment of tribute to Sennacherib (verses 14–16) which is lacking from the Isaiah version. For some scholars, this is sufficient to settle the issue. Jones, for instance, writes: 'it is quite clear that this statement is most fittingly followed in 2 Kgs. 18: 13–16 by the annalistic record which is omitted from Isaiah; this is probably an indication that the original form in 2 Kg. has appeared in an abbreviated form in Isaiah.'[32] Others, however, have argued to the contrary that the verse originally introduced the longer account which follows (2 Kgs. 18: 17–19: 37 = Isa. 36: 2–37: 38), and that this argues therefore for the priority of the Isaiah account.

The course of this debate has been amply documented in Gonçalves's recent study, so that there is no need to retrace the ground here. He also studies the whole issue afresh and at length, and I shall therefore merely summarize his conclusions.[33] He argues first that the date formula in the introductory verse is attested elsewhere in the Deuteronomic History, especially when, as here, an event within a particular reign is being introduced. Moreover,

29 I regret that A. Catastini, *Isaia ed Ezechia: Studio di storia della tradizione di II Re 18–20/Is 36–39* (Rome, 1989), is not accessible to me; for a brief summary, see *ZAW* 102 (1990), 441.

30 For visual presentation of the data, see Wildberger's commentary (pp. 1484–95), as well as the standard synopses of parallel passages in the Old Testament.

31 There is some confusion in the manuscripts about the spelling of Hezekiah's name from which the attempt has been made to argue for the priority of the version in Isaiah as a whole; see S. Norin, 'An Important Kennicott Reading in 2 Kings xviii 13', *VT* 32 (1982), 337–8. However, a broader view of the evidence in the context of the chapter as a whole demonstrates that in this case such a literary-critical conclusion cannot be legitimately drawn from the textual evidence (which is itself in any case disputed); see Gonçalves, *L'Expédition de Sennachérib en Palestine*, 355–7.

32 G. H. Jones, *1 and 2 Kings* (NCB; Grand Rapids, Mich., and London, 1984), 557. This argument is also regarded as decisive by Kaiser (p. 367), following his fuller study, 'Die Verkündigung des Propheten Jesaja im Jahre 701', *ZAW* 81 (1969), 304–15, and Wildberger, 1371.

33 See Gonçalves, *L'Expédition de Sennachérib en Palestine*, 355–61; see also pp. 342–50.

the fifteen years of Hezekiah's prolonged life after illness appears to be calculated by reference to it (2 Kgs. 20: 6; Isa. 38: 5) on the basis of the total duration of Hezekiah's reign (mentioned only in 2 Kgs. 18: 2),[34] a point which demonstrates forcefully that the chronological structure of these narratives must have been written first for their setting within the Deuteronomic History. This, then, militates against any view which would regard the introduction as unsuitable in an annalistic context such as that which immediately follows in the 2 Kings version. (This, of course, is a separate issue from the vexed question of whether the fourteenth year is correct, and, if so, what it refers to.)

From this negative argument, Gonçalves turns secondly to a positive demonstration that the verse in question is more suitable as an introduction to what follows it in 2 Kings than to what follows it in Isaiah. He points out that nowhere else are prophetic stories introduced by a specific date, whereas accounts of invasions comparable with 2 Kgs. 18: 13–16 sometimes are. Next, verse 13 agrees with verses 14–16 in having the whole country as its focus of interest; by contrast, the following stories focus exclusively on Jerusalem, while neither verse 13 nor verses 14–16 show particular interest in the capital. Furthermore, although 2 Kgs. 18: 13 = Isa. 36: 1 inevitably serve to introduce the longer accounts because of their present place in the text, these accounts do not themselves demand knowledge of the introduction. They do not refer back to its substance at all. For instance, had the introduction originally been part of these longer accounts, as in the Isaiah version, one might have expected that the Assyrians would have been portrayed as referring to their conquest of the other cities of Judah in their attempt to break the resolve of the inhabitants of Jerusalem. By contrast, the short account in 2 Kgs. 18: 14–16 positively requires the information included in verse 13 if it is to be intelligible.

In my opinion, Gonçalves has presented a strong case for maintaining that 2 Kgs. 18: 13 = Isa. 36: 1 belonged from the first with 2 Kgs. 18: 14–16 and that it was not originally intended to serve as the immediate introduction to the longer prophetic narrative as it now does in Isaiah 36. Moreover, since there is other material in 2 Kings 18 which is also not found in Isaiah, it is reasonable to suggest that 2 Kgs. 18: 14–16 was deliberately omitted by the Isaiah

[34] See too J. Hughes, *Secrets of the Times: Myth and History in Biblical Chronology* (JSOTS 66; Sheffield, 1990), 212.

redactor; it makes no reference to Isaiah, who was, of course, the focus of the redactor's interest, and he may also have felt that its negative portrayal of the course of events did not fit with his presentation. In addition, he may have thought that it conflicted with the portrayal of Hezekiah that he wished to convey; see Clements's comment on Isa. 38: 3 = 2 Kgs. 20: 3.[35]

A different approach to this material is taken by Seitz (*Zion's Final Destiny*, 51–61). He argues that 2 Kgs. 18: 14–16 is a later, redactional insertion into its present context, motivated by concerns which are peculiar to the Deuteronomic History. Its absence from Isaiah cannot, therefore, be used to argue for the priority (from a literary point of view) of the account in Kings.

For this argument to work, it is necessary, of course, for Seitz to separate 2 Kgs. 18: 13 (which has a parallel in Isaiah) from verses 14–16. It is, therefore, strange that he makes no attempt to answer Gonçalves's points to the contrary which I have summarized above.

More than that, however, his own arguments do not seem convincing. First, he gives some weight to the point about the spelling of Hezekiah's name (see above, n. 31), but is rightly cautious ('Norin may have a point' (p. 54)); the manuscript evidence is too ambiguous (note the inconsistency, for instance, at 2 Kgs. 18: 9–10) and the possibility of scribal inconsistency too high to mount a case on this basis.

Secondly, he finds a striking parallel both form-critically and phraseologically between our paragraph and 2 Kgs. 16: 5, 7–9. This is certainly noteworthy, but it seems to undermine his position, since 2 Kgs. 18: 13 is a significant element in this comparison. It serves to bind verse 13 more closely with 14–16 and to suggest that the paragraph as a whole was framed with the wider concerns of the Deuteronomic History in view. Furthermore, if this paragraph then conflicts with the contrast that is drawn in the book of Isaiah between Ahaz and Hezekiah (p. 57), that can only provide a further reason why 14–16 may have been omitted by the Isaian redactor.

Thirdly, a similar response can be made to Seitz's earlier observation (p. 56) that in verses 14–16 Hezekiah is three times

35 Clements, *Isaiah and the Deliverance of Jerusalem*, 65, and *Isaiah 1–39*, 290; P. R. Ackroyd, 'The Death of Hezekiah: A Pointer to the Future?', in M. Carrez *et al.* (eds.), *De la Tôrah au Messie: Mélanges Henri Cazelles: Études d'exégèse et d'herméneutique bibliques offerts à Henri Cazelles pour ses 25 années d'enseignement à l'Institut Catholique de Paris (Octobre 1979)* (Paris, 1981), 219–26 (220) = *Studies in the Religious Tradition of the Old Testament*, 172–80 (173).

designated as 'the king of Judah' in contrast with 'King Hezekiah' in verses 13 and 17, for he then continues that 'the phrase is well-known from the rubrics that introduce the kings of the northern and southern kingdoms' and so concludes that 'whoever composed 18: 14–16 worked in the same manner . . . as the redactor responsible for 18: 1–2'. If, however, verses 14–16 are inextricably linked with verse 13 (a point which Seitz has unwittingly strengthened by his comparison with 16: 5, 7–9) and yet are closely tied to the primary Deuteronomic editor of Kings,[36] that can only add to the case that the omission of 14–16 in Isaiah must be secondary and derivative.[37]

The conclusion of this discussion of the opening passage in the synoptic parallel is thus that there is a strong case in favour of Isaiah being dependent upon 2 Kings. There is, however, one factor which precludes absolute certainty. Because he is not persuaded that there is adequate motivation for the omission of the material by the Isaiah redactor, Childs has suggested that 2 Kgs. 18: 14–16 may have originally been present in the Isaiah version as well, but that it has been lost in the course of subsequent transmission because of a scribal error. Since both 2 Kgs. 18: 14 and 17 start with the word *wayyišlaḥ*, he thinks that a scribe's eye may accidentally have jumped from one to the other.[38] He admits that this is entirely conjectural, and yet it is a possibility which cannot be totally ruled out. Clearly, if the material once stood in Isaiah, no conclusion could be drawn about dependence either way. Because, as we have seen, there is in fact adequate redactional motivation for the omission of the material in Isaiah (*contra* Childs), I do not rate this possibility very highly. Nevertheless, it would be reassuring if further corroborative evidence could be found.

One possible line of evidence has been mentioned earlier, following Groves—namely, the addition of *ṣᵉbāʾôt* to the divine name in Isa. 37: 16, 32; and 39: 5, since this title is frequent in Isaiah but rare in the Deuteronomic History. This too, however, is somewhat

[36] Seitz (*Zion's Final Destiny*, 59–60) advances further arguments to this effect with regard to verses 14–16 alone.

[37] The question of the historicity of this paragraph, which Seitz rates less highly than many other scholars (ibid. 61–6), is, of course, a totally separate issue, as he himself rightly recognizes elsewhere. See also his article, 'Account A and the Annals of Sennacherib: A Reassessment', *JSOT* 58 (1993), 47–57.

[38] Childs, *Isaiah and the Assyrian Crisis*, 69–70; according to Kaiser ('Die Verkündigung des Propheten Jesaja im Jahre 701', 306), this possibility had already been noted by A. Kuenen.

uncertain, because in such cases the possibility of scribal assimilation to the prevailing literary context cannot be ruled out.

More promising, therefore, is likely to be an examination of the story of Hezekiah's sickness (2 Kgs. 20: 1–11 = Isaiah 38), for it is in this passage that the two accounts diverge most markedly from each other. There are two principal ways in which these accounts differ. They have generally been treated in isolation by the commentators, but, as we shall see, it is probable that they were motivated by the same redactional concern.[39]

The most obvious difference is the addition of the psalm of Hezekiah in Isa. 38: 9–20. This is almost universally regarded as having been added to the account at a late stage in its development; so far as I am aware, even of those who think that this material has been taken over by Kings from Isaiah, only Seitz has suggested that this passage was already in place and was omitted by the Deuteronomic historian, but even then he expresses uncertainty: 'It is impossible to determine whether the psalm of Hezekiah was brought over from Isaiah as part of the original depiction of the DtrH' (p. 187). Moreover, though he suggests that 'its omission is certainly consistent with the other modifications that have occurred in the story of Hezekiah's illness', it is clear that he is working on the basis of the conclusion which he has already reached that the Kings version is dependent on that in Isaiah (a conclusion rejected below). He does not appear to advance any independent arguments to support the proposal that it was deliberately suppressed by the historian.

On the usual view, of course, such an addition presents no difficulty. In addition, however, Ackroyd has made out a case for regarding the inclusion of this psalm as purposeful within the context of the role these chapters play specifically in the book of Isaiah.[40] It is not, he writes, 'simply an appropriately worded psalm of thanksgiving for deliverance in time of distress, here seen as apposite to the recovery of the king. It is a comment on the larger significance of that recovery in the whole context of the book.' He supports this conclusion by the observations that the psalm uses a

39 An attempt to treat these two points together from a redactional standpoint is, however, outlined by Sweeney, *Isaiah 1–4*, 14–15. He approaches the issue from a different set of observations to that advanced below, so that his treatment may be regarded as complementary to mine.

40 Ackroyd, 'An Interpretation of the Babylonian Exile', 165–6; cf. 'Isaiah 36–39', 113.

series of metaphors which speak of restoration to life from the pit, that in Lamentations and parts of Jeremiah these metaphors are used in relation to the experience of exile, and that the climax is reached with the individual joining with the community in worship at the temple. The inclusion of the psalm thus has the effect of heightening the typological significance of Hezekiah's illness. On the one hand, 'the illness of Hezekiah and the death sentence upon him thus become a type of judgment and exile, and in that measure they run parallel to the theme of judgment which is found in the ambassador story which follows'. On the other hand, the conclusion of the psalm points forward to the possibility of restoration for the community. Whereas the Deuteronomic History is reticent about speaking of such restoration, it is entirely suitable within the book of Isaiah. We may conclude, therefore, that the introduction of the psalm is likely to have been consciously effected in order to draw attention to the wider implications of the incident of Hezekiah's illness and recovery.

So far as it goes, this conclusion would fit well with the view that the material in Isaiah 38 has been taken over from Kings. If the psalm was added to fit the wider redactional concerns of the book as a whole, it is likely that the addition was made by the same editor who was responsible for including the narratives in the first place. This falls short of proof, however, because there remains a theoretical possibility that it was added later and separately by someone else who wished to draw out further the implications of the narrative. If that were the case, then borrowing by Kings from Isaiah would still be a possibility.

Besides the addition of the psalm, there are a number of other ways in which Isaiah 38 differs noticeably from 2 Kgs. 20: 1–11. So far as I am aware, these differences have always been treated quite separately from the addition of the psalm (though see above, n. 39, for an exception), but I hope to be able to show that in one respect the two issues are in fact related so closely that both must have been effected together. If that is so, then the case for Isaianic dependence on 2 Kings becomes irresistible.

This second group of differences relates to the fact that the narrative part of the chapter is considerably shorter in Isaiah than in 2 Kings. Not all the minuses should necessarily be accounted for in the same way. For instance, it is possible to believe that 2 Kgs. 20: 4*a* ('And before Isaiah had gone out of the middle court') has been added at a later stage in order to emphasize the speed with which the godly king's prayer was heard,[41] though Sweeney (p. 14) thinks that the Isaianic version has been abbreviated to make the same point. On the other hand, it might be supposed that 2 Kgs. 20: 5's description of Hezekiah as *n$^{e}$gîd-ʿammî* ('the prince of my people'), has been omitted from Isa. 38: 5 because it was thought to detract from the strongly positive portrayal of the king which the Isaianic context requires. It is less easy to explain as a purposeful addition to Kings. However, such small differences are not reliable indicators of dependence when taken alone, since the possibility of accidental loss in the course of transmission must always be borne in mind.

More significant are the differences which result in Isa. 38: 6–7 being so very much shorter than 2 Kgs. 20: 6*b*–11*a*. In the Kings account, as has often been noted, there appear to be two separate narrative elements which are rather roughly juxtaposed. Verses 1–7 are complete in themselves, as they tell of Hezekiah's illness, his prayer, and his recovery through the intervention of the prophet at God's instruction. This comes to a clear literary conclusion in verse 7: 'And Isaiah said, "Take a cake of figs." And they took and laid it on the boil, and he recovered' (*RV*).[42] The climactic 'and he recovered' forms an effective contrast to the 'you shall not recover' in verse 1. To this narrative there is then added in verses 8–11 the account of Hezekiah's request for a sign and the favourable response by the prophet. In the present form of the text, the way for this is partly prepared by the words in verse 5, 'behold, I will heal you; on the third day you shall go up to the house of the Lord'; cf. verse 8. Despite this, however, the request for a sign would logically have been expected before the statement of recovery.

This expected order is what we in fact find in the Isaiah version, where a variant form of 2 Kgs. 20: 7 has been moved to the end of the account in Isa. 38: 21. On this basis, Cogan and Tadmor argue that the Isaiah version must be the later of the two: 'The rearrange-

[41] See Wildberger, 1446. The use of *šwb* (2 Kgs. 20: 5) instead of *hlwk* (Isa. 38: 5) can then be neatly explained as a necessary change consequent upon the addition.

[42] As most commentators recognize, there is no other legitimate way of translating the MT. A number of the English translations seek to harmonize the account with what follows by rendering the *wāw*-consecutive + imperfect verbs as though they continued the imperative mood of Isaiah's direct speech; see e.g. *RSV*: 'Bring a cake of figs. And let them take and lay it on the boil, that he may recover.' Needless to say, without revocalizing, this is unjustified, though the need to harmonize was perceived as early as the LXX and the Peshiṭta.

ment in Isaiah sought to smooth out the difficulty of 2 Kgs. 20: 7 noted above, by removing it to the end of the chapter; therefore the text of Kings is earlier.'[43] Jeremias[44] (whose arguments that Isa. 38: 21 was an original part of the Isaianic text, not a later scribal addition, strongly support Cogan and Tadmor's position) further observes that the removal of 2 Kgs. 20: 7–8 to the end of the chapter has created an unevenness in the representation of who is speaking in Isa. 38: 5–8 (God speaks in the first person through Isaiah in verses 5*b*–6; he is referred to in the third person in verse 7; and the first-person singular in verse 8 is ambiguous, since it could refer either to God or to the prophet). Since in the Kings version the same material exactly all makes sense because it is distributed through more than one scene, Jeremias concludes quite reasonably that this is an indication of an unnoticed difficulty consequential upon the abbreviation in Isaiah.[45]

That conclusion seems convincing so far as it goes,[46] but it does

[43] M. Cogan and H. Tadmor, *II Kings: A New Translation with Introduction and Commentary* (AB 11; New York, 1988), 257.

[44] C. Jeremias, 'Zu Jes. xxxviii 21 f.', *VT* 21 (1971), 104–11.

[45] It is unfortunate that Seitz appears to have been unaware of Jeremias's article. His analysis of Isaiah 38 (*Zion's Final Destiny*, 149–82) proceeds on the assumption that Isa. 38: 1–8 + 21–2 is a coherent narrative which has been confused in Kings (see esp. pp. 162–6). Jeremias has shown, however, that this is not the case; rather, the apparent confusion in Kings is to be explained as due to the juxtaposition of the two narrative blocks in 2 Kgs. 20: 1–7 and 8–11. Isaiah 38 has tried to smooth this out into a single whole, but has thereby unconsciously introduced confusion of a different, and clearly secondary, sort.

[46] A rather different explanation for the present position of Isa. 38: 21 (and 22) is advanced by Talmon, but not in a way which affects the main line of the argument presented above; see F. M. Cross and S. Talmon (eds.), *Qumran and the History of the Biblical Text* (Cambridge, Mass., and London, 1978), 330–1. He observes that the main text of 1QIsa$^{a}$ clearly intended to conclude the 'chapter' at verse 20, for 39: 1 is started on a new line, leaving a space of about three-quarters of a line after 38: 20. The equivalent of 38: 21–2 has been added by a second hand in this space and in the margin. He therefore suggests that the addition of both verses was consciously made at a late stage in the development of the text for structural reasons: 'Together with the main narrative in vv. 1–8, it is intended to form an inclusio-like frame for the inserted prayer-psalm מכתב: while v. 21 (the fig-pad) is a topical doublet of vv. 7–8 (the sun-dial sign), v. 22 links the renewed reference to the King's illness in Is. 39: 1 (= 2 Ki. 20: 12) with the initial narrative, thus arching, as it were, over the intrusive element of the prayer-psalm.' While it is, of course, possible that the present text of Isaiah 38 developed only in stages (to which the postulated *Vorlage* of 1QIsa$^{a}$ *may* serve as a witness), Talmon's explanation of the purpose for the addition of verses 21–2 does not strike me as convincing. It is equally possible that the scribe who copied 1QIsa$^{a}$ omitted verses 21–2 unintentionally, his eye jumping from *'al-bêt yhwh* at the end of verse 20 to *'e'$^{e}$leh bêt yhwh* at the end of verse 22. (Note how a line of comparable length was omitted—clearly accidentally—at 37: 6*b*–7 and then

not account for the whole of the matter. The Isaiah version does, after all, retain Isaiah's offer of a sign to Hezekiah, albeit now in its expected position,[47] but some of the details of what the sign was intended to confirm are systematically eliminated, namely that Hezekiah will be 'healed' and that he will go up to the house of the Lord on the third day. (It is possible that this detail was motivated by the account of Hezekiah's visits to the 'house of the Lord' in the earlier narratives, at 2 Kgs. 19: 1 and 14. Seitz (p. 174) also makes the interesting suggestion that a contrast with the fate of Sennacherib is intended (2 Kgs. 19: 37).) The occurrence of this material in 2 Kgs. 20: 8 is part of a longer passage (verses 6*c*–8), for whose omission we have seen that there were other motives as well, so that not too much should be built upon it. The same does not apply, however, to the excision of the relevant words from verse 5. They could have been left there in the Isaiah version without posing any problem whatever of the sort that we have been examining up till now. Some other explanation must be sought.[48]

I suggest that the answer lies in the new interpretation put upon this whole incident by the inclusion of the psalm of Hezekiah. There, it will be recalled, the climax of the poetic account of the king's restoration comes with the statement that he and his children will give praise to God throughout their lives in the house of the Lord:

> The living, the living, he thanks thee,
>   as I do this day;
> the father makes known to the children
>   thy faithfulness.
> The Lord will save me,
>   and we will sing to stringed instruments
> all the days of our life,
>   at the house of the Lord. (Isa. 38: 19–20)

Whereas in the Kings account the focus of attention is entirely on the individual, Hezekiah, now in Isaiah his restoration is seen

added back in between the lines and in the margin. Similarly, parablepsis from *yābēš ḥāṣîr nābēl ṣîṣ* in 40: 7 to the same phrase in 8 seems best to account for the initial omission of 40: 7*b*–8*a* in an early stage of the text's transmission; see the Appendix.)

47 The fact that in Isaiah Hezekiah is offered a sign without his first requesting one (contrast 2 Kgs. 20: 8) may be due again to the Isaiah version's concern to portray Hezekiah as a wholly pious king (cf. above, n. 35) as well as the desire, already noted, to contrast him with the portrayal of Ahaz in Isaiah 7.

48 There is no evidence for Jeremias's conjecture that 2 Kgs. 20: 5 and 8 were added only later, and so were no part of the Kings text which was copied in Isaiah.

typologically as adumbrating the restoration of the community, characterized by worship in the house of the Lord. In this new context, the reference to a single visit at a particular time to the temple by the king alone as a sign of restoration would have been inappropriate; it was therefore deleted and reinterpreted by the inclusion of the psalm in the manner indicated.

If this is the case, it follows that the reshaping of the first part of Isaiah 38 and the inclusion of the psalm were part of the same process, although, as we have seen, other considerations were also simultaneously at work. Consequently, it is the Isaiah passage which has adapted Kings to its new purpose.

There are, of course, other matters relating to the comparison between these two passages, but there is no need to go into them now. For example, the textual history of these two parallel passages is complicated in the extreme, but Konkel's recent clear study of the matter (above, n. 24) reaches conclusions which are fully in accord with those set out here. Again, the curious addition of verse 22, which makes no sense as it now stands,[49] seems to take note of the very omission which we have analysed, and is generally thought to be a much later scribal note, calling attention to the discrepancy between the two accounts.[50] Again, if *ʾašer yārēdâ bᵉmaʿᵃlôt ʾāḥāz* ('by which it went down on the dial of Ahaz' (2 Kgs. 20: 11)) is a later gloss in Kings by assimilation to the Isaiah text, as many commentators and *BHS* believe (there is LXX support for this view; see Konkel), then its addition in Isa. 38: 8 may be another indication of Isaianic adaptation of its *Vorlage* in the interests of its comparison and contrast with Isaiah 7.[51] Such consequential matters need not detain us now, however. It is sufficient to conclude

[49] I cannot agree with Seitz's attempted explanation of this verse (*Zion's Final Destiny*, 166–9). His treatment of verse 21 is satisfactory: it tells of Hezekiah's healing, which has not been recounted earlier in the chapter. Verse 22, however, has Hezekiah ask what will be the sign that he may return to the temple. Seitz understands this as a further indication of the king's piety, and maintains that the sign is quite separate from that mentioned earlier in the chapter. He does not explain, however, why a sign should be required for what was a matter of standard priestly regulation, nor does he comment on the oddity that no indication is given of what the sign was or whether, indeed, it was ever granted. In Kings, however, the sign is both specified and linked to the promise of a healing miracle, with entry to the temple thereafter as consequential. The secondary nature of verse 22 is clear and acknowledged by all other scholars, including Smelik.

[50] The misguided attempt by *NEB* (followed by *REB*) to restore this verse and the preceding one to their 'proper' place between verses 6 and 7 can only be deplored.

[51] Cf. Ackroyd, 'Isaiah 36–39', 118.

that a study of Isaiah 38 fully confirms our provisional judgement based on 36: 1 above. Isaiah 36–9 was not first composed for its present position in the book of Isaiah, despite some recent suggestions to the contrary; rather, it has been taken, with some modifications, from 2 Kgs. 18–20.

As we saw earlier, the only effective challenge to this conclusion could come from the order of the material, which is certainly not chronological, and which some scholars have thought could only have arisen as a result of a desire to conclude the section with a preview of the Babylonian exile in order to prepare the way for Isaiah 40. Groves, for instance, writes: 'in II Kings 18–20 this climactic awareness of the exile leads to—nothing. Therefore, to detect a purposive ordering of the stories, one must look to the Isaianic setting, where the climax of Isa 39 focuses the reader's attention upon the Deutero-Isaianic deliverance' (p. 196). Smelik (p. 74) makes a similar comment. Such an opinion can be challenged, however, and that from two angles. In the first place, it is not true that the order of the stories in 2 Kings leads nowhere. The work of Clements and others on this material, rather, has shown that there are perfectly sound 'internal' reasons why they assumed their present shape as a collection and furthermore that 2 Kgs. 20: 17–18 specifically prepares for 2 Kgs. 24: 12–16 within the Deuteronomic History.[52] Indeed, Seitz, whom we might otherwise suppose would follow Smelik at this point, is second to none in his conviction that 2 Kgs. 20: 12–19 'has its primary home in the DtrH' (p. 188). Consequently, he rejects Smelik's conclusions concerning the original location of this passage, in contrast with his broad agreement with Smelik over chapters 36–8.

In the second place, while it may readily be agreed that Isaiah 39 functions reasonably well as it stands as an introduction to chapter 40, one might be forgiven for asking whether it could really have

[52] Clements, *Isaiah and the Deliverance of Jerusalem*, 52–71, and 'The Isaiah Narrative of 2 Kings 20: 12–19 and the Date of the Deuteronomic History', in A. Rofé and Y. Zakovitch (eds.), *Essays on the Bible and the Ancient World: Isac Leo Seeligmann Volume*, iii (Jerusalem, 1983), 209–20; C. T. Begg, '2 Kings 20: 12–19 as an Element of the Deuteronomistic History', *CBQ* 48 (1986), 27–38, and 'The Deuteronomistic Retouching of the Portrait of Hezekiah in 2 Kgs 20,12–19', *BN* 38–9 (1987), 7–13. This suggestion is not affected by the recent argument of M. Brettler that 2 Kgs. 24: 13–14 actually refers to the events of 587 rather than 597. His further, and subsidiary, attempt to deny any connection with 2 Kgs. 20: 16–18 seems overly critical, however: see '2 Kings 24: 13–14 as History', *CBQ* 53 (1991), 541–52.

been written specifically to serve that function. As Davies, for instance, points out: 'It is not of course an ideal link, since the fate of the royal family is not something in which these chapters (or those which follow them) show any interest.'[53] On reflection, therefore, it seems to be a case of an intelligible reuse in Isaiah of antecedent material rather than of original composition.

The (somewhat unremarkable) upshot of this lengthy discussion of Isaiah 36–9 is that we have found no evidence for supposing that they were written explicitly for their present position in the book of Isaiah, nor for any kind of rearrangement or addition to them that might be attributed to Deutero-Isaiah such as might have been expected had he been the one responsible for inserting them here as a bridge to the main part of his own composition. They do, however, betray extensive knowledge of the earlier material in Isaiah, while at the same time they manifest a number of characteristics which mark them out as distinctive from the rest of the Deuteronomic History. It is, therefore, likely that they were composed in circles where the prophet's words were valued and were then incorporated as a separate source into the Deuteronomic History. It is difficult now to determine the extent to which the historian himself altered or added to what he thus inherited, but the annalistic introduction (2 Kgs. 18: 13–16) and some of the wording, at least, in the final story at 2 Kgs. 20: 16–18 are obvious places to start looking. Later, they were borrowed from Kings by an editor of the book of Isaiah.[54] Since they serve as a bridge between the two major parts of the book, it is clear (on the hypothesis of the present work) that this must have been some time after the work of Deutero-Isaiah.[55]

It is perhaps worth a somewhat more precise attempt at locating the stage when this borrowing took place. There are two possible

[53] Davies, 'The Destiny of the Nations', 102.

[54] Cf. Mowinckel, *Prophecy and Tradition*, 65: 'This of course does not exclude the possibility that the Isaiah narratives may *also* have existed in a more or less identical complex in the Isaiah tradition circle; but in this definit (*sic*) instance the collectors have not taken these narratives from this assumed tradition, but in the form in which they found it written in the Book of Kings.'

[55] In the concluding chapter of his work, and as a consequence of his case that Isaiah 36–9 concluded the work of First Isaiah before its extension by Deutero-Isaiah, Seitz sketches in avowedly programmatic fashion what he sees as the influence of these chapters on 40–55. So far as I can see, however, none of his examples is limited to 36–9 exclusively, and indeed for most of them I have already argued above, Chapters 3 and 4, that other passages in the earlier part of Isaiah furnish stronger and more direct sources of influence.

indications, though neither can be regarded as decisive. First, we have seen that one of the few purposeful redactional alterations to the Kings text displays an interest in the restored community gathered in worship at the temple. The use of *bayit* for the temple is surprisingly rare in the second half of the book, and only two passages[56] use this designation in a context that is speaking of gathering there for worship, namely 56: 5 and 7 (three occurrences) and 66: 20. (In both places, the passage speaks of the universalizing of the temple worship.) Now, it is often suggested that these two similar passages have been deliberately set at the opening and the close of what we call Trito-Isaiah as part of the final editorial work on that part of the book. Is there a possible hint here that the inclusion of Isaiah 36–9 should be ascribed to this same process? Support for this view comes from Webb's suggestion that 'The eunuchs in view here [i.e. chapter 56] are almost certainly those referred to in 39.7, namely, those who accepted this condition on entering official employment in exile.'[57]

The same conclusion would follow from the second possible indication. Isaiah 39 ends with the expression of Hezekiah's words, 'There will be peace [*šālôm*] and security in my days.' The form of this sentence is slightly different in 2 Kgs. 20: 19, and there is also evidence from the LXX that it did not stand in the original text there; it is another example of an addition made at a later stage in the transmission of the text, based on the Isaiah text.[58] Either way, it appears that the Isaiah editor was interested in this particular sentence. It may be that this should be linked with a most peculiar feature of Isaiah 40–66—namely, that the material is divided into exact thirds by the use of the familiar saying, 'There is no peace, says the Lord (*or* my God), for the wicked' (48: 22; 57: 21). Judging

56 The other references are Isa. 60: 7 (in a passage which, perhaps significantly, Davies ('The Destiny of the Nations', 102 n. 36) sees as reversing 39: 5–7); 64: 10 (which looks back to the destruction of the temple, and which comes in a passage which I have suggested elsewhere was an exilic lament taken up into Trito-Isaiah: see Williamson, 'Isaiah 63,7–64,11'); and 66: 1 (where the importance of the building of the temple is subordinated to the need for a right attitude to God). It is noteworthy that there are no occurrences at all in chapters 40–55.

57 Webb, 'Zion in Transformation', 79 n. 1.

58 The B text translates only the first half of the verse: 'Good is the word of the Lord which you have spoken'; in addition the remainder of the verse was asterisked in the Hexapla. It is thus likely that the second half of the verse was added first in the Isaianic redaction of the text, whence it was added secondarily to MT Kings (and hence to A $bc_2e_2$ etc.). See the comments on the analogous situation at 2 Kgs. 19: 25 above, and Konkel, 'The Source of the Hezekiah Story in Isaiah'.

by the preceding contexts, it is quite clear that this saying was first coined by the author of 57: 21, for its sentiment is carefully based on the previous two verses, whereas it seems to have been only loosely added at the end of chapter 48. Finally, the last verse of the book (66: 24), while using different vocabulary, most certainly reflects the same thought of 'no peace for the wicked'. Again, the verse is not particularly well integrated into its context, though it does have a close relationship to Isa. 1: 2, the very first oracle in the book as a whole ('rebelled against me'). The equal division of the second half of the book in this somewhat artificial manner is curious, but, in view of the evidence for editorial intervention or conscious placement in three, at least, of the four cases, it is hard to escape the impression that it is more than purely coincidental. Clearly, this activity must be part of the latest editorial process in the book, and so it again points to the inclusion of chapters 36–9 at the time of the final arrangement of (40)56–66 (and perhaps too, we may now add, of the present ordering of chapter 1; see above, pp. 153–4). Whether or not this particular conjecture is accepted, it is clear that we may proceed with our main investigation without reference to these chapters.

At the start of Chapter 6, reference was made to the opinion of some commentators that Isaiah 35 was originally part of Deutero-Isaiah's composition. Moving backwards from Isaiah 36–9, the time has now come when that opinion must be examined more closely. In addition, it is frequently maintained that Isaiah 34 belongs with 35 as a single unit of composition, the two chapters together sometimes being styled 'the little apocalypse'.[59] Not surprisingly, therefore, this chapter too has occasionally been claimed for Deutero-Isaiah,[60] so that we shall have to take it into account as well in the course of the discussion.

[59] Clements, indeed, claims that 'the section comprised of 34: 1–35: 10 is recognised by almost all critical scholars to be a unity', though Wildberger is a notable exception; see too H. Donner, '"Forscht in der Schrift Jahwes und lest!" Ein Beitrag zum Verständnis der israelitischen Prophetie', *ZTK* 87 (1990), 285–98. In recent times, the case for unity has been most fully presented by Vermeylen, 437, and B. Gosse, 'Isaïe 34–35: Le Châtiment d'Edom et des nations, salut pour Sion', *ZAW* 102 (1990), 396–404.

[60] For chapter 35 alone, see H. Graetz, 'Isaiah xxxiv and xxxv', *JQR* 4 (1891–2), 1–8; A. T. Olmstead, 'II Isaiah and Isaiah, Chapter 35', *AJSL* 53 (1936–7), 251–3, with references to his earlier indications of this view; R. B. Y. Scott, 'The Relation of Isaiah, Chapter 35, to Deutero-Isaiah', *AJSL* 52 (1935–6), 178–91. For chapters 34

Fortunately, my task in this section has been immeasurably simplified by the appearance of a monograph by Steck devoted entirely to Isaiah 35 (*Bereitete Heimkehr*). Since I am in broad agreement with some major aspects of Steck's thesis, it will be possible to follow his discussion with indications of where some modification may be called for.

As can be seen from the sub-title of his work (*Jesaja 35 als redaktionelle Brücke zwischen dem Ersten und dem Zweiten Jesaja*), Steck's main conclusion is that Isaiah 35 was specifically written to function as a bridge between the two main parts of the book of Isaiah. While accepting that the chapter shows many points of connection with passages throughout Isaiah, he attempts to demonstrate that the closest are with Isa. 40: 1–11 and with chapters 32–4, that is to say, the verse passages which are immediately adjacent to it. We may note in passing here that this conclusion puts chapter 35 in a rather different category from chapters 36–9; there, the connections were more scattered and the passage was seen to function in its present secondary position as a bridge passage, whereas in Isaiah 35 Steck maintains that the chapter was written for its present setting and, indeed, cannot be understood apart from it.

Steck's general arguments with regard to 40: 1–11 are that it is only here that we find such a concentration of parallels with 35, that two of the points of connection are to be found only here, and that the two passages follow the same general order. Moreover, it must be chapter 35 which has borrowed from 40: 1–11 because it also has links with 32–4 which are not shared by 40: 1–11 and because the different way in which some of the elements are used in 35 can be explained contextually by its present position and function.

By way of illustration, Steck's treatment of the first section in chapter 35, namely verses 1–2, may be described in more detail. He has little difficulty in demonstrating some similarities with 40: 3–5. In both passages there is to be a transformation of the *ʿ$^{a}$rābâ* and the *midbār*, the change of subject in 40: 5 is reflected at 35: 2*b*, and part of 40: 5 ('And the glory of the Lord shall be revealed, and all flesh shall see it together') may be compared with the last line of 35:

and 35 together, see H. M. Wiener, *The Prophets of Israel in History and Criticism* (London, 1923), 138; Torrey, 279–301; M. Pope, 'Isaiah 34 in Relation to Isaiah 35, 40–66', *JBL* 71 (1952), 235–43; more tentatively, McKenzie. Torrey's theory was challenged long ago by W. Caspari, 'Jesaja 34 und 35', *ZAW* 49 (1931), 67–86, and by Elliger, *Deuterojesaja in seinem Verhältnis zu Tritojesaja*, 272–8.

2 ('They shall see the glory of the Lord, the majesty of our God'). Other scattered links with both Deutero-Isaiah (not all equally convincing) and with Isaiah 32–3 are then noted.

Next and crucially, Steck seeks to show how the different ways in which the themes indicated by these similarities are handled can be explained by the present position of 35 between 34 and 40. (i) No account of 40: 1–2 is taken at this point, because, according to the end of chapter 33, the guilty status of God's people has already been taken care of. (ii) God's own journey in 40: 3–5 has to drop out because, according to chapter 33, God is envisaged as already enthroned in Zion. The same will be true in 35: 8–10, where the theme of the journey becomes explicit. (iii) The 'levelling' of 40: 4 is omitted because of 34: 3*b*–4*a*, which refers to the melting of the mountains in the context of the judgement of the nations. (iv) In 35: 2 it is the natural elements, not 'all flesh', which see the glory of God, because, according to 34: 2–4, this humanity apart from Israel no longer exists. Furthermore, the line that the reinterpretation should take may have been suggested by 40: 6. (v) The general theme of 35: 1–2 was also suggested by the context: the lands through which chapter 40 envisages the return taking place are destroyed according to chapter 34. Chapter 35, therefore, indicates their restoration in order to overcome this contradiction. Steck thus concludes that chapter 35 only 'works' for those who have already read 33–4 and are going on to read 40.

Steck regards 35: 3–10 as a single section, and it is unnecessary to follow his lengthy discussion of this passage in such detail. He is clearly on firm ground in comparing 35: 4 with 40: 9 and 10–11, slightly less so when he suggests that the three promises of 35: 4*b*, 5–7 and 8–10 have been influenced both formally and in part from the point of view of content by the three promises of 40: 10–11. Once again, he finds a number of connections (some quite striking) with passages in 32–4 (and Jer. 31: 7–22), but then argues in a rather forced (because selective) manner that 35 has followed the general order not only of 40: 1–11 but also of 32–4. This, however, is not strictly necessary for his main argument. (Note, too, his extremely contrived attempt to suggest that 35: 8–10 is based in the detail of its order not only on 40: 11 but also on the closing verses of chapter 34.)

Changes due to context are important for his understanding of this passage too. (i) As before, God is no longer envisaged as participating in the return journey. In verse 4, it is suggested that it is his 'vengeance' and 'recompense' which are regarded as the subject of the verbs, not God himself. (ii) The basis of verses 5–7 is to be found in 33: 23–4,[61] and one of the several reasons why this theme should be particularly emphasized at this point is that 33: 24 has been extended in the light of 32: 2–4 in such a way that the salvation promised to the inhabitants of Zion is now promised also to those who are on the return journey. (This reasoning is similar to that used to explain why chapter 35 did not take particular account of 40: 1–2.) (iii) The need of 35: 5–7 to prepare for the promises of chapter 40 following the devastation foreseen in chapter 34 has already been noted. (iv) If the first three points, based on Isa. 35: 3–7, look back primarily to chapters 32–4, the last part of the chapter, verses 8–10, looks forward rather to 40: 11. It has already been mentioned that Steck's argument here becomes tortuous, as he seeks to establish that the order of the material follows both 40: 11 and 34: 14–15. Even without this, however, the threefold occurrence of *šām* in each of 34: 15–16 and 35: 8–10 remains suggestive.

Even if it is not possible to accept all of Steck's arguments, that need not inhibit us from agreeing that his main conclusion seems to be sound. His arguments are of a cumulative nature, so that disagreement with one or even several of them does not necessarily undermine his position. Important consequences follow from Steck's new understanding of the chapter, and he explores a number of them in the remainder of his monograph. Those which impinge most immediately on our present investigation must be noted.

First, it is clear that Isaiah 35 is dependent from a literary point of view on both Proto- and Deutero-Isaiah, and indeed Steck suggests that it may have been written at the very time when the two separate books were first joined together. In my opinion, however, there never was a separate book of Deutero-Isaiah, and so clearly this suggestion requires modification. The adjustment, however, is not difficult to make. As we shall see later, the main 'problems' which Isaiah 35 sought to solve were raised by the juxtaposition of chapters 34 and 40; those raised by 33 are more apparent than real. The need for 35 may, therefore, have been perceived not so much

[61] The relationship between these two passages is explored in more detail, and with reference to a wider circle of texts both within and beyond the book of Isaiah, by Clements, 'Patterns in the Prophetic Canon: Healing the Blind and the Lame'.

when the two main parts of Isaiah were first joined as when chapter 34 was added. The conclusion will stand, however, that 35 represents a relatively late stage in the composition of the book as a whole, and in particular that it is later than, rather than simultaneous with, the composition of Deutero-Isaiah.[62]

Secondly, this conclusion is supported by the observation that chapter 35 has some links also with Trito-Isaiah. Apart from some scattered parallels, where priority would be difficult to establish either way, Steck points in particular to the similarities between 35: 8–10 and 62: 10–12, and concludes that the form of Deutero-Isaiah which existed at the time of the composition of chapter 35 included the bulk of chapters 60–2 as well. The suggestion that these passages are part of a redactional layer which can be traced through all the major sections of the book of Isaiah is questionable. (Steck draws 11: 11–16 and 27: 12–13 into this discussion, but I attempted to show in Chapter 7 above that this was not convincing.) Nevertheless, the connections between these two particular passages are especially striking, and, when they are combined with the evidence of chapter 34 (see below), which is certainly as old as, and probably earlier than, chapter 35, the evidence seems overwhelming that chapter 35 cannot be dated earlier than parts, at least, of Trito-Isaiah.

Thirdly, then, what are we to say about Isaiah 34, which so many scholars have associated with 35? Steck has two points in particular to say about this chapter.[63] First, it is a separate composition from chapter 35, and, secondly, it may have been an original and inseparable continuation of chapter 33, both chapters forming the conclusion of Proto-Isaiah in the shape which that book had assumed by the time when it was first joined with Deutero-Isaiah.

[62] The similarities between 35 and 40–55, which have been used to suggest identity of authorship (see above, n. 60), are to be explained as later literary allusions, as are the points of contact with the preceding chapters. It is one of the merits of Steck's work that he has shown that this chapter cannot be understood by reference to Deutero-Isaiah alone.

[63] Steck also argues that 34 is a composite text, verses 2–4 and 16–17 being later additions. More speculatively still, he wonders whether verses 2–4 may not be due to the same redactional activity as chapter 35 itself. J. Lust thinks that verse 7 also belongs with 2–4: see 'Isaiah 34 and the *herem*', in Vermeylen (ed.), *The Book of Isaiah*, 275–86. He sees no necessary contradiction between his position and the unity of the final form of the text as urged on rhetorical grounds by J. Muilenburg, 'The Literary Character of Isaiah 34', *JBL* 59 (1940), 339–65 = T. F. Best (ed.), *Hearing and Speaking the Word: Selections from the Works of James Muilenburg* (Chico, Calif., 1984), 59–85.

Both these points raise issues of central concern for our overall hypothesis and must therefore be examined more carefully.

The separation of chapter 34 from 35 has already been discussed to some extent in the context of the examination of the nature of chapter 35, but to this Steck adds some further observations. After maintaining that such links as have been found between the two chapters can all be explained on the theory that 35 was in some measure dependent on 34, he then adds that the links which have been found between 34 and 40–66 are nearly all insignificant, in particular because most of them are also paralleled in other prophetic texts outside the book of Isaiah. They are thus of a different nature altogether from the connections between 35 and 40–66. Only one passage is closely and exclusively paralleled in the second part of the book—namely, 34: 5–6 and 63: 1–6. It has usually been thought that the passage in 34 is dependent on that in 63,[64] but Steck suggests the reverse. Either way, the similarities in outlook and phraseology are so close that a comparable date seems probable. Thus, despite the separation of chapters 34 and 35, a comparatively late date for the former still seems probable.

This conclusion receives support from the observation that, amongst a number of other literary associations, Isaiah 34 seems to be particularly closely linked with Isaiah 13, and in fact to be dependent upon it. Vermeylen points out that the two passages have an identical structure, which he sets out in tabular form as follows:

| | | |
|---|---|---|
| preparation for combat | 13: 2–4 | 34: 1 |
| slaughter of the nations | 13: 5–9, 14–16 | 34: 2–3 |
| cosmic upheaval | 13: 10–13 | 34: 4–5*a* |
| capture of the city and massacre of its inhabitants | 13: 17–19 | 34: 5*b*–8 |
| country turned into desert | 13: 20 | 34: 9–10 |
| wild animals | 13: 21–2 | 34: 11–15 |

There are also a number of words and expressions which the two passages share, among which it is particularly significant to note not only that the list of animals in 13: 21–2 is repeated almost exactly in 34: 11–15 but also that it is there extended by reference to the list of unclean animals in Deut. 14: 12–18 (and cf. Isa. 14: 23;

64 See most recently Gosse, 'Isaïe 34–35'. In this article Gosse builds on two of his earlier studies, 'L'Alliance d'Isaïe 59,21', *ZAW* 101 (1989), 116–18, and 'Detournement de la vengeance du Seigneur contre Edom et les nations en Isa 63,1–6', *ZAW* 102 (1990), 105–10.

Zeph. 2: 14). This observation is strong evidence that it is Isaiah 34 which is dependent on Isaiah 13 (Vermeylen, 440–1). Gosse adds some further evidence, including some from Isaiah 14, though it is not all equally convincing; for instance, compare 13: 20 *lōʾ tiškōn ʿad-dôr wādôr* with 34: 17 *l^edôr wādôr yišk^enû-bāh*;[65] a comparable reversal based on the root *yrš* in 14: 21 and 34: 11, 17; the occurrence of *qippôd* in 14: 23 and 34: 11; and the occurrence together of *pgr* and *šlk* in 14: 19 and 34: 3.[66]

I argued in the previous chapter that the present setting of Isaiah 13–14 was due to the work of Deutero-Isaiah, and that it was of particular significance to him because of its anticipation of the downfall of Babylon. In the light of the dependence of Isaiah 34 upon it, and the latter's shift of focus to Edom, it looks as though we have here a post-exilic development whereby in some circles Edom became a type of the enemy of the people of God, just as Babylon had been.[67] From a redaction-critical standpoint, one can understand Isaiah 34 being put in its present position at this time in order to invite a reading of the main 'Babylonian' section of the book in terms of Edom (hence the reprise of chapter 13) and this being picked up retrospectively in chapter 63. For all these reasons, therefore, Isaiah 34 should be dated to the post-exilic period.[68]

The other matter which arises from Steck's discussion of Isaiah 34 is his suggestion that it is a direct continuation of chapter 33. So far as I am aware, this view has not been presented before, but it naturally has implications for the date of chapter 33 in the light of the points which have just been made. I shall be discussing chapter 33 more fully below, but it is important to establish here whether it is correct to treat it in separation from 34.

65 Vermeylen does not refer to this connection, presumably because, like many other commentators, he regards 34: 16–17 as a later addition. He does, however, point out that *middôr lādôr* occurs in 34: 10.

66 See Gosse, 'Isaïe 34–35', 400–1.

67 Cf. J. R. Bartlett, *Edom and the Edomites* (JSOTS 77; Sheffield, 1989), 184–6, citing also B. C. Cresson, 'The Condemnation of Edom in Post-Exilic Judaism', in J. M. Efrid (ed.), *The Use of the Old Testament in the New and other Essays* (Durham, NC, 1972), 125–48. The juxtaposition of Babylon and Edom is also found in Isaiah 21 and Psalm 137.

68 This is, of course, the common opinion among commentators. Wildberger, for instance, lends it further support by arguing that Isaiah 34 must be later than Obadiah and Ezekiel, while many refer rather more generally to the chapter's 'proto-apocalyptic' character (a rather unsatisfactory description, whose value for dating purposes is questionable). My principal concern above has been the position of Isaiah 34 within the development of Isaiah rather than with absolute chronology.

Steck begins his discussion (pp. 55–6) by conceding that there are no significant verbal or thematic links between the two chapters, which in itself must be regarded as a major weakness in his argument. Positively, he presents the following reasons for his view. (i) The summons in 33: 13 looks forward. Those who are 'near', who are to acknowledge God's might, are the inhabitants of Zion, addressed in 33: 17–24. (Steck agrees with Vermeylen that verses 14–16 are a later addition.) Those who are 'far off', who must listen to what God has done, are the peoples who are addressed in 34: 1, 5–15. This is supported by a comparison between the formulation of 33: 13 and 34: 1; compare the use of *šmʿ* in both verses and the summons in 34: 1 to those who are, *ex hypothesi*, 'far off', to 'draw near' (*qirᵉbû*). (ii) Since chapter 33 probably refers to the destruction of Babylon as the enemy of God's people, the two chapters together provide the Babylon–Edom development which we have seen is attested elsewhere. (iii) Both chapters take account of the preceding context.[69]

This third point proves nothing, however, for we have repeatedly seen that it is a feature of many passages which have been added to the basic core of Proto-Isaiah to refer to earlier material. The chief value of the evidence (and, to be fair, the one which Steck principally refers to) is to show that chapter 34 looks backwards rather than forwards, from a literary point of view. It thus belongs more with what precedes than with what follows, and in this way differs from chapter 35. While in the light of my comments above concerning the redactional function of chapter 34 this judgement perhaps requires some modification, Steck's main point here may be accepted. That has nothing to do, however, with establishing that it is part of the same composition as chapter 33.

Steck's second argument, too, is weak in the extreme. The Babylon–Edom juxtaposition can as well be accounted for by addition in the light of developing circumstances as by unity of authorship. The two nations are not brought together in 33–4 in such a close way that the reference to the one demands a reference to the other.

This leaves only the first argument, which is clearly the strongest.

[69] Steck (*Bereitete Heimkehr*, 50 n. 24) compares 34: 8 with 32: 10; 34: 9 with 30: 33; 34: 5–6 with 31: 8; 34: 12 with 32: 1; 34: 11–15 with 32: 13–14; and he also notes the links with chapter 13. On p. 56 he compares 33: 1 with 21: 1; 33: 5–6 with 32: 15 ff.; and 33: 17 ff. with 32: 8.

It is, however, precarious to base a case on a specific interpretation of 33: 13, since there is no agreement as to the precise function of that verse. Steck asserts, without supporting reasons and with no reference to contrary views, that 'Die Aufforderung 33,13 hat vorausweisenden Charakter' (p. 55), and he further sees two separate groups being addressed, the 'far off' and the 'near'. Neither point is certain, however. Kaiser, Wildberger (p. 1296), and Roberts,[70] among others, have argued that the verse looks back to what precedes as a conclusion, rather than forward to what follows, and Wildberger further suggests that the 'far off' are the peoples of verse 12 and the 'near' are those addressed in the second-person plural in verse 11, namely, the people of Ariel (cf. verse 7), that is, Zion. Others, however, such as Auvray and Vermeylen,[71] regard the verse more as a transition, linking together the peoples of the previous section and the 'sinners in Zion' of verses 14–16. Thus Vermeylen, who in any case believes that verses 13–16 are a later addition, writes that 'Le compilateur ménageait ainsi une transition entre la parole adressée aux nations (vv. 10–12; cfr *rᵉḥôqîm*, "les éloignés") et la requête des Juifs fidèles prêts à pénétrer dans le sanctuaire (v. 14; cfr *qᵉrôbîm*, "les proches")' (p. 433).[72] Finally, among those who take the verse as forward-looking in its entirety, Caspari[73] suggests that the 'near' are addressed in verses 14–19 and the 'far off' in verses 20–3.

It may also be questioned whether it is correct to distinguish so sharply between two separate groups of people in this verse. There are undoubtedly a number of passages where the expression 'near and far' is used as a merismus to express totality,[74] and, in view of the synonymous parallelism in the rest of this verse, the same seems likely to be true here as well, without a need to distinguish too

70 J. J. M. Roberts, 'Isaiah 33: An Isaianic Elaboration of the Zion Tradition', in C. L. Meyers and M. O'Connor (eds.), *The Word of the Lord Shall Go Forth: Essays in Honor of David Noel Freedman in Celebration of His Sixtieth Birthday* (Winona Lake, Ind., 1983), 15–25.

71 Childs seems to take a similar position, though this is neither clear nor explicit: see *Isaiah and the Assyrian Crisis*, 116.

72 Kaiser moves a step in this direction when he observes that the reversal of the usual order of near and far is a means of preparing for the following stanza (verses 14–16).

73 Caspari, 'Jesaja 34 und 35', 86.

74 See Deut. 13: 7; Isa. 57: 19; Jer. 25: 26; Ezek. 6: 12; 22: 5; Dan. 9: 7; Est. 9: 20; and A. M. Honeyman, '*Merismus* in Biblical Hebrew', *JBL* 71 (1952), 11–18; Irwin, *Isaiah 28–33*, 149; Zimmerli, *Ezechiel*, 155–6 = *Ezekiel 1*, 191; R. Gane and J. Milgrom, 'קרב', *TWAT* vii, cols. 156–7.

sharply between gentile nations and the people of God. It is the latter who are primarily addressed. In sum, whichever of the approaches sketched out above is adopted (and the last one seems most probable to me), no continuation of 33: 13 in the terms of 34: 1 is to be expected.

This conclusion receives support from the fact that the construction of the passage which Steck proposes would appear to be unparalleled. There are numerous examples of such summonses to appear as witnesses, to receive instruction, or for some other purpose,[75] but in none of them, so far as I am aware, are those mentioned addressed separately in the way that Steck suggests, still less is a second introduction of the sort proposed for 34: 1 inserted resumptively before the address to the second group. The balance of probability thus strongly favours the usual view that 34: 1 introduces a new literary unit.[76] The different form and themes of the two chapters, acknowledged by Steck, thus come as no surprise.

It may thus be concluded from this examination of Isaiah 34 and 35 that they are both to be regarded as post-exilic additions to the book of Isaiah, but that this does not necessarily apply to chapter 33. Despite the probability which Steck has demonstrated that the two chapters were not originally written as a single piece and that 35 in particular has been written to serve as a bridge between what precedes and chapters 40–55(66), they cannot have been included in the form of the book which Deutero-Isaiah knew or was responsible for. In particular, I have modified Steck's position by suggesting that the need for the addition of chapter 35 became apparent only after chapter 34 had been inserted (his arguments to this effect with regard to chapter 33 will be examined below). The insertion of chapter 34 reflects a post-exilic development of the identity of the enemy of God's people (from Babylon to Edom, possibly viewed typologically) and owes its position to the desire to reinterpret the Babylon of chapter 13 in Edomic terms before the main 'Babylonian' section of the book in chapters 40–55 is read. In different ways, therefore, both chapters presuppose a form of the book in which the main parts of Proto- and of Deutero-Isaiah were present.

[75] C. Hardmeier (*Texttheorie und biblische Exegese: Zur rhetorischen Funktion der Trauermetaphorik in der Prophetie* (BEvT 79; Munich, 1978), 302–16) stresses the variety of the relevant material against attempts to limit them to two or three form-critical categories only.

[76] Hardmeier (ibid. 302 n. 66) points out that in the vast majority of cases the summons to hear marks the start of a new textual unit.

They, too, may thus be eliminated from our enquiry as we look for the point at which Deutero-Isaiah himself joined the bulk of his work to the edited form of the literary deposit of Isaiah of Jerusalem.

We come finally, then, to an examination of Isaiah 33. While most scholars still recognize the importance of Gunkel's study, in which he suggested that the form-critically disparate parts of the chapter could be held together under the rubric of a 'prophetic liturgy',[77] there remains the widest possible spectrum of opinion with regard to date and setting. Authorship by Isaiah himself is defended anew by Roberts,[78] an exilic date has been proposed by Barth[79] and Clements, (unconsciously?) following such older commentators as Dillmann-Kittel and König, a setting in the Persian period is advocated by Wildberger, while a Hellenistic date (slightly modifying the Maccabean date previously suggested by Duhm, Marti, and Scott) is still favoured by Kaiser.

An important fresh approach to the chapter has recently been advocated by Beuken.[80] Rather like Steck in his work on Isaiah 35,[81] Beuken insists that it has developed within the context of the literary development of the book as a whole. Because it reflects a number of passages which both precede and follow it, and because it tells a 'story' which is suitable at this point in the general movement or plot of the book by its recall of the earlier sections and anticipation of the later, he compares it to the genre of a 'mirror

[77] H. Gunkel, 'Jesaja 33, eine prophetische Liturgie: Ein Vortrag', *ZAW* 42 (1924), 177–208; for a fundamental modification of Gunkel's work, see R. Murray, 'Prophecy and the Cult', in R. Coggins, A. Phillips, and M. Knibb (eds.), *Israel's Prophetic Tradition: Essays in Honour of Peter R. Ackroyd* (Cambridge, 1982), 200–16. While Murray has demonstrated some significant connections with other Old Testament liturgical material, especially Psalm 46, it is not possible to follow him in most of the more far-reaching speculations in which he indulges. Wildberger finds three major and separate sections in the chapter (verses 1–6, 7–16, 17–24), but nevertheless maintains that they all come from the same setting and the same author (p. 1286). As was noted above, Steck (Bereitete Heimkehr, 55) regards verses 14–16 as a later addition, though this does not seriously affect the fundamental unity of the chapter. Only Vermeylen seems to have returned to a more radical literary division of the chapter.

[78] Roberts, 'Isaiah 33: An Isaianic Elaboration of the Zion Tradition'.

[79] Barth, *Die Jesaja-Worte in der Josiazeit*, 46–7, 287–8.

[80] W. A. M. Beuken, 'Jesaja 33 als Spiegeltext im Jesajabuch', *ETL* 67 (1991), 5–35.

[81] Though, unlike Steck, Beuken does not focus particularly on the immediately adjacent material, nor does he argue from similarities of arrangement.

text', 'an artistic device, which is found in the world literature of all times'.[82] It is therefore misguided to search after an independent *Sitz im Leben* for this chapter; one can speak only of its *Sitz im Prophetenbuch*.

Beuken's study, parts of which will be examined in detail below, suggests the possibility that chapter 33 may indeed function in the manner that we suggested earlier was to be expected at this point where we anticipate a shift from the edited version of the earlier Isaianic literary deposit to the substance of Deutero-Isaiah's own composition. In what follows, I shall seek to defend the thesis that in fact this is precisely the case. The argument will fall into three main parts. First, I shall discuss the general suitability of the chapter in its overall shape for this purpose; secondly, I shall examine some significant items of detail in the chapter which point towards the hand of Deutero-Isaiah as the one responsible for its inclusion here; and, thirdly, I shall look in detail at the verbal links which Beuken has presented, to see whether any of them (such as those suggested with Trito-Isaiah) are problematic for my case.

The chapter opens with a 'woe!' oracle pronounced against a 'destroyer' and a 'treacherous one'. At the present, he has not yet been destroyed or dealt with treacherously, but the time is coming when the tables will be turned on him. Though not referred to by name, the Babylonians would seem to be the intended nation (whether or not an earlier, authentic oracle of Isaiah against the Assyrians underlies the verse, as advocated by Vermeylen). This is most strongly suggested by the close parallel with 21: 2, to which all commentators draw attention, and it receives support also from the use of the same language with reference to the Chaldeans in Hab. 1: 13 (and cf. 2: 5); in addition, the exact reversal of fortunes is of the same nature as that predicted for them in Hab. 2: 6–19. As the empire which had destroyed Jerusalem, a major focus in the remainder of the chapter, no other power seems so suitable in the present context. The near anticipation of Babylon's overthrow is similar to what was seen in parts of chapters 13 and 14, to say nothing of its echoes in Deutero-Isaiah. This verse, therefore, provides a significant clue for the dating, historical standpoint, and outlook of the chapter as a whole.

Following this confident introduction, the prophet turns to speak on behalf of the community, using through much of the

[82] Cf. Beuken's English summary: 'Jesaja 33 als Spiegeltext', 35.

remainder of the chapter elements which from a form-critical perspective are all characteristic of the lament, but not in their expected order.[83] Thus, verse 2 represents the request for salvation itself, but the lament proper is found only in verses 7–9 (Wildberger's suggestion that verses 3–4 serve to fulfil the function of the lament seems less well founded). The 'expression of certainty' is clearly present in verses 5–6, and it may well be that verses 3–4 (which occupy something of an intermediate position; so Kaiser) should be taken along with them. Verses 10–12(13) are an oracle in which God responds to the petitioners' lament, announcing that he is about to rise up to act on their behalf, and this is (ultimately) developed in verses 17–24 with an extended assurance of salvation, something which moves beyond the category of lament, but which is not unrelated, of course, to the expression of certainty (cf. verse 22, for example). Prior to that, however, verses 14–16 take the form of an entrance liturgy,[84] responding to the question who is worthy to participate in the future blessed state of Zion. This short passage is set apart somewhat from the prevailing context, both because it derives from a different category of Psalm altogether and because it is suggestive of a division within the Zion community, whereas the rest of the chapter speaks rather in terms of a Zion-gentile division. It is thus understandable that some commentators should have regarded these verses as a later addition. On the other hand, there are a number of close connections in thought between these verses and the surrounding context (e.g. cf. 14*b* with 12; 16*a* with 5 and 10), and, as we have already seen, the writer has clearly used considerable freedom in altering the usual liturgical forms to suit his purpose. Furthermore, an 'internal' examination is not necessarily inappropriate at this point before the future state of salvation is described. A decision on these verses is thus best left open.

Reflection on this outline suggests that both thematically and form-critically it is entirely appropriate at this point in the book, on the assumption that Deutero-Isaiah was here effecting a transition to his material in chapters 40–55. As Beuken has pointed out, the fundamental shape of the chapter is one of progression from a situation of judgement to one of salvation. The lament of the

[83] It should be remembered, however, that the Psalms of lament in the Psalter itself manifest a considerable degree of flexibility in the order in which the various elements occur; for a recent summary, see Day, *Psalms*, 19–38.

[84] Cf. Day, *Psalms*, 60–1.

people is answered by God's emphatic assertion that he is about to move in judgement upon the oppressors (10–12) and that the result will be salvation for Zion and its inhabitants. Similarly, we may add, much of the material which Deutero-Isaiah inherited spoke of God's indictment of his people which had brought them to the point of exile in which lament was the only appropriate response. This seems to be the setting presupposed by verse 1. Then, speaking in the very broadest terms, he follows this in chapters 40–8 with God's assertion that he is about to move decisively against Babylon, while in 49–54 the major theme moves on to the restoration of Zion.

Form-critically, the nature of this chapter is by no means totally unexpected to anyone familiar with chapters 40–55. Although the question of the structure of the sections of that material remains a matter of ongoing research and discussion, there is a considerable measure of agreement that in some passages, at least, shorter units which are patterned on elements which we find in the Psalms are joined together to construct longer sections which have a new unity and coherence of their own.[85] In addition, it is particularly significant that only in Deutero-Isaiah do we find the oracles and assurances of salvation which respond to the laments of the people. As is well known, it was long suspected that such oracles must have been given by priests or prophets in the temple cult in Jerusalem, since only so could the sharp changes in tone from lament to confidence in a number of the Psalms of individual lament be explained,[86] but it was not until the work of Begrich, developed by Westermann and Schoors,[87] that it was appreciated that many of Deutero-Isaiah's oracles could be seen as furnishing precisely this missing element in our knowledge of the Israelite liturgy. Isaiah 33, I suggest, falls into a similar category. Although God's oracle in

[85] Thus, for instance, though he disagrees quite substantially with many details of Westermann's analysis, Melugin nevertheless accepts that 'the prophet fused and transformed genres, often to the extent that the structure is essentially his own creation'. But he continues: 'Nevertheless, his short utterances are capable of standing alone by the test of both form and content' (*The Formation of Isaiah 40–55*, 175).

[86] For a summary of the scholarly debate, see W. H. Bellinger, *Psalmody and Prophecy* (JSOTS 27; Sheffield, 1984).

[87] See J. Begrich, 'Das priesterliche Heilsorakel', *ZAW* 52 (1934), 81–92, and *Studien zu Deuterojesaja* (BWANT 4/25; Stuttgart, 1938); C. Westermann, 'Das Heilswort bei Deuterojesaja', *EvTh* 24 (1964), 355–73; 'Sprache und Struktur' (and see too the introduction to his commentary); Schoors, *I am God your Saviour*.

verses 10–12, which so clearly answers to the lament of the people (e.g. verse 5), has its parallels in a few of the communal laments of the Psalter (e.g. especially Ps. 12: 6), the same cannot be said of the more far-reaching promises of verses 17–24. Whilst this passage does not follow the stereotyped form of many of the oracles and assurances of salvation, it nevertheless functions in the same way in the context of the chapter as a whole.[88] Of course, if the oracles of salvation in Deutero-Isaiah do *not* reflect pre-exilic cultic practice, as urged recently by Conrad and Day,[89] then the relationship between Isaiah 33 and Deutero-Isaiah will be even more marked.

Secondly, we may note a number of particular points which make this chapter peculiarly suitable as a link with chapters 40–55, which originally will have followed it directly. (i) The last verse leads straight into 40: 1–2: 'And no inhabitant will say, "I am sick"; the people who dwell there will be forgiven their iniquity' (33: 24).[90] The passive participle construction of the final phrase, *n*ᵉ*śu' 'āwōn*, does not in itself determine whether a past or future reference is intended. Within the context of the verse, one might suppose that this is a promise of future forgiveness, as rendered by the *RSV*. This is rare for the passive participle, but not impossible if the context so demands; cf. 2 Sam. 20: 21 and GK §116*p*. On the other hand, 40: 1–2 promises comfort to Jerusalem on the ground that already her iniquity (*'ᵃwōnāh*) has been pardoned. Another way of approaching the problem, however, is to follow Wildberger in his insistence that the last clause of 33: 24 is meant to serve as a grounding for the first: because of forgiveness, there will be freedom from sickness. It then functions in exactly the same way as the comparable clause in 40: 2, where the introductory *kî* makes clear that forgiveness is the ground for the announcement for comfort. The two passages thus fit together perfectly in sequence. Steck's contrary position is here to be challenged. It will be recalled that

88 For Deutero-Isaiah's freedom with regard to these forms, see e.g. Westermann on Isa. 51: 9–52: 3 (and esp. on verses 12–16). The question at the end of 51: 13 may be compared with 33: 18.

89 E. W. Conrad, 'Second Isaiah and the Priestly Oracle of Salvation', *ZAW* 93 (1981), 234–46; 'The "Fear Not" Oracles in Second Isaiah', *VT* 34 (1984), 129–52, developed and modified in *Fear Not Warrior: A Study of 'al tîrā' Pericopes in the Hebrew Scriptures* (Brown Judaic Studies, 75; Chico, Calif., 1985), 79–107; Day, *Psalms*, 30–2.

90 Rendtorff ('Zur Komposition des Buches Jesaja', 305) notes that 'Der Schluß von Kap. xxxiii läßt vermuten, daß auch dieses Kapitel eine bestimmte Funktion innerhalb der Gesamtkomposition des Jesajabuches hat.'

this was one of the points where he finds a contradiction between chapters 33–4 and 40. He thinks that in 33 the people of Jerusalem are already in a state of forgiveness, whereas this is still a future promise in 40 (see p. 17). In fact, as we have seen, however, 40: 2 also speaks of forgiveness as something already effective, though not yet appreciated, while in 33: 24 it is timeless, but announced as the basis for a future promise of healing. Naturally, in each case it is inappropriate to speak of 'tenses' in quite the way that we usually do in Western languages. What matters is that the indication of forgiveness in 33: 24 is then 'firmed up' by its announcement in 40: 2, in both cases the main point being that it undergirds the wider promise of blessing.

(ii) A significant element in the last section of chapter 33 is the emphasis on the kingship of God. He is referred to as *melek* in both verses 17[91] and 22, the latter being an especially forceful expression, and a number of attributes and functions go along with this characterization, not the least of which is salvation itself. Elsewhere in Isaiah 1–39, only chapter 6 speaks unequivocally of God as king, and it is likely that 33: 17 has this passage in view with its promise that now not just the prophet's eyes but those of the people of Zion as a whole[92] 'will see the king in his beauty'; contrast 6: 5. Elsewhere in the first half of the book, the title *melek* is applied to the Davidic king and to the one of his line who it is hoped will in future fulfil the often frustrated hopes of the present. In particular, chapter 32 looks forward to the benefits of his coming rule, some of which overlap with those of the reign of God in chapter 33; cf., for example, 32: 1–3, 16–18, and 33: 5–6, 16, 20, 22–4. Chapter 33 thus presents a different expectation from that which is characteristic of the rest of 1–39. As we saw in an earlier chapter, Isaiah 6 exercised a profound influence on Deutero-Isaiah, and in his writing we find a number of passages where God is entitled king; see 41: 21; 43: 15; 44: 6; and especially 52: 7, which again refers to his work of salvation (and cf. 52: 10). When this is combined with Deutero-Isaiah's well-known 'democratization' of the Davidic hope in 55: 3–5 (see above, p. 112), we must conclude that the thought of chapter 33 is entirely of a piece with his thought in this particular, and that

91 For a recent discussion, rightly concluding that this verse indeed refers to God and not a human king, see M. Brettler, *God is King: Understanding an Israelite Metaphor* (JSOTS 76; Sheffield, 1989), 173.

92 The second-person singular suffix on 'your eyes' is clearly to be taken as a collective.

by its juxtaposition with chapter 32 it prepares the way well for what is to follow. Finally, it may perhaps be significant that God is never styled *melek* in Trito-Isaiah. There are a couple of passages where royal language is used in association with him, of which 66: 1 is the most obvious. Here, however, the emphasis of the passage is not on God's royal attributes as such; they are introduced, rather, as part of the rhetorical build-up to the positive teaching of the passage which follows in verse 2: God is not so concerned with a physical temple, viewed as a divine throne room, but rather, 'this is the man to whom I will look, he that is humble and contrite in spirit, and trembles at my word'. The structure of this passage is thus exactly like 57: 15, which equally refers in its introduction to Isaiah 6 before going on to make the new claim that God dwells also 'with him who is of a contrite and humble spirit' (see further below, pp. 232–3). In both cases, therefore, it is probable that the introduction is picking up on a well-known characteristic of God as known from earlier in the book in order to emphasize the new point which follows. Trito-Isaiah is thus not interested in God's kingship as such; he refers to it only in order to deny the consequences which might normally be expected to follow from it. The comparability of chapter 33 with the thought of Deutero-Isaiah within the book as a whole thus stands out all the more clearly.

(iii) The phraseology of 33: 2, which encapsulates the people's lament as they await God's salvation, is also ideally suited to express the longings whose fulfilment, it seems, Deutero-Isaiah intended to announce. In a general way, as Westermann in particular has shown, he frequently picks up the language of such laments in order to reverse them, and on a number of occasions these laments are either the same as, or else very similar to, ones which are preserved for us in the Psalter. The same point applies to the present case; cf., for example, Pss. 4: 2; 6: 3; 31: 10; and 123: 3. Beyond that, however, the expression 'we wait for thee', while also reminiscent of some passages in the Psalter, may point in particular to Isa. 8: 17, whose importance and links with 40: 31 and 49: 23 were noted in Chapter 5 above. Similarly, the plea 'be thou our arm* every morning' is close to the lament cited by Deutero-Isaiah at 51: 9, the request for salvation is abundantly answered in chapters 40–55, and 'the time of trouble', though not paralleled there in terms of its wording, is close in thought to the situation whose end is announced in 40: 2 (contrast 46: 7). Not for one moment, of course, am I suggesting that such sentiments and expressions are unique to Deutero-Isaiah; on their own, they could not prove anything. Nevertheless, when read in the context of his work as a whole, their suitability cannot be denied.

(iv) Isa. 33: 5 and 10 both refer to the Lord's exaltation. In verse 5, it is stated as a fact; in verse 10, he himself emphasizes that now he will arise, lift himself up, and be exalted. The thought and language are reminiscent of chapter 2 (see especially verses 11 and 17) as well as of the start of chapter 6. This theme was discussed in Chapter 3 above (see pp. 38–41), and it is sufficient to refer back to the treatment there.

(v) In Isa. 33: 20, the future security of Zion is described by way of the metaphor of a tent: 'a quiet habitation, an immovable tent, whose stakes will never be plucked up, nor will any of its cords be broken'.[93] This is an unusual usage; as might be expected, tents are elsewhere more noted for their vulnerability; cf. Jer. 4: 20; 10: 20; Ps. 52: 7. It is closely paralleled, however, in Isa. 54: 2, where Zion (not mentioned by name, but clear from the context) is told: 'Enlarge the place of your tent, and let the curtains of your habitation be stretched out; hold not back, lengthen your cords and strengthen your stakes.' It is true that in the immediate context the emphasis is on the number of Zion's inhabitants rather than on her security,[94] but the latter theme also becomes prominent later in the chapter, while Zion's unexpected extent (54: 3) is itself anticipated in 33: 17. It is thus surprising that in his article on Isaiah 33 (p. 26) Beuken dismisses the similarity between these two passages as insignificant.[95]

(vi) The fact that chapter 33, which rounds off a major section in the book, finds a number of parallels and echoes in 54, which similarly completes a section before the final exhortation in chapter 55, prompts a reflection on the possible links with Isa. 2: 2–4. It was suggested in Chapter 6 above that this latter passage was purposefully placed at the start of the work which Deutero-Isaiah edited

[93] The curious juxtaposition of this image with its surrounding context was noted by Gunkel, 'Jesaja 33', 184–5.

[94] On this theme, cf. M. Callaway, *Sing, O Barren One: A Study in Comparative Midrash* (SBLDS 91; Atlanta, 1986), 59–72.

[95] It may further be noted that both chapters pick up in a small way the theme of 1: 21; see 33: 5 and 54: 14. Indeed, the whole atmosphere of 33: 17–24, with its joy in the physical appearance of Jerusalem and its confidence in her security is broadly echoed in chapter 54, especially verses 11–17.

and added to in order to set out in programmatic fashion the vision towards which he saw history developing and to which his interpretation of the events of his own time and those of a former generation were together moving. Chapters 33 and 54 seem to mark important steps along that pathway. Thus in 33 there may be echoes of the opening vision (2: 2–3) in verses 5–6 and 22 in particular, while other aspects of it, especially 2: 4, may have influenced the formulation of 54: 16–17.

Finally, this way of looking at chapter 33 helps us to answer the other of Steck's points regarding what he sees as a 'contradiction' between 33 and 40–55, which he thinks chapter 35 was framed to deal with. This concerns the emphasis on the presence of God enthroned as king in Zion in 33 contrasted with his coming to Zion, accompanied by the returning exiles, in chapter 40. Although it is possible that a later reader might have perceived a difficulty here, it may be doubted whether Deutero-Isaiah himself would have done. As we have already had occasion to observe (see above, p. 151), not only in chapter 54, but in some other passages as well (e.g. 49: 14–26; 51: 1–52: 2; 52: 7–10), he projects himself forward to the time when the people will be restored in Zion with God in their midst, even though this is interspersed with other passages which still look forward to the return (e.g. especially 52: 11–12). In view of the wider literary context which precedes chapter 33, there is thus no difficulty in believing that he could have done the same here; indeed, since the starting-point of the chapter is, as we have seen, to look back to the situation envisaged by so much of the judgemental material in Isaiah's own words, it would have been incomprehensible if he had done otherwise. Rather as in the manner of the opening of chapter 2, he then looks forward to the outcome of God's final work of salvation before 'backtracking' in chapter 40 to indicate in more detail the steps that should lead towards the fulfilment of that vision.

So far, we have examined various matters relating to the general theme of Isaiah 33, its setting in the book, and a number of its details in terms of content and language which have led to the suggestion that it would have served admirably to act as a transition from the edited work of Isaiah of Jerusalem to the substantive part of Deutero-Isaiah's composition. Before we conclude that this is the most reasonable way of understanding the chapter, however, we must look thirdly and finally at the various connections which

Beuken has described between this chapter and other parts of the book (see above, n. 80). Some of these have already been discussed in the previous section, and so they will only be mentioned here for completeness sake. Others will add to our appreciation of the chapter's links with other parts of Isaiah 1–39, to which we have not so far given much attention. Yet others, however, will require more detailed study; these are the cases where Beuken finds evidence of a connection with Trito-Isaiah. Clearly, if these are convincing, and if it is Isaiah 33 which is dependent on Trito-Isaiah, then our thesis will have to be modified accordingly. In fact, however, we shall see that the few links which Beuken suggests with this particular body of material are more remote than those which we have examined so far, that some of them do not stand up to examination at all, and that those where some association may be presumed can all be easily explained in ways other than postulating dependence of Isaiah 33 on Trito-Isaiah. I shall follow Beuken's enumeration throughout, and refer to all the passages which he mentions.

(i) Isa. 33: 1 and 21: 2. Beuken demonstrates convincingly that 33: 1 is dependent on 21: 2, and the significance of this for the setting and function of chapter 33 has already been discussed above. Since 21: 2 can be dated to the exilic period,[96] this fits well with our overall hypothesis. An isolated voice to the contrary is that of Vermeylen, who, as we have seen, ascribes 33: 1 to Isaiah himself but dates 21: 2 to the post-exilic period. It may be significant, however, that Vermeylen does not discuss the relationship between the two verses, something which is so uncharacteristic of his usual procedure that the suspicion cannot be avoided that he was aware of its embarrassment to his conclusions reached on other grounds.

(ii) Isa. 33: 2 and 8: 17; 12; 25: 9; 51: 5; 59: 11. The last three passages referred to are associated with 33: 2 by Beuken for the following reasons: the use in each verse of the verb *qwh* and derivatives of the root *yšʿ*; the use of *yd* (25: 10) and *zrwʿ* (33: 2; 51: 5) as God's instrument; and what he calls 'das bekennende Element', which in 33: 2 takes the form of the vocative *yhwh* and the inverted word order *lᵉkā qiwwînû*, in 51: 5 the comparable inversion whereby *ʾēlay* and *ʾel-zᵉrōʿî* stand first in their respective clauses, and in 59: 13 the contrasting expressions 'denying the Lord' and

96 See Wildberger and Clements; note too the dependence of Jeremiah 50–1 on Isaiah 21, as observed by Macintosh (*Isaiah xxi. A Palimpsest*, 113–15), especially significant if the usual exilic dating of the Jeremiah passage is correct.

'turning away from following our God'. Of these three points, the second two are so weak that they cannot be admitted. With regard to the use of 'arm', only 33: 2 and 51: 5 may be compared; 25: 10 (note, not verse 9) uses the different word, 'hand', while in chapter 59 Beuken has to appeal to verses 1 (hand) and 16 (arm), which are too remote from verse 11 to be allowed. In the case of 'das bekennende Element', only 33: 2 and 51: 5 share the inversion; in chapter 59 Beuken already has to move on two verses to 13, and even then he is unable to find what he wants but has to appeal to a phrase which refers to the opposite of the other verses. In fact, 59: 13 links most closely with 25: 9 (note the use of *yhwh* and *'ᵉlōhênû*). Thus on two of the three points, 33: 2 may be compared with 51: 5 but not with 25: 9 or 59: 11. In the case of the first argument, the only remaining one, the two words in question are so common in Isaiah as a whole that it may be seriously questioned whether their occurrence together is in itself a sufficiently strong indication that the verses must have been phrased in conscious dependence on one another.

The rest of Beuken's discussion of these passages traces a development through the book of Isaiah, based primarily on the theme of 'waiting' for God. In this connection, it might be supposed that 30: 18–19 has exerted a stronger influence on 33: 2 than any of the passages listed. Beuken indeed refers to it, but has presumably not included it in his heading to this section because it uses *ḥkh* rather than *qwh* (but note also the repeated use of *ḥnn* here and its occurrence in 33: 2 and the image of God exalting himself in 30: 18 and 33: 3). Furthermore, it emerges that 25: 9 is more strongly linked with 8: 17 and chapter 12 than with 33: 2. I therefore conclude that there can be no talk of citation in the case of the passages discussed, that the vocabulary links are at best weak, but that if anything the closest association of 33: 2 is with 30: 18–19 and with 51: 5. Furthermore, the appeal to chapter 59 is the most remote of all, while there is no reason why the possible allusions in chapter 25 should not be of the same sort that we saw characterized chapters 24–7 as a whole. For what it is worth, this example fits well with my overall hypothesis.

(iii) Isa. 33: 3–4 and 30: 27–33. Beuken finds in these two passages the only occurrences in Isaiah of 'nations' and 'peoples' in parallel in a context where they are spoken of negatively (though, as he points out, the theme itself is common enough). To this he adds the use of *qwl* and *zrwʿ* in each passage. The point of chapter 33 is to transfer the judgement pronounced against Assyria in chapter 30 to the oppressor in 33. On the basis of verse 1 in comparison with 21: 2, Beuken sees here a reference to the Persians, but I have already argued that Babylon is more likely. This example as a whole does not seem particularly strong, but even if Beuken is right in seeing a reflection of 30: 27–33 in 33: 3–4, it causes no difficulty for my case: most commentators accept that 30: 27–33 is pre-exilic, whether from Isaiah himself (so, for instance, Wildberger) or from the so-called Josianic redactor (so Barth[97] and Clements).

(iv) Isa. 33: 5–6 and 11: 1–10. Before discussing the two main passages indicated in this section, Beuken points out briefly that 33: 5 also has some associations with 2: 11, 17; 12: 4; and 57: 15, 'aber nicht im Sinne eines Kommentares oder der Antizipation eines bestimmten Textes'. The first three verses cited do not in any case pose any problem for our understanding of chapter 33. The case of 57: 15 is different, however, and the evidence seems to me to point rather strongly towards deliberate borrowing from chapter 33 by Trito-Isaiah. If that could be established, it would, of course, be important both in terms of upholding a date for 33 earlier than Trito-Isaiah and of suggesting, contrary to Beuken's theory, that 33 does not 'mirror' the whole of the rest of the book of Isaiah but rather a more limited portion of it. We must, therefore, look at this verse more carefully.

Isa. 57: 15 comprises six half-lines, which for convenience we may label and set out as follows:

A 1 For thus says the high and lofty one
2 who inhabits eternity, whose name is holy:
3 'I dwell in the high and holy place,
B 1 and also with him who is of a contrite and humble spirit,
2 to revive the spirit of the humble,
3 and to revive the heart of the contrite.'

It is clear that, despite the beginning of the divine speech at A3, the real contrast in the verse is between the sections which I have labelled as A and B. The first three half-lines dwell on God's exaltation, while the second three introduce the new, and initially surprising, thought that he also condescends to the contrite and humble. Now, within the context of the book of Isaiah, the first half of the verse presents us with the view of God's character and status

[97] Barth, *Die Jesaja-Worte in der Josiazeit*, 92–103.

which we have been led to expect, and it is this which, from a rhetorical point of view, enables the writer to introduce his new appreciation with such effective impact. In order to make this point, we should observe, the writer draws nearly all the significant phrases in A from the earlier part of the book. Thus, as we saw in Chapter 3 above, A1 is a clear and direct quotation from 6: 1 (*rām wᵉniśśā'* ('high and lifted up/high and lofty one)); A2's 'whose name is holy' is doubtless an allusion to the favourite Isaianic title, 'the holy one of Israel' (and see also 40: 25), while 'I dwell in the high . . . place' (*mārôm . . . 'eškôn*) in A3 is, as Beuken has seen, related closely with 33: 5 (*šōkēn mārôm*) and also with 33: 16 (*hû' mᵉrômîm yiškōn*). This leaves only the first phrase in A2 without an obvious antecedent in the earlier parts of Isaiah, though its general thought comes as no surprise in the context. It thus seems highly probable that the close association of this verse with 33: 5 and 16 is to be explained by way of citation on Trito-Isaiah's part rather than the reverse.

Turning now to the echoes of 11: 1–10 in 33: 5–6, we may readily acknowledge that in some cases the evidence seems compelling, and indeed it has frequently been noted by previous commentators. This would be a problem for the view of Isaiah 33 being defended here were it certain that 11: 1–10 as a whole is post-exilic, as a number of scholars have argued. Nowadays, however, the situation is less clear-cut, for there is an increasing body of opinion amongst even some usually more radical scholars that the first five verses of chapter 11 are earlier (though not necessarily Isaianic), and that this was then expanded by the addition of verses 6–9(10) to give the passage its present shape.[98] The connection of the opening of chapter 11 with the end of the previous chapter is the single most significant factor in this re-evaluation. Now, it is noteworthy that, although he does not pass comment on the fact, the significant connections which Beuken finds between chapters 11 and 33 are, in fact, confined to 11: 1–5. His comparison of 33: 5*b* ('he will fill Zion with justice and righteousness') with 11: 9 is limited to the verb 'fill' (*ml'*), even though the objects in each passage are completely different. It is much more probable that 33: 5*b* has been influenced

[98] See e.g. Barth, *Die Jesaja-Worte in der Josiazeit*, 57–76; Vermeylen, 269–76; Nielsen, *There is Hope for a Tree*, 123–40, all with further bibliography. It should be noted, however, that these scholars do not agree among themselves in many respects.

in this regard rather by 1: 21 ('How the faithful city has become a harlot, she that was full of justice! Righteousness lodged in her, but now murderers') and 1: 27 ('Zion shall be redeemed by justice, and those in her who repent, by righteousness').[99] It may, therefore, be concluded that the links between 33: 5–6 and 11: 1–5 do not rule out the possibility of a late exilic date for 33, and that the reference to 33: 5*a* in 57: 15 positively favours it.

(v) Isa. 33: 7–12 and 29: 1–8 (note especially the apparent play on the enigmatic *'ᵃrî'ēl* of 29: 1 in 33: 7). There is no need to discuss this example in detail, since it clearly poses no problem for the view I am defending.

(vi.1) Isa. 33: 7 and 9: 5–6; 52: 7; 53: 5. These connections are based on the occurrence of *šālôm*, distinguished from other uses of this word in Isaiah mainly by the association with messengers or heralds. The point of comparison is weak at best, and one might have supposed that Beuken would also have referred to 40: 9, which at any rate suggested itself to Wildberger (p. 1294). In that case it would be possible to regard 33: 7 as the negative side ('the ambassadors of peace weep bitterly') of that which will become positive in chapter 40. However, it would be hazardous to build any conclusion on this example, which in any case is not related to Trito-Isaiah.

(vi.2) Isa. 33: 8*a* and 40: 3; 49: 8–11; 57: 14; 59: 7; 62: 10. These passages have the word 'highway(s)' in common, which on its own is quite insufficient to establish a pattern of dependence, if, indeed, there is any dependence at all. Rather, it is preferable to link this with the preceding example and to see 33: 7–8 as together providing part of the negative background which 40: 1–11 will reverse. Taken with other connections, such as that noted between the end of chapter 33 and the opening of 40, this contributes to the suggestion that 33 may have been framed in part to provide for the transition between the two major parts of the book as fashioned by Deutero-Isaiah.

(vii) Isa. 33: 8*b*–9 and 24: 3–7; 35: 1–2; 40: 3. Here, there are some close phraseological connections with chapter 24, such as *hēpēr bᵉrît* in 33: 8 and 24: 5 (nowhere else in Isaiah), and *'ābal 'umlᵉlâ 'āreṣ* (33: 9) with *'ābᵉlâ nābᵉlâ hā'āreṣ 'umlᵉlâ nābᵉlâ tēbēl* (24: 4, and cf. verse 7). However, although Beuken proposes a

[99] There are some minor textual issues raised by both these verses, but they do not affect the point under discussion.

reading on the basis of the present arrangement of the book of Isaiah, there is no evidence here to suggest that this is not just another of the number of allusions in chapters 24–7 to other parts of the book as collected by Sweeney (see Chapter 7 above). Taken by themselves, the two passages do not indicate which is dependent on which, so that the broadly based conclusions about the method of composition in the Isaiah Apocalypse should take priority. The dependence of 35: 1–2 (the list of place names) is likely to be the same, as has been argued by Steck.[100] The only connection with 40: 3 is the single word *ʿ$^{a}$rābâ*, which again by itself is not much to go on, though, taken in association with what was suggested at vi.1 and vi.2 above, is possibly another slight example of the preparatory function of chapter 33 for the passage which once immediately followed it.

(viii) Isa. 33: 10–13 and 2: 6–22; 40: 21, 28. Beuken's suggestion that God is represented in chapter 33 as saying that 'now' he will do what was foretold in chapter 2 is certainly possible, and it fits well with the general function which I have argued for with regard to the chapter as a whole—namely, a closure of the first part of the book and preparation for the new announcement in the second. (The possible allusion in 33: 11 to 5: 24 is similar.) In addition, Beuken includes verse 13 in this paragraph (*contra* Steck), taking the perfect *ʿāśîtî* as a 'perfectum instans'—'what I am doing'. Noting that only in this verse and at 40: 21 and 28 do we find the verbs *šmʿ* and *ydʿ* in parallel in the book of Isaiah, and noting in addition that in 33: 13 they are part of a summons to recognize what God is doing whereas in chapter 40 they form part of a rhetorical question, asking whether the reader has not perceived how God works, he concludes that it looks as though 'die exklusive semantische Übereinstimmung zwischen diesen beiden Texten auf der Ebene einer Anspielung zu liegen'. Needless to say, this conclusion fits well with my understanding of the chapter.

(ix) Isa. 33: 14–16 and 2: 10 (=19, 21); 1: 12–17; 26: 2–11. These verses in Isaiah 33 are frequently compared with the so-called entrance liturgies of Pss. 15 and 24, and Beuken further compares Lev. 6: 2 and Deut. 32: 22 as other passages outside the book of Isaiah which evidence some slight connection with these verses. In none of these cases, however, are the links sufficiently strong to suggest particular literary dependence. Rather, he finds more sig-

[100] Steck, *Bereitete Heimkehr*, 16.

nificant the fact that only here and at 2: 10, 19, and 21 is the root *pḥd* ('fear, terror') associated with the appearance of God in the book of Isaiah, and the possibility that these uses are related is strengthened by the fact that other echoes of chapter 2 have already been noted elsewhere in chapter 33. By contrast, where the root occurs in other places in the book, it is to emphasize that Israel need not fear (12: 2; 44: 8; 51: 13) whereas other nations and idol worshippers must (19: 16–17; 24: 17–18; 44: 11). Similarly, though less strikingly, the 'sinners' of 33: 14 may recall 1: 28. Finally the fire imagery of verse 14*b* may echo 29: 6 and 30: 27, 30 (again, passages which have been seen above to have other links with chapter 33). So far as possible verbal allusions in this passage are concerned, therefore, it can be seen that they all come from earlier parts of the book and are thus fully compatible with the approach to chapter 33 being defended here.

Beuken maintains that the significance of these verses for his thesis lies not so much in the realm of verbal correspondence as in their contribution to the 'story' of the book of Isaiah which was discussed above; they describe the response of 'the sinners' to the fact that 'now' God is going to arise as previously he had promised he would. Because verse 14*b* reports the words of the people concerned, there is a clear difference from the entrance liturgies in the Psalter. Verses 15–16 then outline the prophet's answer to the people's question, using material partly culled from earlier in the chapter. In all this, Beuken finds some points of connection with 1: 12–17 and 26: 2–11.

I have already indicated that I find this aspect of Beuken's analysis helpful in terms of its contribution to the elucidation of the function of chapter 33 between the two main parts of the book as a whole. Furthermore, his reference to chapter 1 (much of which is probably extracted from sayings of Isaiah which will originally have been located elsewhere in the book) usefully serves to show that this element need not necessarily presuppose a setting later in the post-exilic period, as some commentators have suggested. Beyond that, since there is no indication of specific dependence on chapter 26, no problem seems to be raised by the data presented by Beuken in this section for our overall argument.

(x.1) Isa. 33: 17 and 6: 4 (52: 7–8); 26: 11.

(x.2) Isa. 33: 22 and 2: 4; 66: 16. These two verses may be taken together because of their most distinctive common element, namely the ascription of the title 'king' to God. This was discussed earlier in this chapter (see above, pp. 226–7), where it was suggested that there were grounds for detecting here a characteristic emphasis of Deutero-Isaiah. Beuken's analysis seeks to draw something of a distinction between the relevant passages by pointing out that most of the references in Deutero-Isaiah lack the notion of 'seeing' the king (shared by 6: 4 and 33: 17), but he accepts that even this detail is present at 52: 7–8.

The remaining passages which Beuken relates to these two verses are less noteworthy. Isa. 26: 11 is referred to because, like 33: 17, it uses the verb *ḥzh* for seeing God's activity. However, although some other possible links between chapters 26 and 33 have been noted, the distinctive feature of the kingship of God is lacking in chapter 26, and the use of the verb alone is not much to go on. The other titles for God in 33: 22 are thought to provide some further textual associations, but again it may be questioned how significant they are; at any rate, it does not seem possible to establish dependence one way or the other. For 'the Lord is our judge', it is noted that the verb occurs with God as subject at 2: 4 and 66: 16 (though in both places the reference is universal, whereas in 33: 22 the emphasis falls rather on his action on behalf of his own people. In addition, reference might have been made to 51: 5 and the theme, at least, of the trial speeches in Deutero-Isaiah); nowhere else is God called 'our lawgiver [*RSV*: ruler]', though the root *ḥqq* is used with God as subject in a different sense at 49: 16; and, for 'he will save us', Beuken refers back to his discussion at point (ii) above. In contrast with what must be regarded as weak parallels at best, the significant emphasis of 33: 22 is its radical theocentricity, and this is certainly fully in line with the thought of Deutero-Isaiah.

(xi) Isa. 33: 19 and 28: 11. Many other commentators too have noted the apparent dependence of 33: 19 on 28: 11; naturally, it poses no problem for our immediate purpose.

These, then, are the passages by which Beuken seeks to establish his interpretation of Isaiah 33 as a 'mirror' text within the book of Isaiah as a whole.[101] This discussion has inevitably been somewhat tedious, but there have been several gains in terms of our under-

[101] He mentions, only to dismiss, two other possible elements: 33: 20 with 1: 14, 21, 26; 32: 18; 54: 2; and 33: 23*b* with 9: 2 and 53: 12. I have already referred to the first of these in the discussion above, while the second would again pose no difficulty for my position.

standing of the chapter. Negatively, it has been shown that there is nothing which demands that Isaiah 33 knew of Trito-Isaiah or Isaiah 24–7, so that the initial impression that might be gained from Beuken's work and which would rule out an earlier date for chapter 33 is shown to be misleading. Positively, the evidence so carefully marshalled by Beuken can serve to strengthen the case for its shaping and inclusion at this point by Deutero-Isaiah. In particular, we have noted that there are some striking points of dependence upon earlier material in the first part of the book, a feature which has been seen to be characteristic of this prophet; in addition, some of his themes with which we are familiar from chapters 40–55 are alluded to here; and, finally, we have found some minor elements in the chapter (in addition to those collected by Beuken) which suggest that it was particularly suitable as a transition from the earlier Isaianic material to the new announcement in chapter 40. Thus, while there are aspects of Beuken's theory with which I am unable to agree, there is much in his presentation which can in fact be turned to favour the alternative hypothesis which I advanced earlier in this chapter.

In conclusion, therefore, it may be repeated that chapter 33 serves admirably as the point of original connection between the literary deposit of Isaiah of Jerusalem and the material which Deutero-Isaiah added to it in chapters 40 and following. As we saw in chapters 1–12 and again in 13–14, he has intervened in the earlier material at the start and the close of the major sections as part of the process by which he bound the earlier work and his own material together into a new unity.[102] (In this connection, it may be significant that chapter 32 is reckoned by many to have formed the conclusion of the work of Isaiah as edited in the late pre-exilic period.) How much of chapter 33 he inherited and how much was his own composition it is hard now to say; the liturgical-type language makes the disentangling of 'source' and 'redaction' un-

[102] This is not to rule out the possibility of Deutero-Isaianic redaction in the immediately preceding chapters as well. Mowinckel (*Prophecy and Tradition*, 76) has raised the question whether 32: 15–18 might be considered here, as has Laberge ('Is 30, 19–26: A Deuteronomic Text?') with regard to 30: 19–26 (p. 40). See, too, Jeppesen's discussion of the possible relocation of 28: 16 in 'The Cornerstone (Isa. 28: 16) in Deutero-Isaianic Rereading of the Message of Isaiah'. The 'double therefore' and content of 30: 18 are also suggestive. My concern has been to outline the main shape of this redaction, however, not to discuss every possible example of its occurrence.

usually problematical in this chapter. Fortunately, it is not necessary for our present purposes to seek to resolve this particular issue; it is sufficient for us to be able to affirm his responsibility for the final form and the present setting of the chapter as a whole.

# 9

# Conclusions

'THE theory is unlikely, impossible to prove, and suffers from a circularity of logic.' Thus Seitz dismisses the early suggestion of de Lagarde that the material of Isaiah 1–39 comprises a chrestomathy of earlier prophetic texts edited by Deutero-Isaiah with the aim of encouraging belief in the new promises which he proclaimed.[1] That the theory is 'impossible to prove' in the strict sense of the words may be readily accepted, as was noted already at the start of Chapter 6, but it remains for the reader who has followed the arguments of the preceding discussion to decide whether that also renders the suggestion unlikely and suffering from a circularity of logic. As with most theories in biblical scholarship, probability would seem to be a more appropriate yardstick by which to judge, and here appeal may be made to the criterion whether the theory adequately accounts for the data in the most economical manner.

In response to the questions raised by the survey of research in Chapter 1, I have argued for three main proposals in the course of this book, namely (i) that Deutero-Isaiah was especially influenced by the literary deposit of Isaiah of Jerusalem (Chapters 3–4), (ii) that he regarded the earlier work as in some sense a book that had been sealed up until the time when judgement should be passed and the day of salvation had arrived, which day he believed himself to be heralding (Chapter 5), and (iii) that in order to locate his message in relation to the earlier and continuing ways of God with

[1] Seitz, *Zion's Final Destiny*, 27 n. 1, with reference to P. de Lagarde, *Symmicta*, i (Göttingen, 1877), 142. De Lagarde's suggestion was raised in a footnote as an explanation for the order of the prophetic books (Jeremiah; Ezekiel; Isaiah) in a manuscript he was discussing. He implies that he will advance arguments in support of the suggestion elsewhere ('wie ich nachweisen werde'), but despite searching I have not been able to find any such discussion. Furthermore, in *Semitica*, i (Göttingen, 1878), 1, he refers back to this passage in *Symmicta*, i, with the words 'meine . . . grundanschauung vom buche Isaias habe ich in meinen Symmicta 142 kurz angegeben', which implies that he did not regard further argumentation as necessary.

Israel he included a version of the earlier prophecies with his own and edited them in such a way as to bind the two parts of the work together (Chapters 6–8).[2]

Inevitably, in relation to a book which has been studied so intensively as Isaiah, these proposals will be subject to a host of objections and counter-proposals. I attempted in Chapter 2 to deal with some of these in a preliminary manner, sufficient at least to enable the discussion to get started, while throughout the remaining chapters I have sought to defend my position against a representative selection of alternative approaches on matters of detail.[3] In conclusion, however, two wider questions which are raised by this discussion need to be briefly examined.

First, why should Deutero-Isaiah have been particularly influenced by Isaiah of Jerusalem? In answering this question, it must first be stressed that there is no intention of underestimating his debt to other authors and streams of tradition. It is well known, for instance, that many of the Psalms, which probably represent the tradition of the Jerusalem cult, have exerted considerable influence upon him both in his phraseology and in the forms with which he chose to give expression to his message of salvation. Similarly, in a way that was quite foreign to Isaiah of Jerusalem,[4] he appealed to the accounts of the Exodus and wilderness wanderings as a foil to his announcement of a new release and journey back to Zion, while he also shows himself aware of the more nearly contemporary work of Jeremiah and Ezekiel. It would be extremely difficult to attempt to quantify these various sources of influence, not least because of the problems of method which would need to be tackled. If I have been right in my analysis of the material in Chapters 3–5 above, however, it should nevertheless be clear that the exilic form of Isaiah 1–39 would be near the top of any such list.

A probable solution to this question must be sought in terms of what would enable him to speak most forcefully to his contemporaries in the present situation. So far as we can judge, the liturgy of the Babylonian exiles continued to be based squarely upon those

[2] Clifford ('The Unity of the Book of Isaiah', 2) has recently raised some of these conclusions as a possibility for consideration without, however, attempting a detailed demonstration.

[3] Naturally, a comprehensive coverage of the secondary literature is out of the question. I hope at least that I have not overlooked any major or widely adopted position which would be fatally damaging to the case being presented.

[4] Though, again, see Clifford, 'The Unity of the Book of Isaiah'.

forms which are known to us from the pre-exilic and exilic Psalms. A prominent component of this liturgy was what we may very loosely call the Zion tradition, so that any prophet faced with the task of moving the faith of the exilic community forward in response to the imminent demise of Babylonian supremacy would have been obliged to reinterpret this tradition in a way that took account of its severe reversal in the fall of Jerusalem and yet retained those elements which, despite the apparent contradiction of recent events, still spoke so eloquently to the despair of the people. In such circumstances, where else could a prophet look if not to the work of Isaiah of Jerusalem as by then developed? Jeremiah and Ezekiel both worked too closely under the immediate impact of the fall of Jerusalem to give them that sense of perspective which was required, their role too much that of interpretation and explanation. It is in Isaiah alone that the larger sweep of God's dealings with Zion in both judgement and mercy is to be found, and, as has already been indicated several times, the process of relating this to the Babylonian conquest had already begun prior to Deutero-Isaiah. It is thus difficult to see where else he could have gone for an accepted and authoritative setting for his own work on the literary level, while the presentation of that work in terms of familiar but transformed liturgical forms stands in no tension with this conclusion. Of course, he could not ignore the Exodus traditions, which by now had become an accepted part of the 'southern' community's religious heritage, but his use of them (in which he had already been anticipated by others) is more by way of illustration, contrast, and example than of furnishing him with the theological groundwork on which he built.

The suggestion that there is influence from the first part of the book of Isaiah on the second is by no means new, and my discussion of it makes no claim to be more than a modest development of the direction of much recent research—an attempt to set it on the basis of a sounder method, to gather the examples into a single presentation and to add some further passages for consideration. The proposal that Deutero-Isaiah also edited a form of the earlier work is more controversial, however (though again not entirely original), and it raises a second and more serious general question. Since it is known from Isaiah 56–66 that there was at least one other who closely imitated the style of Deutero-Isaiah, how can we be sure that it was Deutero-Isaiah and not some other imitator who was responsible for those parts of Isaiah 1–33 which seem to come closest to his outlook and way of speaking?

The answer is that clearly we cannot be sure, but there are some indications which make the proposal more attractive than the alternative. First, the alternative does not take account of the argument I have advanced for the rationale behind the literary activity of Deutero-Isaiah—namely, that he regarded himself as 'opening' a book which (on his understanding) had long been closed. Without some such rationale, the historical-critical method, which has brought us to our present understanding of the major divisions of the book and which cries out for an advance towards a historical explanation of the many elements which also serve to unite it, would seem to fail us; we should be reduced to the level of observing chance similarities and massive coincidences. For some, this might be a welcome concession of defeat. Most scholars, however, would probably rather cling to the hope that literary unity in historical diversity has some rational explanation, even if we cannot always yet discover it. The case advanced above for understanding a major stage in the growth of the book of Isaiah at least makes a proposal for such an explanation which the hypothesis of later imitators cannot.

Secondly, it has been argued throughout Chapters 6–8 that the redactional layer there described is to be located in a situation which looks back on judgement and which anticipates salvation as something imminent and thus still future. Of course, there is an important sense in which Isaiah 56–66 serves to throw the promised salvation off into the future yet again, but we have not found evidence in the work of our redactor for the obvious devices by which this shift is accomplished. Everything seems to point to one who was working at the close of the exilic period, and this is supported by the fact that chapters 34–5, which indeed stand much closer to the world of Trito-Isaiah, are already to be dated after his work. In such a case the most natural identification by far is with Deutero-Isaiah.

Finally, the point may be stressed again that this seems to furnish the most economical hypothesis which has yet been advanced. No one who has struggled with the plethora of secondary literature on Isaiah 1–39 will need any convincing that many of the proposals for the exilic and post-exilic redaction of the work are of the greatest complexity. Not all these complexities by any means are eliminated on the present suggestion, for I have made clear that there is still a good deal in Isaiah 1–39 which post-dates the close of the exile. Nevertheless, it is likely that any streamlining of this process will be welcome, just as has been the case with the separate proposal for a Josianic redaction to account for much of the pre-exilic form of the work.

I therefore continue to regard the Deutero-Isaianic hypothesis as more probable than that of the imitator, but even should this be mistaken the hope may be expressed that the redactional layer which has been uncovered and which seems to show a consistent literary method and theological outlook will in any case help to advance our understanding of this part of the work.

The book called Isaiah has undoubtedly had a long and sometimes complex history of growth. Increased awareness of this paradoxically makes the task of reading more difficult. A number of voices have been raised in recent years to explore strategies whereby an informed reader can seek to do justice both to a historical reading of the work of Isaiah of Jerusalem and to a reading which arises out of its growth in later periods. If the arguments of the present work were to be accepted, a major consequence would be to attempt such a reading specifically from within the standpoint of Deutero-Isaiah. The present work has been devoted only to laying the critical foundations for such an interpretation, though the shape and direction which it might take have been indicated at some of the major turning-points in the text. To undertake that task in full, however, would require a commentary rather than a monograph, and thus it is a task which must await another day.

# APPENDIX

1: 7 The last clause of the verse—ושממה כמהפכת זרים—is rendered in the *RV* as 'and it is desolate, as overthrown by strangers'. Elsewhere, מהפכה always refers to the overthrow of Sodom and Gomorrah (cf. Deut. 29: 22; Isa. 13: 19; Jer. 49: 18; 50: 40; Amos 4: 11), while the use of זרים in the present verse comes under suspicion as being clumsily repetitious of זרים in the previous line. In addition, the point of comparison, 'as overthrown by strangers', is inappropriate, since according to the earlier part of the verse it is in fact strangers who are doing the overthrowing. Consequently, most commentators conjecturally emend זרים to סדם here. It may be assumed either that a scribe was unconsciously influenced by the earlier occurrence of זרים, or that it was originally a marginal correction of that occurrence which then mistakenly replaced סדם on the 'cuckoo' principle (cf. L. C. Allen, 'Cuckoos in the Textual Nest', *JTS* NS 22 (1971), 143–50, and 'More Cuckoos in the Textual Nest', *JTS* NS 24 (1973), 69–73). This certainly seems preferable to alternative emendations which have been proposed, such as זרם, 'an inundation' (Lowth—though at least he recognized the problem), זדים, 'insolent ones' (N. H. Tur-Sinai, 'A Contribution to the Understanding of Isaiah i–xii', *ScrH* 8 (1961), 156), or alternatively reading וְשָׁמוּהָ instead of ושממה (A. B. Ehrlich, *Randglossen zur Hebräischen Bibel*, iv (Leipzig, 1912), 4, and Kissane). Recent attempts to defend the MT are not convincing, in my opinion; see J. T. Willis, 'An Important Passage for Determining the Historical Setting of a Prophetic Oracle—Isaiah 1. 7–8', *ST* 39 (1985), 151–69, and Watts.

In addition, the clause as a whole is not well integrated into the poetic structure of the passage (see the lineation in *BHS*; contrast H. W. M. van Grol, 'Paired Tricola in the Psalms, Isaiah and Jeremiah', *JSOT* 25 (1983), 63) and it hangs limply in the immediate context because of the way that it backtracks to שממה at the start of the verse. Since Sodom is mentioned later on, in vv. 9 and 10, it is attractive to regard this clause as an exegetical gloss, whose purpose was to indicate that the שממה of v. 7*a* was to be compared with the destruction of Sodom in v. 9. The *wāw* may be regarded as explicative, '*even* a desolation like . . .'. It is impossible, of course, to tell when the gloss was incorporated into the text, though it is already attested by the earliest textual witnesses (LXX and 1QIsa$^{a}$; on the latter's reading, see J. Koenig, *L'Herméneutique analogique du Judaïsme antique d'après les témoins textuels d'Isaïe* (SVT 33; Leiden, 1982), 218–21).

2: 12 The last word in the MT of this verse is highly problematic. After learning that the day of the Lord is directed 'against all that is proud and haughty [גאה ורם] and against all that is lifted up', we expect another adjective descriptive of pride to complete the parallelism. This is reinforced by the observation that the following verses (13–16) continue with a further string of nouns which illustrate the pride of man, all introduced by 'and against' (ועל), not one of which is qualified by a comment that 'it will be brought low' such as concludes v. 12. ושפל is, therefore, out of context, it disturbs the parallelism, and, lacking as it does a proper subject, it is not integrated into the syntactical flow of the passage. Translations which retain it are thus obliged to mark it as parenthetical (see recently Oswalt).

The Septuagint includes a translation of ושפל (καὶ ταπεινωθήσονται), but also inserts before it καὶ μετέωρον. While this may just be an expansion by the translator under the influence of what he might have regarded as a stereotyped phrase (cf. v. 13 and Ziegler, *Untersuchungen zur Septuaginta des Buches Isaias*, 61), it is generally reckoned to represent וְגָבֹהַּ, a word whose plural is rendered in the same way at 5: 15. Such a reading certainly supplies what we expect (cf. the use of the same root in vv. 11, 15, and 17), though if it stood in the *Vorlage* of the Septuagint, we should note that ושפל also stood there alongside it. This is clearly not the case of one word being mistakenly substituted for another.

Commentators have not generally paused to ask how ושפל entered the text and ultimately displaced וגבה. While I cannot explain the second part of this process, there are two possible ways of explaining the first. (i) It may originally have been intended as a marginal correction (read as ישפל) to the שפל of v. 11. We should certainly expect the verb there to be imperfect (cf. the doubtless secondary תשפלנה of 1QIsa[a]), and the slightly awkward singular might be the result of influence from the preceding אדם (cf. GK §146*a*) and/or a desire to retain syntactical parallelism with the singular ושח. Alternatively, שפל in v. 11 may have been an infinitive absolute (so J. Huesman, 'Finite Uses of the Infinitive Absolute', *Biblica*, 37 (1956), 287), a fact not appreciated by the putative glossator. (ii) Another possibility is that ושפל was added as an exegetical gloss to supply a cross-reference to 40: 4. Knowing the promise that 'every mountain and hill shall be made low [ישפלו]', the commentator may have wished to point the reader forward to God's future activity. There are certainly other features of chapter 2 which might have drawn the opening of chapter 40 to his attention (note, for instance, the use of הר and גבעה in 2: 14 and 40: 4), so that one is even tempted to suppose that he could have confused the גאה of the earlier part of 2: 12 with the גיא of 40: 4 and so read ורם as יָרֻם.

Finally, it is not impossible that these two explanations should be combined. A marginal correction ישפל to שפל in v. 11 was misunderstood by a later scribe as a reference forward to 40: 4, so causing him to include the word (read as ושפל) in its present inappropriate setting.

2: 13 הרמים והנשאים. These words seem to disturb the rhythm (not to say the metre) of the passage. In vv. 12–16 ten items are listed, each one being introduced by ועל כל, and each one consisting of two words (either noun plus adjective or two nouns in a construct relationship). The two words in question intrude into this pattern and break the close parallelism between 'all the cedars of Lebanon' and 'all the oaks of Bashan'. Furthermore, like the ships of v. 16, the cedars of Lebanon do not require such a descriptive qualification. The words are therefore usually, and surely rightly, regarded as a gloss, since it is difficult to believe that they entered the text as the result of mechanical error alone.

The words occur in the singular in the preceding verse and in the plural in the following verse; it therefore seems probable that in v. 13 they represent an early fragment of exegetical activity, explaining to the reader that the generalized description of v. 12 is now being illustrated by the specific items which follow. Appropriately, therefore, the gloss qualifies the first of these items to be listed. (A different, but not incompatible, approach is taken by J. Blenkinsopp, 'Fragments of Ancient Exegesis in an Isaian Poem (Jes $2_{6-22}$)', *ZAW* 93 (1981), 51–62.) The date of the gloss cannot be determined; in principle, there is no reason why it should not be extremely early.

5: 8 והושבתם. A number of older commentators, such as Marti and Gray, were suspicious of the text at this point, both because of the change of person to second plural and because of doubts about the force of the hoph'al of ישב (elsewhere found only—and perhaps significantly—at 44: 26). Neither objection seems compelling, however. The switch from third to second person is attested elsewhere, especially in הוי oracles; see GK §144*p*, and in particular D. R. Hillers, '*Hôy* and *Hôy*-Oracles: A Neglected Syntactic Aspect', in C. L. Meyers and M. O'Connor (eds.), *The Word of the Lord Shall Go Forth: Essays in Honor of David Noel Freedman* (Winona Lake, Ind., 1983), 185–8. Its effect is to render the oracle as a whole as a vocative. As to the hoph'al, it is probably supported by LXX and Vg., which translate as a question (i.e. reading MT as הישבתם; the other versions apparently presuppose the qal—וישבתם—and 1QIsa[a]'s reading וישתם is doubtless a misreading of the same; cf. Wildberger). It seems to make sense ('and you are made to dwell alone') and should be preferred over the qal as a *lectio difficilior*. It may be suggested that the hoph'al was chosen deliberately to act as a reminder that all land was ultimately a gift from God (cf. Lev. 25: 23) and so to emphasize the culpability of the large estate builders. (Maintaining that 'the semantic field of *yšb* includes ownership of land', D. N. Premnath renders 'And you have become possessors of land all by yourselves in the midst of the land'. Although his article includes other helpful discussion, this particular point seems weak, since it fails to explain, or even take account of, the use of the hoph'al; see 'Latifundialization and Isaiah 5. 8–10', *JSOT* 40 (1988), 49–60.)

5: 9 The first line of the verse, באזני יהוה צבאות, lacks a verb and so makes no sense: 'In my ears the Lord of Hosts'. Because of the אם־לא following, we expect something like לכן נשבע ('Therefore (the Lord of Hosts) has sworn (in my hearing)'), and this is the emendation which is generally adopted. It is also usual to appeal to the LXX for indirect support: its reading here, ἠκούσθη γὰρ, could reflect כי נשמע, which itself could be a corruption of לכן נשבע. The other versions are also cited by some; Targ., for instance, could be thought to reflect a comparable Hebrew text to that of the LXX, despite its characteristically paraphrased rendering: 'The prophet said, With my ears I heard [הויתי שמע] when this was decreed by (from before) the Lord of Hosts', while Wildberger also cites Pesh. *'eštᵉmaʻ* in support. Vg., by contrast, is clearly working with MT, with which 1QIsa[a] is also identical at this point.

While these conjectures are plausible, and may even be right, the possibility should also be borne in mind that the versions may equally well have had a text approximating MT as their *Vorlage*, which they were then obliged to translate *ad sensum*: given באזני, the rest follows almost automatically. If we are going to emend, as emend we must, it is perhaps not necessary to appeal to the versions to bolster a conclusion reached on other grounds and for which they offer only questionable, and at best indirect, support. In that case, it becomes attractive as an alternative to observe the close parallel to our verse at 22: 14, . . . ונגלה באזני יהוה צבאות אם ('And the Lord of Hosts revealed himself in my ears, Surely . . .') (on אם and אם לא as simple particles of asseveration, see GK §149*e*). The meaning, of course, is not seriously affected, so that for convenience I have kept with the majority (and *RSV*) in the text used above, p. 52.

5: 30 The general purport of the second line of this verse is clear enough, but there can be no certainty with regard to several of its details. (i) ונבט is either niph'al or pi'el, but this common root is everywhere else used only in the hiph'il. Though very few commentators remark on the fact, it would therefore be attractive to follow Vg. in vocalizing as a first-person plural hiph'il: וְנַבֵּט ('and if we look . . . '). The involvement of the author and his readers in this concluding and summarizing addition does not seem impossible. (ii) In the middle of the line, the Masoretes join צר וחשך both by vocalization and punctuation. The resultant suggestion that the one viewing the earth sees an alternation of 'tribulation and light', stoutly defended by Delitzsch, probably depends upon the 'optimistic' interpretation of the first line of the verse, which I have argued is mistaken. The widely proposed redivision of the line (moving the *zāqēph qāṭôn* to צר and vocalizing וָאוֹר) is to be preferred. (iii) Though עריף is a *hapax legomenon*, the root is well attested and emendation seems unnecessary (cf. Wildberger). With but slight alterations to the vocalization, the line may then be rendered: 'And if we look to the land, behold darkness closing in [cf. *REB*, *or* 'distressful darkness'], and the light grows dark because of its [i.e. the earth's] clouds.' While in the case of a line such as this prudence demands the minimum of emendation, the possibility that there has been some more deep-seated corruption cannot be avoided. Comparison with 8: 21–2 suggests that there may once have been a reference to 'looking up' as well as 'looking to the earth' and perhaps even that עריפיה may have arisen by corruption of מעוף; but clearly any restoration based on such possibilities would be wholly conjectural. Even then, the overall sense of the line would not be significantly altered.

6: 11 תשאה. The MT must be construed as a niph'al of שאה I (for the root, see K.-M. Beyse, 'שאה', *TWAT* viii, cols. 898–901) followed by שממה as an accusative of result after the passive of the verb: 'be ruined (and become) a desolation'; cf. GK §121*d*. The niph'al of this root does not occur elsewhere, however (or if it does, at 17: 12, it has a different meaning, as noted by Gray, 111). It is also repetitious of the qal of the same root in the first line of the verse, but, since it there has ערים ('cities') as its subject, but here האדמה ('the land'), it is difficult to see how the same meaning could comfortably be ascribed to both occurrences. The Masoretic vocalization may, therefore, be an artificial device to avoid this difficulty. The LXX καταλειφθήσεται suggests the very slight emendation to תשאר ('and the land is left desolate'), and this has been adopted by the overwhelming majority of commentators from Lowth to Wildberger. This may be another example of the type of scribal error noted at 1: 7, where the occurrence of a word has caused assimilation to it of another similar looking word shortly after.

9: 2 הגוי לא. As vocalized and punctuated by the Masoretes, לא is the negative particle and is to be construed with the second half of the line, 'You have not increased the joy', which is clearly impossible in the context. The *qere* לו is equally unsatisfactory since it lacks any possible antecedent (העם in v. 1 governs plural verbs in what follows). More recent attempts to construe the consonantal text are also unconvincing: e.g. C. Schedl, 'Nochmals Jes $9_2$: הגוי לא', *ZAW* 94 (1982), 293, who, following Dahood, suggests a Hebrew word לָא ('victor'), here construed as a vocative. The old and well-nigh universally adopted emendation הגילה is surely right. It makes for perfect parallelism with השמחה in the second half of the line, and the two verbal forms of these roots are then picked up in reverse order in the following two lines: שמחו in *2b* and יגילו in *2c*. Against B. Becking's suggestion ('Der Text von Jesaja $9_{2a}$', *ZAW* 92 (1980), 142–5) to read הגוי הלאה ('the tired people'), see the remarks of W. Rudolph, 'Lesefrüchte', *ZAW* 93 (1981), 292.

11: 11 There are two ways in which sense can be made of the MT as it stands. One is to suppose that יוסיף governs the infinitive לקנות and that ידו is an adverbial accusative, as in the marginal reading of the *RV*: 'And it shall come to pass in that day, that the Lord shall again the second time recover with his hand the remnant of his people.' Such a rendering (which is not supported by the LXX; see below) appears to be forced, however, for it gives peculiar sense ('to recover with his hand') and results in a strange word order, the effect of which is to emphasize ידו in a manner which is not developed in the context. An additional difficulty is that שנית is redundant after יוסיף. (J. G. Janzen has commented privately to me that יוסיף עוד is common in biblical Hebrew, and that this aspect of the present text need not be considered strange by analogy. But the absence of parallels to the usage of our verse suggests that יוסיף שנית may have been as unlikely in Hebrew as would be the English 'again a second time' by comparison with the expected 'yet again'.)

The alternative way to explain the MT is to assume that ידו is the direct object of יוסיף and that it has the meaning 'his strength'. This is the approach adopted by Targ. ('The Lord will add [יוסיף] his strength [גבורתיה] a second time . . .'). In support of this approach, appeal might be made to יסיף אמץ in Job 17: 9, though the sense required there ('will grow stronger') is hardly suitable with the Lord as its subject.

It is thus difficult to escape the conclusion that the LXX was probably right to find in שנית an infinitive that could both be dependent upon יוסיף, used as an auxiliary verb in its commonest sense, and govern ידו as its accusative object. LXX has τοῦ δεῖξαι ('to show') (LXX's continuation τὴν χεῖρα αὐτοῦ τοῦ ζηλῶσαι clearly arises from reading לקנות in the light of קנא rather than קנה), and, although it is not attested elsewhere as a translation of נשא (see E. Hatch and H. A. Redpath, *A Concordance to the Septuagint* (Oxford, 1897), 286), commentators have generally used this evidence to support an emendation of שנית to שְׂאֵת. נשא יד occurs in a closely comparable context at 49: 22, and the proposed emendation removes the grammatical difficulties already noted, overcomes, of course, the oddity of שנית following יוסיף, and is sufficiently close to the consonantal text of the MT to be explained as a scribal slip in the course of the transmission of the text.

This seems the most likely solution to me, though not surprisingly other suggestions have been advanced. (For Vermeylen, see above; for some others that do not require discussion, see Wildberger.) The most influential alternative has been that of D. W. Thomas ('The Root שנה = *sny* in

Hebrew II', *ZAW* 55 (1937), 174–6), who attempted to relate שנית to a root שנה in Hebrew which he and a number of other scholars have argued has cognates in Arabic, Syriac, and, probably, Ugaritic, and which means 'to be, or become, high, exalted in rank; to shine'; if שנית be read as the piʿel infinitive construct שַׁנּוֹת, it gives us a meaning apparently similar to שׂאת but has the advantage of keeping closer to the MT.

While many now accept the existence of this root in Classical Hebrew (see J. J. Stamm *et al.*, *Hebräisches und Aramäisches Lexikon zum Alten Testament*, iv (Leiden, 1990), 1477–8, though it is rejected by Wildberger), Thomas's proposal for our particular verse has not found such favour; see, for instance, J. A. Emerton's review of the evidence which supports the probability of a root שנה II in Hebrew while nevertheless retaining the MT of Isa. 11: 11 ('The Meaning of *šēnā*' in Psalm cxxvii 2', *VT* 24 (1974), 15–31). (Emerton defends the MT on the ground that 'it would not be surprising if there were an otiose expression in a late prophetic verse like Isa. xi 11' (p. 28). He does not explain, however, why late prophetic verses should be more susceptible to otiose expressions than others.) Indeed, it is not certain that the postulated root, which seems usually to relate to being high in the sense of exalted of rank, also had the meaning of being physically high. Of course, the two ideas are closely related, as נשׂא itself shows, but the development required to make sense of Isa. 11: 11 adds a further hypothetical element which contrasts with the solid attestation of the expression נשׂא יד and the support of the close parallel with 49: 22.

**12: 1** The last two verbs in this verse (ישב and ותנחמני) are pointed as jussives by the Masoretes. Elsewhere in this psalm, however, the substantiation of the call to praise is consistently perfect or *wāw*-consecutive + imperfect, and LXX, Pesh., and Vg. treat the verbs as such in this verse also; we should therefore probably read וַיָּשָׁב וַתְּנַחֲמֵנִי (see Gray, *contra* Wildberger), or perhaps even better retain ישב as a jussive for imperfect (see GK §109*k*) with perfect force; cf. Deut. 32: 8, 18; Hos. 6: 1; Ps. 18: 12, etc. (Even if some of these passages are corrupt, as Gray implies, they presumably still attest an intelligible form of Hebrew.) The fact that Targ. alone agrees with the Masoretic vocalization strengthens the case for regarding the latter as deliberately interpretative; cf. GK §107*b* n. 2, and above, Ch. 6 n. 9.

**24: 16** This verse bristles with textual difficulties, but fortunately not all need to be resolved here. The main issue which concerns us is the relationship between the first and second lines.

The first line concludes the passage introduced in v. 14 which speaks of those who sing universal songs of joy and praise. צבי לצדיק ('honour to the Righteous One') appears to be a quotation from the songs which 'we' have heard.

There then follows the obscure passage ואמר רזי לי רזי לי אוי לי בגדים בגדו. Three main approaches have been adopted to this line.

(i) Gray notes that the LXX has a much shorter text and that it appears to read אוי לבגדים in place of אוי לי בגדים. He therefore retains only these two words ('woe to the disloyal') as an antithetic parallel to צבי לצדיק. (He suggests that רזי לי may be the work of a later glossator; see also E. Liebmann, 'Der Text zu Jesaia 24–27', *ZAW* 23 (1903), 209–86 (239)). On this view, 16*b* (or, at least, the two words of it which are retained) are simply an integral part of 16*a*.

(ii) Most of the ancient versions saw in רז the Aramaic loan-word meaning 'secret, mystery'. Their lead has not often been followed (though see Procksch and Kaiser), but J. Niehaus ('*rāz-p*$^{e}$*šar* in Isaiah xxiv', *VT* 31 (1981), 376–8) has sought to uphold it on the basis of a formal comparison of Isa. 24: 16*b*–18 and Dan. 5: 25–8. In his view, the רז is contained in the first three words of v. 17 and their פשר ('interpretation') is given in v. 18. Verse 16*c* (whose opening has again to be emended to אוי לבגדים) parallels 17*b* and identifies the targets of the רז, while 16*b* introduces the whole. On this view, there is, therefore, no strong connection between 16*a* and 16*b*; the latter introduces a new literary section, even though Niehaus finds a general contrast between 14–16*a* and 16*b*–18. Despite the ingenuity of this proposal, however, it overlooks several difficulties. I. Willi-Plein ('Das Geheimnis der Apokalyptik', *VT* 27 (1977), 62–81) (to which Niehaus does not refer) has raised serious doubt (pp. 71–3) about whether רז can here refer to a 'secret' and has also adduced considerations which render questionable a dependence on the LXX for emendation at this point. Furthermore, these verses seem to be a pastiche of citations from other prophetic passages (principally Isa. 21: 2, 33: 1, and Jer.48: 43–4), which, in common with other such citations in Isaiah 24–7, they interpret in a universalizing direction (see Sweeney, 'Textual Citations in Isaiah 24–27', 44–5). It is precisely v. 16*b* which is the new element introduced by our writer; it is difficult to see, however, how a text already substantially present in Jeremiah could now be introduced as a רז, which by definition should be unfamiliar and mysterious.

(iii) The usual modern understanding of this verse takes רזי as an abstract noun from the root רזה ('to grow lean'), with its associated adjective רָזֶה ('lean'). It is true that a noun רזון is attested from this root, but in view of the marked proclivity for word-play in Isaiah 24–7 (not least in the present passage), it is not impossible that the form רזי was preferred as a contrast with צבי in the previous line. *RSV* offers a paraphrase based on this approach: 'But I say, "I pine away, I pine away, Woe is me! For the treacherous deal treacherously . . .".' There is much to be said in favour of this view: it does not involve emendation, and it makes for a good contrast with the previous line, which the introductory ואמר leads us to expect. I therefore conclude that 16*b* relates to 16*a* as a rejection by the prophet of what he regards as the inappropriate optimism of the preceding lines.

27: 12 The ambiguities in the first line of this verse and probable clues to their resolution are well set out by Gray. חבט can mean both 'to beat off' (e.g. of olives from a tree) and 'to beat out' (of grain), while שבלת means either 'flowing stream' or 'ear of grain' (listed as homonyms by BDB). The line may thus be rendered either 'The Lord will beat out (grain) from the corn-ears of the River to (those of) the Wady of Egypt', or 'The Lord will beat off (olives) from the current of the River to the Wady of Egypt'. Although not completely decisive, the only pointer towards a resolution of this dilemma comes with the use of לקט ('to pick, gather, glean') in the next line, an activity which would be expected to precede the beating-out of grain but to follow the beating-off of olives. The latter is therefore more appropriate in the context, which entails as a consequence that שבלת here means stream or current.

A further oddity is that the מ(ן) on שבלת is matched by עד in the next phrase, and so might be expected immediately before הנהר, and indeed this transposition is sometimes proposed conjecturally (e.g. by Procksch, Wildberger, and *BHS*). A consequence of that, however, would be that שבלת would then have to refer to an ear of grain, which we have seen is less probable. (Gray also observes that שבלת is nowhere else used as a collective, as such an emendation demands.) On the whole, therefore, MT is to be preferred, perhaps with the meaning 'from the flowing River', as suggested by Johnson (*From Chaos to Restoration*, 108), and the explanation proposed that שבלת was included before הנהר in order to give poetic balance to the נחל before מצרים.

30: 7 רהב הם שבת. Attempts to retain MT fail to convince, either because they rest on highly questionable philological speculations (Irwin, *Isaiah 28–33*, 77–8, who postulates a noun הם meaning 'roaring') or because they give unsatisfactory sense (Donner, *Israel unter den Völkern*, 158: 'Rahab sind sie? Untätigkeit!', followed by Kaiser). Many emendations have therefore been proposed (see the surveys in Wildberger, and Day, *God's Conflict*, 89), of which the simplest and most widely adopted is to run the last two words together and to vocalize הַמָּשְׁבָּת. I have no fresh considerations to add to Day's in favour of this emendation.

30: 8b The ugly sound of the Masoretic vocalization לָעַד עַד־עוֹלָם cannot be right. When these two nouns are combined for superlative effect, the forms are consistently לעד לעולם or (more usually) לעולם ועד; עד־עולמי עד occurs once (Isa. 45: 17), but even that avoids עַד repeated in immediate proximity. All the versions except the LXX render the first עד as 'witness', and two Hebrew manuscripts actually read לְעֵד (see *BHS*); this vocalization is undoubtedly correct, as all modern commentators agree.

32: 3 The vocalization of תשעינה appears to associate the word with שעה ('the eyes of those who see will not gaze'), but this makes little sense in itself and is emphatically contradicted by the wider context (vv. 3*b*–4). The proposal that לא = לו ('And him [i.e. God] the eyes of those, that see, shall regard') (so Lowth), is improbable: שעה is followed elsewhere by אל, על, or ב, never ל, and, besides, the wider context does not lead us to expect such a specification of the object of sight. Nor is לו ('if') (so Irwin, *Isaiah 28–33*, 121) appropriate, since the supposed apodosis in v. 5 is not logically connected with the protasis, and in any case v. 5 clearly belongs with v. 6. Most of the versions saw in תשעינה a form of the verb שעע ('be smeared over, blinded'), and in this they were surely right. The only uncertainty is whether to vocalize as a qal, תְּשֹׁעֶינָה, or as a hoph'al, תֻּשָׁעֶינָה. The latter is supported by the use of the hiph'il at 6: 10, which this verse is clearly reversing, and the former by the otherwise unattested qal of קשב in the parallel half of the line. The meaning is not affected by this uncertainty, however.

33: 2 זרעם. Wildberger's discussion of this word is entirely satisfactory. He rightly rejects both A. Poynder's suggestion('"Be Thou their Arm every Morning": Isaiah xxxiii. 2', *ExpT* 13 (1901–2), 94) that זרע here does not have its usual meaning, 'arm', but by reference to Arabic means 'scatterer' or 'assailant', and various appeals to the enclitic *mēm* to resolve the problem of the word's suffix; see H. D. Hummel, 'Enclitic *mem* in Early Northwest Semitic, Especially Hebrew', *JBL* 76 (1957), 85–107 (95); M. Dahood, 'Some Ambiguous Texts in Isaias', *CBQ* 20 (1958), 41–9 (45); Irwin, *Isaiah 28–33*, 138. The parallel ישועתנו, which agrees with the first-person-plural verbs in the first line, makes the third-person-plural suffix impossible, however. Pesh., Targ., and Vg. are to be followed and זרענו ('our arm') restored. R. Weiss ('On Ligatures in the Hebrew Bible (ם = נו)', *JBL* 82 (1963), 188–94) has convincingly demonstrated how easily these consonants could be confused in certain forms of the script.

40: 6 חסדו. The meaning of חסד in this context has given rise to far more discussion than can be conveniently surveyed here, and a firm decision is not required for the purpose of the argument above, p. 78. Briefly, commentators adopt one of two main approaches. (i) There are those who believe that the word here cannot have its usual meaning and who observe that the ancient versions have not used their normal translation equivalents. They therefore emend the text, either taking their cue from LXX, Pesh., and Vg. (all of which refer to 'glory') and so suggesting הודו, הדרו, or חמדו, or else following the lead of Targ. ('and all his strength') and proposing חסנו (noting that Targ. also uses תוקף to render חסן at 1: 31). (ii) Other scholars, however, insist that the meaning of חסד can itself include such ideas as 'strength, reliability, steadfastness', and that this is suitable in the present context; see especially N. H. Snaith, 'The Exegesis of Isaiah xl. 5, 6', *ExpT* 52 (1940–1), 394–6; L. J. Kuyper, 'The Meaning of חסדו Isa. xl 6', *VT* 13 (1963), 489–92; C. F. Whitley, 'The Semantic Range of *Ḥesed*', *Biblica*, 62 (1981), 519–26; rather differently H. J. Stoebe, 'Zu Jesaja 40, V. 6', *Wort und Dienst*, N.F. 2 (1950), 122–8, and G. Gerlemann, 'Das übervolle Mass', *VT* 28 (1978), 151–64 (158).

40: 7–8 LXX and 1QIsa[a] (first hand) lack an equivalent of v. 7 (or of 7*b*–8*a*), and a second hand has added the lacking portion of MT between the lines and down the margin of 1QIsa[a]. Before the discovery of 1QIsa[a], the suggestion that LXX represents a defective text, a scribe's eye having accidentally jumped from 7*a* to the identical 8*a*, was reasonable (so, for instance, Ziegler, *Untersuchungen zur Septuaginta des Buches Isaias*, 47). That this should have independently happened twice, though possible (so Elliger), is less probable. Moreover, J. Koenig ('Récouverture du débat sur la première main rédactionelle du rouleau ancien d'Isaïe de Qumrân (I Q Is A) en 40, 7–8', *RQ* 11 (1983), 219–37) has emphasized the point that paleographically the second hand is considerably later than the first, thus ruling out the possibility that the first scribe simply made an error in copying which was immediately (so Elliger) corrected. It is certainly more probable that LXX and 1QIsa[a] (first hand) testify to an alternative shorter text which enjoyed wide circulation. That conclusion does not of itself, however, resolve the issue whether the shorter text derived at an earlier stage from the longer by accidental omission or whether the longer MT developed by accretion from the shorter text.

One consideration which might be thought to favour the latter conclusion is the widespread view that the last three words of v. 7 are a gloss; they are held to disturb the metre and to use עם as a general word for mankind whereas Deutero-Isaiah restricts its use to Israel. These arguments are less than convincing, however, since עם is certainly used in a general sense at 42: 5 and because the use of an extra stich in a line (including an element of repetition, as in v. 7) is securely attested at 40: 9 (הרימי אל־תיראי) just following.

The most weighty consideration, however, and one which vitally affects the question of whether priority should be given to the longer or shorter version of vv. 7–8, is exegetical, and this, it seems to me, decisively favours MT in its present form (so too correctly in this respect Merendino, *Der Erste und der Letzte*, 47–62). In the shorter text, the change in mood from despair in vv. 6–7*a* (or 8*a*) to confidence in 8*b* is abrupt and unexplained, for in this form of the text only one voice speaks (the unresolved question whether ואמר in v. 7 should be revocalized to first-person singular does not affect this point). In the longer form of the text (MT), however, everything makes sense. In response to the summons to 'cry' (6*a*), the first speaker replies in pessimistic mood through the remainder of v. 6 and most of v. 7;

mankind's weakness appears to make the enterprise worthless. Then with אכן, however, the mood changes and another voice (presumably the one which first said 'cry') responds. It is conceded that mankind is like grass (resuming both 6*b* and 7*a*) which will only wither and fade (resuming 7*a*), *but* 'the word of our God will endure for ever'. אכן, standing first in the sentence, has a strong asseverative force (cf. BDB 38B), and could be paraphrased 'yes indeed' or even 'yes, I know that . . .'. On this view, the repetitions are a significant part of the speaker's rhetoric, whereas without them the passage remains confused. (For a less prosaic exegesis, see S. A. Geller, 'Were the Prophets Poets?', *Prooftexts*, 3 (1983), 211–21.)

41: 22 ונדעה אחריתן. The order of clauses in lines *b* and *c* of this verse has a chiastic structure and, as North emphasizes, leaves no doubt that the suffix on אחריתן refers to הראשנות, not to הבאות. It is not certain, however, that these observations are strong enough to outweigh the arguments for inverting the order of clauses in line *c*. Verse 23 continues the syntactic structure of 22*b* in both its lines: an imperative followed by a final clause. Both verses must, therefore, be taken closely together as a single unit. In that case the apparent chiasmus in v. 22 breaks down and 22*c* uncomfortably disrupts a regular pattern. A contributory consideration is that the conjectured inversion results in a more satisfactory rhythmic balance. Furthermore, even with the order of clauses inverted, the evident meaning of the passage is sufficiently clear to ensure that the antecedent to the suffix on אחריתן is not confused.

42: 16 The repetition of לא ידעו in the first and second halves of the line is suspicious and seems to overload the first half metrically. Most recent commentators, therefore, delete it and vocalize the previous word בַּדֶּרֶךְ in consequence, despite the lack of ancient textual support (exceptions include Bonnard, and Merendino, *Der Erste und der Letzte*, 263). The proposal to delete both occurrences, however (so, for instance, Elliger), seems less probable, not least because there is then no explanation as to where the phrase came from in the first place.

42: 19 At first sight, the only problem posed by this verse is the meaning of the word משלם. On the assumption that it is not here a proper name, it has the form of a puʿal participle, either of שָׁלֵם ('be performed (of a vow), be repaid, requited'), or of a denominative verb from שלום, hence 'one in a covenant of peace' (though neither the piʿel nor the puʿal of this denominative is otherwise attested). This has often been linked in the past with Arabic *muslim* ('one who trusts in God') (so again Z. W. Falk, 'Hebrew Legal Terms: II', *JSS* 12 (1967), 241–4), to give rise to such translations as 'my dedicated one' (*RSV*), 'the surrendered one' (Cheyne), or 'the confidant of God' (Delitzsch). Suggestions that attempt to stay closer to the attested meanings of the root in Hebrew include 'he who has been granted my covenant of peace' (North), 'day labourer' (de Boer, not justified: presumably 'one who gets paid'), 'the one who is to be restored' (Snaith, 181; cf. Bonnard, 137: 'le Réintégré'), and 'he who has been requited' (L. G. Rignell, *A Study of Isaiah Ch. 40–55* (Lund, 1956), 36, followed by W. Eisenbeis, *Die Wurzel* שלם *im Alten Testament* (BZAW 113; Berlin, 1969), 78–9, 323–4; cf. Merendino, *Der Erste und der Letzte*, 275–7: 'Da, der Vergeltung erfahren hat!').

Before any attempt is made to choose between these or comparable proposals, however, it should be noted that upon closer inspection the MT reveals other peculiarities, including (i) the abrupt switch from the first-person divine address in the first line of the verse to the third-person עבד יהוה in the second; (ii) the threefold repetition of עור, coupled with the fact that the last phrase of the verse is effectively completely repetitive of the first; (iii) however it is understood, משלם contrasts with the other nouns with which it is apparently parallel in having no suffix or dependent noun to qualify it; and (iv) the ancient versions do not all follow MT. The evidence is set out comprehensively in Elliger, but the consequences he draws from it do not inspire confidence. On the basis of LXX and Vg. he believes that the כי אם of the first phrase was repeated in the second; of כמלאכי, that leaves only כ and ל to be accounted for. Putting these two consonants together with אשלח, he then eliminates the א as an inevitable consequence of the shift to the first person once כמלאכי was read, the כ may have been confused with an original מ and the ח with ה; this enables him to postulate an original משליהו (cf. LXX οἱ κυριεύοντες αὐτῶν), which, unlike LXX, he links with משל I, to give 'seine Spruchmacher', i.e. those who mock, and so oppose, the prophet (cf. p. 285). The second line of the verse (where Pesh.'s שליטא recognizes the root משל) is then completely redundant; משלם was originally a corrective gloss on the confused ending of the previous line, and the rest of line *b* then developed secondarily around it. In support, it is noted that the first half of line *b* was not represented in the original form of the LXX. Despite Elliger's ingenuity, however, his starting-point is weak, for it is doubtful whether LXX and Vg. need have read כי אם twice in the first line: in this respect their renderings represent the evident sense of the MT. Moreover, he has to clutch at straws to get the desired meaning out of his postulated משליהו. Without such conjectures the first-person suffixes of the first line are guaranteed by אשלח and the line as it stands makes excellent sense; it seems wiser to leave it intact.

This does nothing, however, to relieve the problems of the troublesome second line. Since none of the proffered explanations of the MT commends itself, resort to conjecture is frequently made. *BHS* represents that most widely accepted—namely, משלחי ('my sent one', parallel with 'my messenger (whom) I send' in the first line) for משלם, and חרש for the second

עור, with appeal to Symmachus and two Hebrew manuscripts. While it might be possible to reinforce this second point by appeal to the scribal quirk noted at 1: 7 and 6: 11 above, the first is pure conjecture and moreover introduces an otherwise unattested meaning for the puʿal participle of שלח (contrast 16: 2; 27: 10; Prov. 29: 15). In addition, the suggestion does not explain the abrupt change from first to third person.

The alternative approach to this line is to regard it as an interpretative gloss on the first line. On this view, taking the absence of the first half of the line from the LXX seriously, ועור כעבד יהוה will have been added initially as an explanatory comment on the first part of the verse; the need was felt to ensure that the first-person pronominal suffix was correctly understood. I suggest that the first half of the line was added subsequently as a cross-reference to עבד משלים in 49: 7 (cf. Volz). It has long been recognized that there has been some such cross-referencing following the two servant passages in chapters 42 and 49 (see especially 42: 6 and 49: 6 and 8), and 50: 10–11 may reflect a similar process. It looks as though the occurrence of עבדי in the first line of our verse may have triggered a comparable expansion. (Whether the gloss has itself been subsequently corrupted, perhaps when it was drawn in as part of the text, need not be further considered.)

42: 20 The main problems are (i) the abrupt change from second to third person within the verse (though GK §144*p* lists other possible examples of this), (ii) the *kethib/qere* variant in the first word, which indicates consciousness of a difficulty, and (iii) the evidence of the versions, which tend to offer the second person throughout, though sometimes in the plural.

Modern commentators divide into two groups, according to whether they favour the second or third person consistently. Thus North, Muilenburg, de Boer, and Westermann, for instance, follow the *kethib* רָאִיתָ and emend ישמע to תשמע (with a number of manuscripts). This is thought to follow well from the second-person imperatives in v. 18. Against this, however, it should be noted that the imperatives are plural, not singular, so that a further change of person is thereby introduced, that a third-person rendering could equally easily follow after v. 19*a*, and that there is no explanation why the last word of the verse should have been corrupted in this way; on this view, a scribe would have had the second-person singular firmly in mind, so that a corruption to third person at the end of the verse is unlikely.

There is thus much to be said for following Volz, Torrey, Elliger, *BHS*, and others in reading רָאוֹת with the *qere* and emending תשמר to ישמר. (H. J. van Dijk ('Does Third Masculine Singular **taqtul* Exist in Hebrew?', *VT* 19 (1969), 440–7) suggests that MT may itself be a third-person masculine singular form, but his theory as a whole has not attracted much support.) ראות is an unusual (though possible; see GK §75*n*) form of the infinitive absolute, and this makes a good parallel with פקוח; it also enjoys considerable manuscript support (see Elliger). At the same time, it is not difficult to imagine that because the form was unfamiliar there was a ו/י confusion, so giving rise to the *kethib*. Once this had happened (and the evidence of the versions, including 1QIsa[a]'s ראיתה, indicates that it was early), it is easy to understand why ישמר* should have been altered to תשמר in most manuscripts. The manuscripts which read תשמע at the end of the verse show this process continuing, whereas MT's *apparently* more difficult reading tells strongly in its own favour. (G. R. Driver's more radical proposals ('Linguistic and Textual Problems: Isaiah i–xxxix', *JTS* 38 (1937), 36–48 (48)) do not, therefore, seem necessary.)

43: 9 ישמיענו. Commentators generally find the plural form of the verb difficult following the singular יגיד in the first half of the line and so propose a small change in vocalization in order to eliminate the problem: יַשְׁמִיעֵנוּ (see *BHS*). However, since the next line undoubtedly continues in the plural, and since in principle a plural verb is acceptable (though unusual) following מי ב׳ (cf. 36: 20), this solution only postpones rather than resolves the difficulty. Indeed, 1QIsa[a] moves in the opposite direction, reading the plural יגידו for the MT's singular יגיד. Perhaps, however, it is unnecessary to look for complete consistency in this respect. Though not an exact parallel, Mal. 1: 10 also mixes singular and plural verbs after מי גם בכם, and this suggests the possibility that, while מי בהם governs both halves of the line, its force is slightly different in each: 'Oh that even one of them would declare this and that they would show us the former things.'

Some also find the first-person-plural suffix difficult. North and Elliger, for instance, prefer to follow 1QIsa[a] in omitting the נ so as to read ישמיעו. However, since, as already noted, 1QIsa[a] has יגידו in the first half, it is difficult to be sure that its text has not arisen by a process of editorial tidying-up. (The versions generally show sufficient diversity in these matters to preclude the possibility of a firm alternative textual tradition.) In 41: 21–6 the first person plural also features in a closely comparable context, so that its presence here is not disturbing. While clearly neither the proposed emendations nor 1QIsa[a] are impossible, it is not certain that they are to be preferred to the MT (Volz).

44: 7b De Boer seeks to retain the MT: 'what is more than my establishing a lasting people and things to come.—Let them report to him over what shall come to pass.' Apart from the inelegant awkwardness of this rendering, it implies a very compressed form of expression in Hebrew; what justification is there, for instance, for supplying 'what is more'? In addition, עם עולם is referred to Israel, whereas, in the only other passage where the phrase occurs (Ezek. 26: 20), it clearly refers to those who are long dead, probably the antedeluvians. This latter consideration led

Delitzsch to follow the Masoretic punctuation of the line and so to render: '(And who proclaims as I . . .) since I founded the people of the primeval world? And future things, and what is coming, let them declare.' This leaves the first phrase of the line unusually dependent on the opening words of the verse with the rest of the first line intruding uncomfortably, however, while in the second line rhythmic balance certainly requires ואתיות to be joined to the first half, against the Masoretic division.

In view of these difficulties, nearly all commentators emend in one of two ways. (i) Most (cf. *RSV*, *BHS*, and the detailed justification in Elliger) follow Oort's proposal to read מי השמיע מעולם אותיות ('who has announced from of old the things to come?'). This stays close to the consonantal text (which is generally supported by the versions; cf. Schoors, *I am God your Saviour*, 230, who, however, prefers ישמיע to השמיע) and makes excellent sense in the context. (ii) In order to keep even closer to the consonantal text, Torrey suggested משמיע and North משמיעי for the first word; it is construed as a *casus pendens*, serving as a protasis in a conditional sentence 'with the force of "those who ages ago announced coming events should be able to tell us (. . .) what the future still holds"'. The main problem with this proposal, however (apart from the somewhat strained syntax), is that it does not furnish the required sense: Deutero-Isaiah never concedes, as this rendering implies, that the idol gods have been able long ago to announce coming events (see, for instance, v. 8). The first, and most widely adopted, conjecture is thus to be preferred. (*Pace* North, the plural יגידו is not impossible following מי, even with the singular השמיע intervening; see somewhat similarly on 43: 9 above. Against M. J. Dahood's proposal (*Ugaritic–Hebrew Philology: Marginal Notes on Recent Publications* (Biblica et Orientalia, 17 (Rome, 1965), 32), see Schoors, *I am God your Saviour*, 231.)

**44: 26a** Many commentators emend the singular עבדו to plural עבדיו, principally because of the parallelism with מלאכיו. The evidence in support from manuscripts and the ancient versions is slight, as Elliger candidly admits: 'Rein vom Gesichtspunkt der Textüberlieferung aus wäre eher den letzteren [i.e. sing.] zu folgen.' In any case, Berlin (*The Dynamics of Biblical Parallelism*, 49–50) shows that the versions were not sensitive to this type of 'singular-plural parallelism', of which there are many well-attested examples. If satisfactory sense can be made of the MT, it should, therefore, be preferred as the more difficult reading, and a sizeable minority of commentators have always accepted this. On the suggestion advanced in the course of the present work, that is indeed the case.

**44: 26b** With its three main phrases, this line is surprisingly long in the context of this passage (vv. 24*b*–28), which otherwise has balanced rhythm. In addition, the suffix on חרבותיה must refer to Jerusalem of the first clause, not 'the cities of Judah' of the second. It is, therefore, probable that this latter represents a later expansion of the line (cf. North, Whybray, Elliger, Schoors, *I am God your Saviour*, 269, *BHS*, etc.). The further issue of whether 28*b* (which has textual difficulties of its own) should be moved and merged with this line, so perhaps easing the problem just noted (see Marti), is more speculative, and need not be discussed here.

45: 9 The first line of this verse has been much discussed. As it stands, the MT has הוי followed by a singular participle רב (a plural participle in this position is more common, but the singular is by no means impossible; cf. v. 10 immediately following, Jer. 22: 13, and the series of הוי oracles in Habakkuk 2), which governs את as a frequent alternative to עם ('with') in this construction. In the second half of the line, את then has to have the extended meaning of 'with' = 'together with, among'. The line may thus be rendered, 'Woe unto him that striveth with his Maker! a potsherd among the potsherds of the earth!' (*RV*), and this has been found acceptable to many, including Marti, North, Bonnard, Schoors, *I am God your Saviour*, 259–62, H. Leene, 'Universalism or Nationalism? Isaiah xlv 9–13 and its Context', *Bijdragen*, 35 (1974), 309–34, Whybray, and, most recently, Hermisson. On this approach, even Torrey's slight emendation of חַרְשֵׂי to חֲרַשׂ (construct of חָרָשׂ), which apparently lies behind *RSV*'s 'an earthen vessel with the potter!', is unnecessary; the point of the MT is that the one contending with his maker is not in any special position to do so: he is but one of the hundreds of sherds that were strewn over any inhabited site in antiquity.

Many wish to emend more radically; cf. Volz; G. R. Driver, 'Linguistic and Textual Problems: Isaiah xl–lxvi', *JTS* 36 (1935), 396–406 (399), and 'Isaianic Problems', 49–51; C. F. Whitley, 'Textual Notes on Deutero-Isaiah', *VT* 11 (1961), 457–61 (458–9) (followed by Naidoff); *BHS*. They all, however, take as their starting-point the proposal to read הֲיָרִיב instead of הוי רב, either because it is thought that Deutero-Isaiah could not have used הוי, or to 'improve' the parallelism with היאמר at the start of the next line. Both points, however, are adequately answered by the observation that the verse has been influenced by reflection on 29: 15–16, so that it seems unnecessary to go into further detail here.

For ידים = 'skill' at the end of the verse, cf. G. R. Driver, 'Isaianic Problems', 51 (following Delitzsch), and Hermisson (for 'handles', as in *RSV*, ידות would be expected; cf. GK §87*o*); see also D. F. Payne, 'Old Testament Exegesis and the Problem of Ambiguity', *ASTI* 5 (1966–7), 48–68 (57–8).

45: 11 The second line of the MT apparently says, 'Ask me the future concerning my children, and command me concerning the work of my hands'. תצוני is not, of course, an imperative but must be construed as a second-person jussive with imperatival force, something which, if not impossible, is certainly awkward. The principal difficulty with the MT, however, is that it completely contradicts the argument of the context, which is stressing the sovereignty of the creator over the creature and the inscrutability of his ways; cf. Leene, 'Universalism or Nationalism?' Three main proposals have been advanced to overcome these difficulties. (i) Some, such as North, observe that the LXX (ὁ ποιήσας τα ἐπερχόμενα) and 1QIsa$^{a}$ (יוצר האותות) have made האתיות into the object of יוצר*. They therefore take this word with the first line of the verse (2: 2: 2) and maintain that without it על־בני fits more comfortably after שאלוני. However, MT's ויצרו should probably be retained: it fits the context extremely well, applying the reasoning of v. 9*b* (where יצרו in fact occurs) to Israel itself and thus requiring the retention of the suffix as its object. (יצר is, of course, used in several of Deutero-Isaiah's introductory formulae with regard to Israel.) Most important, however, is that this proposal still leaves the problem of the clash between שאלוני and the prevailing context. To treat it as an ironical statement (so North) is unsatisfactory. (ii) A once popular proposal, following Ehrlich, *Randglossen*, iv. 166, was to emend the start of line *b* to האתם תשאלוני ('will you question me . . .'). This conjecture removes the main problems of the MT, and furthermore it is noted that Targ. also renders this line as a question. This last point is blunted, however, by the fact that Targ. also clearly retains an equivalent of האתיות (דעתידן למיתי). Something very close to the traditional consonantal text is thus attested by all the versions, so that a proposal which remains closer to it is to be preferred. (iii) Such a proposal has been advanced, apparently independently, by G. R. Driver ('Studies in the Vocabulary of the Old Testament. V', *JTS* 34 (1933), 33–44 (39)) as a conjecture, and by Skehan ('Some Textual Problems in Isaia', 54–5), on the basis of 1QIsa$^{a}$ (האותות שאלוני) with only a different word division, namely הא(ו)תי תשאלוני ('will you ask *me* . . .'). The emphasis on the object (God) is very suitable in the context, the problem of תצוני at the end of the verse is removed, and the conjecture remains extremely close to the consonantal text. Not surprisingly, it has been widely adopted (e.g. *BHS*, Whybray, Hermisson; against Koole's renewed attempt to defend MT ('Zu Jesaja 45, 9ff.'), see Naidoff, 'The Two-Fold Structure of Isaiah xlv 9–13', 181 n. 8). It also seems contextually superior to Whitley's suggestion ('Textual Notes on Deutero-Isaiah', 459), האתות תשאלוני ('Do ye ask me signs (concerning my sons)?'), a question supposedly answered in the next verse.

49: 5 וישראל לא יאסף. To make sense of the *kethib* in this context, אסף must have the sense of 'gather and take away', hence 'remove': 'and (that) Israel be not removed, swept away.' This is certainly an attested meaning of the word (cf. BDB 62B), despite G. Widengren's cavalier assertion to the contrary: see 'Yahweh's Gathering of the Dispersed', in W. B. Barrick and J. R. Spencer (eds.), *In the Shelter of Elyon: Essays on Ancient Palestinian Life and Literature in Honor of G. W. Ahlström* (*JSOTS* 31; Sheffield, 1984), 227–45 (233). Despite this, the *qere* is better supported by the versions, including 1QIsa$^{a}$ (לו) and LXX (πρὸς αὐτόν), and it is found in nine Hebrew manuscripts. It also makes for more straightforward parallelism with אליו in the first half of the line (though cf. 45: 1*c* for the *kethib*'s form of parallelism); hence, 'and that Israel be gathered to him' (*RSV*). R. Tournay's suggestion ('Quelques relectures bibliques antisamaritaines', *RB* 71 (1964), 504–36 (529–30)) that the *kethib* represents a later, anti-Samaritan reinterpretation ('but Israel [= the northern kingdom] will not be gathered') cannot be sustained, however. It is decisively contradicted by v. 6*b*, and in addition would have involved the curious understanding of Jacob as Judah in the first half of the line.

49: 12 The returning exiles are said to be set to arrive from four different directions. The first, מרחוק ('from afar'), is unspecified, but the second and third, מצפון ומים, clearly indicate the north and west respectively. מארץ סינים could thus theoretically refer to either east or south. Many earlier scholars from the sixteenth century on thought of China (see the impressive list in Schoors, *I am God your Saviour*, 102), while others preferred Syene (סונה) as representing the southernmost point at which there was known to be a Jewish colony (cf. Jer. 44: 1; Ezek. 29: 10; 30: 6; and the evidence of the Elephantine papyri); cf. Lowth, who cites J. D. Michaelis and J. C. Doerdelein amongst his predecessors. Vg. and Targ. refer to the south, and 1QIsa$^{a}$ (which distinguishes י from ו) clearly reads סוניים; see plate xli in M. Burrows (ed.), *The Dead Sea Scrolls of St. Mark's Monastery*, i (New Haven, Conn., 1950), *contra* the printed text on the facing page. (For a discussion of this form, see F. Rundgren, 'Elephantine-Aramäisches *mallāḥ dī mayyā* und altägyptisches *mw byn*, "Katarakt"', *Studia Linguistica*, 11 (1957), 57–60 (59).) There is absolutely no evidence that the Jewish dispersion had reached as far as China by this time, and it is extremely doubtful whether even the name could have been known to Deutero-Isaiah; see G. Lambert, 'Le Livre d'Isaïe parle-t-il des Chinois?', *NRT* 75 (1953), 965–72; E. J. Kissane, '"The Land of Sinim" (Is. 49: 12)', *ITQ* 21 (1954), 63–4. My former colleague, Dr M. A. N. Loewe, has informed me that the 'name derives from Ch'in, the title of a dukedom, later a kingdom, that may have been founded in 897 BC, and succeeded in 221 BC in conquering all rival kingdoms and founding the first of the empires. There is nothing to show that the name Ch'in (in the sixth century BC pronounced, perhaps, as dz'i̯ĕn) was ever used for denoting the whole land, as a collective; and as the Ch'in empire has for 2000 years been subjected to harsh criticism it has never been adopted by the Chinese themselves, who subsequently called themselves after two later dynasties (Han or T'ang)'. The reading סונים is overwhelmingly probable, and מרחוק will then refer to the east in consequence.

49: 19 *RSV* renders the MT as it stands:

> Surely your waste and your desolate places
> and your devastated land —
> Surely now you will be too narrow for your inhabitants
> and those who swallowed you up will be far away.

On this view, the first line has to be understood as a somewhat unconnected introduction to contrast with what follows: 'Instead of the three subjects, "thy ruins" etc., the comprehensive "thou" is employed permutatively, and the sentence commenced afresh' (Delitzsch). The MT is simply assumed to be correct, even by a number of commentators who normally pay careful attention to the problems of the Hebrew text (e.g. North, Bonnard, and Schoors, *I am God your Saviour*, 104).

To others, however, the text as it stands is impossible: 'It is sufficiently obvious that something is wrong with the text of the first half of this verse. See any good commentary. As the words are now pointed, we have what sounds like a mere fragment, part of which is obscure, to say the least.' Torrey's solution to the difficulties which he thus perceives is ingenious; he revocalizes the three nouns as verbs (the actual forms he gives are partly erroneous; they are correctly given in *BHS*: חֲרַבְתִּיךְ, שִׁמַּמְתִּיךְ, and הֲרַסְתִּיךְ) and takes ארץ as an accusative, to give: 'I devastated thee, laid thee waste, razed thee to the ground.' *BHS* adopts this proposal, and recommends also deleting ארץ on the basis of the LXX. This last point is very questionable, however, both because in rendering the words as nouns the LXX may simply have run ארץ הרסתיך together as τὰ πεπτωκότα and because ארץ is required by the regular metre of this passage. Even then, however, there are difficulties with Torrey's suggestion. As Whybray points out, such a heavy emphasis on the afflictions of the past is inappropriate in the context, and in addition the sequence of tenses assumed by the emendation is irregular.

Another possible approach to this verse is to assume that something may have dropped out. Duhm noted further that v. 18*b* is overloaded, and so attempted a major reconstruction of these two lines. Such a radical solution is not acceptable today (any more than is Volz's proposal to move 19*a* to follow 16), but a more modest version that takes account of his observations could be attempted. I note כי כלם and ככלה in 18*b* and כי at the start of 19; perhaps יִכָּלוּ (niph'al of כלל ('to complete, perfect')) has been lost from the start of v. 19. The verb occurs in only one other passage (Ezek. 27: 4, 11), again in a context of building. Its loss could be explained in one of two ways. (i) A simple case of haplography, probably aided by the rarity of the word. On this view, חי אני נאם יהוה at the start of 18*b* is an anacrusis, and the rest of the line is a 3: 2 in keeping with the lines which follow. (ii) Alternatively, ותקשרים ככלה may not have been in the original text, but may have been added in the margin as a cross-reference to 61: 10. At a later stage of copying, it may then have replaced יכלו* on the cuckoo principle (see on 1: 7 above). On this view, חי אני נאם יהוה would have been included in the passage's rhythmical structure and 18*b* would have been a 3: 3 in keeping with the lines which precede.

So long as the MT of 19*a* is regarded as acceptable, there is no need to entertain this conjecture; I offer it only as a simple and intelligible solution if the problems of 19*a* are considered insuperable. Either way, ושממתיך need not be changed.

50: 4 לשון למודים. It is *possible* (but by no means certain) that this first occurrence of למודים is an abstract noun ('teaching'), so that the whole phrase means 'an expert tongue'; cf. Torrey; G. R. Driver, 'Linguistic and Textual Problems: Isaiah xl–lxvi', 406; North; Whybray. If correct, this first occurrence would be semantically closer to Jer. 2: 24, though the second would still mean 'disciples' or the like, as at 8: 16. Nevertheless, 'the tongue of those who are taught' is not, perhaps, as obscure an expression as some of these commentators imply, and indeed others continue to make good sense out of it; cf. Westermann, and, more generally, D. F. Payne, 'Characteristic Word-Play in "Second Isaiah": A Reappraisal', *JSS* 12 (1967), 207–29.

52: 13 The usual understanding of this verse as a description of the servant's success and exaltation has been challenged in particular by G. R. Driver, 'Isaiah $52_{13}$–$53_{12}$: The Servant of the Lord', in M. Black and G. Fohrer (eds.), *In Memoriam Paul Kahle* (BZAW 103; Berlin, 1968), 90–105 (90–1); see also J. Morgenstern, 'The Suffering Servant—A New Solution', *VT* 11 (1961), 292–320, 406–31 (313). He argues first that such a description is out of place in this context ('the time to speak of his success and prosperity is at the end of the poem') and second that 'השׂכיל is inappropriate to the Servant's circumstances, inasmuch as it expresses not plain success or prosperity, for which הצליח is the proper word (s. $53_{10}$), but success as the result of wise or clever provision, i.e. worldly success, which is out of the question'. Driver's solution is then to revocalize the verb as יְשֻׂכַּל ('he will be bound') (cf. Akkadian *šakkilū* ('bandage, scarf', as something tied round the head); Hebrew שִׂכֵּל ('crossed' of hands); and Arabic *šakala* ('bound, tied')), and then to understand the following verbs as a reference to 'the lifting up of the Servant after being bound as a form of punishment, such as hanging'. He thus arrives at the translation (p. 103): 'Lo! my servant shall be bound and lifted up, | he shall be raised aloft, very high.'

This radical reinterpretation of the verse is unnecessary, however. The verb השׂכיל is not limited to 'worldly success'. At Josh. 1: 7–8, for instance, it is twice said to result from careful attention to the (book of the) Torah (and in v. 8 it is parallel with הצליח, which Driver thinks would be 'the proper word' to describe the servant's success; note too that Targ. of Isa. 52: 13 translates ישכיל by יצלח), while at 1 Sam. 18: 14 David's success (משכיל) is attributed to the fact that 'the Lord was with him'. Furthermore, there need be no objection to a reference to the servant's success in the introduction to the poem. It is not uncommon in the Hebrew Bible to state the result of an action first and then to trace the path by which this result is attained. The consequential tripartite nature of many narratives is thus reflected in Isa. 52: 13–53: 12 as well; see O. H. Steck, 'Aspekte des Gottesknechts in Jes 52,13–53,12', *ZAW* 97 (1985), 36–58; G. Fohrer, 'Stellvertretung und Schuldopfer in Jes $52_{13}$–$53_{12}$', in *Studien zu alttestamentlichen Texten und Themen (1966–1972)* (BZAW 155; Berlin, 1981), 24–43 (29); more cautiously, J. Koenig, *Oracles et liturgies de l'exil babylonien* (Paris, 1988), 178–80; on the servant's success and reward, see further H.-J. Hermisson, 'Der Lohn des Knechts', in J. Jeremias and L. Perlitt (eds.), *Die Botschaft und die Boten: Festschrift für Hans Walter Wolff zum 70. Geburtstag* (Neukirchen-Vluyn, 1981), 269–87. Finally, the consistent use of the verbs in the second half of the verse elsewhere in Isaiah, as described in Chapter 3 above, suggests strongly that they should be understood in the same way in the present passage. The traditional understanding of Isa. 52: 13 should thus be retained.

The proposal to delete one of the three verbs in the second half of the verse on the ground that the LXX has only two verbs is also to be rejected; it rests on a misunderstanding of the LXX's translation practice; see O. Hofius, 'Zur Septuaginta-Übersetzung von Jes 52,13b', *ZAW* 104 (1992), 107–10.

54: 14 רחקי. An imperative (literally, 'be far from me'), used as sometimes elsewhere to express a distinct assurance or promise; cf. GK §110*c*. The slight emendation to imperfect תרחקי (see *BHS*), therefore, seems unnecessary, and does not materially alter the meaning (cf. S. R. Driver, *Tenses*, §57; Glaßner, *Vision eines auf Verheißung gegründeten Jerusalem*, 80). North captures the sense well with 'so far from oppression that you will not need to fear'.

# BIBLIOGRAPHY


ACKROYD, P. R., 'A Note on Isaiah $2_1$', *ZAW* 75 (1963), 320–1.

—— 'An Interpretation of the Babylonian Exile: A Study of II Kings 20, Isaiah 38–39', *SJT* 27 (1974), 329–52.

—— 'Isaiah i–xii: Presentation of a Prophet', in *Congress Volume: Göttingen 1977* (SVT 29; Leiden, 1978), 16–48.

—— 'The Death of Hezekiah: A Pointer to the Future?', in M. Carrez *et al.* (eds.), *De la Tôrah au Messie: Mélanges Henri Cazelles: Études d'exégèse et d'herméneutique bibliques offerts à Henri Cazelles pour ses 25 années d'enseignement à l'Institut Catholique de Paris (Octobre 1979)* (Paris, 1981), 219–26.

—— 'Isaiah 36–39: Structure and Function', in W. C. Delsman *et al.* (eds.), *Von Kanaan bis Kerala: Festschrift für Prof. Mag. Dr. Dr. J. P. M. van der Ploeg O.P. zur Vollendung des siebzigsten Lebensjahres am 4. Juli 1979* (AOAT 211; Neukirchen-Vluyn, 1982), 3–21.

—— *Studies in the Religious Tradition of the Old Testament* (London, 1987).

ALBERTZ, R., 'Das Deuterojesaja-Buch als Fortschreibung der Jesaja-Prophetie', in E. Blum, C. Macholz, and E. W. Stegemann (eds.), *Die Hebräische Bibel und ihre zweifache Nachgeschichte: Festschrift für Rolf Rendtorff zum 65. Geburtstag* (Neukirchen-Vluyn, 1990), 241–56.

ALLEN, L. C., 'Cuckoos in the Textual Nest', *JTS* NS 22 (1971), 143–50.

—— 'More Cuckoos in the Textual Nest', *JTS* NS 24 (1973), 69–73.

ALLIS, O. T., *The Unity of Isaiah* (London, 1951).

ALONSO-SCHÖKEL, L., 'Is 12: De duabis methodis pericopam explicandi', *VD* 34 (1956), 154–60.

ALT, A., 'Jesaja 8,23–9,6: Befreiungsnacht und Krönungstag', in *Festschrift Alfred Bertholet, zum 80. Geburtstag gewidmet* (Tübingen, 1950), 29–49 = *Kleine Schriften zur Geschichte des Volkes Israel*, ii (Munich, 1953), 206–25.

ANDERSON, B. W., 'Exodus Typology in Second Isaiah', in B. W. Anderson and W. Harrelson (eds.), *Israel's Prophetic Heritage: Essays in Honor of James Muilenburg* (New York, 1962), 177–95.

—— 'Exodus and Covenant in Second Isaiah and Prophetic Tradition', in F. M. Cross, W. E. Lemke, and P. D. Miller (eds.), *Magnalia Dei: The Mighty Acts of God: Essays on the Bible and Archaeology in Memory of G. Ernest Wright* (Garden City, NY, 1976), 339–60.

—— '"God with Us"—in Judgment and in Mercy: The Editorial Structure of Isaiah 5–10(11)', in G. M. Tucker, D. L. Petersen, and R. R. Wilson (eds.), *Canon, Theology, and Old Testament Interpretation: Essays in Honor of Brevard S. Childs* (Philadelphia, 1988), 230–45.

ANDERSON, G. W., 'Isaiah xxiv–xxvii Reconsidered', *Congress Volume: Bonn, 1962* (SVT 9; Leiden, 1963), 118–26.

AUVRAY, P., *Isaïe 1–39* (Sources bibliques; Paris, 1972).

BALTZER, D., *Ezechiel und Deuterojesaja: Berührungen in der Heilserwartung der beiden großen Exilspropheten* (BZAW 121; Berlin, 1971).

BARR, J., *The Variable Spellings of the Hebrew Bible* (Oxford, 1989).

BARSTAD, H. M., *A Way in the Wilderness* (*JSS* monograph, 12; Manchester, 1989).

BARTH, H., *Die Jesaja-Worte in der Josiazeit: Israel und Assur als Thema einer produktiven Neuinterpretation der Jesajaüberlieferung* (WMANT 48; Neukirchen-Vluyn, 1977).

BARTLETT, J. R., *Edom and the Edomites* (JSOTS 77; Sheffield, 1989).

BARTON, J., *Amos's Oracles against the Nations: A Study of Amos 1.3–2.5* (SOTSMS 6; Cambridge, 1980).

—— *Reading the Old Testament: Method in Biblical Study* (London, 1986).

BEALE, G. K., 'Isaiah vi 9–13: A Retributive Taunt against Idolatry', *VT* 41 (1991), 257–78.

BECKER, J., *Isaias—der Prophet und sein Buch* (SBS 30; Stuttgart, 1968).

BECKING, B., 'Der Text von Jesaja $9_{2a}$', *ZAW* 92 (1980), 142–5.

BEGG, C. T., '2 Kings 20: 12–19 as an Element of the Deuteronomistic History', *CBQ* 48 (1986), 27–38.

—— 'The Deuteronomistic Retouching of the Portrait of Hezekiah in 2 Kgs 20,12–19', *BN* 38–9 (1987), 7–13.

—— 'Babylon in the Book of Isaiah', in Vermeylen (ed.), *The Book of Isaiah*, 121–5.

BEGRICH, J., 'Das priesterliche Heilsorakel', *ZAW* 52 (1934), 81–92.

—— *Studien zu Deuterojesaja* (BWANT 4/25; Stuttgart, 1938).

BELLINGER, W. H., *Psalmody and Prophecy* (JSOTS 27; Sheffield, 1984).

BERLIN, A., *The Dynamics of Biblical Parallelism* (Bloomington, Ind., 1985).

BETTENZOLI, G., *Geist der Heiligkeit: Traditionsgeschichtliche Untersuchung des QDŠ-Begriffes im Buch Ezechiel* (Quaderni di Semitistica, 8; Florence, 1979).

BEUKEN, W. A. M., '*Mišpāṭ*: The First Servant Song and its Context', *VT* 22 (1972), 1–30.

—— 'Jes $50_{10-11}$: Eine kultische Paränese zur dritten Ebedprophetie', *ZAW* 85 (1973), 168–82.

—— *Jesaja II–III* (De Prediking van het Oude Testament, 4 vols; Nijkerk, 1979–89).

—— 'Isa. 56: 9–57: 13—An Example of the Isaianic Legacy of Trito-

Isaiah', in J. W. van Henten *et al.* (eds.), *Tradition and Re-interpretation in Jewish and Early Christian Literature. Essays in Honour of Jürgen C. H. Lebram* (SP-B 36; Leiden, 1986), 48–64.
—— 'The Main Theme of Trito-Isaiah: "The Servants of YHWH"', *JSOT* 47 (1990), 67–87.
—— 'Isaiah Chapters lxv–lxvi: Trito-Isaiah and the Closure of the Book of Isaiah', in J. A. Emerton (ed.), *Congress Volume: Leuven 1989* (SVT 43; Leiden, 1991), 204–21.
—— 'Jesaja 33 als Spiegeltext im Jesajabuch', *ETL* 67 (1991), 5–35.
BEYSE, K.-M., 'שאר', *TWAT* viii, cols. 898–901.
BLENKINSOPP, J., 'Fragments of Ancient Exegesis in an Isaian Poem (Jes $2_{6-22}$)', *ZAW* 93 (1981), 51–62.
BOER, P. A. H. DE, *Second-Isaiah's Message* (*OTS* 11; Leiden, 1956).
BONNARD, P.-E., *Le Second Isaïe: Son disciple et leurs éditeurs: Isaïe 40–66* (EB; Paris, 1972).
BREKELMANS, C. H. W., 'Deuteronomistic Influence in Isaiah 1–12', in Vermeylen (ed.), *The Book of Isaiah*, 167–76.
BRENNER, M. L., *The Song of the Sea: Ex 15: 1–21* (BZAW 195; Berlin, 1991).
BRETTLER, M., *God is King: Understanding an Israelite Metaphor* (JSOTS 76; Sheffield, 1989).
—— '2 Kings 24: 13–14 as History', *CBQ* 53 (1991), 541–52.
BROCKELMANN, C., *Hebräische Syntax* (Neukirchen, 1956).
BROWN, W. P., 'The So-Called Refrain in Isaiah 5: 25–30 and 9: 7–10: 4', *CBQ* 52 (1990), 432–43.
BROWNLEE, W. H., *The Meaning of the Qumrân Scrolls for the Bible, with Special Attention to the Book of Isaiah* (New York, 1964).
BUDDE, K., *Jesajas Erleben: Eine gemeinverständliche Auslegung der Denkschrift des Propheten* (Gotha, 1928).
BURNEY, C. F., 'The "Boot" in Isaiah ix 4', *JTS* 11 (1910), 438–43.
BURROWS, M. (ed.), *The Dead Sea Scrolls of St. Mark's Monastery*, vol. i (New Haven, Conn., 1950).
CALLAWAY, M., *Sing, O Barren One: A Study in Comparative Midrash* (SBLDS 91; Atlanta, 1986).
CANNAWURF, E., 'The Authenticity of Micah iv 1–4', *VT* 11 (1961), 26–33.
CARR, D., 'Reaching for Unity in Isaiah', *JSOT* 57 (1993), 61–80.
CARROLL, R. P., *When Prophecy Failed: Reactions and Responses to Failure in the Old Testament Prophetic Traditions* (London, 1979).
CASPARI, W., 'Jesaja 34 und 35', *ZAW* 49 (1931), 67–86.
CATASTINI, A., *Isaia ed Ezechia: Studio di storia della tradizione di II Re 18–20/Is 36–39* (Rome, 1989).
CAZELLES, H., 'Qui aurait visé, à l'origine, Isaïe ii 2–5?', *VT* 30 (1980), 409–20.

CHEYNE, T. K., *The Prophecies of Isaiah* (London, 1880).
—— *Introduction to the Book of Isaiah* (London, 1895).
CHILDS, B. S., *Isaiah and the Assyrian Crisis* (SBT 2nd ser., 3; London, 1967).
—— *Introduction to the Old Testament as Scripture* (London, 1979).
CHISHOLM, R. B., 'Structure, Style, and the Prophetic Message: An Analysis of Isaiah 5: 8–30', *BibSac* 143 (1986), 46–60.
CLEMENTS, R. E., 'Patterns in the Prophetic Canon', in G. W. Coats and B. O. Long (eds.), *Canon and Authority: Essays in Old Testament Religion and Theology* (Philadelphia, 1977), 42–55.
—— *Isaiah 1–39* (NCB; Grand Rapids, Mich., and London, 1980).
—— *Isaiah and the Deliverance of Jerusalem: A Study of the Interpretation of Prophecy in the Old Testament* (JSOTS 13; Sheffield, 1980).
—— 'The Prophecies of Isaiah and the Fall of Jerusalem in 587 B.C.', *VT* 30 (1980), 421–36.
—— '"A Remnant Chosen by Grace" (Romans 11: 5): The Old Testament Background and Origin of the Remnant Concept', in D. A. Hagner and M. J. Harris (eds.), *Pauline Studies: Essays Presented to Professor F. F. Bruce on his 70th Birthday* (Exeter, 1980), 106–21.
—— 'The Unity of the Book of Isaiah', *Interpretation*, 36 (1982), 117–29.
—— 'The Isaiah Narrative of 2 Kings 20: 12–19 and the Date of the Deuteronomic History', in A. Rofé and Y. Zakovitch (eds.), *Essays on the Bible and the Ancient World: Isac Leo Seeligmann Volume*, iii (Jerusalem, 1983), 209–20.
—— 'Beyond Tradition-History: Deutero-Isaianic Development of First Isaiah's Themes', *JSOT* 31 (1985), 95–113.
—— 'Patterns in the Prophetic Canon: Healing the Blind and the Lame', in G. M. Tucker, D. L. Petersen, and R. L. Wilson (eds.), *Canon, Theology, and Old Testament Interpretation: Essays in Honor of Brevard S. Childs* (Philadelphia, 1988), 189–200.
—— 'Isaiah 14,22–27: A Central Passage Reconsidered', in Vermeylen (ed.), *The Book of Isaiah*, 253–62.
CLIfford, R. J., 'The Function of Idol Passages in Second Isaiah', *CBQ* 42 (1980), 450–64.
—— *Fair Spoken and Persuading: An Interpretation of Second Isaiah* (New York, 1984).
—— 'The Unity of the Book of Isaiah and its Cosmogonic Language', *CBQ* 55 (1993), 1–17.
CLINES, D. J. A., *Job 1–20* (WBC 17; Dallas, 1989).
COGAN, M., and TADMOR, H., *II Kings: A New Translation with Introduction and Commentary* (AB 11; New York, 1988).
CONRAD, E. W., 'Second Isaiah and the Priestly Oracle of Salvation', *ZAW* 93 (1981), 234–46.

—— 'The "Fear Not" Oracles in Second Isaiah', *VT* 34 (1984), 129–52.

—— *Fear Not Warrior: A Study of 'al tîrā' Pericopes in the Hebrew Scriptures* (Brown Judaic Studies, 75; Chico, Calif., 1985).

—— 'The Royal Narratives and the Structure of the Book of Isaiah', *JSOT* 41 (1988), 67–81.

—— *Reading Isaiah* (OBT; Minneapolis, 1991).

CRESSON, B. C., 'The Condemnation of Edom in Post-Exilic Judaism', in J. M. Efrid (ed.), *The Use of the Old Testament in the New and other Essays* (Durham, NC, 1972), 125–48.

CROSS, F. M., 'The Council of Yahweh in Second Isaiah', *JNES* 12 (1953), 274–7.

CROSS, F. M., and TALMON, S. (eds.), *Qumran and the History of the Biblical Text* (Cambridge, Mass., and London, 1978).

CRÜSEMANN, F., *Studien zur Formgeschichte von Hymnus und Danklied in Israel* (WMANT 32; Neukirchen-Vluyn, 1969).

DAHOOD, M. J., 'Some Ambiguous Texts in Isaias', *CBQ* 20 (1958), 41–9.

—— *Ugaritic–Hebrew Philology: Marginal Notes on Recent Publications* (Biblica et Orientalia, 17; Rome, 1965).

DAVIES, G. I., 'The Destiny of the Nations in the Book of Isaiah', in Vermeylen (ed.), *The Book of Isaiah*, 93–120.

DAVIS, E. F., *Swallowing the Scroll: Textuality and the Dynamics of Discourse in Ezekiel's Prophecy* (JSOTS 78; Sheffield, 1989).

DAY, J., 'A Case of Inner Scriptural Interpretation: The Dependence of Isaiah xxvi. 13–xxvii. 11 on Hosea xiii. 4–xiv. 10 (Eng. 9) and its Relevance to some Theories of the Redaction of the "Isaiah Apocalypse"', *JTS* NS 31 (1980), 309–19.

—— Review of Macintosh, *Isaiah XXI*, in *JTS* NS 34 (1983), 212–15.

—— *God's Conflict with the Dragon and the Sea: Echoes of a Canaanite Myth in the Old Testament* (Cambridge, 1985).

—— 'Pre-Deuteronomic Allusions to the Covenant in Hosea and Psalm lxxviii', *VT* 36 (1986), 1–12.

—— 'Prophecy', in D. A. Carson and H. G. M. Williamson (eds.), *It is Written: Scripture Citing Scripture: Essays in Honour of Barnabas Lindars, SSF* (Cambridge, 1988), 39–55.

—— *Psalms* (Sheffield, 1990).

—— Review of Brenner, *The Song of the Sea*, in *ExpT* 103 (1991), 82.

DELCOR, M., 'Les Sources du Deutéro-Zacharie et ses procédés d'emprunt', *RB* 59 (1952), 385–411.

DELITZSCH, F., *Commentar über das Buch Jesaia* (Leipzig, 1889[4]) = ET *Biblical Commentary on the Prophecies of Isaiah* (Edinburgh, 1890).

DIAKONOFF, I. M., 'Media', in I. Gershevitch (ed.), *The Cambridge History of Iran, ii. The Median and Achaemenian Periods* (Cambridge, 1985), 36–148.

DIETRICH, W., *Jesaja und die Politik* (BEvT 74; Munich, 1976).
DIJK, H. J. VAN, 'Does Third Masculine Singular **taqtul* Exist in Hebrew?', *VT* 19 (1969), 440–7.
DILLMANN, A., *Der Prophet Jesaia* (Kurzgefasstes exegetisches Handbuch zum Alten Testament; Leipzig, 1890; 6th edn. by R. Kittel, Leipzig, 1898).
DONNER, H., *Israel unter den Völkern* (SVT 11; Leiden, 1964).
—— '"Forscht in der Schrift Jahwes und lest!" Ein Beitrag zum Verständnis der israelitischen Prophetie', *ZTK* 87 (1990), 285–98.
DRIVER, G. R., 'Studies in the Vocabulary of the Old Testament. V', *JTS* 34 (1933), 33–44.
—— 'Linguistic and Textual Problems: Isaiah xl–lxvi', *JTS* 36 (1935), 396–406.
—— 'Linguistic and Textual Problems: Isaiah i–xxxix', *JTS* 38 (1937), 36–49.
—— 'Isaianic Problems', in G. Wiessner (ed.), *Festschrift für Wilhelm Eilers* (Wiesbaden, 1967), 43–57.
—— 'Isaiah $52_{13}$–$53_{12}$: The Servant of the Lord', in M. Black and G. Fohrer (eds.), *In Memoriam Paul Kahle* (BZAW 103; Berlin, 1968), 90–105.
DRIVER, S. R., 'Professor Franz Delitzsch', *ExpT* 1 (1889–90), 197–201.
—— *A Treatise on the Use of the Tenses in Hebrew* (Oxford, $1892^3$).
—— *The Book of the Prophet Jeremiah* (London, 1906).
—— *An Introduction to the Literature of the Old Testament* (Edinburgh, $1913^9$).
DUHM, B., *Das Buch Jesaja übersetzt und erklärt* (HK 3/1; Göttingen, 1892; 4th edn., 1922).
DUMBRELL, W. J., 'The Purpose of the Book of Isaiah', *TynB* 36 (1985), 111–28.
—— *The Faith of Israel: Its Expression in the Books of the Old Testament* (Leicester, 1989).
EATON, J. H., 'The Origin of the Book of Isaiah', *VT* 9 (1959), 138–57.
—— *Festal Drama in Deutero-Isaiah* (London, 1979).
—— 'The Isaiah Tradition', in R. Coggins, A. Phillips, and M. Knibb (eds.), *Israel's Prophetic Tradition: Essays in Honour of Peter R. Ackroyd* (Cambridge, 1982), 58–76.
EHRLICH, A. B., *Randglossen zur Hebräischen Bibel* (Leipzig, 1912).
EICHHORN, J. G., *Einleitung ins Alte Testament* (Leipzig, $1787^2$).
EICHRODT, W., *Der Herr der Geschichte: Jesaja 13–23 und 28–39* (BAT 17/II; Stuttgart, 1967).
EISENBEIS, W., *Die Wurzel* שׁלם *im Alten Testament* (BZAW 113; Berlin, 1969).

EISSFELDT, O., 'The Promises of Grace to David in Isaiah 55: 1–5', in B. W. Anderson and W. Harrelson (eds.), *Israel's Prophetic Heritage: Essays in Honor of James Muilenburg* (New York, 1962), 196–207.

ELLIGER, K., *Deuterojesaja in seinem Verhältnis zu Tritojesaja* (BWANT 63; Stuttgart, 1933).

—— *Deuterojesaja*, i. *Jesaja 40,1–45,7* (BKAT xi/1; Neukirchen-Vluyn, 1978).

EMERTON, J. A., 'The Textual Problems of Isaiah v 14', *VT* 17 (1967), 135–42.

—— 'Some Linguistic and Historical Problems in Isaiah viii. 23', *JSS* 14 (1969), 151–79.

—— 'The Meaning of *šēnā*' in Psalm cxxvii 2', *VT* 24 (1974), 15–31.

—— 'The Translation and Interpretation of Isaiah vi.13', in J. A. Emerton and S. C. Reif (eds.), *Interpreting the Hebrew Bible: Essays in Honour of E. I. J. Rosenthal* (Cambridge, 1982), 85–118.

ENGNELL, I., *The Call of Isaiah: An Exegetical and Comparative Study* (Uppsala Universitets Årsskrift 1949: 4; Uppsala and Leipzig, 1949).

ERLANDSSON, S., *The Burden of Babylon: A Study of Isaiah 13: 2–14: 23* (ConB, OT Ser., 4; Lund, 1970).

—— 'Jesaja 11: 10–16 och dess historike bakgrund', *SEÅ* 36 (1971), 24–44.

ESCHEL, H., 'Isaiah viii 23: An Historical–Geographical Analogy', *VT* 40 (1990), 104–9.

EVANS, C. A., 'On the Unity and Parallel Structure of Isaiah', *VT* 38 (1988), 129–47.

—— *To See and Not Perceive: Isaiah 6.9–10 in Early Jewish and Christian Interpretation* (JSOTS 64; Sheffield, 1989).

EXUM, J. C., 'Isaiah 28–32: A Literary Approach', in P. J. Achtemeier (ed.), *Society of Biblical Literature 1979 Seminar Papers*, ii (Missoula, Mont., 1979), 123–51.

FALK, Z. W., 'Hebrew Legal Terms: II', *JSS* 12 (1967), 241–4.

FEY, R., *Amos und Jesaja: Abhängigkeit und Eigenständigkeit des Jesaja* (WMANT 12; Neukirchen-Vluyn, 1963).

FISCHER, J., *Das Buch Isaias* (HSAT 7; Bonn, 1937).

FISHBANE, M., *Biblical Interpretation in Ancient Israel* (Oxford, 1985).

FOHRER, G., *Das Buch Jesaja* (3 vols., Zürcher Bibelkommentare; Zurich and Stuttgart, 1964–$7^2$).

—— 'Entstehung, Komposition und Überlieferung von Jesaja 1–39', in *Studien zur alttestamentlichen Prophetie (1949–1965)* (BZAW 99; Berlin, 1967), 113–47.

—— 'Jesaja 1 als Zusammenfassung der Verkündigung Jesajas', *ZAW* 74 (1962), 251–68 = *Studien*, 148–66.

—— 'Stellvertretung und Schuldopfer in Jes $52_{13}$–$53_{12}$', in *Studien zu*

*alttestamentlichen Texten und Themen (1966–1972)* (BZAW 155; Berlin, 1981), 24–43.
FRANKE, C. A., 'The Function of the Satiric Lament over Babylon in Second Isaiah (xlvii)', *VT* 41 (1991), 408–18.
FRYE, R. N., *The History of Ancient Iran* (Munich, 1984).
GALLING, K., 'Ein Stück judäischen Bodenrechts in Jesaia 8', *ZDPV* 56 (1933), 209–18.
GAMMIE, J. G., *Holiness in Israel* (OBT; Minneapolis, 1989).
GANE, R. and MILGROM, J., 'קרב', *TWAT* vii, cols. 147–61.
GELLER, S. A., 'Were the Prophets Poets?', *Prooftexts*, 3 (1983), 211–21.
GERLEMANN, G., 'Das übervolle Mass', *VT* 28 (1978), 151–64.
GITAY, Y., 'Deutero-Isaiah: Oral or Written?', *JBL* 99 (1980), 185–97.
—— *Isaiah and his Audience: The Structure and Meaning of Isaiah 1–12* (SSN 30; Assen, 1991).
GLASSNER, G., *Vision eines auf Verheißung gegründeten Jerusalem: Textanalytische Studien zu Jesaja 54* (ÖBS 11; Klosterneuburg, 1991).
GONÇALVES, F. J., *L'Expédition de Sennachérib en Palestine dans la littérature hébraïque ancienne* (EB NS 7; Paris, 1986).
GOSSE, B., *Isaïe 13,1–14,23 dans la tradition littéraire du livre d'Isaïe et dans la tradition des oracles contre les nations* (OBO 78; Freiburg and Göttingen, 1988).
—— 'L'Alliance d'Isaïe 59,21', *ZAW* 101 (1989), 116–18.
—— 'Detournement de la vengeance du Seigneur contre Edom et les nations en Isa 63,1–6', *ZAW* 102 (1990), 105–10.
—— 'Isaïe 34–35: Le Châtiment d'Edom et des nations, salut pour Sion', *ZAW* 102 (1990), 396–404.
—— 'Isaïe 14, 24–27 et les oracles contre les nations du livre d'Isaïe', *BN* 56 (1991), 17–21.
—— 'Isaïe 52,13–53,12 et Isaïe 6', *RB* 98 (1991), 537–43.
—— 'Isaïe vi et la tradition isaïenne', *VT* 42 (1992), 340–9.
GRAETZ, H., 'Isaiah xxxiv and xxxv', *JQR* 4 (1891–2), 1–8.
GRAY, G. B., 'The Parallel Passages in Joel and their Bearing on the Question of Date', *Expositor*, 8 (1893), 208–25.
—— *A Critical and Exegetical Commentary on the Book of Isaiah I–XXVII* (ICC; Edinburgh, 1912).
GROL, H. W. M. VAN, 'Paired Tricola in the Psalms, Isaiah and Jeremiah', *JSOT* 25 (1983), 55–73.
GROVES, J. W., *Actualization and Interpretation in the Old Testament* (SBLDS 86; Atlanta, 1987).
GUNKEL, H., 'Jesaja 33, eine prophetische Liturgie: Ein Vortrag', *ZAW* 42 (1924), 177–208.
HAAG, H., *Der Gottesknecht bei Deuterojesaja* (Erträge der Forschung, 233; Darmstadt, 1985).

HABEL, N., 'The Form and Significance of the Call Narratives', *ZAW* 77 (1965), 297–323.

HARAN, M., 'The Literary Structure and Chronological Framework of the Prophecies in Is. xl–xlviii', *Congress Volume: Bonn 1962* (SVT 9; Leiden, 1963), 127–55.

—— 'Book-Size and the Device of Catch-Lines in the Biblical Canon', *JJS* 36 (1985), 1–11.

HARDMEIER, C., *Texttheorie und biblische Exegese: Zur rhetorischen Funktion der Trauermetaphorik in der Prophetie* (BEvT 79; Munich, 1978).

—— Verkündigung und Schrift bei Jesaja: Zur Entstehung der Schriftprophetie als Oppositionsliteratur im alten Israel', *TGl* 73 (1983), 119–34.

—— 'Jesajaforschung im Umbruch', *Verkündigung und Forschung*, 31 (1986), 3–31.

HARRISON, R. K., *Introduction to the Old Testament* (London, 1970).

HASEL, G. F., *The Remnant: The History and Theology of the Remnant Idea from Genesis to Isaiah* (Andrews University Monographs, 5; Berrien Springs, Mich., 1972).

HATCH, E., and REDPATH, H. A., *A Concordance to the Septuagint* (Oxford, 1897).

HAYES, J. H., and IRVINE, S. A., *Isaiah, the Eighth-Century Prophet: His Times and his Preaching* (Nashville, 1987).

HEIDER, G. C., *The Cult of Molek: A Reassessment* (JSOTS 43; Sheffield, 1985).

HENRY, M.-L., *Glaubenskrise und Glaubensbewährung in den Dichtungen der Jesajaapokalypse* (BWANT 86; Stuttgart, 1967).

HERMISSON, H.-J., 'Der Lohn des Knechts', in J. Jeremias and L. Perlitt (eds.), *Die Botschaft und die Boten: Festschrift für Hans Walter Wolff zum 70. Geburtstag* (Neukirchen-Vluyn, 1981), 269–87.

—— *Deuterojesaja 45,8–25* (BKAT 11/7; Neukirchen-Vluyn, 1987).

—— 'Einheit und Komplexität Deuterojesajas: Probleme der Redaktionsgeschichte von Jes 40–55', in Vermeylen (ed.), *The Book of Isaiah*, 287–312.

HILLERS, D. R., '*Hôy* and *Hôy*-Oracles: A Neglected Syntactic Aspect', in C. L. Meyers and M. O'Connor (eds.), *The Word of the Lord Shall Go Forth: Essays in Honor of David Noel Freedman* (Winona Lake, Ind., 1983), 185–8.

HOʾUS, O., 'Zur Septuaginta-Übersetzung von Jes 52,13b', *ZAW* 104 (1992), 107–10.

HØGENHAVEN, J., 'On the Structure and Meaning of Isaiah viii 23b', *VT* 37 (1987), 218–21.

—— *Gott und Volk bei Jesaja: Eine Untersuchung zur Biblischen Theologie* (Acta Theologica Danica; Leiden, 1988).

HOLLADAY, W. L., *Isaiah: Scroll of a Prophetic Heritage* (Grand Rapids, Mich., 1978).
—— *Jeremiah 1* (Philadelphia, 1986).
HONEYMAN, A. M., '*Merismus* in Biblical Hebrew', *JBL* 71 (1952), 11–18.
HOUSE, P. R., *The Unity of the Twelve* (JSOTS 97; Sheffield, 1990).
HUBBARD, R. L., *The Book of Ruth* (NICOT; Grand Rapids, Mich., 1988).
HUBER, F., *Jahwe, Juda und die anderen Völker beim Propheten Jesaja* (BZAW 137; Berlin, 1976).
HUESMAN, J., 'Finite Uses of the Infinitive Absolute', *Biblica*, 37 (1956), 271–95.
HUGHES, J., *Secrets of the Times: Myth and History in Biblical Chronology* (JSOTS 66; Sheffield, 1990).
HUMMEL, H. D., 'Enclitic *mem* in Early Northwest Semitic, Especially Hebrew', *JBL* 76 (1957), 85–107.
HURVITZ, A., 'The Chronological Significance of "Aramaisms" in Biblical Hebrew', *IEJ* 18 (1968), 234–40.
—— *The Transition Period in Biblical Hebrew: A Study in Post-Exilic Hebrew and its Implications for the Dating of Psalms* (Hebrew; Jerusalem, 1972).
IRWIN, W. H., *Isaiah 28–33: Translation with Philological Notes* (Biblica et Orientalia, 30; Rome, 1977).
JANZEN, W., *Mourning Cry and Woe Oracle* (BZAW 125; Berlin, 1972).
JENKINS, A. K., 'The Development of the Isaiah Tradition in Isaiah 13–23', in Vermeylen (ed.), *The Book of Isaiah*, 237–51.
JENNI, E., 'Jesajas Berufung in der neueren Forschung', *ThZ* 15 (1959), 321–39.
JENSEN, J., *The Use of* tôrâ *by Isaiah: His Debate with the Wisdom Tradition* (CBQMS 3; Washington, 1973).
—— 'Yahweh's Plan in Isaiah and in the Rest of the Old Testament', *CBQ* 48 (1986), 443–55.
JEPPESEN, K., 'Call and Frustration: A New Understanding of Isaiah viii 21–22', *VT* 32 (1982), 145–57.
—— 'The Cornerstone (Isa. 28: 16) in Deutero-Isaianic Rereading of the Message of Isaiah', *ST* 38 (1984), 93–9.
—— 'The *maśśā' Bābel* in Isaiah 13–14', *PIBA* 9 (1985), 63–80.
—— 'From "You, My Servant" to "The Hand of the Lord is with my Servants"', *SJOT* (1990/1), 113–29.
JEREMIAS, C., 'Zu Jes. xxxviii 21 f.', *VT* 21 (1971), 104–11.
JOHNSON, D. G., *From Chaos to Restoration: An Integrative Reading of Isaiah 24–27* (JSOTS 61; Sheffield, 1988).
JONES, D. R., 'The Traditio of the Oracles of Isaiah of Jerusalem', *ZAW* 67 (1955), 226–46.
JONES, G. H., 'Abraham and Cyrus: Type and Anti-Type?', *VT* 22 (1972), 304–19.

—— *1 and 2 Kings* (NCB; Grand Rapids, Mich., and London, 1984).

JOÜON, P., *Grammaire de l'Hébreu biblique* (Rome, 1923).

KAISER, O., 'Die Verkündigung des Propheten Jesaja im Jahre 701', *ZAW* 81 (1969), 304–15.

—— *Der Prophet Jesaja Kapitel 13–39* (ATD 18; Göttingen, 1973) = ET *Isaiah 13–39: A Commentary* (London, 1974).

—— *Das Buch des Propheten Jesaja Kapitel 1–12* (ATD 17; Göttingen, 1981⁵) = ET *Isaiah 1–12: A Commentary* (OTL; London, 1983²).

KAPLAN, M. M., 'Isaiah $6_{1-11}$', *JBL* 45 (1926), 251–9.

KELLERMANN, D., 'גור', *TWAT* i, cols. 979–91.

KELLERMANN, U., *Messias und Gesetz: Grundlinien einer alttestamentlichen Heilserwartung: Eine traditionsgeschichtliche Einführung* (BSt 61; Neukirchen-Vluyn, 1971).

KENNETT, R. H., 'The Prophecy in Isaiah ix 1–7', *JTS* 7 (1906), 321–42.

KESSLER, W., *Gott geht es um das Ganze: Jesaja 56–66 und Jesaja 24–27* (BAT 19; Stuttgart, 1967²).

KIESOW, K., *Exodustexte im Jesajabuch: Literarkritische und motivgeschichtliche Analysen* (OBO 24; Fribourg and Göttingen, 1979).

KILIAN, R., *Jesaja 1–39* (Erträge der Forschung, 200; Darmstadt, 1983).

KIRKPATRICK, A. F., *The Book of Psalms* (CBSC; Cambridge, 1902).

—— *The Doctrine of the Prophets* (London, 1917³).

KISSANE, E. J., *The Book of Isaiah* (Dublin, 1941).

—— 'The Land of Sinim (Is. 49: 12)', *ITQ* 21 (1954), 63–4.

KNIERIM, R., 'The Vocation of Isaiah', *VT* 18 (1968), 47–68.

KOENEN, K., *Ethik und Eschatologie im Tritojesajabuch: Eine literarkritische und redaktionsgeschichtliche Studie* (WMANT 62; Neukirchen-Vluyn, 1990).

KOENIG, J., *L'Herméneutique analogique du Judaïsme antique d'après les témoins textuels d'Isaïe* (SVT 33; Leiden, 1982).

—— 'Récouverture du débat sur la première main rédactionelle du rouleau ancien d'Isaïe de Qumrân (I Q Is A) en 40, 7–8', *RQ* 11 (1983), 219–37.

—— *Oracles et liturgies de l'exil babylonien* (Paris, 1988).

KÖHLER, L., *Deuterojesaja (Jesaja 40–55) stilkritisch untersucht* (BZAW 37; Giessen, 1923).

KÖNIG, E., *Stilistik, Rhetorik, Poetik in Bezug auf die biblische Litteratur komparativisch dargestellt* (Leipzig, 1900).

—— *Das Buch Jesaja, eingeleitet, übersetzt und erklärt* (Gütersloh, 1926).

KONKEL, A. H., 'The Sources of the Story of Hezekiah in the Book of Isaiah', *VT* 43 (1993), 462–82.

KOOIJ, A. VAN DER, *Die alten Textzeugen des Jesajabuches: Ein Beitrag zur Textgeschichte des Alten Testaments* (OBO 35; Freiburg and Göttingen, 1981).

KOOLE, J. L., 'Zu Jesaja 45,9 ff.', in M. S. H. G. Heerma van Voss *et al.* (eds.), *Travels in the World of the Old Testament: Studies Presented to Professor M. A. Beek on the Occasion of his 65th Birthday* (Assen, 1974), 170–5.

KORNFELD, W. J., 'QDŠ und Gottesrecht im Alten Testament', in J. A. Emerton (ed.), *Congress Volume: Vienna 1980* (SVT 32; Leiden, 1981), 1–9.

KOTTSIEPER, I., *Die Sprache der Ahiqarsprüche* (BZAW 194; Berlin, 1990).

KRATZ, R. G., *Kyros im Deuterojesaja-Buch* (Forschungen zum Alten Testament, 1; Tübingen, 1991).

KRAUS, H.-J., *Psalmen* (BKAT 15; Neukirchen-Vluyn, $1961^2$) = ET *Psalms 60–150* (Augsburg, 1989).

—— *Geschichte der historisch-kritischen Erforschung des Alten Testaments* (Neukirchen-Vluyn, $1969^2$).

KUNTZ, J. K., 'The Contribution of Rhetorical Criticism to Understanding Isaiah 51: 1–16', in D. J. A. Clines, D. M. Gunn, and A. J. Hauser (eds.), *Art and Meaning: Rhetoric in Biblical Literature* (JSOTS 19; Sheffield, 1982), 140–71.

KUYPER, L. J., 'The Meaning of חסדו Isa. xl 6', *VT* 13 (1963), 489–92.

LAATO, A., *Who is Immanuel? The Rise and Foundering of Isaiah's Messianic Expectations* (Åbo, 1988).

LABERGE, L., 'Is 30, 19–26: A Deuteronomic Text?', *Église et théologie*, 2 (1971), 35–54.

LACK, R., *La Symbolique du Livre d'Isaïe: Essai sur l'image littéraire comme élément de structuration* (AnB 59; Rome, 1973).

LAGARDE, P. DE, *Symmicta*, i (Göttingen, 1877).

—— *Semitica*, i (Göttingen, 1878).

LAMBERT, G., 'Le Livre d'Isaïe parle-t-il des Chinois?', *NRT* 75 (1953), 965–72.

LEENE, H., 'Universalism or Nationalism? Isaiah xlv 9–13 and its Context', *Bijdragen*, 35 (1974), 309–34.

—— *De vroegere en de nieuwe dingen bij Deuterojesaja* (Amsterdam, 1987).

LESCOW, TH., 'Jesajas Denkschrift aus der Zeit des syrisch-ephraimitischen Krieges', *ZAW* 85 (1973), 315–31.

L'HEUREUX, C. E., 'The Redactional History of Isaiah 5.1–10.4', in W. B. Barrick and J. R. Spencer (eds.), *In the Shelter of Elyon: Essays on Ancient Palestinian Life and Literature in Honor of G. W. Ahlström* (JSOTS 31; Sheffield, 1984), 99–119.

LIEBMANN, E., 'Der Text zu Jesaia 24–27', *ZAW* 23 (1903), 209–86.

LIEBREICH, L. J., 'The Compilation of the Book of Isaiah', *JQR* NS 46 (1955–6), 259–77; 47 (1956–7), 114–38.

LINDARS, B., 'Good Tidings to Zion: Interpreting Deutero-Isaiah Today', *BJRL* 68 (1985–6), 473–97.

LINDBLOM, J., *Die Jesaja-Apokalypse: Jes. 24–27* (Lund and Leipzig, 1938).

LINDENBERGER, J. M., *The Aramaic Proverbs of Ahiqar* (Baltimore and London, 1983).

LORETZ, O., 'Die Gattung des Prologs zum Buche Deuterojesaja (Jes $40_{1\text{-}11}$)', *ZAW* 96 (1984), 210–20.

—— *Der Prolog des Jesaja-Buches (1,1–2,5): Ugaritologische und kolometrische Studien zum Jesaja-Buch* (UBL 1; Altenberge, 1984).

LOWTH, R., *Isaiah: A New Translation; with a Preliminary Dissertation, and Notes, Critical, Philological, and Explanatory* (London, 1824).

LUST, J., 'Isaiah 34 and the *ḥerem*', in Vermeylen (ed.), *The Book of Isaiah*, 275–86.

MACINTOSH, A. A., *Isaiah XXI: A Palimpsest* (Cambridge, 1980).

MCKANE, W., *A Critical and Exegetical Commentary on Jeremiah*, i (ICC; Edinburgh, 1986).

MCKENZIE, J. L., *Second Isaiah: Introduction, Translation, and Notes* (AB; Garden City, NY, 1968).

MARGOLIOUTH, G., 'Isaiah and Isaianic', *The Expositor*, 7th ser., 9 (1910), 525–9.

MARTI, K., *Das Buch Jesaja* (KHAT 10; Tübingen, 1900).

MARTIN-ACHARD, R., 'Esaïe 47 et la tradition prophétique sur Babylone', in J. A. Emerton (ed.), *Prophecy: Essays Presented to Georg Fohrer on his Sixty-Fifth Birthday 6 September 1980* (BZAW 150; Berlin, 1980), 83–105.

—— 'Esaïe liv et la nouvelle Jérusalem', in J. A. Emerton (ed.), *Congress Volume: Vienna 1980* (SVT 32; Leiden, 1981).

MATHEUS, F., 'Jesaja xliv 9–20: Das Spottgedicht gegen die Götzen und seine Stellung im Kontext', *VT* 37 (1987), 312–26.

—— *Singt dem Herrn ein neues Lied: Die Hymnen Deuterojesajas* (SBS 141; Stuttgart, 1990).

MEADE, D. G., *Pseudonymity and Canon: An Investigation into the Relationship of Authorship and Authority in Jewish and Earliest Christian Tradition* (Grand Rapids, Mich., 1987).

MEIER, S. A., *Speaking of Speaking: Marking Direct Discourse in the Hebrew Bible* (SVT 46; Leiden, 1992).

MELAMED, E. Z., 'Break-up of Stereotype Phrases as an Artistic Device in Biblical Poetry', *ScrH* 8 (1961), 115–53.

MELUGIN, R. F., *The Formation of Isaiah 40–55* (BZAW 141; Berlin, 1976).

MERENDINO, R. P., *Der Erste und der Letzte: Eine Untersuchung von Jes 40–48* (SVT 31; Leiden, 1981).

METTINGER, T. N. D., *The Dethronement of Sabaoth: Studies in the Shem and Kabod Theologies* (ConB, OT Ser., 18; Lund, 1982).

—— *A Farewell to the Servant Songs: A Critical Examination of an Exegetical Axiom* (Lund, 1983).

MILGROM, J., 'Did Isaiah Prophesy during the Reign of Uzziah?', *VT* 14 (1964), 164–82.

MILLAR, W. R., *Isaiah 24–27 and the Origin of Apocalyptic* (HSM 11; Missoula, Mont., 1976).

MISCALL, P. D., *Isaiah* (Sheffield, 1993).

MONTGOMERY, J. A., *A Critical and Exegetical Commentary on the Book of Daniel* (ICC; Edinburgh, 1927).

MORGENSTERN, J., 'The Suffering Servant—A New Solution', *VT* 11 (1961), 292–320, 406–31.

MOSCATI, S., 'I sigilli nell'Antico Testamento', *Biblica*, 30 (1949), 314–38.

MOWINCKEL, S., *Jesajadisiplene: Profitien fra Jesaja til Jeremia* (Oslo, 1926).

—— *Prophecy and Tradition: The Prophetic Books in the Light of the Study of the Growth and History of the Tradition* (Oslo, 1946).

—— 'Die Komposition des Jesajabuches Kap. 1–39', *ActOr* 11 (1932–3), 267–92.

MUILENBURG, J., 'The Literary Character of Isaiah 34', *JBL* 59 (1940), 339–65 = T. F. Best (ed.), *Hearing and Speaking the Word: Selections from the Works of James Muilenburg* (Chico, Calif., 1984), 59–85.

—— 'The Book of Isaiah, Chapters 40–66', in G. A. Buttrick (ed.), *The Interpreter's Bible*, v (New York and Nashville, Tenn., 1956), 381–773.

MULLEN, E. T., *The Divine Council in Canaanite and Early Hebrew Literature* (HSM 24; Chico, Calif., 1980).

MÜLLER, H.-P., 'Glauben und Bleiben: Zur Denkschrift Jesajas Kapitel vi 1–viii 18', in *Studies on Prophecy: A Collection of Twelve Papers* (SVT 26; Leiden, 1974), 25–54.

MURRAY, R., 'Prophecy and the Cult', in R. Coggins, A. Phillips, and M. Knibb (eds.), *Israel's Prophetic Tradition: Essays in Honour of Peter R. Ackroyd* (Cambridge, 1982), 200–16.

NA'AMAN, N., 'Literary and Topographical Notes on the Battle of Kishon (Judges iv–v)', *VT* 40 (1990), 423–36.

—— 'The Kingdom of Judah under Josiah', *Tel Aviv*, 18 (1991), 3–71.

NAIDOFF, B. D., 'The Two-Fold Structure of Isaiah xlv 9–13', *VT* 31 (1981), 180–5.

NIEHAUS, J., '*rāz-pešar* in Isaiah xxiv', *VT* 31 (1981), 376–8.

NIELSEN, K., *There is Hope for a Tree: The Tree as Metaphor in Isaiah* (JSOTS 65; Sheffield, 1989).

NORIN, S., 'An Important Kennicott Reading in 2 Kings xviii 13', *VT* 32 (1982), 337–8.

NORTH, C. R., 'The "Former Things" and the "New Things" in Deutero-Isaiah', in H. H. Rowley (ed.), *Studies in Old Testament Prophecy* (Edinburgh, 1957), 111–26.

—— *The Second Isaiah: Introduction, Translation and Commentary to Chapters xl–lv* (Oxford, 1964).

O'CONNELL, R. H., 'Isaiah xiv 4B–23: Ironic Reversal through Concentric Structure and Mythic Allusion', *VT* 38 (1988), 407–18.

OLMSTEAD, A. T., 'II Isaiah and Isaiah, Chapter 35', *AJSL* 53 (1936–7), 251–3.

OSWALT, J. N., *The Book of Isaiah, Chapters 1–39* (NICOT; Grand Rapids, Mich., 1986).

OTZEN, B., *Studien über Deuterosacharja* (Acta Theologica Danica, 6; Copenhagen, 1964).

—— 'Traditions and Structures of Isaiah xxiv–xxvii', *VT* 24 (1974), 196–206.

PARDEE, D., 'Troisième réassemblage de RS 1.019', *Syria*, 65 (1988), 173–91.

PAYNE, D. F., 'Old Testament Exegesis and the Problem of Ambiguity', *ASTI* 5 (1966–7), 48–68.

—— 'Characteristic Word-Play in "Second Isaiah": A Reappraisal', *JSS* 12 (1967), 207–29.

PETERSEN, D. L., *The Roles of Israel's Prophets* (JSOTS 17; Sheffield, 1981).

—— *Haggai and Zechariah 1–8: A Commentary* (OTL; London, 1984).

PFEIffer, R. H., *Introduction to the Old Testament* (London, 1952).

POPE, M., 'Isaiah 34 in Relation to Isaiah 35, 40–66', *JBL* 71 (1952), 235–43.

PORTER, J. R., 'The Supposed Deuteronomic Redaction of the Prophets: Some Considerations', in R. Albertz, F. W. Golka, and J. Kegler (eds.), *Schöpfung und Befreiung: Für Claus Westermann zum 80. Geburtstag* (Stuttgart, 1989), 69–78.

POYNDER, A., '"Be Thou their Arm every Morning": Isaiah xxxiii. 2', *ExpT* 13 (1901–2), 94.

PREMNATH, D. N., 'Latifundialization and Isaiah 5.8–10', *JSOT* 40 (1988), 49–60.

PREUSS, H. D., *Verspottung fremder Religionen im Alten Testament* (BWANT 92; Stuttgart, 1971).

PROCKSCH, O., *Jesaia I* (KAT 9/1; Leipzig, 1930).

PURVIS, J. D., *The Samaritan Pentateuch and the Origin of the Samaritan Sect* (HSM 2; Cambridge, Mass., 1968).

QUELL, G., 'Jesaja 14, 1–23', in J. Herrmann (ed.), *Festschrift Friedrich Baumgärtel zum 70. Geburtstag, 14. Januar 1958* (Erlanger Forschungen, Reihe A, 10; Erlangen, 1959), 131–57.

RAD, G. VON, 'Die Stadt auf dem Berge', *EvTh* 8 (1948–9), 439–47 = *Gesammelte Studien zum Alten Testament* (ThB 8; Munich, 1958), 214–24 = ET 'The City on the Hill', in *The Problem of the Hexateuch and other Essays* (Edinburgh and London, 1966), 232–42.

REIMER, D. J., *The Oracles against Babylon in Jeremiah 50–51: A Horror among the Nations* (San Francisco, 1993).

RENAUD, B., *Structure et attaches littéraires de Miché iv–v* (Cahiers de la *RB* 2; Paris, 1964).

RENDTORFF, R., *Das Alte Testament: Eine Einführung* (Neukirchen-Vluyn, 1983) = ET *The Old Testament: An Introduction* (London, 1985).

—— 'Zur Komposition des Buches Jesaja', *VT* 34 (1984), 295–320.

—— 'Jesaja 6 im Rahmen der Komposition des Jesajabuches', in Vermeylen (ed.), *The Book of Isaiah*, 73–82.

RIGNELL, L. G., *A Study of Isaiah Ch. 40–55* (Lund, 1956).

RINGGREN, H., 'Some Observations on Style and Structure in the Isaiah Apocalypse', *ASTI* 9 (1973), 107–15.

—— 'Israelite Prophecy: Fact or Fiction?', in J. A. Emerton (ed.), *Congress Volume: Jerusalem 1986* (SVT 40; Leiden, 1988), 204–10.

ROBERTS, J. J. M., 'Isaiah in Old Testament Theology', *Interpretation*, 36 (1982), 130–43.

—— 'The Divine King and the Human Community in Isaiah's Vision of the Future', in H. B. Huffmon, F. A. Spina, and A. R. W. Green (eds.) , *The Quest for the Kingdom of God: Studies in Honor of George E. Mendenhall* (Winona Lake, Ind., 1983), 127–36.

—— 'Isaiah 33: An Isaianic Elaboration of the Zion Tradition', in C. L. Meyers and M. O'Connor (eds.), *The Word of the Lord Shall Go Forth: Essays in Honor of David Noel Freedman in Celebration of his Sixtieth Birthday* (Winona Lake, Ind., 1983), 15–25.

ROBERTSON, D. A., *Linguistic Evidence in Dating Early Poetry* (SBLDS 3; Missoula, Mont., 1972).

ROBINSON, H. W., 'The Council of Yahweh', *JTS* 45 (1944), 151–7.

RUDOLPH, W., *Micha—Nahum—Habakuk—Zephanja* (KAT 13/3; Gütersloh, 1975).

—— *Haggai—Sacharja 1–8—Sacharja 9–14—Maleachi* (KAT 13/4; Gütersloh, 1976).

—— 'Lesefrüchte', *ZAW* 93 (1981), p. 292.

RUNDGREN, F., 'Elephantine-Aramäisches *mallāḥ dī mayyā* und altägyptisches *mw byn*, "Katarakt"', *Studia Linguistica*, 11 (1957), 57–60.

SAEBØ, M., 'Grenzbeschreibung und Landideal im Alten Testament mit besonderer Berücksichtigung der min-'ad-Formel', *ZDPV* 90 (1974), 14–37.

SAWYER, J. F. A., 'Daughter of Zion and Servant of the Lord: A Comparison', *JSOT* 44 (1989), 89–107.

SCHEDL, C., 'Nochmals Jes $9_2$: הגוי לא', *ZAW* 94 (1982), 293.

SCHMIDT, W. H., 'Wo hat die Aussage: Jahwe "der Heilige" ihren Ursprung?', *ZAW* 74 (1962), 62–6.

—— 'Die deuteronomistische Redaktion des Amosbuches', *ZAW* 77 (1965), 168–93.

—— *Alttestamentliche Glaube und seine Umwelt: Zur Geschichte des alttes-*

*tamentlichen Gottesverständnisses* (Neukirchen-Vluyn, 1968) = ET *The Faith of the Old Testament: A History* (Oxford, 1983).

—— 'Die Ohnmacht des Messias', *Kerygma und Dogma*, 15 (1969), 18–34.

SCHMITT, H.-C., 'Prophetie und Schultheologie im Deuterojesajabuch: Beobachtungen zur Redaktionsgeschichte von Jes 40–55', *ZAW* 91 (1979), 43–61.

SCHOORS, A., 'Les Choses antérieures et les choses nouvelles dans les oracles deutéro-Isaïens', *ETL* 40 (1964), 19–47.

—— *Jesaja* (Boeken van het Oude Testament, 9; Roermond, 1972–3).

—— *I am God your Saviour: A Form-Critical Study of the Main Genres in Is. xl–lv* (SVT 24; Leiden, 1973).

SCHREINER, J., 'Das Buch jesajanischer Schule', in J. Schreiner (ed.), *Wort und Botschaft: Eine theologische und kritische Einführung in die Probleme des Alten Testaments* (Würzburg, 1967), 142–62.

SCHULZ, H., *Das Buch Nahum: Eine redaktionskritische Untersuchung* (BZAW 129; Berlin, 1973).

SCHUNCK, K.-D., 'Jes $30_{6-8}$ und die Deutung der Rahab im Alten Testament', *ZAW* 78 (1966), 48–56.

SCHWARTZ, G., 'Jesaja $50_{4-5a}$: Eine Emendation', *ZAW* 85 (1973), 356–7.

SCORALICK, R., *Trishagion und Gottesherrschaft: Psalm 99 als Neuinterpretation von Tora und Propheten* (SBS 138; Stuttgart, 1989).

SCOTT, R. B. Y., 'The Relation of Isaiah, Chapter 35, to Deutero-Isaiah', *AJSL* 52 (1935–6), 178–91.

—— 'The Book of Isaiah, Chapters 1–39', in G. A. Buttrick (ed.), *The Interpreter's Bible*, v (New York and Nashville, Tenn., 1956), 151–381.

SEELIGMANN, I. L., *The Septuagint Version of Isaiah: A Discussion of its Problems* (Leiden, 1948).

SEITZ, C. R., 'The Divine Council: Temporal Transition and New Prophecy in the Book of Isaiah', *JBL* 109 (1990), 229–47.

—— *Zion's Final Destiny: The Development of the Book of Isaiah: A Reassessment of Isaiah 36–39* (Minneapolis, 1991).

—— 'Account A and the Annals of Sennacherib: A Reassessment', *JSOT* 58 (1993), 47–57.

SEKINE, S., *Die Tritojesajanische Sammlung (Jes 56–66) redaktionsgeschichtlich untersucht* (BZAW 175; Berlin and New York, 1989).

SELLIN, E., and FOHRER, G., *Einleitung in das Alte Testament* (Heidelberg, $1965^{10}$) = ET G. Fohrer, *Introduction to the Old Testament* (London, 1970).

SELMS, A. VAN, 'The Expression "The Holy One of Israel"', in W. C. Delsman *et al.* (eds.), *Von Kanaan bis Kerala: Festschrift für Prof. Mag. Dr. Dr. J. P. M. van der Ploeg O.P. zur Vollendung des siebzigsten Lebensjahres am 4. Juli 1979* (AOAT 211; Neukirchen-Vluyn, 1982), 257–69.

SHILOH, Y., and TARLER, D., 'Bullae from the City of David: A Hoard of Seal Impressions from the Israelite Period', *BA* 49 (1986), 196–209.
SIMON, U., 'Ibn Ezra between Medievalism and Modernism: The Case of Isaiah xl–lxvi', in J. A. Emerton (ed.), *Congress Volume: Salamanca 1983* (SVT 36; Leiden, 1985), 257–71.
SKEHAN, P. W., 'Some Textual Problems in Isaia', *CBQ* 22 (1960), 47–55.
SKINNER, J., *The Book of the Prophet Isaiah, Chapters I.–XXXIX. with Introduction and Notes* (CBSC; Cambridge, 1897).
SMELIK, K. A. D., 'Distortion of Old Testament Prophecy: The Purpose of Isaiah xxxvi and xxxvii', *OTS* 24 (1986), 70–93.
SMITH, W. R., *The Prophets of Israel and their Place in History* (London, 1895²).
SNAITH, N. H., 'The Exegesis of Isaiah xl. 5, 6', *ExpT* 52 (1940–1), 394–6.
—— 'Isaiah 40–66: A Study of the Teaching of the Second Isaiah and its Consequences', in H. M. Orlinsky and N. H. Snaith, *Studies on the Second Part of the Book of Isaiah* (SVT 14; Leiden, 1977²), 135–264.
SPYKERBOER, H. C., *The Structure and Composition of Deutero-Isaiah, with Special Reference to the Polemics against Idolatry* (Meppel, 1976).
STADE, B., 'Deuterozacharja: Eine kritische Studie', *ZAW* 1 (1881), 1–96.
STAMM, J. J. *et al.*, *Hebräisches und Aramäisches Lexikon zum Alten Testament* (4 vols.; Leiden, 1967–90).
STANSELL, G., *Micah and Isaiah: A Form and Tradition Historical Comparison* (SBLDS 85; Atlanta, 1988).
STECK, O. H., 'Bemerkungen zu Jesaja 6', *BZ* N.F. 16 (1972), 188–206.
—— *Friedensvorstellungen im alten Jerusalem* (ThSt 111; Zurich, 1972).
—— 'Beiträge zum Verständnis von Jesaja 7,10–17 und 8,1–4', *ThZ* 29 (1973), 161–78.
—— 'Aspekte des Gottesknechts in Jes 52,13–53,12', *ZAW* 97 (1985), 36–58.
—— *Bereitete Heimkehr: Jesaja 35 als redaktionelle Brücke zwischen dem Ersten und dem Zweiten Jesaja* (SBS 121; Stuttgart, 1985).
—— *Studien zu Tritojesaja* (BZAW 203; Berlin and New York, 1991).
STOEBE, H. J., 'Zu Jesaja 40, V. 6', *Wort und Dienst*, N.F. 2 (1950), 122–8.
STUHLMUELLER, C., '"First and Last" and "Yahweh-Creator" in Deutero-Isaiah', *CBQ* 29 (1967), 495–511.
—— 'Deutero-Isaiah: Major Transitions in the Prophet's Theology and in Contemporary Scholarship', *CBQ* 42 (1980), 1–29.
SWEENEY, M. A., 'New Gleanings from an Old Vineyard: Isaiah 27 Reconsidered', in C. A. Evans and W. F. Stinespring (eds.), *Early Jewish and Christian Exegesis: Studies in Memory of William Hugh Brownlee* (Atlanta, 1987), 51–66.
—— *Isaiah 1–4 and the Post-Exilic Understanding of the Isaianic Tradition* (BZAW 171; Berlin, 1988).

—— 'Textual Citations in Isaiah 24–27: Toward an Understanding of the Redactional Function of Chapters 24–27 in the Book of Isaiah', *JBL* 107 (1988), 39–52.

TALMON, S., 'Synonymous Readings in the Old Testament', *ScrH* 8 (1961), 335–83.

THOMAS, D. W., 'The Root שנה = *sny* in Hebrew II', *ZAW* 55 (1937), 174–6.

TIDWELL, N. '*Wā'ōmar* (Zech. 3: 5) and the Genre of Zechariah's Fourth Vision', *JBL* 94 (1975), 343–55.

TOMASINO, A. J., 'Isaiah 1.1–2.4 and 63–66, and the Composition of the Isaianic Corpus', *JSOT* 57 (1993), 81–98.

TORREY, C. C., *The Second Isaiah: A New Interpretation* (Edinburgh, 1928).

—— 'Isaiah 41', *HTR* 44 (1951), 121–36.

TOURNAY, R., 'Quelques relectures bibliques antisamaritaines', *RB* 71 (1964), 504–36.

TUR-SINAI, N. H., 'A Contribution to the Understanding of Isaiah i–xii', *ScrH* 8 (1961), 154–88.

VAN WINKLE, D. W., 'The Relationship of the Nations to Yahweh and to Israel in Isaiah xl–lv', *VT* 35 (1985), 446–58.

VERMEYLEN, J., *Du prophète Isaïe à l'apocalyptique: Isaïe, I–XXXV, miroir d'un demi-millénaire d'expérience religieuse en Israël* (EB; 2 vols.; Paris, 1977–8).

—— 'Le Motif de la création dans le Deutéro-Isaïe', in P. Beauchamp (ed.), *La Création dans l'Orient Ancien* (LecD 127; Paris, 1987), 183–240.

—— (ed.), *The Book of Isaiah* (BETL 81; Leuven, 1989).

—— 'L'Unité du livre d'Isaïe', in Vermeylen (ed.), *The Book of Isaiah*, 11–53.

VIEWEGER, D., '"Das Volk, das durch das Dunkel zieht . . ." Neue Überlegungen zu Jes (8,23ab)9,1–6', *BZ* N.F. 36 (1992), 77–86.

VINCENT, J. M., *Studien zur literarischen Eigenart und zur geistigen Heimat von Jesaja, Kap. 40–55* (BET 5; Frankfurt am Main, 1977).

VOLLMER, J., 'Zur Sprache von Jesaja $9_{1-6}$', *ZAW* 80 (1968), 343–50.

—— *Geschichtliche Rückblicke und Motive in der Prophetie des Amos, Hosea und Jesaja* (BZAW 119; Berlin, 1971).

VOLZ, P., *Jesaia II* (KAT 9; Leipzig, 1932).

WADE, G. W., *The Book of the Prophet Isaiah* (London, $1929^2$).

WAGNER, M., *Die lexikalischen und grammatikalischen Aramaismen im alttestamentlichen Hebräisch* (BZAW 96; Berlin, 1966).

WASCHKE, G., 'קוה', *TWAT* vi, cols. 1225–34.

WATSON, W. G. E., *Classical Hebrew Poetry: A Guide to its Techniques* (JSOTS 26; Sheffield, 1984).

WATTS, J. D. W., *Isaiah 1–33* and *Isaiah 34–66* (WBC 24–5; Waco, 1985 and 1987).

—— *Isaiah* (Word Biblical Themes; Dallas, 1989).

WATTS, R. E., 'Consolation or Confrontation? Isaiah 40–55 and the Delay of the New Exodus', *TynB* 41 (1990), 31–59.

WEBB, B. G., 'Zion in Transformation: A Literary Approach to Isaiah', in D. J. A. Clines, S. E. Fowl, and S. E. Porter (eds.), *The Bible in Three Dimensions: Essays in Celebration of Forty Years of Biblical Studies in the University of Sheffield* (JSOTS 87; Sheffield, 1990), 65–84.

WEGNER, P. D., 'Another Look at Isaiah viii 23B', *VT* 41 (1991), 481–4.

WEISER, A., *Die Psalmen* (ATD 14/15; Göttingen, $1959^5$) = ET *The Psalms: A Commentary* (OTL; London, 1962).

WEISS, R., 'On Ligatures in the Hebrew Bible (נו = ם)', *JBL* 82 (1963), 188–94.

WERNER, W., *Eschatologische Texte in Jesaja 1–39: Messias, Heiliger Rest, Völker* (Forschung zur Bibel, 46; Würzburg, 1982).

—— *Studien zur alttestamentlichen Vorstellung vom Plan Jahwes* (BZAW 173; Berlin, 1988).

WESTERMANN, C., 'Das Heilswort bei Deuterojesaja', *EvTh* 24 (1964), 355–73.

—— 'Sprache und Struktur der Prophetie Deuterojesajas', in *Forschung am Alten Testament* (ThB 24; Munich, 1964), 92–170.

—— *Das Buch Jesaja Kapitel 40–66* (ATD 19; Göttingen, $1981^4$) = ET *Isaiah 40–66: A Commentary* (OTL; London, 1969).

WHEDBEE, J. W., *Isaiah and Wisdom* (Nashville and New York, 1971).

WHITLEY, C. F., 'The Call and Mission of Isaiah', *JNES* 18 (1959), 38–48.

—— 'Textual Notes on Deutero-Isaiah', *VT* 11 (1961), 457–61.

—— 'The Language and Exegesis of Isaiah $8_{16-23}$', *ZAW* 90 (1978), 28–43.

—— 'The Semantic Range of *Ḥesed*', *Biblica*, 62 (1981), 519–26.

WHYBRAY, R. N., *Isaiah 40–66* (NCB; London, 1975).

WIDENGREN, G., 'Yahweh's Gathering of the Dispersed', in W. B. Barrick and J. R. Spencer (eds.), *In the Shelter of Elyon: Essays on Ancient Palestinian Life and Literature in Honor of G. W. Ahlström* (JSOTS 31; Sheffield, 1984), 227–45.

WIENER, H. M., *The Prophets of Israel in History and Criticism* (London, 1923).

WIERINGEN, A. L. H. M. VAN, 'Jesaja 40, 1–11: Eine drama-linguistische Lesung von Jesaja 6 her', *BN* 49 (1989), 82–93.

WIKLANDER, B., *Prophecy as Literature: A Text-Linguistic and Rhetorical Approach to Isaiah 2–4* (ConB, OT Ser., 22; Uppsala, 1984).

WILCOX, P., and PATON-WILLIAMS, D., 'The Servant Songs in Deutero-Isaiah', *JSOT* 42 (1988), 79–102.

WILDBERGER, H., 'Die Völkerwallfahrt zum Zion: Jes. ii 1–5', *VT* 7 (1957), 62–81.

—— 'Gottesnamen und Gottesepitheta bei Jesaja', in *Jahwe und sein Volk: Gesammelte Aufsätze zum Alten Testament* (ThB 66; Munich, 1979), 219–48.

—— *Jesaja*, i. *Jesaja 1–12* (BKAT 10/1; Neukirchen-Vluyn, 1980[2]).

—— *Jesaja*, ii. *Jesaja 13–27* (BKAT 10/2; Neukirchen-Vluyn, 1978).

—— *Jesaja*, iii. *Jesaja 28–39. Das Buch, der Prophet und seine Botschaft* (BKAT 10/3; Neukirchen-Vluyn, 1982).

WILLI-PLEIN, I., 'Das Geheimnis der Apokalyptik', *VT* 27 (1977), 62–81.

WILLIAMSON, H. G. M., *Ezra, Nehemiah* (WBC 16; Waco, 1985).

—— 'The Concept of Israel in Transition', in R. E. Clements (ed.), *The World of Ancient Israel: Sociological, Anthropological and Political Perspectives* (Cambridge, 1989), 141–61.

—— 'Isaiah 63,7–64,11: Exilic Lament or Post-Exilic Protest?', *ZAW* 102 (1990), 48–58.

WILLIS, J. T., 'An Important Passage for Determining the Historical Setting of a Prophetic Oracle—Isaiah 1.7–8', *ST* 39 (1985), 151–69.

WILSON, R. R., *Prophecy and Society in Ancient Israel* (Philadelphia, 1980).

WOLFF, H. W., *Dodekapropheton 4: Micha* (BKAT 14/4; Neukirchen-Vluyn, 1982) = ET *Micah: A Commentary* (Minneapolis, 1990).

—— 'Schwerter zu Pflugscharen—Missbrauch eines Prophetenwortes?', *EvTh* 44 (1984), 280–92 = *Studien zur Prophetie: Probleme und Erträge* (Munich, 1987), 93–108.

YOUNG, E. J., *Studies in Isaiah* (London, 1954).

ZIEGLER, J., *Untersuchungen zur Septuaginta des Buches Isaias* (Münster, 1934).

ZIMMERLI, W., 'Der "neue Exodus" in der Verkündigung der beiden grossen Exilspropheten', in *Gottes Offenbarung*: Gesammelte Aufsätze zum Alten Testament (ThB 19; Munich, 1963), 192–204.

—— 'Zur Sprache Tritojesajas', in *Festschrift für Ludwig Köhler* (Bern, 1950), 62–74 = *Gottes Offenbarung: Gesammelte Aufsätze zum Alten Testament* (ThB 19; Munich, 1963), 217–33.

—— *Ezechiel* (BKAT 13, 2 vols.; Neukirchen-Vluyn, 1969) = ET *Ezekiel* (2 vols.; Philadelphia, 1979 and 1983).

# INDEX OF PASSAGES CITED

# INDEX OF MODERN AUTHORS

DATE DUE

| | | | |
|---|---|---|---|
| | | | |
| | | | |
| | | | |
| | | | |
| | | | |
| | | | |
| | | | |
| | | | |
| | | | |
| | | | |
| | | | |
| | | | |
| | | | |
| | | | |
| | | | |
| | | | |
| | | | |